D1572461

SCANDALS IN THE HOUSE OF BIRDS

Photo by Nathniel Tarn

The Mam or "Maximón"

NATHANIEL TARN WITH
MARTÍN PRECHTEL

SCANDALS

IN THE

HOUSE OF BIRDS

Shamans and Priests
on Lake Atitlán

MARSILIO

Scandals in the House of Birds:
Shamans and Priests on Lake Atitlán

Copyright © 1997 Nathaniel Tarn

Marsilio Publishers
853 Broadway, Suite 604
New York, New York 10003 USA

ISBN 1-56886-044-7

Printed in the United States of America.
All Rights Reserved.

Library of Congress Cataloging-in-Publication Data

Tarn, Nathaniel.
    Scandals in the house of birds : Shamans and priests on Lake
Atitlán / NathanielTarn
        p.   cm.
    Includes bibliographical references.
    ISBN 1-56886-044-7 (alk. paper)
    1. Tzutuhil sculpture--Guatemala--Santiago Atitlán.   2. Tzutuhil
Indians--Religion.   3. Tzutuhil Indians--Rites and ceremonies.
4. Art thefts--Guatemala--Santiago Atitlán.   5. Santiago Atitlán
(Guatemala)--Religious life and customs.   6. Santiago Atitlán
(Guatemala)--Social life and customs.
    II. Title.
F1465.2.T9T37   1998
972.81'6400497415--dc21
                                                                        98-4887
                                                                          CIP

Table of Contents

Contents

About the Authors

NATHANIEL TARN, born in Paris, France, was educated at Cambridge University; the Ecole des Hautes Etudes, Paris; the University of Chicago; the London School of Economics and the London School of Oriental & African Studies. He is a poet, translator, editor, critic and anthropologist. He has published some twenty books of poetry; many volumes of translation, among which three best-selling collections of Pablo Neruda's, and *Views from the Weaving Mountain*, a volume of thirty years' essays in literary and cultural criticism. As an anthropologist, he is an expert in the Highland Maya area and South East Asia and has also worked in the Himalayan Region, China, Japan, Cuba and Alaska. Tarn has read his work and lectured world-wide. His poetry has been translated into some two dozen major languages. He has taught, *inter alia*, at the Universities of London, Princeton, Colorado, Pennsylvania and Jilin (P.R.China). Tarn retired as Professor Emeritus of Modern Poetry, Comparative Literature and Anthropology, Rutgers University, in 1985.

MARTIN PRECHTEL was born in New Mexico and raised there, to a great extent on the Santo Domingo Reservation. A Keresan speaker, he attended Santa Fe's branch of St. John's College for a year where he published a small volume of verse. He went to Guatemala in 1976 to help in earthquake relief work and stayed on. Settling in Santiago Atitlán, he mastered the language, married a native woman, apprenticed himself to leading shamans and healers, began practicing natural medicine and participated in Atiteco ritual, initially as a flutist. He eventually rose in the Native hierarchy and, in 1979, crowned his career by being appointed

Primer Mayor, the official responsible for the major event of the Atiteco year: the vast complex of Holy Week rituals. Soon after, the Civil War in Guatemala sent him into hiding until he was able to return to this country. As a musician, Prechtel formed and led various bands and has records of his music in and outside Guatemala. As a painter, he has exhibited many times in Guatemala and all over the United States. He has continued his activity in healing, the men's movement and the arts.

Acknowledgements

As this book tells it, very soon after Tarn's 1959 arrival in Atitlán, Prechtel and he began, without much ceremony, to work together and have remained friends ever since. Although all the writing has been done by Tarn, it seemed only natural and just that Prechtel should be offered joint authorship of the book. It is very likely they both feel, as son and grandson to Nicolás Chiviliu, that *this* great shade is the true author of this work.

When thanking individuals or groups, we immediately face the fact that Guatemala today is a tragic place, perhaps as tragic— the other candidate may be Cambodia—as any since the Nazi era in Europe. Wealth and Power are in the hands of a miserably small minority which continues to oppress indigenous peoples with far more cruelty, perhaps, than even the Conquistadores ever devised. It brings no comfort to American writers to know that their country has for a long time been an accomplice, even a guiding light in this state of affairs. The masquerade that is "democracy" in Guatemala today is a shameful crime against Native American humanity. One continues to pray for change and there are signs that a peace process recently completed may be accounted progress.

For this reason, it will be mainly in the last chapter entitled *Memorial to the Dead of Atitlán* where our thanks to Atitecos will be enshrined. The safety of those still living demands no less and their names have been changed in this book.

For the rest, Nathaniel Tarn wishes to express heartfelt gratitude to the following friends and colleagues: the late Drs. Robert Redfield, J.E.S. Thompson, S. de Borhegyi, Fred Eggan, Juan de Dios Rosales and Joaquín Noval, and Drs. Robert Carmack,

Acknowledgements

Ricardo Falla, Gary Gossen, Alain Ichon, Henri Lehmann, Christopher Lutz, Tim Knab, Robert Carlsen, James Mondloch, Cherry Pancake, Benjamin Paul, Flavio Rojas Lima, Barbara and Dennis Tedlock, Norman Hammond, Sister Alice Zachmann. Thanks also for aid in the various research stages to: the Ford Foundation; the Wenner Grenn Foundation for Anthropological Research and the Social Science Research Council. Eliot Weinberger's encouragement and editorial help in giving its present form to this book was invaluable. Janet Rodney Tarn's leading role in everything to do with this book, from research to writing, should be abundantly clear.

So many people help one over such a long period of time. May those whose names may have inadvertently been omitted here forgive us.

We dedicate this book to all Atitecos, past, present and future, with especial affectionate reverence to the men women and cadets of the "Royal Tzutujil Navy." Above all, may the Maya, however long it takes, triumph over repression, imperialism and tourism in their own magnificent and immemorial land.

SCANDALS IN THE HOUSE OF BIRDS

Map of the Lake Atitlán Area
Department of Solola, Highland Guatemala

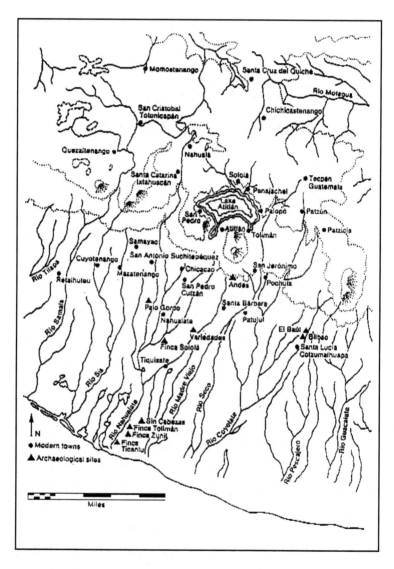

Southwestern Guatemala. Adapted from McBryde 1947.

Detail of the Lake Atitlán Area
Department of Solola, Highland Guatemala

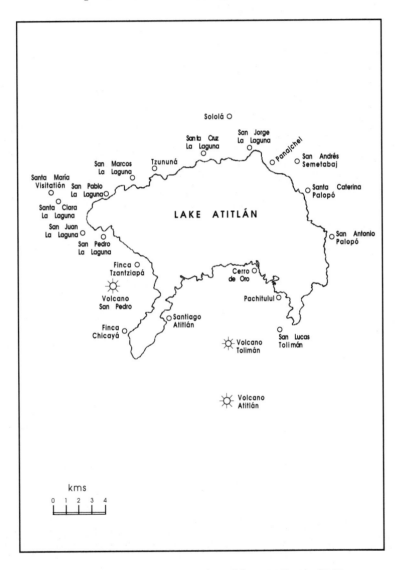

Southwestern Guatemala. Adapted from McBryde 1947.

ONE

The Maximón Scandals

We are on Lake Atitlán in the Department of Sololá, Guatemala, Central America. It is one of the most beautiful lakes in the world, ringed with hills and three majestic volcanos, home to several Tzutujil and Cakchikel Maya Indian villages. The Maya here speak two of the languages in the Quichean group. Many of the dialects within the languages differ noticeably.

Writing in 1952–53, Tarn described a major religious icon of the Tzutujil village of Santiago Atitlán: the Maximón. In the description, the word cofradía refers to a small brotherhood of Indian officials, elected for a year at a time, who keep the images and maintain the rituals of a particular village saint both in the village church and in their own small chapel:

Tarn, 1952–3:

As nearly as one can discover from conflicting evidence, the Maximón is, basically, a flat piece of wood about two and a half feet high and six to eight inches thick. A little jar or enamelled iron cup is strapped to the top end and contains the base of another piece of wood, or possibly gourd, which forms the core of the head. At the bottom end, two jars contain the wooden legs. The whole contraption is kept in a bundle above the roof trellis of *cofradía* Santa Cruz (the Holy Cross) towards which all who enter cross themselves and under which the largest candles always stand. When dressed for *fiestas*, the core is wrapped in rags and corn-husks, held together with string and fitted with boots. In this *cofradía*, there is a dresser or *telinel*, an official attached to the *cofradía*: he is an *aj'kun*, a native priest; the office was permanent until 1950 but is now yearly. The *telinel* covers the resultant bundle with a minimum of two or three sets of clothes offered by Atitecos and pilgrims from other villages. A doll emerges, some four and a half feet tall, clothed in shirt, belt and pants of Atiteco style plus a Texan size fifty-five hat, a blue serge jacket and a bib of some thirty silk scarves. A crude wooden mask covers the head core.

Such a puppet had, rather surprisingly, attracted the attention of no less an international periodical than the Latin American Edition of *Time Magazine* for April 2nd, 1951. It describes some events of 1950 and their repercussion in 1951:

DEVILISH DEITY

The raw-boned Tzutujil Indians of mountain-bound Santiago Atitlán (pop. 10,000) have a religion of their own, a mixture of undigested bits of Roman Catholicism and queer survivals of paganism. Their favorite deity is a raffish, four foot idol named Maximón, who smokes cigars, wears four hats and a leer. Smoking is the least of Maximón's vices. With gleeful perversity, the Indians assign to him an uninhibited libido and a rollicking disregard for the Ten Commandments.

Last week was Maximón's annual festival, culminating on Good Friday with drunken dances, a caricature of a Passion Play, and special offerings to the idol. Outside the village church, where the villagers also worshipped as sometime Christians, Maximón was installed for the occasion in a tiny chapel. His guards posted by haughty Nicolás Chiviliu, village brujo (witch doctor), swung censers, cranked huge wooden noisemakers. They were guarding Maximón from the priest. Most years the Indians have invited a Roman Catholic cleric to help during Holy Week in their mixed pagan-Christian ceremonies. Last year, they asked Dominican Padre Godofredo Recinos on the other side of Lake

Atitlán. He was shocked by Maximón. When he tried to set the idol afire, the guards chased him away. Then he fired three shots at Maximón. He missed. Next morning, Good Friday, he delivered an ultimatum: 'Either that pagan idol goes, or I do.'

'Have a good trip,' said Nicolás. Six weeks later, Padre Recinos came back across the lake with his father superior in a motor launch. Robes aflutter, the priests dashed into the village. They chopped Maximón's wooden head from his straw body with a machete and sped away.

The Indians were enraged. They made a new head, but it was a poor substitute for the original. When Padre Recinos turned up in Santiago Atitlán last week uninvited, he was met with silence and sullen stares. The padre hopefully offered to say Good Friday Mass without payment if someone would offer him food and lodging. He was answered with cold silence. Turning to go, the padre shook his fist at leering Maximón. 'That,' he cried, 'is the work of the devil.' 'Padre,' said brujo Nicolás, 'we are sons of the devil.'

Tarn, whom Nicolás considers as his apprentice, reads this to Nicolás as soon as he sees it. Nicolás is a tall, broad, leonine, immensely handsome man with a regal bearing. Nicolás loves it. He doesn't even bridle at the word *brujo*, although normally he gets furious at any confusion between *aj'kun* (shaman, prayer-maker, native priest) and *aj'itz* (witch, sorcerer, evil magician). No doubt he accepts *brujo* as the normal foreigner's usage.

"Well, I never said that we were sons of the devil! Can you imagine me saying *that*? But he did have a pistol, that's true. Only thing is: the *cofrades* rushed him before he could fire. One bullet fell on the ground and we now have it at the bottom of the Mam's clothes box!" Nicolás does not use the name "Maximón." He would accept "the Mam" or "Don Pedro" or "the Old Guy." But not "Maximón."

TWO

Stories of the Early Earth, I: The Ancients Who Made the Mam

Tarn, writing in 1952–53, records the following story by his teacher Nicolás Chiviliu:

Tarn, 1952–3:

In the very old days, when men were small, dirty and poor, we the Atitecos were capable of prophecy and knowing about the rain before it came. Among these ancients there were—now . . . was it twelve or six? It was six, yes, six—who used to go on regular trips east to Antigua which, in those days, was the Capital of Guatemala. You know the town, it is still there, tourists love it. The ancients were traders and fishermen and, after fishing the fish from the Lake, they went on three day journeys to Antigua and then came back to Atitlán. They did the journey very quickly until they arrived at the two Volcanos. These men had six sisters (some say wives) who were very clever but also poor and dirty. At Antigua, the men were always treated as 'Indios' and 'Ixtis' and 'dirty people.' . . .

[We are trying to put together a great sequence of stories by entering it at one point or another. Bear in mind the importance of Lake Atitlán in those old days—now reduced by pollution and decreasing fish populations—as well as the solid trading relationship which has always existed between the Pacific Coast and Atitlán. We will tell the stories in different voices, sometimes going over an episode from different points of view.]

In 1979, Pascual Mendoza is talking. He is a small, quiet man, a great shaman and "miracle worker" but given to frequent outbursts of crying when emotionally beleaguered. Atitecos make plentiful use of nicknames: Pascual's is "Weep Wizard":

Weep Wizard, 1979:
We have a group of women, the *nawal taq exki* or *taq iyoma'*, the Power-Women. They are pure, steadfast, ideal women. They have their husbands—the Power-Men, the *nawal taq achi*—although they are as solid as old maids. We call old maids *rilaj q'apoja'*: venerable maids. These women used to go southwest to the Coast every day, taking the road past the cross-roads, the *kolo' be*, as you leave the village, passing Xokexom and Chicacao and then on down to San Miguel Panaj and San Antonio Suchitepéquez. That road is a killer. Most men who go down in Holy Week, for instance, take three days. A woman doing it today is unthinkable.

Our Power-Women go down carrying huge baskets. They are winds and clouds going down to the Coast and coming back by return flight that very day. They take salt down from Sacapulas in the North and trade it for cacao. Also tropical fruit.

Tarn's Diary, 1952–53:
I learned the only lesson in economics of my whole life. I carried a bunch of bananas on foot from the Coast to Santiago. At the bottom they were worth five cents, at the top seven cents. On the way down, I saw Catleya orchids all along the path: a glorious blaze of purple. If only I could get them to the northern cities! I picked one: it wilted within five minutes.

Weep Wizard, 1979:
At the same time as the Power-Women travelled southwest, their men would catch fish in the Lake and take them

all the way east to Patzún, on the way to Antigua. It's said
they went so fast, the fish were still alive and jumping when
they got into the highlands. Some of them would go as far
as Panq'an, which is our old name for Antigua. Some would
go to Sololá and Chimaltenango. They would pick up
Sacapulas salt which Atitlán did not have in those days and
bring it back for the women to take to the Coast. This was
old-time salt: now no one trades for salt to the north any
more. They would also bring lime from the north. Everything was bartered: even today people can remember how
much a pound of corn was worth, a pound of salt, a pound
of fish.

Prechtel, 1979:
Weep Wizard is not saying it in the story, but the men put
one foot on one volcano then the other foot on the next,
then another, then another. The story only says that they
went very quickly so that the fish would remain fresh. The
men and women moved in a continuous cycle. When the
men came back in the early morning, the women would
have already gone. And when the women came back in
the afternoon, the men were already gone. Some say the
men and women were siblings, and they each had husbands and wives. Most say that the men and women were
married but did not see each other too often. *Cabecera [the
Head of Atitlán's Indian officials]* says they made love only
once every twenty days—the Maya calendric cycle has
twenty days, O.K.?

Tarn, 1952–53:
Now it happened that one of the men realized that there
was another guy sleeping with his wife in his absence. And
when he would come back from a trip, someone would
tell him to beware of his wife because she was having an
affair. Once, the wife heard her husband coming and said

to her lover, 'You had better hide under the bed and then you can escape when my husband comes in or, if he sleeps or goes out to piss, you can slip out on tiptoe.' The husband entered his house but, as he had the power of clairvoyance, he knew all about the man under the bed. He had brought bread and chocolate and liquor with him and invited the other man to come out from under the bed and share their meal. But the lover was afraid and didn't budge.

The husband said, 'It doesn't matter: my wife is only a fruit, you have been helping her in this matter and I forgive you.' After much pleading, the lover came out and shared the food and drink, then thanked the husband and went on his way. And the husband said, 'If you come back tomorrow, it will not matter, it will be O.K.' On the next trip by the merchant, however, someone said to all the men that all their wives had lovers. 'Yes, we know,' they said, 'and this time, we are going to do something about it.'

Weep Wizard, 1979:
In the story of the Power-Women, we have the Power-Men passing between the Volcanos: Volcano-Volcano, Volcano Atitlán, and Volcano-Her-Children, Volcano Tolimán. They would make for a place called Sajkab, near Agua Escondida in the neighborhood of the Palopó villages on the Lake's east side. There is a white cliff thereabouts; the place of lime talc or white rock. This is the *cal* they would cook with beans and give to pregnant women and use for spinning. They would rest here and talk and make their plans for Patzún and Antigua. There was also a place, below Sajkab, where they would test their weapons. The weapons were called *hwit*, they were magic sticks or staffs. They would throw a *hwit* at a wall and it would boomerang back: the wall would be all sliced up. They had no other weapons since all other arms were prohibited by the government.

The Power-Men went up every day and could read their own palms. They could also make their *hwit* stand up and this would divine for them what was happening at home. One day, they were at Tz'anch'oj which is just behind Volcano-Her-Children.

The Power-Men are going along. Some say there are twelve men and some say three. The older people seem to prefer three. The first man was Poklaj, Dust; the second Batzin, Thread; and the third was Ch'eep, the Ultimo. Well, they are climbing away and the older brother Dust says to the younger, 'Hey, don't you feel a bit ridiculous, a bit ashamed?' The Ultimo asks why. 'Well, because there is another man messing around with your wife,' says Dust. 'I didn't know that,' says the Ultimo.' 'I think we should "play a game" on the next trip, don't you?' said Dust. So they agreed on it.

The next trip, the Ultimo left in his house the box that we usually place inside our carrying frame. When they got to Tz'anch'oj, he turned back, leaving the other two to go on to Godinez and sleep there. At midday, the Ultimo gets home and knocks on the door. No answer. He knocks again. Eventually, his wife's voice, asking 'Ooooooooooo-uuuu! What are you doing here?' 'I just forgot my box,' says the Ultimo. The wife goes on delaying by asking questions and he says she should just let him in to get his box.

She lets him in; he has liquor and some food. He tells her to tell the friend to come out. '*Friend,*' she says, '*what* friend? What do you mean? Whom do you mean?' 'Oh, the guy lying under the bed wrapped in a mat of course,' says the Ultimo. 'Is that what you do to your friends, is that how you treat your turkeys, shoving them under the bed?' he asks his wife. The wife begins to apologize; her husband tells her not to worry; they should all have lunch together and then he will be off again. The lover comes out all colors, feeling terrible: the husband tells him to sit down and not feel bad and not run away. The husband offers the lover a drink; the lover thinks he is going to kill him with that drink. 'Why should I kill you?' says the Ultimo. 'You are a man just like I am. You saw a fruit, you smelled it, you found it good and wanted to eat it. Any man would have done the same: there is no fault in you.' The wife is crying; he tells her to pass the food and liquor around; they all get soaked. The Ultimo then picks up his box and departs.

He gets back to his brothers; they talk about it. The brothers argue that they cannot let this go on: pretty soon the whole village will be at it. Obviously the wife is informing on them and has joined the 'other side'; she has turned *q'isoum*, transforming witch. They will have to be cunning, to 'play a game,' *tz'aniem*, and risk themselves against these devils. But they cannot do it alone. They will have to make a form, toy, doll, instrument, weapon: an *itzbal*.

Juan Ajcot is a thick-set man who seems very slow on a first encounter but quickly reveals a formidable wit. He has a reputation as a great ladies' man. His nickname is "Red Banana":

Red Banana, 1979:
There were six Power-Men called *aj'biaj*, men of travel, *biaj*: from Spanish *viaje*, travel. But no one travels except for trade, so: traders, merchants. Now these six travelled so much that no one remembered they were Atitecos any more. They hardly remembered it themselves.

While they were on the Coast, a man would come and enjoy their wives. They had always earned a good living but now, when they went home, they would be given shitty food. They couldn't figure it out. The lover would go one week with one wife, the next with another.

One day, they were on the Coast and they felt they had woken up with a bad dream. They went into a bar to drink it off. They only went in one at a time so that their gear outside the bar could be watched and protected. When they had all gotten their drinks, one guy asked the other if he felt anything strange or untoward. They began to compare notes. 'I think we are all *nikanik ali*, crazy guys,' said one. 'I think there is somebody messing around with the *rilaj vinaq*, the venerable person, the old lady.'

Nabeyal, First Merchant, decided they would have to check the situation out, so they bought their chile in San Antonio and went home. Perhaps, since they were doing well at business, someone was spreading rumors to do them harm, *Nabeyal* suggested. He said, 'Go into your own house, each one of you, and see what's what.'

So the Ultimo, who reached home first, knocked on the door of his house and his wife didn't want to open up. *(Usual dialogue.)* 'Aren't you going to offer me any coffee?' he said. 'There is no coffee,' she answered, 'Why don't you make your own?' 'Great!' thought the Ultimo. 'What about a little of your good food?' said the Ultimo. 'Well, there are some small tortillas made days ago,' she said—these are *ko'ol way*, small tortillas, like *ko'ol q'ij*, small, old, dead winter sun. 'Grrrrrrrreat!' thought the Ultimo. He didn't make any comments but when he wanted to sleep with her, she gave him a mat on the floor. 'Suuuuuuuper!' thought the Ultimo. 'This is really something else!'

The next man went into his house and the foods were cooking on the fire but the wife was gone. There was no sign of her. He made his own breakfast and ate. His wife came in from the market beaming all over her dial. 'Ooooo-oooops, what are you doing here?' she said. (Same story.)

The Power-Men realized what was going on and they felt terrible. Up in Patzún, soon afterwards, they swapped stories and felt even worse. 'It would be one thing if the women had boy friends but we still ate well and were

looked after,' said one, 'but we are eating like pigs and that
is unforgivable!' 'Here we are, earning their *living* and *they*
are eating our food,' said another. This lover was eating
their food: you understand it means that the lover is 'eating' their wives.

Weep Wizard, 1979:
Now Dust, Thread and Ultimo decide they will have to
call a convention of the Power-Men and, after selling their
wares in Antigua, they make for Atitlán and on to the Center of the world. We call that Center Cerro de Burro. It's a
small hill among those that separate us from the Coast,
just southwest of our village. There they call all the Power-
Men and Power-Women together. All the stories give different line-ups but the men are likely to be: Diego Batzin,
Juan Batzin; Diego Tzruy, Juan Tzruy; Diego Tz'aaj, Juan
Tz'aaj; Diego Poklaj, Juan Poklaj; Matek Staka and so forth.
Matek Staka is a dance king in our *fiesta* dances; all those
figures are Power-People. The women are likely to be:
Yamri Kmo'; Yamri Tz'ubtz'ub, Yamri Pixnaq and so forth:
these are either names of fruit or names of parts of the
loom. There are twenty-four Power-People in all *(here, you
see, the tale is reverting to twelve men, twelve women).*

Then, they all give *razón*, which is like they're saying
what should be done about a case and why, and Diego
Poklaj, Dust, is first: some even call him Santiago because
Santiago is our 'first' saint. Dust-man they call him: which
is also what they sometimes call the Mam. 'Well,' someone begins, 'it seems as if the earth has gotten a little different: the "sons-and-daughters" *(the ordinary people at large,
especially the uninitiated)* have gotten out of hand a little bit
and the order of things is beginning to break up. Virgin
boys are starting to marry widows and widowers take virgin
girls to wife; married men are sleeping with other men's

wives; people are taking things that don't belong to them; Indians are trying to be *ladinos* . . . All this has got to stop and we are the ones who must stop it.'

Each one gives his or her views. This is where the story of the great bull of Xechivoy comes in with some story-tellers, the animal that scared people so much no one would venture out at night. One of the Power-Women told a story about her human husband: how he got worms in his testicles so that they rattled and how she cured him. This, like the bull business, was a case of female witchcraft: it was the work of the *q'isoma'*, female transforming witches. The whole village was suffering from female witchcraft as a matter of fact and that is why the Mam was created. Well, in one way or another, enough evidence was collected at this power-conference for something to get done.

The man who was *Telinel* (the official responsible for dressing the Mam) in 1979 is a quiet, powerful man who always speaks with great calm. His gestures have a curious elegant tenderness about them which no one would expect from his tough physique. His nickname is Malvex, "Loincloth." He tells the story very differently:

Loincloth, 1979:
A long time ago, there were many Power-Men. And there was one woman: María Magdalena. She was very powerful: number one crazy-woman and also an incredible witch. She would spend eight nights with a man and then switch to another and so on down the line. She would get hold of someone's husband and run him so ragged he would turn into a *nikanik*, a crazy guy, a kind of village idiot, and very soon die. But the guy who was looking after her more than most was Diego Tz'aaj—for he was very rich and lived inside a hill. No one could help being attracted to her. And the world had only just begun.

12

There were three shamans, diviners-of-days, who wanted to cure this woman and set the world straight: while this woman was on the world with all these guys buzzing around her nothing could happen right. The best thing they could do, they thought, was to put her in a sweatbath. To sweat her up. That is the way you get rid of *ch'ojlal*: the crazy lust sickness. They tried it one time: when they woke up, all the men were tucked inside the sweatbath and she was gone! Another time, one of the three diviners became her lover, he was that attracted. He was also very strong and told her, no matter what happened, she would not be able to do him in. But she got him alright: she slowly turned him into a *nikanik*. Once he tried to get her with the *isote* plant—which was used against transforming witches and had been used against the great bull—but she turned it around against him and drove him crazy.

It was at that point that they decided on making the Mam.

[At first sight, this does not seem to be so much a tale of the world's beginning but rather a tale about social order breaking down when men are too long away from home. The story may reflect the problems of a society of traders or of a society under stress, either in the distant past or more recently. Insofar as powerful people, natural or supernatural, are often thought of as ladino, *the lover or lovers may have been plantation owners. Insofar as female witchcraft is often associated with the Coast—where Atitlán had dependencies until recent times—it suggests that the lover or lovers may have been Coastal men.*

Tropical fruit is brought up to Atitlán from the coastal region during the rituals of Holy Week, to be offered to the Mam who is said to "smell," "eat," or "sleep with" these fruit. To complicate matters, the Mam is often thought of as a ladino. *If we are dealing with relatively recent myth, plantation owners, usually coastal as it happens, may be the villains. If we are dealing with relatively older myth, the fruit may have originally represented wives (fruit = women = wives) sent by coastal vassals to Atiteco overlords. One wonders then whether our stories involve a kind of vassals' vengeance*

SCANDALS IN THE HOUSE OF BIRDS

against Atitlán: coastal men lost their women to Atitlán and took Atiteco women ("illegally" from the Atiteco point of view) in exchange? It would be understandable if, indeed, the wife-givers turned out to be also the source of female witchcraft.

Of course, the main parts of the story of the Mam do involve the origin of order in the world as a whole—a major, if not the major, story told by virtually all tribal origin myths. Moreover, there is reason to believe the Mam myth may be relatively ancient or, at least, may well contain very ancient lore.]

THREE

1950–53: Stolen Masks

There is a contemporary account of the theft of the masks. The tone is reminiscent of Spanish Colonial chronicles. It was written by Agustín Pop, in his Field Diary for April 22nd, 1950. Pop was an anthropologist from San Pedro la Laguna, neighbor village to Atitlán, almost certainly a Protestant at the time and working for the *Instituto Indigenista Nacional*, the National Indigenist Institute. Tarn's present comments are in italics:

> A religious conflict according to the information received from various villagers to whom the matter was of some moment: they say that on Holy Wednesday 1950, the priest arrived in Santiago Atitlán to say mass. The priest was called in by a rich person called J.S. who gave 150 quetzales for the mass—so that he was not called by the village but by one Atiteco.
>
> The priest had come overland from San Lucas Tolimán and met with an Atiteco [*probably a Protestant*] who had come from Cerro de Oro to preach the Gospel of Our Lord Jesus Christ. The priest already knew what the people did with Maximón during Holy Week, for as soon as he met this man he began asking him about it. The man gave him a very good account of the Maximón customs and added that the non-Christian villagers thought of him as their only god. The priest replied that he knew all this and that he had come this year to prevent this cult and to burn the Maximón. But the man told him not to burn it, for the people would become alarmed and could go as far as to take the priest's life: better to be wise and not court such a danger.
>
> The priest arrived in the Roman church and found it

well and truly adorned but he saw a group of men, and behind them a multitude of people were adoring the Maximón, so that he got furious and broke down the wooden arrangements which had been set up to receive the Maximón and threw them over the church porch. People got extremely angry and were ready to set about killing the priest so someone fetched the literate boys and told them to tell the priest to leave the Maximón alone, for he was their god, and that the priest would go mad and die should he persist.

The priest answered that he didn't give a fig about going mad, but that he would not allow them to worship the man who had been Christ's worst enemy before the crucifixion. [*The priest was speaking of the Maximón as Judas Iscariot.*] The people's temper got considerably worse and some shouted that the priest should be put to death because he wasn't a Catholic but a Protestant. The priest ran over to the convent to get his pistol and made as if to shoot the people, shouting 'I die for the truth but let's see that you go too, and to hell at that for the pack of idolaters and savages that you are!'

But when the priest went back to the convent, then the people set up the stones again and then placed Maximón there with a golden [*golden!?*] incense burner, liters of aguardiente and especially thick candles. When the priest came back out, he kicked the incense burner and candles, but as he was holding his pistol the guardians endured all this without moving. All of this was witnessed by the *Catequista* leader of San Pedro. [*The* Catequistas *were usually young men trained in literacy and Catholicism by priests inspired by the movement* Acción Católica, *a conservative organ of the Roman Church which began having great influence in Guatemala around 1945.*]

When the priest had finished his business, he came to the beach to go to San Pedro. The idolaters took fright and said that the Last Judgement or Deluge was upon them. J.S.

began collecting money from the villagers—the money which he had paid for the mass—because the mass had not been said: they came to the beach with the Mayor of the village and the priest gave the money back without a fuss. But the Mayor told them that if they had thus given alms to God, then they should respect the priest and not take it back.

They understood and tried to give the money back but the priest refused and they had to put it by force into his bag. In the end, they convinced him to say the mass, but he accepted only on condition that they should not adore the Maximón. In the end, they put the Maximón in its place but did not adore it; only while the priest took breakfast, a few ran to adore him, but, while the priest was in church, they did nothing.

When they told him that he would go mad, he said: 'All right, all right!: let them take me to the lunatic asylum, or let them put Maximón in my sleeping quarters, and I will prove that all this is arrant nonsense.' But the people remained very much upset.

At the moment among the Roman Catholics, there is a split: one side agrees with the priest and his anti-idolatrous sermons; the other is against him and against the truth. The priest promised to hold a session in the Parochial House in Sololá and to make all those who were agreed against the Maximón to sign a paper to that effect. Some of the San Pedro la Laguna people here who believe in the Maximón are against the priest and what he did in Atitlán.

Juan Sisay, the painter of Atiteco scenes in a "primitive" style, and, presumably, the J.S. of Pop's account, is sounding off to Tarn, three years after the event, about the values of old customs. This is the moment to put in the big question. Tarn: "Why then did you do what you did in 1950? People say it was you who helped the priests take the mask?" As usual with Juan, he maintains that his role has been completely misrepresented:

Juan Sisay, 1953:

This is my story. One day, not long after that Holy Week in 1950, I met the priest at a *Catequista* wedding in San Pedro. The priest had told me to tell Atitecos that they should evacuate the Maximón from *cofradía* Santa Cruz and adore him with all their customs if they wanted to— as long as it was *not* done in the same house with the Holy Burial, the *Santo Entierro*. You know that *cofradía* Santa Cruz has Crosses, a Holy Burial—a dead Christ in a glass case—and the Maximón up in the trellis. If they did not obey was his sense of it, he would have to notify the Archbishop in Quetzaltenango and *he* would come and destroy the Maximón.

The Archbishop had already written me, as it happens, asking me for details, but I was worried about acting without authority and suggested holding a session of the elders, the *principales*. At this meeting, one of the sacristans assaulted me and almost hit me, saying that I was a criminal to try to do away with such old customs.

He accused me of just having sold a painting of the Maximón to a hotel in Panajachel across the Lake and poured scorn on me for trying to destroy what he called 'the shirt on my back and the food in my belly.' Well, I didn't answer but I was very hurt that this had been witnessed by so many people. Perhaps I was too sensitive about such things. But I was also angry. I phoned the priest who told me that the Archbishop was coming.

The Archbishop was prevented from getting here by a violent rainstorm so that only three priests arrived: a Father Superior, Father Recinos and a third man. I met them on arrival and they went to see the Town Mayor. The Mayor happened to be away and they spoke to a senior officer, the First *Regidor* who happened to be Andrés Tzina. He was violent with the priests and refused them any aid in their plans to burn the Maximón in the market place.

Finally, they rushed over to *cofradía* Santa Cruz taking with them a group of junior officers, the *alguaciles*. They prayed for a while and exorcised the house. I stood at the door, not wishing to interfere in such delicate matters. Then they looked for the head and masks of Maximón and took them away.

Later there was a great outcry in the village and people wanted to kill the priests. But it was too late. Their anger did not turn against me until some time later. As for the masks, they were taken to Sololá, Quetzaltenango, and finally Guatemala City, where they were burned.

The sexton Salvador Pospoy told Tarn that the date for the theft was June 6, 1950. Nicolás Chiviliu had come back from a trip to Guatemala City on the same boat as the priests and had gone to his own house, suspecting nothing. He was told later that Juan Sisay, two policemen and the priests had stolen the masks from *cofradía* Santa Cruz.

Pascual Ixbalan, son of the Francisco Ixbalan who had been *alcalde* Santa Cruz, i.e. leader of that *cofradía*, in June 1950 (his own age being about thirteen), claims in 1979, nearly thirty years later, that his father had been away at the Coast and had left relatives in charge of the *cofradía*. Pascual remembered three *ladinos* coming, none of whom he knew; also one priest, a Padre Simeon, two armed policemen, and Juan Sisay with his side-kick Domingo. Juan Sisay went into the *cofradía*, asked for the *alcalde* as is the custom, and was told he was away.

Then Juan took the initiative of climbing up the ladder himself, got the head out, put it in a case and gave the case to one of the policemen. He also took hold of another mask which he gave to another person in the raiding party: the head, Pascual assumed, already bore one mask. Then the party left. The second mask was found in the *urna*, Maximón's glass case. It is very hard to say which of the two masks was the one which Tarn eventually found but it was probably the one on the head at the time of the theft.

Padre Simeon was later transferred to Tzununa and died in a boat accident on the lake. Padre Godofriedo Recinos was the man behind the deed: a Salvadorean who had tried to get rid of the Maximón while stationed in Atitlán. It is hard to know whether Recinos was present or not: accounts vary. Padre Simeon may have been the "third priest" in Agustín Pop's *Instituto Indigenista* account. Pascual Ixbalan's account of "three *ladinos*" is confusing: he was probably seeing three priests in civilian dress—although *Time* talks of "robes aflutter."

As we shall see, one mask was returned to Atitlán at the time Pascual Ixbalan told his story in 1979. As it was being admired in *cofradía* Santa Cruz as a very old one, it was said that various *principales* had believed this mask to be the *ch'eep* (smallest or last-born) of a group of three—but this turned out not to be the case. It was the middle one. The first one was thought to have been "bearded and mustachioed and very ancient."

It was also claimed that the head had been a curious three-piece affair, something like "a little chair on the back of which a Mam face was carved and into which a mask was fitted as if the mask were seated." It is also possible that there may have been some sort of "chair" for the body.

The ease with which Juan Sisay took the head was said by the *Telinel* 1979 to have been connected to the Mam's being kept fully formed ("*armado*") for one half of the year: if the head was taken in June (the rainy season), the Mam must therefore have been kept loose in three pieces during the dry season. Chiviliu is on record as having been the one to argue successfully that the head should be kept attached to the body at all times: presumably this was *after* the theft.

■　　■　　■

A few days after the theft, the Director of the *Instituto Indigenista* sends Agustín Pop back to Atitlán with a questionnaire:

1) What percentage of the population was in favor of the Maximón before the event?
— 95% for (*ladino* and Indian),
5% against (all Protestants).
2) What percentage afterwards?
— 15% for,
85% against.
3) What do the people think happened to the Maximón?
— A rumor ran that the Pope had heard of the great fame of the Maximón and had sent for him to adore him.

The statistics strain credulity. Even if this rumor did run, it hardly satisfies Atitlán for long. Two or three deputations go to Sololá, achieving nothing. An edict is issued against the Maximón and, after inventory, he is moved from *cofradía* Santa Cruz and sent to the house of another *principal*. He stays there during six months and fines are allegedly levied against any one found "worshipping him" (i.e. specifically, one would think, placing candles, offering incense, tobacco, alcohol, and praying). After this time, the Maximón goes back to *cofradía* Santa Cruz as if nothing had happened.

1951: Holy Week comes around and no one knows what to do.

Nicolás Chiviliu steps right into the breach. He is never tired of telling how, on Holy Tuesday, after "fortifying myself with a glass of 'champagne' drunk with the *ladino* shopkeeper and politico Ramíro Ramírez," he had sent off a telegram to the President of the Republic:

Urgent. Santiago Atitlán, 3/19/51. 14.00 hours. To: Constitutional President of the Republic Jacobo Arbenz Guzmán: respectfully beg your orders continuation vestment of San Simon and celebration Major Holy Week ceremonies forbidden to us by priests. Beg you to intervene. We greet you. Nicolás Chiviliu, via Salvador Pospoy (sic).

Salvador Pospoy & Companions. Santiago Atitlán. Yours received 19.30 hours National Palace. Departmental Governor has instructions to intervene in your case. Sincerely. Jacobo Arbenz.

Followed one hour later by a message from the Departmental Governor in Sololá telling our friends to proceed. Nicolás dresses the Mam alone in the *cofradía*, and takes him to the small chapel on the left of the church esplanade—the last of four such chapels and survivor of the earthquakes of some years before. On Holy Wednesday, Atitecos find their Maximón not far from the usual place he would have occupied on such a day: his traditional station to the right of the church door on the covered porch.

■ ■ ■

1952: The priest complains that the small chapel, being opposite his room in the convent to the church's left is too noisy what with the prayers and drunken singing. He is losing his sleep. The Mam is accordingly moved to a position in the market place and it is here he is expected to go in 1953. The market place position, however, is frowned upon in that it is close to the place in the plaza where they sell pigs.

During Tarn's first months in Atitlán in 1952, he is befriended by Juan Sisay and his *Catequista* friends; he also hears a constant stream of accusations against them and plumbs the depths of ill feeling which the Maximón events have generated. These accusations on the part of the traditionalists are obsessive and the stories are told over and over again. A great deal of diplomacy is required to maintain friendships on all sides, even considering the no-man's-land position an outsider might be assumed to occupy.

The message from the elders is that Juan and his friends are just *patojos*, children, and have no right to interfere. Besides which, as painters, Juan and his friend Domingo are making money out of things which they have set out to destroy.

The traditionalists, however, lack leadership because the then

Cabecera is not a strong one and because the Town Mayor is a *Catequista*. Clearly, politics are involved. A further complication is that the Protestants, often nicknamed the Hallelujahs in the village, are waiting in the wings. *Both* the traditionalists and the *Catequistas* being Catholic, neither party wants Protestant interference.

In an effort to defuse the situation, the elders and, especially, the shamans, the *aj'kuna*, vie with each other in declaring that the Maximón is not a power any more and that, above all, he is not the "person who sold Jesus Christ."

To wit:

Third Cofradía Santa Cruz, 2/11/1952:
The priest said that Maximón sold Jesus for thirty pieces of silver or gold, but this one we have here is not the one who sold him: he is only his representative and one has to keep him because he is ancient and cannot be separated from *cofradía* Santa Cruz.

Nicolás Chiviliu, 4/8/1952:
During Holy Week, the priest spoke about Maximón and mentioned the three Simons: Simon Sametaya [*Thaddeo?*] who was in paradise; Simon Peda [*Pedro?*] and the Maximón who was the 'image, adornment or representation of the Simon in paradise'—but the priest was not clear about which one had sold Christ.

Pedro Mendoza, aj'kun friend of Chiviliu's, 3/24/1953:
To suppose or make believe that Maximón speaks to contemporary man as he once spoke to the ancient ones is to fool the people. I am fifty-six years of age and I have never had a single word from Maximón. Because he is the most sacred god, he does not talk.

Andrés Tzina, 4/2/1953:
'Look, look, we are adoring him! What are all these candles for? It's all wrong, it's a sin!' [*A moment later.*] 'Well, perhaps

23

it is alright after all, perhaps it doesn't matter: we say nothing and he says nothing and nothing really happens no
ways!' Tzina is drunk. (Tzina, furiously anti-*Catequista* but
also a disbeliever in the Mam, is sitting in front of the
Maximón in church 'like a ferocious rabbit in front of
a still more ferocious snake,' says Chiviliu, with ill-dis-
guised contempt.)

At the time, Tarn associates all these remarks about the Mam
not talking any more with a theme which comes up very frequently
in conversation with the elders regarding some kind of "death of
the world" which is occurring at this time, or has recently occurred.
This, in turn, Tarn relates to the Mam's nature as a vortex of conflict between Maya and Catholic beliefs engendered at the time of
the Conquest and operative ever since and of a vortex of doubts
about the continued validity of traditional rites and world-views.
In 1979, however, keeping in view the evidence about *aj'kuna*
talking with the Mam as part of their healing and divining prac-
tices, the "death of the world" theme seems more like a red her-
ring trailed under the nose of a friendly outsider during a time of
trouble. On the other hand, traditionalists do feel that these are
"latter days" and that a *juicio* or judgement—the end of a cosmic
era if a big judgement—may be occurring or about to occur. One
major sign of this in the 1970s is the manifest splitting up of the
ancient religion into three branches: the traditional Catholic; the
Catequista Catholic; and the Protestant.
Surprisingly, the "judgement" theme is already aired by Juan
Sisay at a moment when he can glimpse a triumph of his *Catequistas*
in 1953:

Juan Sisay, 1953:
The old people have to be helped for they are worried about
the spread of Protestantism. There happens to be a man
curing and doing 'miracles' in Guatemala City and Catholics are converting in droves after seeing him. One convert

even wants to take an organ back that he lent us *Catequistas*, though his daughter, for instance, says *she* would die if she ever had to change her religion. So, you see, it is dividing families! Wouldn't it be terrible if the *Cabezera* fell ill and was cured by a Protestant? No, it would even be better for him to go to hospital and fall into the hands of a doctor!

■   ■   ■

Late in January 1953, the traditionalists make a move:

Tarn, 1/25/1953:
An infernally tricky day. The sexton Salvador Pospoy is in to my house around nine this morning. They are going to *pedir milagro* (ask for a miracle) at *cofradía* Santa Cruz and they are going to dress the Maximón. Why don't I come and take advantage of the situation with my cameras? Surprising!

The *cofradía* looks and feels like the Pentagon and everyone is playing at being general. Most people are absolutely against any priest coming anywhere near Atitlán in Holy Week. It is feared, however, that the *Catequistas* have already asked one to come. Comments are made about him—the one who comes from Sololá—charging higher and higher fees for his masses and still insisting on booting out the old rituals, the *costumbres*.

The Town Mayor is also decried as a turncoat who had stood by the old guys during the Scandals and had then told them, yes, to take the Mam to the market place. Pospoy proposes that a memorandum be drawn up citing all the facts. Perhaps Ramíro Ramírez, the *ladino* who had been village Secretary, could be asked. Maybe I could type a letter to the President of the Republic.

Then *Telinel* sets up candles and does a long prayer. At the end, he takes a large candle and calls *Alcalde de cofradía* over, placing the candle against his forehead center, then

25

to right and left, then to right and left shoulders, then holding it to be kissed. Repeated with all *cofrades*.

Later ritual, *costumbre*, includes songs and prayers by Pospoy and *Telinel*. Pospoy gets everyone to kneel, then tells the story of the theft at great length. Recites a complete list of *fiestas cofradía* Santa Cruz is responsible for celebrating, plus a list of men from San Pedro and San Juan Sacatepéquez, San Raymondo, Antigua, Patzún, Patzicía, Panajachel, Sololá *et al* who have promises made to do *costumbre* here during Holy Week. He invokes blessings on all present here by name—as in an *aj'kun costumbre*. He ends by asking good fortune during Holy Week against the Spaniard, the Foreigner, the Infidel (the Sololá priest is a Spaniard).

There is no Maximón dressing (perhaps because I am here?) and the question of their trust in me is not finally settled. We all go to church around 5:30. The *Catequistas* are there with the Town Mayor in front of the main altar. We move to the altar of Santa Cruz. The *Catequistas* are all dressed up nice and neat, led by Domingo, Juan Sisay's friend, in their staggeringly dull *Salve Marias*. The *cofrades* are straggling behind Pospoy howling his head off above the *Catequista* din.

Telinel, no doubt trying to be funny, sends our censer off with Sixth *Cofrade* to the Mayor, Juan, Domingo and Juan Mendoza. They are embarrassed by their rosaries but can't refuse to pass the censer under their armpits—as any one would have to do when offered the censer in a *cofradía* . . .

On February 8th, 1953, it is announced that the priest at Sololá has sent a letter forbidding the Maximón to be placed at his old position on the church porch during Holy Week. Doubts are expressed about the letter: Juan Sisay is accused of listening in on the meetings of *principales* and then reporting to the priest. Meeting after meeting is held without any agreement. The *ladinos* are said to be stepping in with their own likes, dislikes and demands.

Individuals rant and rave about going to Guatemala City to see presidents and lawyers, then backtrack out of fear of officialdom or financial burdens.

Every conceivable document to every conceivable recipient, from President of the Republic to Sololá priest, is dreamed up, discussed at appalling lengths, then abandoned. Nothing happens except that the traditionalists are gradually sinking into lethargy and despair. Much hinges on whether masses are to be requested of the priest and there is heated debate as to their cost. Frequent comparison is made between the high financial demands of the priest and the relatively modest ones of the *aj'kuna*: implicitly, sometimes explicitly, their respective deities are involved as well. *Telinel* threatens not to dress Maximón at all or to dress him but let him stay in the *cofradía* rather than allow him to go to the pigs. Individuals come in at all times of the day, crying that they want to go see the President who would surely be kind to his "Indian Children" but that they are being prevented—by lack of money, fear of the police or the supplications of their fearful families: Indians do not take risks lightly and they are right. The traditionalists cannot get it together and they are at their wits' ends. The *Catequistas* are being magnanimous: always a bad sign. The whole case is going to collapse by default into their hands.

■   ■   ■

Six days before this, Tarn is in Guatemala City on February 2nd, 1953. He is advised by his friend the French Consul General that a Father Teste, Order of Lazarists, native of Clermond Ferrand, France, is in town at the Pauline Fathers' House on 12th street.

Teste is a very lively, also very nervous little gentleman, with French rusty from twenty-one years of service in Central America. He confirms that Father Recinos, now in El Salvador, had given Santiago Atitlán an ultimatum of one month to move the Maximón out of *cofradía* Santa Cruz. Also that three priests took two masks. One was given to the Archbishop. "One" (laughing) "is in my possession." Tarn now believes that Teste was the third priest.

Times, Teste claims, were difficult. This was just before a presidential election and there was something of a campaign against priests. The leftist Arbenz regime was about to come into power. The priests had had to go to the *Instituto Indigenista Nacional*. [*The Director of the I.I.N. at the time tells Tarn that the priests refused to let any notes be taken on what they said.*]

March 6th, 1953: The mask is obtained from Father Teste as an object of ethnographical value on Teste's condition that it should not be returned to Atitlán. Tarn, "saving the mask for science," sees no alternative to it not being returned and suggests that it go to a prominent European museum, the museum where he had first been trained. The mask is in pretty bad condition, visibly full of worms, with a piece of one lip falling out. It needs museographic attention.

Father Teste says that the villages have been left so long without regular resident priests that the visiting priests can hardly cope when on circuit. Priests, confronted with an enormous amount of stubbornness, may have lost patience and done some things ill-advisedly. Priests are only human after all.

The mask is duly delivered in Guatemala City to a representative of the museum, a good buddy of Tarn's, and duly deposited in Europe where it undergoes disinfection, delousing and mild restoration.

A photo of the mask eventually appears on the cover of an anthropological work, *Los Escándalos de Maximón* by the anthropologist E. Michael Mendelson [*known as "Miguel Sol" in Atitlán*]. The book is published many years after these events: in 1957 in Guatemala City.

FOUR

Stories of the Early Earth, II: The Finding of the Mam

Weep Wizard, 1979:
In the great council room which was this area of the Lake, the Power-Men and the Power-Women were debating. Francisca Batz'bal, that is Francisca Thread, gets up and says, 'I believe that we should make a form.'

Red Banana, 1979:
    'I believe we should make a *ch'ajalniel ruchiliev*; a guard-ian of the earth,' said First Merchant. 'Let's make a helper, a machine; let's ask a tree—we'll make an image from the tree and give him wisdom and set him up as caretaker of the earth.'

Weep Wizard, 1979:
Another answers, 'Yes, but with what?' Francisca says, 'Let's try rock.' And they tried rock and the rock wouldn't stand up. They tried mud, rubber and other substances. Then, they saw that the obvious thing was to make it of wood like a *santo*. 'O.K., let's do that,' said one, 'let's use cedar.' The women said that cedar was too purely good: it lacked spunk, fire, death—and how would they get rid of female magic if they used cedar? But nevertheless they went to the place Xejuyu to ask the cedar. They talked to him, gave him food and candles, but he said no. He did not want to have anything to do with woman-magic.

Red Banana, 1979:

The merchants, on their way to the Coast, stop at Xejuyu: underneath the hill. It is where the hill drops off, on the southern rim, dipping towards the Coast.

Loincloth intervenes, 1979:

The three diviners and counters of days were Hyeronimo Ixtulul, Jacobo Tz'aaj and Jacobo Okuy. There were two old ladies: Juana Batz'bal, a grandmother, and Juana Pnem, a mother. The plants started coming to them: the first was an *isote* plant and the second was a large banana plant. All the plants they knew the names of came to them. But they could not help to set the world aright so they began to look for the names of the plants they did not know. They divined the trees one by one with their divining beans. These were not coral beans yet, I don't exactly know what they were at that time. But tree after tree was failing them.

They couldn't live in the village anymore. One got a bow, another a lance, the third a blowgun. They hunted birds in the hills. Juana Batz'bal and Juana Kinom went with them. The women said, 'We have an idea. Let's make a being who is a woman and can cure the world.' They looked at the diviners and asked how they would do it. 'We'll make her out of mud,' they said. But the being couldn't stand up. They threw it away: it had no *naoj*, no intelligence, it was a purely dumb thing. They went tentatively from tree to tree, carving a little here and there to check things out. They shot birds by day and ate crickets and other darkness animals at night. There were no tortillas left at all because they had left the village . . .

Weep Wizard, 1979:

The session went on as they discussed each wood in turn. 'Let's try the cypress,' they said. The cypress said that he had killed the jaguar in the old days but he was no good at killing woman-magic. So they said, 'Well, let's go talk to the *tz'aaj*.' So Diego Tz'aaj, one of the Power-Men, went to talk to Juan Tz'aaj/Diego Tz'aaj the tree. And the tree said he was good for beds and house-corners because he didn't rot, but he also didn't move very fast and no, thank you!

[*Tarn in discussion with Prechtel, 1979: So a formula like Juan Tz'aaj/Diego Tz'aaj indicates completion, a complete unit of function say, just like 12/13 in an enumeration . . . Also, it is beginning to look as if the Power-Men are the trees and vice versa. This may make sense when you remember the claim that the first beings on earth were vegetal.*]

Red Banana, 1979:
The merchants come upon six coastal trees: the white guayava, the guanacaste, the ceiba, the chicharro, the cedar, and one other I forget. They talk to each tree in turn, making their offerings and ceremonial speeches and requests. Each tree says he cannot give up his own spot: his boss will be mad at him is the excuse. The trees are thrones of the rain angels. The last tree says, 'Why don't you try *P'ko'k?*'— that is: the Corral—which is the name we give here to the home area around the Lake.

So, the merchants go to *P'ko'k* at Xesiwan; they talk to *chaj*, the pine tree, to *k'sis*, the cypress, the *okuy*, the *kuxin*, and the *tz'aaj*. But each of these trees is a throne. Better: the thrones are connections between sky and earth, like ladders going up to heaven. The upper part of the tree, where the angel sits invisible, belongs to sky; the lower part to earth. It is like an office: the angel sits in the tree and picks up his mail. The ladder going up into the Mam's trellis in *cofradía* Santa Cruz is also a *palbal*, a throne . . . The *palbal Mam* made of *tz'aaj*.

*[Tarn to Prechtel in discussion, 1979:
So: Power-Man = tree = throne. From there it is a small step to seeing
that the Power-People are the rain-angels' representatives on earth, or better: their earthly forms.]*

Weep Wizard, 1979:

So each tree claimed to have its own work to do and to be
already busy in helping the world to thrive. They went to
the bat tree who said, 'I glow at night in the people's fires:
what would they say if I became a killer?' They went to the
pine tree who said that he lit fires and kept them going in
the hearths and adorned all the fiestas and celebrations:
how could he mess with woman-magic? There would be
no good odors in the forest anymore! And the *okuy* tree
also refused. And all these Power-Men were trees, you
understand, so what they were actually doing was asking
each other.

Now the Power-Men were moving counter-clockwise
round the Lake, starting from the Center at Cerro de Burro.
They started from Xejuyu near the Center and went on to
Bajlam Che and Tokenawa 'Alebal and Xetuk, towards
Xokexom, Mesebal and finally Chokox Aq'oum, the Mushroom Place. In each place there was a *mesa*, a table, and a
palbal, a throne, and finally a cross: table-tree-throne-cross
make up one unit. So they worked their way round in the
neighborhood of the coast road, on the southern rim of
the Lake perimeter.

As they got to the south side of Volcano-Volcano, they
found the *hornillo* tree, from which they make the marimba
and some of the drums. They said, 'This tree's wood is
hard; he has a note and can sing: his secret is that he is the
spirit of the men of song.' And they asked him. But the
hornillo tree said no. He would willingly help to make the
form stand up if they ever found it, but, as for him, he was
hot shit and used only by angels. The *hornillo* is the two-

tongued drum, the *k'unk'un*, he doesn't want to have anything to do with earth things: he only calls the heavenly rain.

Red Banana, 1979:
The tz'aaj says the same. 'We can't believe it! We have been through eleven trees!' say the merchants. They are giving the whole thing up for lost, walking around in circles, their arms behind their backs, shaking their heads. Suddenly, the merchant Tz'aaj has an idea. 'I have a friend who lives on Volcano-Her-Children,' he says. 'He's over there and maybe *he'll* do it.' 'Where? where?' say the merchants. 'Over there, he is quite small,' says Tz'aaj. They wander around, up through Bekan and Chupral, they go all over that place but they can't see anything special. Then they come on an alder tree, a smooth tree with few leaves.

Right next to it stands a *tz'ajtel*, a coral tree—but it has bad wood, is dumb-looking and soft. 'This is just the worst scene possible,' they think, so they go through the whole business with the alder. They begin to hear the coral tree panting uneasily: its heart is almost jumping out of its body, it is so anxious to talk to them. As for the alder, it claims to belong to 'the sons and daughters' to keep them warm: it will definitely not give up its body to the merchants. But the coral tree seems to be more than willing.

FIVE

A Sudden Interference

On March 1st, 1953, the Maximón affair takes the most surprising turn. A group of influential Protestants suddenly interferes
on the side of *cofradía* Santa Cruz and the elders. They begin a
determined battle against the *Catequistas*. The conflict turns out
to have roots in politics as well as religion and illustrates beauti-
fully how political rivalry can channel itself into already existing
factional lines: in this case religious ones. It makes common sense
that if the Protestants are going to fight Catholicism properly,
they have to fight the *Catequistas* first and foremost.

The background for the purpose of hearing out this case is as
follows:

1] In 1944, national power is gained by Arevalo's *Frente Popular Libertador*. The successors of Ubico's dictatorship are defeated.

2] Pedro Ramírez Mendoza, (nicknamed Ma Hallelujah by
1979), a young Protestant leader (and a prime collaborator and
friend), enters the *F.P.L.* in 1945 "because I wanted progress and
this was the party that had won the Guatemalan Revolution."
Later, the *F.P.L.* splits into many sub-parties.

3] In 1950, Jacobo Arbenz Guzmán becomes President after
Arevalo. Pedro joins the *Partido de Renovación Nacional (P.R.N.)*
and Juan Sisay does also. Pedro: "I became a *regidor* in the
municipality but stayed out of politics; I believed the job should
be non-political—that is the office and the party affiliation should
not mix. But I watched Juan Sisay and Manuel Rianda, Nicolás
Chiviliu's relative, receive money from the *P.R.N.* and keep it for
themselves. There were quarrels and then separation in 1952. Juan
took his *Catequistas* and illiterates into the *Partido de Acción Revolu-
cionaria (P.A.R.)*. I took the most progressive elements into the

Partido Revolucionario Guatemalteco (P.R.G.). The *P.R.N.* clung on very enfeebled, with Andrés Tzina as its secretary—but it had no influence in Atitlán."

4] *P.A.R.* wins the elections for municipal office in 1952: an election in which, like most others, less than 10% of the population casts a vote. All municipal officials, except Third *Regidor,* belong to *P.A.R.* In the *P.R.G.* list, at least two of the high officials are relatives of Pedro's.

5] Pedro claims that *P.A.R.* won because of intimidation at the ballot boxes. He is in the process of bringing suit against the *ladino* Municipal Secretary who is also secretary of the local *P.A.R.* For some unfathomable reason, the judge in Sololá has refused to try the case and has sent it to a judge in San Lucas Tolimán. In San Lucas, Pedro's opponent is being defended by his own aunt; the San Lucas Secretary is a relative and the San Lucas Mayor is a *P.A.R.* member. Pedro feels that the odds are long against him. There are other problems arising out of the now vengeful actions of the Mayor of Santiago who is *P.A.R.*, of course, and also the President of the *Catequistas.* This is our friend the *Catequista* Pedro Sosof.

So: on this morning of March 1st 1953, Sixth *Cofrade* Santa Cruz passes by Tarn's window and tells him that the *cofrades* have been summoned by a private party with a view to getting back the Mam where he belongs. The meeting place is a Pentecostal church to which Pedro's family belongs or—this happens with the Protestants here—which belongs to Pedro's family. Only the *cofrades* and some eight or nine Protestants are there. But everyone is very enthusiastic. Pedro briefs Tarn:

Pedro Ramírez Mendoza, 3/1/1953:
O.K., so: in the Constitution it says that everyone has freedom of belief but the *principales* here need help because they are ignorant and afraid. The Maximón is an ancient thing of this town and is not only loved by Indians but liked by tourists as well. People here hate Juan Sisay because

he curses the Maximón while selling paintings of him for a living.

Now: *Why* are the *principales* so afraid of this little bunch of *Catequistas*? Because the Town Mayor, Pedro Sosof, is one of them. Why are the *principales* not afraid of accepting help from us? Because they can see perfectly well that we don't envy their images and in fact don't give a damn about them! Tarn: I see your point about the two Catholicisms here and that the traditionalist majority should have its way unless—if ever—the *Catequistas* win out. I agree, that makes perfect sense.

After explaining the business about the *P.A.R.* and the *P.R.G.*:

Pedro Ramírez Mendoza:
What we want to do is to get a man over from Panajachel who is in charge of Tourism there and he'll make out a memorandum for us to the Archbishop of Guatemala— *not* Quetzaltenango, mind you, but Guatemala. This Señor Palmieri is a *P.R.G.* man and it was he who helped us get a tractor for the construction of the Tolimán-Atitlán road. We asked him for a football and some football clothes and equipment. They arrived. Now we want to get his help on the Maximón issue since the Maximón is such a great tourist attraction. We want to get an order from such a high place in the Church that the Sololá priest will be put right out of action.

It also happens to be the case that Palmieri is a great admirer, and favorite, of President Jacobo Arbenz.

Pedro Ramírez Mendoza:
What's with this Maximón? The Indians want to keep it in memory of the fact that there was once a man who sold Christ for thirty pieces of silver. Someone, Indian or priest,

has told them the Maximón is Judas. Of course, it was the *priests* who were responsible in the first place for Christ's betrayal, right? Because *they* had bribed Judas! Anyway, all this stuff about his being hung up in church is in the Bible, but since most of us are ignorant and analphabetic, we just don't know that.

Hearing that the treason happened sometime around Holy Week, the *cofrades* put the Maximón and the Judas together at some point in time although originally they had nothing to do with each other. [*Silent admiration for Pedro's deductive powers on the part of Tarn.*] Of course, they are now denying that the Maximón is Judas because the *Catequistas* are making such a big point of it!

By the way, it was Andrés Tzina of the *P.R.N.* who suggested the letter to the Archbishop: he can't stand the Town Mayor and that's why he's helping us.

By the next day, there is strong excitement in the village. Juan Sisay is as mad as a wild boar and has threatened the Santa Cruz people with dire penalties. Pedro is in touch with the Governor of Sololá who has told him not to bother the President of the Republic on such minor matters. The priest makes an appearance to say a requiem mass but leaves hastily after consulting with the *Catequistas*. Pedro's father, Francisco, an ex-*aj'kun*, adds this to the briefing:

Francisco Ramírez, 1953:
When Sisay exploded at the *cofrades*, he said they were little more than drunken pigs. I told him off violently for an intolerant and uncharitable young man. The Town Mayor got scared and told him off also. They finally reached agreement on the priest not coming so as to avoid conflict during the *fiesta*. But the Memorandum to the Archbishop will be drawn up by the Tourism official.

You see, this is a great opportunity to show the Catholics

that we Protestants practice the toleration we preach. Some
have been poking fun at me for wanting to help, but I say
that anyone who pokes fun at a man's religion has no religion himself. I myself have no anger or jealousy against
the Judas: the custom is harmless and amusing, it may as
well go on.

By March 11th, after trips back and forth to Sololá by Pedro
and the *cofrades*, the following paper is in hand at *cofradía* Santa Cruz:

Ten cent form no.788061; Register 788223; Quinquennial
1948–1952; Governor's Office, Sololá.
   The Government of the Department of Sololá grants this
license to Salvador Pospoy so that he might, as Secretary of
the *cofradía* of the image of Santa Cruz, carry out, in the village of Santiago Atitlán, with the customary ritual, the celebration of Holy Week beginning on the 29th day of this
month and continuing until the 5th of April next, during
which time they may take into the streets whatever procession they are used to having, augmented by regional music
and they can also take out the 'Judas' in the same manner
during those days. Señor Pospoy will be held responsible for
any disorder that might occur in the village. Police take note.
Sololá, March 10th, 1953. Note taken (Police).

Tarn observes that the paper does not specify the exact place-
ment of the Maximón.
   At the same time, another paper prepared by one of Señor
Palmieri's legal staff is also in hand:

Ten cent form no.C1636502; Register 1636834; Quinquen-
nial 1953-1957.
   Archbishop Raymundo Mariano Rosell y Arellano,
Guatemala:
   The undersigned, all of legal age, Catholics, villagers of
Santiago Atitlán, department of Sololá, come before you

with all due respect to explain: that by as many means as we have had at our disposal we have kept up the purity of our religious rituals—especially those related to the celebration of Holy Week in these parts, included in which is the 'hanging of Judas' which has now been forbidden to us by the priest in charge of the parish of Sololá.

Such intolerance shown by the said minister of our Holy Mother the Catholic Church motivates the decay of religious feelings among our people insofar as we consider that, if we are not given clear explanations of the meaning and content of the sacrifice of Jesus Christ for the salvation of Humanity, so much the less should we be prevented from holding our own very elementary interpretation of the same, and to this effect we beg you, Archbishop, to give orders to the aforementioned priest so that he does not interfere in our *costumbres*, depriving us from celebrating the *fiestas* ordained by the Catholic Church as we have been in the habit of doing for more than two hundred years.

We pray you will accept our petition, Santiago Atitlán, March 7th, 1953. Salvador Pospoy.

Thumbprints already appended: Juan Quieju, Diego Chiquita, José Alvarado, Diego Ajchomajay, Salvador Marroquin, Claro Vicente Tuiz, Gregorio Pablo, Nicolás Pablo, Juan Cristóbal, Gaspar Boron.

Nicolás Chiviliu signs a little later. By the 13th, there are seventy-five signatures; by the 14th, one hundred fifty. The petition is sent off. Tarn notes with concerned amusement the heavy hand of *ladino* interpretation in causing Indians to claim that their views on religion are "elementary."

From this time until the celebration of Holy Week, no official response appears to have arrived from any source. Speculation continues to run rife. At various times it is said that the Archbishop will himself appear, *Deus ex Machina*, or the Governor of Sololá, in personal epiphany. A drunken *Cabecera* moans on March 11th about the difficulties of making any move whatsoever without consulting everybody, once more refuses Tarn permission to see the town Title on that count—it had always been kept with "superstitious" secrecy in a great box—speculates that Sisay's father's sins have been visited on his son, and wonders whether the time of the Lord Mam might not really be up after all.

The *Cabecera* has not yet heard about the *cofradía* Santa Cruz Memorandum. When he does, he flies into a rage at Santa Cruz bypassing his authority. The Santa Cruz *cofrades* are still unsure of their success and it only takes a drop of drink to waft them back to their obsessions about the destruction of the ancient ways and their interminable recitals of the archtraitor's deeds. The strain tells above all on Salvador Pospoy: the documents after all make him responsible for any mishap.

Pospoy is a man of medium build who struggles to maintain great dignity against the bearing of a clown and a set of difficult features: a nose worthy of Jimmy Durante; twinkling eyes; broad lips always cracking fiendishly conspiratorial smiles over very irregular teeth. Pospoy has been getting loaded more often than usual, vociferating about the supremacy of Santa Cruz over all other *cofradías* and exalting his own role as *Cofradía* Secretary (*Escribano*). He makes violent speeches about "passing everybody under the swords" and envisages "legions of thousands of millions" of Atitecos massacring the fifty-odd *Catequistas* if they should interfere with the Mam. His mind is an armory of pistols, guns, rifles, swords, and razor blades which he enumerates in his prayers as magical instruments.

On March 26th, 1953, Nicolás Chiviliu is discovered around midday in the *ladino* Ephraín Arteaga's restaurant where he sometimes has a bite to eat with his clients: in this case a man, his wife and three children from San Pedro Sacatepéquez. Nicolás is taking it easy, chugging at some refined *gaseosa* (soda pop) or other, and tells of a broil that morning with the *Telinel*, the latter having objected to Nicolás putting on the Mam some clothes which customers had brought him. This is one of a series of broils between the Chiv—who considers himself *Telinel*-For-Life—and whoever happens to be "usurping" the office at the time. Nicolás recounts how he threatened to go to the police, evict the *Telinel* and carry the Mam himself during this Holy Week. Enter to him Pospoy:

Tarn, 1953:

We all move out and, on the way to *cofradía* Santiago, meet *Alcalde, Juez*, First and Fifth Santa Cruz, assembled for some reason in a bar and being showered with drinks by a belligerently sozzled Pospoy. Pospoy orders beers for Nicolás and for Tarn, then begins to bear-hug Nicolás, making as if to lift him from the ground, grabbing him in the crotch and holding on. He makes a variety of jokes about Nicolás's 'bird.' Nicolás says the bird is asleep or on a trip; *Juez* tells him he has great good fortune in having such an oversized one—and so on and so forth.

Suddenly, Pospoy beckons Nicolás outside and starts a *sotto voce* conversation with him. He is exhibiting various documents to Nicolás and telling him things which make Chiviliu look incredulous. Tarn overhears him saying, as he moves on cat's paws to join them, that he, Tarn, possesses copies of these documents but will be given no more to pass on to Juan Sisay.

Pospoy then blows up good and proper to the effect that Tarn is a *gringo jodido*, a goddamned foreigner, a tourist, a thief, vagabond and good-for-nothing, that he has taken these documents to pass on to the enemy, that the *principales* now hate and abominate him and will never have anything more to do with him and that Tarn has had it in general and in particular since he, Pospoy, is going to get the police with whips, swords and pistols to drive the wretch out of town. He brandishes an imaginary arsenal of weapons as if he had them on hand.

More than amazed, Tarn at first answers calmly that he really doesn't know what to do with this nonsense then bethinks himself to fly into an exemplary rage, shouting that if he had wanted to screw Santa Cruz it would have been the easiest thing in the world to write to the Archbishop himself without stooping to the use of treacherous and off-color tricks.

Tarn stomps off in a calculated rhetorical gesture and, as he turns around, finds an energetic scuffle going on between Salvador and Nicolás for the possession of what turns out to be a common or garden Missal. Nicolás had mentioned this volume before as containing prayers to all the saints, including the Mam, and had told Tarn that he might want it back. Pospoy won't let go, but kicks, punches and shouts in and out of the bar while *cofrades* try to help the Chiv: it is the nearest thing to a fight that Tarn has ever witnessed in these parts.

Finally, Pospoy, gives the book a resounding kiss, then slams it down furiously onto a window ledge. Exit Nicolás wild-eyed and dishevelled from the bar, half-disbelieving that he has the book back.

Nicolás recovers from the scuffle while at *cofradía* Santiago. He repeats over and over that he had loaned this book to Pospoy (having owned three copies on which he had at one time spent $7.50) because Pospoy had no money but required the book as a *sacristán*. He had also bought the ungrateful wretch a jacket. Now the Missal was his again, would stay with him forever: he had decided to repossess it: 'It is unique, the book of books; it contains *everything*; all the prayers; all the world's manifold secrets,' and so on and so forth.

On and off during the day the memory of his bout came back to him and he wove it into his *costumbre*, weeping a ritual dirge: 'Ay, Don Pedro, Lord San Simon . . . (sob) . . . it hurts . . . (sob) . . . it hurts bitterly,' enumerating Pospoy's evil dispositions in his prayers and altogether managing to sound most lamentable to any saint within earshot. All of this interspersed, as usual, with fits of good humor in which he was as boisterous and amusing as ever.

He was taking Tarn's side in the quarrel, bemoaning the fact that such a 'good person' should be put into such a 'choler,' eliciting the tenderness of women present towards Tarn and finally placing the book on the mane of Santiago's horse very solemnly, leaving it there awhile and then taking it down with a closing, definitive flourish. He drew Tarn more explicitly than ever into his *costumbre*, calling him *zahorín* and *aj'kun*, evoking San Bernadino, the Sun saint, on Tarn's behalf and getting his clients to pay Tarn respect as well as choking him with his incense.

That evening, as Tarn was getting ready to leave for Santa Cruz, invited after a chance meeting with *cofrades* in the street who seemed anxious about some offense done to him, Nicolás stomps in, his son in tow. In a curious mood, a Tzutujil King Lear, roaring with laughter then muttering moodily and taking swigs from a bottle of 'fine wine' he is carrying.

Pospoy had cited him, he declares, and a policeman had arrived to summon him to the municipality at 8:00 a.m. on the 27th. It is agreed that nothing should be said about Tarn's part in the scuffle because of the Mayor's relations with the *Catequistas*. Tarn, however, does offer to go as witness for the Chiv. Spying a Mexican dagger on Tarn's desk, Nicolás picks it up and pockets it (he is not averse to helping himself to things in this way), then declares with somber mien that he would never carry *estas mierdas* (this shit) and puts it down with a flourish.

March 27th: Chiviliu comes for Tarn at 8:20, brandishing a paper proving that he had given Pospoy eight *quetzales* for a coat some four years before. The little procession runs into *Juez*, First and Sixth Santa Cruz who all side with it, together with Pedro Ramírez Mendoza and the Protestants who ridicule Pospoy and threaten to give him a hearty dressing down. The idea of such a fuss when all is going so well! What bugs everyone is that Pospoy should have assaulted Chiviliu after offering him drinks!

The party waits at the *Juzgado*. The Town Mayor is out on an errand. Pospoy blunders in half-drunk at about 10:30, shakes hands with Nicolás and smiles, ostentatiously showing off a torn pocket. They both go before an Assistant Mayor.

Pospoy starts drawing out a host of irrelevant papers, including his Holy Week permits, and complains that Nicolás has done him irreparable damage. Nicolás explains his side of the affair very quietly. The Assistant Mayor looks at his fingernails as if in extreme pain, murmuring about friendship all the way through and Tarn is trying his utmost not to burst a gut. The two gentlemen are put into the poky to cool off until the Mayor's return.

Tarn returns to the municipality at 11:30 and finds that Pospoy has apparently done what he should have done in the first place for he is clowning in front of the Municipal Secretary, withdrawing his complaint on the grounds of piteous drunkenness, begging pardon on his knees with eyes lifted to the ceiling in a saintly mode, cross-chatting most amicably with his erstwhile foe. If Nicolás is Lear in all this, Pospoy has something of Falstaff.

But the almighty Law has been disturbed and both our friends are ordered to pay one *quetzal*. Nicolás lends Pospoy his *quetzal* and accepts judgement very meekly, either because Pospoy is in truth a friend or because the principle that it takes two to disturb the peace is firmly anchored and accepted. After they have paid up, Nicolás takes Pospoy off to the tailor to have his coat pocket repaired.

On a later occasion, Tarn sees Pospoy using a Missal that is the spitting image of the one he had had to give up.

On March 27th, during the hearings on the Chiviliu-Pospoy affair, a messenger informs the Assistant Mayor that a priest is in

Sololá, will be in San Lucas Tolimán on the 28th and in Atitlán on Sunday 29th. After this, the Town Mayor, Juan Sisay, Domingo, and some *Catequistas* are seen waiting for messages in the Post Office. Rumor is rife as to the origin of this new priest: Cuba and the Netherlands are two places mentioned. He arrives on the morning of the 28th and Pospoy, as sacristan, is carrying his bag. He watches the doings of the fruit procession from the church esplanade in the company of Juan Sisay.

That same afternoon, Juan and Sixth Santa Cruz drop by almost at the same time. Juan: "The priest is Colombian. He is very interested in witnessing the *fiesta* and he won't interfere with the Maximón." Juan sounds almost content! Is it sheer relief? Sixth: "This *padre* has been sent by the Archbishop of Guatemala and that means the Archbishop has okayed our request. Nicolás's son has overheard the Mayor and the priest agreeing to have the Mam in church."

The priest, when finally met with, is in effect a charming and peaceful person, sent to Atitlán with instructions to avoid all open conflict. It is hard to imagine him combative even without instructions. He says that he has spoken with the Sololá priest and found him quite "brusque." He is determined "not to be thrown out of town" but seems rather surprised at hearing that it would be a distinct possibility.

He restricts his comments, such as they are, to mild sermonizing and exhorts his flock to give thought to the inner life. Nicolás and everyone else are delighted with him: there are rumors that he will be permanently appointed to Santiago. They do not materialize.

The Holy Week doings proceed normally, with the Mam hung in the church porch as usual. Nicolás stays away from most of it, though he takes an active part in guiding the Wednesday procession of the Mam to the municipality and the church and takes over physically from the *Telinel* when the great icon is finally strung up. A very small change is introduced at the priest's request so that the church door be left free of encumbrances: that the post should be set up at the second pillar south of the entrance door rather than at the first.

Accusations are deflected from the priest to the *Catequista* Vice-President—but no one can work up too much steam over it. That anyone should have cared at all at this point perhaps illustrates a principle: that insecurity over custom and the knowledge of custom generates interminable finickiness over the observance of detail—as if it were important to remember that there is something to remember more than to remember exactly what that thing might have been.

Two months later, a letter arrives from the Sololá priest enumerating a certain number of grumbles. In short, he is furious over what has happened. The *Catequistas* meet in church and the Town Mayor resigns his presidency, claiming he has enough to do with his job, the road building commission and his enemies in the P.R.G. Domingo, Juan Sisay's friend, suggests that everyone resign and Juan Sisay follows suit rather than be left alone. Juan speaks to the theory that only large scale indoctrination will change the situation, not individual attacks on particular facets of ritual behavior.

From now on, the *Catequistas* will be seen to be working on a new, fairly innocuous policy to get elders such as Nicolás properly married in church. No move to reconstitute the *Catequistas* occurs for the rest of Tarn's stay.

[*It will take until the mid-1980s for the* Catequistas *finally to follow the road Pedro and the Protestants had already foreseen in the 1950s. After the disasters of the Civil War and the continuing inroads of Protestantism, backed more and more by substantial American capital, the* Catequistas *finally begin to realize—and not in Atitlán alone but all over Guatemala—that their real enemies are not the Catholic traditionalists (or* Costumbristas *as they have come to be called) but the Protestants. The Church needs all the allies it can get and the young* Catequistas *are seen desperately learning* costumbre *before the elders who can teach them vanish from the face of the earth.*

TWO ENDNOTES:

1) By 1979, the 1950s Town Mayor, Pedro Sosof, is a leading Protestant.

2) It is clear from a number of sources that the question of the Mam is not a new one. Published in 1929, Samuel K. Lothrop's *Further Notes on Indian Ceremonies in Guatemala* informs us: "About fifteen years ago (circa 1914), a Bishop arrived in Atitlán during Holy Week and was duly horrified to find his flock worshipping an image of Judas. He thereupon issued orders that the figure be burned. But before this could be done, the people assembled in great numbers, armed with clubs and machetes, and shortly the Bishop had to flee from the town with a mob of enraged Indians howling at his heels."

S I X

Stories of the Early Earth, III
The Making of the Mam

Weep-Wizard continues the story of the trees, 1979:
They had gone to twelve trees. It is the three main Power-Men and the three main Power-Women who are dealing with this now: the others had given up; their trees had been left behind.

Loincloth, 1979:
One night, they will come to a very big flowering tree which they won't be able to name. They will become intoxicated by it and fall asleep under its shade. Then the first diviner, Axrom Ixtulul, will ask the tree its name, but the tree will answer that it has no name. 'You are lying,' Axrom will say, 'I will find out your name.' Axrom will look into his divining kit and will say 'What is your name? Ha! I have it here!' Axrom will be trying to outfox the tree. The tree will say, 'My name is Yaxwan Kinom, the *Jocote tree.*' 'You're not Yaxwan Kinom, we have that name here!' Axrom will say. The next day the tree will say that its name is Diego Tz'aaj, the Red *Taxicoba* tree, and so on, through a whole bunch of names.

Then the diviners will start divining how many days it would be before the head of the figure would be made. The time will be coming close so they will know that this tree has power. The tree will have these very heavy, very full flowers. 'What is your real name?' they will ask it the next day. 'My name is Juan Tz'ajtel', John Coral Tree,' it will finally say. And they won't catch on yet—because they

48

don't yet know what the coral tree is. Then, on another day, the tree will change its name again. It will call itself Axrom Ixtulul! 'This tree is getting darned uppity,' the men will say. 'The tree speaks each one of our names and claims to be each one of us. Yet he is a tree and won't tell us his real name!'

Weep Wizard, 1979:
One of the Power-People had a dream. Some say it was the first Power-Man, some say the Ultimo and some say María Castellana: one of them had a dream. They would find what they wanted in a place struck by lightning, said the dream. Well, let's say it was Diego Poklaj: he walked along the ridge of Volcano-Volcano and on down to Volcano-Her-Children. There he was caught by a strong south whirlwind rain until he took refuge under a tree. He got soaked. A big lightning struck there and he knew it was a sign, but a sign of what he didn't know.

Red Banana, 1979:
Well, the merchants make to go home and the coral tree is weeping and weeping. 'Why don't they talk to me?' he says and, as they go off, he whistles. So the First Merchant calls to his Ultimo and says, 'Hey, did you whistle, Ultimo?' Well, they find out it isn't Ultimo, it's the tree. They tell this tree he's no good, he rots, he's soft, he's valueless, he won't burn. 'Yeah, I know,' says the tree, 'but I'll do the job you need.' So First Merchant has a list of questions: 'Well, are you ready to take pain? Fire? Glass? Bullets? The heat of day? The cold of night? Wet? Damp? Mud? Slings? Arrows? Outrageous fortune? Everything?'

'Yeah, yeah, yeah, I am I am I am,' says the coral tree.

'Are you ready to turn into a man? Into a woman? To do everything we say?'

'IamIamIam,' says the tree very quickly.

49

'Without slipping in anything that *you* want to do yourself?'

'Yeah, yeah, yeah,' says the tree, quicker and quicker.

'Without getting paid? Without any reward? Without anything to show for anything?'

'Yesyesyes! Absolutely! I'm just sick and tired of being here and nobody wanting me!' says the tree.

'O.K.' say the merchants. And they quit questioning the tree.

Weep Wizard, 1979:
In the afternoon, the sun came up and nearby where Diego Poklaj, Diego Dust, had taken shelter and had his dream, there was this very old, beaten up tree: a *tz'ajtel* tree, an old one, really cut to pieces and hacked about. Diego Poklaj looked at it and said to himself, 'Christ! They couldn't mean *this* thing, it's a mess, it's far too soft, it sucks!' And he passed it by. So he heard a whistle behind him. He went back to the tree and asked, 'What's the big idea?' The tree just grunted back. 'Are you the chosen one?' said Poklaj. The tree just grunted. So Poklaj took out his stone hatchet and chopped.

[*Prechtel: They make him, you see. They chop up the tree and tie up all the pieces together. A dinky, two-foot high little guy comes out of this. Another version: They make him. He is already formed inside the hollow tree. He is peering out. They cut around his outline and haul him out whole.*]

Weep Wizard, 1979:
Poklaj chopped seven times and each chop had a name, a syllable. *Jun di klaj ki du bey bu ba* it went. And Dust said, 'Are you the one who has been chosen for this?' The tree said, 'Haaaa! I'm number one! I can play any game you want, I'm the best player of them all! I can chase anything

on earth, go faster than the wind, I am hotter than the sun and colder than death!' the tree said.

Red Banana, 1979:

So the merchants go home and they get something to eat. 'He doesn't look so good, he doesn't cut much of a figure,' they decide, 'but he's our boy.' They all get their files the next day, to sharpen their machetes. But the Ultimo has had a dream. 'This tree doesn't want sharp machetes: rub them on rocks to make them dull,' he tells them. It's true: if you put a sharp machete into coral wood, it will stick just like cork. So First Merchant comes up to the tree and asks if he is ready for this pain. The tree says he is. 'Remember everything we told you yesterday because we are your makers and we will take you apart if you disobey us,' First Merchant says.

So they give him a first stroke on his feet, plaaaam. With each chop, they give him an order. They get to his head and the head is going up and down, nodding, like this. Plaam. 'You feel that?' they ask. At every stroke they hear the tree going, 'A! E! O! Oh! Ay! Ou! A! E!' while they are making and shaping him. When they have finally carved him out, he is about this big. 'Well, can you stand up now?' they ask. 'He looks pretty good this man made of pain,' they say to themselves in congratulation.

Weep Wizard, 1979:

Then Dust called all the Powers and they came in a big wind. Dust announced that they had found 'it.' '*This?*' the Powers asked, sardonically. But Thread came forward and said, 'Yes, yes, yes. This is him, I recognize him perfectly! O.K. Everyone in order give him seven strokes of the hatchet.' So Thread directed the making of the figure; it was not Dust who did it.

Loincloth, 1979:

At this point, the old ladies, the Power-Women, will come and say, 'This tree will be the one to cure our world because all it does is to tell lies and that is exactly what we need! We need something that can put witchcraft into something else and kill it.' They will divine the right day on which to make the figure. The women will say that it cannot be carved—it has to be sung into being. They will charm it with the first song. With each cut, they will make a prayer and will work inside clouds to be invisible. The diviners will teach the women to get food each day from the village: they will not be hunting anymore. And also to bring them their pipes, and chocolate and liquor. With each word there will be 260 questions [*a calendrical number*], with each cut they will ask him:

'Are you willing to go inside a man and kill him?'
'Yes.'
'Are you willing to become a wall?'
'Yes.'
'Are you willing to become a spine?'
'Yes.'
'A woman?'
'Yes.'
'A man?'
'Yes.'
'A wasp?'
'Yes.'
'Smoke?'
'Yes.'
'Are you willing to become all things that have smell and taste on the face of the earth?'
'Yes.'
'Are you willing to go up? Are you willing to go down?'
'Yes.'

'Are you willing to go underwater? Under the trees?'

'Yes.'

'And under the earth?'

'Yes.'

And so on, and on, until the end of the questions. So, finally, they will come to an end but the figure will not be able to stand up. The two women will take off their headbands, wrap them round the legs and up the body and round the arms and head: and the figure will move. They will sing; it will stand up and begin to dance. The headbands will give it the power as they do in the tales of how the hoes worked by themselves. Then they will begin to test him.

Weep Wizard, 1979:

She makes him. It is her child until it is made and then it is her husband. That's why it's called boy/man. So they go, 'Da, da, da, da, da, da, dum—dum,' because that is his song, seven notes plus one. This first song is called *cabildo mayor* or *nabe palacio*: the first palace. The second song is called *cabildo real*, the royal palace. The third song relates to a woman, perhaps the moon. Three songs to the figure, followed by three songs to the Martín. [*This, as we'll see, is the great Power of Nature inside the Martín bundle in cofradía San Juan.*] These are the songs we still play on the *marimba* in the *cofradía*. So each Power is giving him his magic. And Dust, of course, is giving him the power of dust, earth, and dryness.

Nicolás Chiviliu, 1953:

They make him. In the beginning, he doesn't whistle, he cries like a baby. When they finish, he is an old grump and will not talk at all. Each one of his songs represents four hundred 'suns': the old men say it used to be a form of calculating time.

Weep Wizard, 1979:

Batzin gives him the power to tie knots; Ikaj, the axe, the power to chop, cut and make lightning; and so on down the Powers. One gives *naoj*, intelligence, savvy, the power to connive and be wily: some say this is Dust and some say it's Tz'aaj. Many of these things we do not remember exactly any more. They give him the power to name the days and divine: his is the tree of the divining seeds which, from now on, will be taken from the coral. They give him the power to make rain, wind, lightning, storm and to ruffle the waters.

When the Power-Men have given him their powers, the Power-Women line up and give him theirs. They give him the power to turn into a woman, to make himself beautiful and to change forms. They give him food, drink and clothing. 'You have a thousand faces, forms, words, prayers, of each a thousand,' they say. 'A thousand prayers, a thousand songs, a thousand compassions [*mil oraciones, mil compasiones*],' as the *aj'ukna* later say. 'You can be the head of butterfly, of bat, of hawk, of double-headed eagle, of jaguar, of snake, bee, wasp, and all these woman powers.'

Nicolás Chiviliu, 1953:

After he is made, he is very, very hot: his chest grows into a hot Sun disc, his face and chest are glowing; he is bright like the Sun. He thinks he is the Sun. Later, they will have to blow mist into his eyes—when they begin to punish him: they will have to blow clouds over the Sun. [*We remember all those characters in* Popol Vuh *who mistakenly believe they are the Sun.*]

Weep Wizard, 1979:

'You are our dog, our servant,' they make sure to tell him. He is feeling a bit inflated because he has not yet gotten up. They begin to play the second song. Francisca Thread gives the last cuts on his feet, forms them, sings, 'Stand up, boy, stand up, man!' So he stands up. They ask him if he can talk. 'Ha! Ha! I'm the best of speakers! I speak better than any of those sons of bitches!' he cries out. 'Can you think?' they ask him. 'Ha! Ha! I'm the best for thoughts! I think better than any of those sons of bitches!' he cries out. So they said that they would have to test him.

They went to the village and found a *nikanik ala*, a real dumb little guy who had never opened his mouth and they brought him to the Mushroom Place. Well, the new figure gave this guy a piece of mushroom with mineral water—kneeling down and praying over him before he did that—and, suddenly, no question about it, the guy could *speak*! The figure had turned instantly into a sort of demigod. Then they had to make him dumb again and so they blew mist into his eyes. The guy could still talk and so on, but he no longer had that divine knowledge.

Francisca Thread said they had to dance the figure a second time and they created the second song. They danced him in the four directions in order to orient him: 'This is where your father comes from and this is where your mother rests,' they said to him. The third song was for the woman: she picked him up on her shoulders and danced with him, just like a *telinel* does today. [*Which answers to a strong suggestion that the* telinel *is a 'wife' to the Mam.*]

They created a table for burning candles and incense there and wanted to test him some more. His root stock stayed there—and is still there at the Mushroom Place up high, back of the village—but they sent him to the south side of Volcano-Her-Children and told him to make rain. He made rain after flying there like the wind, but he stood under the rain and got all wet. They all roared and roared with laughter and asked him what sort of a god he was, the knucklehead, the *rubenom acha*, the manufactured man, the one who had not been born, who couldn't get out from under his own rain!

'You don't have any flesh—where the hell are you?' they laughed and laughed. 'You will kill yourself if you make lightning and it shoots you yourself!' they roared and laughed at him. 'When you make rain, stand *on top* of the clouds,' they said to him. 'Oh! I didn't know that!' said the being. So they made him try it again while he was all still wet and shivering.

Then they told him to come down out of there and instructed him to change into a dog, a man, a leaf, a woman and all sorts of various things. Then the Ultimo asked him if he remembered his wife—the Ultimo's of course—and the figure said yes, he did. 'How the hell can you *remember*?' said the Ultimo, but the other just went, 'Ooouuuuuuu-uuuuuuuu. . . .' Then the Ultimo told him to get on his wife's case because she had messed him up. 'But I thought you were going to . . .' said the older brother. But the Ultimo said, 'Well, no, we have a form now,' so the figure went down the hill. They were having this great procession, they were going to carry him into town. So he went down the hill to do his first job and he met the woman.

[*Prechtel: I have heard that he is made in a place near Cerro de Oro and taken to the Mushroom Place to stand up. Another version: he is made in the Mushroom Place but not finished and taken over to a spot close to Chukumuk, on the other side of Tzalin Abaj, up by Chikoy. And that is where he was first tested, chasing Evil-Person out of Volcano-Her-Children and not, as someone said, out of Volcano-Volcano.*]

And this figure is the one that is called the Mam.

■   ■   ■

The Making of the Mam

[Some notes from *Popol Vuh*, in Dennis Tedlock's translation:

When Hurricane had spoken with the Sovereign Plumed
Serpent, they invoked the daykeepers, diviners, the midmost
seers:
　　There is yet to find, yet to discover how we are to model
a person, construct a person again, a provider, a nurturer,
so that we are called upon and we are recognized: our
recompense is in words.

★

'You have been called upon because of our work, our design.
Run your hands over the kernels of corn, *over the seeds of the
coral tree*, just get it done, just let it come out, *whether we
should carve and gouge a mouth, a face in wood,*' they told the
day-keepers.

★

'Just let it be found, just let it be discovered,/say it, our ears
are listening,/may you talk, may you speak,/*just find the wood
for the carving and sculpting*/by the builder sculptor.

★

'It is well that there be your manikins, woodcarvings, talking, speaking, there on the face of the earth.'
　　'So be it,' they replied. The moment they spoke it was
done: the manikins, woodcarvings, human in looks and
human in speech.
　　This was the peopling of the face of the earth.
　　They came into being, they multiplied, they had daughters, they had sons, these manikins, woodcarvings. But there
was nothing in their hearts and nothing in their minds, no
memory of their mason and builder. They just went and

walked wherever they wanted. Now they did not remember the Heart of Sky.

And so they fell, just an experiment and just a cutout for humankind. They were talking at first but their faces were dry. They were not yet developed in the legs and arms. They had no blood, no lymph. They had no sweat, no fat. Their complexions were dry, their faces were crusty. They flailed their legs and arms, their bodies were deformed.

★

The man's body was carved from the wood of the coral tree by the Maker, Modeler. And as for the woman, the Maker, the Modeler needed the pith of reeds for the woman's body. They were not competent, nor did they speak before the builder and sculptor who made them and brought them forth, and so they were killed, done in by a flood. (Our italics. *P.V.*, pp.80-86; c.f. Edmonson, *P.V.*, pp.20-31; Recinos, *P.V.*, pp.86-90).

So we have the Mam, a powerful deity, made of wood, but, in Atitlán, not multiplied into a people as in Popol Vuh *and not destroyed (just as his Christian manifestation, Judas, is not burned there—though it is burned in other villages—but always kept in* cofradía *Santa Cruz). A deity whom, we will later hear, is the last of the gods made, the Ultimo of the gods, and joins the Rain Angels as such. But also a god who, in the cyclical terms that govern these myths, becomes at various times, the* First *god, Angel or what have you. (Miguel Arcángel, first of the angels; Pedro, first of the Apostles, etc. are also Christian forms of his.) A god who, as the Ultimo in the Sweatbath stories we will tell in another book, becomes a monkey at the hands of his elder brothers—the monkey being the present day form of the destroyed wooden men in* Popol Vuh—*but who, like all the Ultimos, always seems to come up trumps just like the Sun setting splendidly over the west.*

A god who, as Judas, has an extraordinarily intimate relationship to Jesucristo, enabling Jesucristo to live out his destiny and who, perhaps, can

58

eventually succeed Jesucristo as the next Sun. A divine wooden being who is more complex and more informative than the wooden beings in Popol Vuh, so that Atiteco data actually adds to our knowledge of that book. A god, perhaps, who exemplifies the last of created beings: the Indians of Atitlán, who will one day take over from their oppressors, the conquistadors of all creeds, nations and origins.]

SEVEN

Rebels in Trouble

Tarn, 1952-53:
There was a strong desire for change among certain Atitecos at the time of my stay. Before Atitlán's coastal dependencies had been assigned to the coastal Department of Suchitepéquez in the 1920s, the village had benefited from a steady flow of visitors on their way through Santiago to Sololá: there had been a hotel, better houses and shops, more social life among the educated and semi-educated. It was felt in a variety of quarters that Atitlán was ripe for a renewal of prosperity.

A group of *ladinos*, especially members of the political party that had won the election, took up a plan, dormant for some time, to build a road between Atitlán and San Lucas Tolimán. When recourse to the government proved only partially successful, they organized their own committees and went to work themselves with teams of *alguaciles*, *ladino* and Indian volunteers. A scheme for building wells was also afoot though nothing materialized during my stay.

In the school, the Director had freed some teachers by persuading reluctant Indian parents that boys and girls could be taught together and, in 1953, the first batch of 6th grade students was able to apply for scholarships to higher institutions. Governmental plans for adult education had some repercussions in the village and, by the time I left, two or three night classes were being run, mostly attended by Protestants and *Catequistas*. In the course of these, I taught elements of Maya history.

Political party strife had entered Atiteco life not long after the Revolution against the Dictator President Ubico in 1944. This activity did not go far beyond fitting itself into patterns of rivalry already established in the village, but it was a beginning. In November 1952, a committee for the operation of the Agrarian Reform Laws of the Arbenz government was elected in Santiago. Many opined that the laws hardly applied to Atitlán: communal lands would always remain such and available for distribution to the poor. If an Atiteco needed land, he could always get it and no one was ever allowed to starve.

Most of the older Atitecos could not see the need for these laws, but then, 'the government orders and the people obey.' As for 'socialism' or 'communism,' people knew little about them and the priest had an easy job of strengthening their dislike and distrust of anything that smacked of change. At various times, political party leaders from the capital visited the village and helped to organize varied activities. But they were not very successful unless the activity coincided in some way with already existing and more intimate interests. In July 1953, for instance, some *P.A.R* speakers came to organize an agricultural co-operative group. The Vice-President of the *Catequistas* and Domingo publicly refused offices. Juan Sisay tried to get out of the post of 'Secretary of Culture' but was finally induced to accept.

The Maximón Scandals, however, make it clear that religious conflict proved a fertile field for the awakening of non-religious interests. They show the extent to which personal quarrels and rivalries, cast in the mould of religious affairs, transformed themselves along the same lines when politics entered the field and determined to a large extent the political affiliations of the respective parties.

In a sense the true battle was fought along religious divisions between progressive Catholics and progressive

Protestants with traditionalist Catholics—the *cofrades* Santa Cruz and some *aj'kuna*—as little more than pawns in the hands of the Protestants. The progressive Catholics were interested in the struggle from a purely religious point of view at first. But the Protestants were no longer interested in Catholicism: to leave Catholicism meant leaving the whole politico-religious hierarchical organization of the village and its responsibilities in order to concentrate more closely on one's own well-being, that of one's family and co-religionists. It also meant abandoning the traditional world view and what they would pejoratively call '*aj'kunery.*'

Consequently, Protestants could afford to use any and all intra-Catholic squabbles for their own ends. Gifted with well-educated youngsters, prosperous traders and firmly convinced parents, their party could win hands down over the progressive Catholics who were at odds with their elders, seldom prospered materially and were mostly less sophisticated than the average Protestant.

Catequistas showed psychological stress in a number of ways above and beyond the stress exhibited by other parties in the Scandals. The case of one young *Catequista* leader is recalled:

Nicolás Lakan was poor in 1952: some six years before (1946), the family had had to sell the site of their hut in order to find money for the burial of a younger brother and Nicolás often spoke of his having to go earn a living on a plantation, though never liking the thought of leaving home. He was extremely naive, but intelligent and, with the *Catequistas*, he rose to the post of Sacristan and Secretary (*Escribano*) of *cofradía* Concepción. He loved his faith with true fervor and spoke of the traditionalists as of people belonging to a different world. But the *Catequistas* had a grievance about a drinking problem of his and his drinking in church with Salvador Pospoy when fulfilling a sacristan's duty to the dead.

One day, as I sat in church during my first talk with *Cabecera* 1952, Nicolás came in weeping: he wept as soon as drunk. 'One cannot trust friends; they are doing me wrong by saying that I am profaning the church by drinking in here. They have set spies on me. But what can I do about it? Don't they know I am poor and have to earn my miserable living on a plantation? And how can I possibly afford to go to prison? And how do they know enough to judge anyway, how can anyone know what to do, when the *ladinos*, the tourists, everybody says that we Indians are nothing more than animals? What can I do when I am swimming in drink, swimming in sin? Does one have to abandon the old customs? What did you say about it once? What should I choose?'

Cabecera told me to tell him and, as he cried on my shoulder, I tried to quiet him down and soothe this guilt which was so obviously eating him up. As I spoke of allegiance to the elders, he started up again: "But, I want to know the truth, the real truth and I want the truth also for Santiago Atitlán; I want us to rise like Quetzaltenango! We must have ambition! Change is coming . . . the future . . . the Catholic religion . . . my friends!'

Later in the afternoon, he seemed happy enough after singing awhile, but, suddenly, Pospoy must have angered him for he rushed out crying, 'For me there is no authority, there is no one who commands!' A moment later, he was back, shook hands with me briskly, said he would come and pay his respects some other time and departed for the day. Other instances of this kind of behavior convinced me that he would not soon be rid of this misery, but later in my stay he was quieter and attended night classes with obvious pleasure and benefit.

Other *Catequistas*, though far more stable in their attitudes towards social change and orthodox Catholicism, exhibited stress in a number of ways.

Tarn, 1952-53:

Domingo often quarrelled violently with Juan Sisay and, though naturally abstemious, went on drinking bouts for two or three days during which he became quite unlike his usual quiet, rather abstracted self, and often violent. His marital life was subject to much strain and it became clear over time that he had been seduced into a very close relationship by Juan. Despite attempts at secrecy in their little workshop near the plaza, most of the village seemed to know about this.

Salvador Sisay Petzey, a relative of Juan, was always afraid of people 'talking' and was full of 'being strong in one's own house against evil spirits and evil talkers.' He cultivated acquaintances with as many *ladinos* as would accept him and one of his reasons for working with me was that, he said, 'You might teach me the nature of things as you have travelled a great deal about the world.' He was one of the strongest supporters of the night class movement.

Both Domingo and Salvador were well aware that they did not wish to rise in society through the *cofradía* system. Domingo was a sacristan and Salvador admitted that he would probably try to make his way on the political ladder alone. On one occasion, I gave Salvador a copy of the Declaration of the Rights of Man, issued by the United Nations, scarcely suspecting that he would read it.

On one occasion, however, when the Town Mayor and *mayores* were teasing him about working with me, he demanded respect from them for his 'job' since, after all, his work was not paid and could be looked at as a free service to the community in recording their rights and

customs. He then explained the Declaration to them, opin-
ing that it had been made law in the United States. Opposition from their elders on such issues as the Maximón
Scandals helped in directing the attention of such youths
toward the political field.

In some cases, there was an obvious desire on the
Catequistas' part to imitate *ladinos* and even join in their ceremonies. This was best seen at Christmas. Juan Sisay and
Domingo were constantly in attendance on the *ladino* procession of the Virgen Concepción and had been given
charge of the '*Convite*,' a dance connected with the *ladino*
cofradía elections in which some *ladinos* dressed up as Indians. Though *ladinos*, in private, did not appreciate Juan's
talents as a decorator, he helped them all in the minor deco-
rative tasks in church and home, attended their parties and
even danced, on one occasion, with a *ladino* girl. He was
the only Indian to build a crib in his plaza workshop and
he gave a little party there for municipal officials.

Juan was reticent about his feelings towards *ladinos*.
Something can be guessed at from such chance remarks as,
'Indians have animal hair and eyes compared to *ladinos*.'
Unlike certain Protestants, however, Juan was afraid to wear
ladino dress for fear fellow Indians should mock at him.

Another glimpse of *Catequista* ambivalence can be obtained
from looking at the case of Manuel Rianda, a Chiviliu relative
and alleged enemy of his. In 1950, Manuel, jealous of Chiviliu,
had proposed his services or arranged to be proposed as *telinel*. He
was opposed by Chiviliu and others who thought of him as a
"trouble maker" or thought that "he did not have the manner of
the job." Though his physical strength was certainly up to the
task, he was not made *telinel*. Furious against *cofradía* Santa Cruz,
Manuel joined the *Catequista* faction to the extent of signing the
paper agreeing to the fines imposed on anyone found "worship-
ing the Maximón." Afterwards, the Town Mayor set spies on the

temporary home of the Mam—and "Manuel was caught red-handed doing *costumbre!* Imagine, he was so base that he made his clients pay the fine and he went free of charge!"

Manuel's remarks about "one-year Catholics" such as *cofrades* and other officials in the politico-religious hierarchy subsequently continued to be very contemptuous:

Tarn, 1952-53:

Manuel said: 'I was an *aj'kun* in the past and also a merchant in the capital but I always had bad luck. I could not understand this ill luck heaped on an *aj'kun* and concluded little by little that God did not like my work. So I went to church and confessed. I have not practiced as an *aj'kun* for five or six years now and feel much better for it, even though some people say that I am a "lost man."

'You see, there are two words: the word of God and the word of the world (*mundo*). This latter is the root of the world, it is very ancient and is kept alive by the words and prayers of the *aj'kuna*. The village cannot go on living without it because it is an original thing; it is tied to the beginning of the world. Its path is large and straight like the royal road, the *camino real*. The word of God, on the other hand, is a thorny, obscure, hidden path difficult to tread and is known to very few people, least of all the *aj'kuna*, but it is the true Catholic path and is represented by the Lord's Prayer, the Salve Maria and other such sacred recitations.'

Sore trials, including the loss of a son in a bus crash, had not helped to settle Manuel's constant anxiety, most times disguised as aggression. His behavior exhibited much of the fear of persecution found in *aj'kuna* probably since the time of Ubico (it was untrue that he had not practiced for the last five or six years), fear of witchcraft accusations, loss of paraphernalia and the like, as well as fear of the mysterious political processes taking place under

Arbenz—all of these found also in the life of Nicolás Chiviliu—but, additionally, his lack of confidence in regard to what should or should not be conceded to orthodox Catholicism placed him in striking contrast to Chiviliu.

In short, it seemed that there were three possible attitudes to progress and tradition at this time: there were those who continued the traditional life without question; those who were totally converted to progressive Christianity, mainly Protestants; and those caught in the vortex—*Catequistas*, some *aj'kuna*, and various other actors in the drama of the Maximón Scandals—who vacillated in the middle.

Writing up the first field work in 1952-53, it made sense to divide people into the "Men of Martín," the "Men of Jesucristo," and the "Men of Maximón"—with Maximón as an impure, ambivalent figure, less "native" than Martín, less "Catholic" than Jesucristo. Maximón might then be seen as a vortex of conflict conceivably extending back in time through Atiteco history and representing everything which, in Maya-Christian syncretism, had never properly functioned, fused or formed itself into a unified whole.

Later understandings, in 1979 and beyond, were to dispel this tidy scheme in most of its details though, at the time, it remained a major organizing principle for a very large mass of information.

A final question which could not help arising under the circumstances was still a question in 1979: How did the Scandals avoid outbreaks of violence? In 1990, with massive nation-wide repressive violence behind us and still with us, the question continues to be of interest, especially when Civil War violence erupting into Indian communities has often been seen as governed there by local rivalries and enmities.

Again, from the point of view of the first field work:

Tarn, 1952-53:
There are many factors in the everyday life of Atitlán which tend to impede conflict. A strong sense of privacy and the

absence of any widespread habit of visiting other peoples' compounds restricts social intercourse to the essential economic, political and religious activities. Restraints about visiting compounds when husbands are away at work are very marked. Respect for elders and generalized consideration for peoples' property and their right to dispose of it as they please helps too. Rules governing the division of labor among the sexes (including a woman stepping aside to let a man pass on the road; a woman's non-interference in male affairs; a woman's subordination to her husband at the expense of relations with her own family; as well as a number of taboos women must observe vis a vis men) help to prevent friction in this domain.

Elaborate politeness and protocol in eating, drinking and ritual activities; the toleration of obsessional behavior and mild aggression in certain stages of inebriation linked with ritual; the habit of speaking in agreement with others and working toward the consensual rather than antagonism in group decisions; indeed all ritual 'acquiescence' or 'confirmatory' behavior and conversation, can also be cited as means of conflict avoidance where parties live together in very close proximity with ever-shrinking access to land and living space. Any repression can, of course, be held to create extra pressure and provoke violence: it seems true that when an Atiteco breaks loose he does so suddenly and spectacularly. But repression in normal circumstances prevents such outbreaks from being indulged in lightly and I frequently saw men who had succumbed bitterly regret it afterwards.

In most cases of eventual conflict avoidance after initial spats, the injured parties complained to third parties or got drunk and accused groups of people or factions or parties rather than specific individuals. I did not study witchcraft accusations *per se* but it is probable that in less recent times, these were used as a means of letting off steam in as imprecise and uninvolved a fashion as possible. [*1989: demographic pressure and civil violence appear to have increased the incidence of witchcraft accusations as might well have been foreseen.*]

During the Scandals, several factors were at work: *Catequistas* feared family dissension and their elders' disapproval, as well as the *pronunciamentos* of their leaders and priests. The *Cabecera* feared opposition to his precarious authority if he veered too far to one side or another; the *cofrades* feared the Town Mayor's political power; and the Mayor, no doubt, feared for his political future. I also have the feeling that many of those whose ideals were at odds nevertheless felt affection for each other and this may have been the case especially when they were related. Nicolás Chiviliu and Manuel Rianda; Juan Sisay and Pedro Ramírez Mendoza; *Cabecera* 1952 and his son; Salvador Sisay Petzey and his Protestant sister, were all people whose relations were uneasy because they were kin as well as religious or political opponents.

Nor should ideas about toleration, man's fate and retribution be forgotten. When it is believed that each person has a God-given 'fate' or *suerte* to live out as best he can; when toleration towards other ideas than one's own are evinced; when it is thought that the moral powers in the universe will be displeased with anti-social behavior and sometimes go to brutal lengths to punish it, individuals will not lightly interfere with one another, quarrels will tend to be soon forgotten, people will sit back and let events pass and a friendly smile will mask the bitterest of enmities. There is, when all is said and done, nowhere else to go: Atitecos, after all, are Atitecos for life.

The channeling of religious conflict into political conflict, happening very gradually after an initial reverse situation, may have helped to prevent violence. For in party politics, it is normal to find oneself in opposition to others and men like Juan Sisay and Pedro Ramírez were well aware of this. Accusations here need not be levelled on supernatural grounds (witchcraft especially) nor can they be anonymous since everyone is aware of who is fighting whom. If the Scandals did not manifest the element of violence which is said to have attended previous manifestations of this type of conflict, it may be because the leading spirits in the struggle had begun to realize that, from the political point of view, conflict was the normal and inevitable outcome of life in society.

Juan Sisay was still causing trouble in 1979. In September of that year, the Guatemalan National Tourist Board had promoted a very large procession of *costumbristas* from all over the area in Sololá. *Cabecera* 1979, though not preventing it, had been most put out by Juan Sisay's appearing in full *principal* regalia to join the Atiteco delegation. Juan had tried to take over the delegation, given them orders, treated them like children.

When an issue regarding the future of *cofradía* Rosario came up at the end of the month, Juan came in to a meeting before being called, told the Council of *principales* he had a new *alcalde* for them and that they should find the *cofrades*. This was after offering to be *alcalde* himself, something nobody wanted. Juan was then accused in Council of trying to sell a *cofradía* to a rich *compadre* of his with whom he had trade and land deal relations in order that the moneybags should give "immodest *fiestas*"; of offering to pay for things and then not paying; of getting money from city *ladinos* on false pretexts as well as the usual accusation of living off the *santos*. It was also whispered that he was turning up at Santa Cruz and offering a jacket to the Mam for Holy Week 1980 in order to get the Mam on his side politically.

At one point, Juan claimed that a small statue of Rosario was his. *Cabecera* finished splendidly with "O.K. Take it away and keep it! You wore the *mangax* black wool coat of a *principal* in Sololá, but you would not dare to wear it here! You have not felt the breath of alcohol, the breath of smoke; you have not felt the north wind; you have not felt the breath of the Sun—[*i.e. you have not gone up through the ranks and done your services*]—and yet you try to impose a candidate on us!"

We'll end here with some doings recorded by Domingo about an unfortunate defense put up by Juan Sisay in 1979, when still anxious to shuck off his perceived responsibility for the Scandals. It is clear that Domingo is no longer a bosom friend of Juan's.

Domingo is telling an involved story about a spot of trouble between the then American priest and his parishioners. As in so many cases throughout this history, Juan Sisay is again involved. Father Gaspar Culan Yataz, an Atiteco native padre of somewhat extreme views, has just given a sermon during the time of the *fiesta* San Antonio to the effect that, if the people really thought all the gods and *santos* were in these wooden church altar statues, then why were certain craftsmen and artists, like Juan Sisay, making money out of restoring them?

The best thing to do now, Culan had said in anger, was for people to take down the cross and saints, chop them up, use them for firewood and cook tortillas on the fire. This shocked people and recalled both the threat of damage to the Mam way back in the 1950s and Juan Sisay's role at the time.

Domingo, 1979:

Well the only thing the *principales* remembered about the complex sermon was the bit about chopping up Jesucristo and the only thing Juan Sisay remembered was that this priest was a damned acute and intelligent threat to his money-making machinations. They had a hell of a meeting after that mass but didn't get much done. The next week there was another one which was really vicious. They called in all the *cofrades* and also Juan. Nicolás Pedro, *Alcalde* San Antonio, whose mass it had been, got up and said that the native priest was just a kid and that at one time, he Nicolás Pedro had been a kid *Catequista* saying they should chop up the *santos*—and now look at him, he was an *alcalde de cofradía*. This awoke memories of the *Catequistas* being accused of acting like ignorant kids during the Scandals . . .

So Juan Sisay got up and stormed up and down recalling how the people said he had stolen the head, which was not true: it was the priest who had stolen it and now this American priest was letting this young native priest get away with murder also! So he took people over to his own mansion—an enormous two-storeyed palace compared to most Atiteco buildings—and created a document and got many people drunk, after which they signed it. But that gets us into another story . . .

During Nicolás Pedro's speech, Juan looked hysterical, like some angry woman in a marketplace squabble. He cried that if he and his friends had done something terrible to the Mam in the old days, they would have suffered for it. And he said, 'Well, look at me now, I'm fine, I'm successful, I am a famous artist, I have a fine mansion, I have fine suits of clothes and, ahem . . . , er. . . .' And everybody was breaking up because two of his seven kids are paralyzed and walking crooked and here he is with this great big house!

It all goes to show that what you do now you pay for later. Juan was always saying, 'It wasn't me, it wasn't me, it was the *padre* who did it!' Everybody said, 'What do you mean, you showed him where to go? Dammit! if you go into the mountains and all of a sudden you find yourself inside a cave by accident, well that is one thing, but it's very different if, all of a sudden, you say, "Hey, come here, look at this," and then you lead people into a hole . . . and that is what you guys did . . .'

The retributions for that behavior during the Scandals are cited over and over even today and it is said that even the culprits recognize what happened. Some died. One man has broken his leg over and over again. One man's children have come down with polio. And so forth. The sins of the fathers visited far on down. Memory softens slowly.

EIGHT

Stories of the Early Earth, IV: Husbands and Lovers

Red Banana shakes his shoulders, sighs deeply, chugs at his beer, spills a drop on the earth giving it to drink, propels more drops to the four directions with the index finger and thumb, takes up the Mam's tale:

Red Banana, 1979:
Now when they had made the Mam, the merchants wanted him to go into the village to deal with their wives. He should see if they indeed had lovers because they were themselves unable to see. 'Just take a look,' they said to the Mam, 'but don't do anything to anyone.' The Mam stood outside the Ultimo's house for a while and saw a man go in. 'Well, we cannot judge by that alone,' said the Mam to himself, and changed himself into an exact replica of that man who went in. Identical.

The next day, the Mam comes in early and knocks on that woman's door. 'Oh, it's you!' she says, welcomes him and sits him down. The Mam is feeling silly because, though he looks like the lover, he cannot act like him. He just sits there and sits there, doing nothing, saying nothing. 'What's wrong with you?' says the wife. 'Do you want coffee?' 'No, no, I can't drink coffee,' says the Mam: he doesn't know how. 'Breakfast?' 'No.' 'What's come over you? Are you mad?' 'No.' Well, the woman is mightily perplexed.

In a little while, the lover comes in. He sees this guy who looks just like him. 'Boy!' thinks the lover, sitting

74

down next to the Mam. The woman is perplexed out of her mind. 'Which one is the real one? Which one do I feed? Which one do I make love with?' She is going nuts.

'Er . . . And what are you doing here?' says the lover to the Mam.

'Oh, just came in to see her for a while.'

'Oh . . . Yeah . . . You have no business, no message?'

'Er . . . No . . . And what about you?'

'Just came to give her the weekly money . . .'

'Ah . . . Yes . . . And where do you sleep?'

'Well, sure as hell, not on the floor! And where do you sleep?'

'Oh, I don't sleep, I never get tired, I'm always walking around,' says the Mam.

So the Mam ends up by wishing them good day and leaves after giving the woman some money for the week. He goes outside and stands all afternoon on top of the *tuj*, the sweatbath. He cannot figure out what else to do. At night he pulls out a big cigar and lights up. There he is all night, on top of the *tuj*.

The next morning he sees the lover leave and moves over to the next lady's house. He witnesses her scene and goes back up the hill to the waiting merchants. They had left again for the Coast but he catches up with them on the road. They listen to his news, tell him he has done well and that he is now ready for his second job. Which is to punish the lover. Punish but not kill, they say. 'And the women?' says the Mam. 'Aren't they just as bad?' 'Do nothing to *them*,' the merchants say. And when the Mam protests: 'You are our servant, it is not for you to judge.'

He goes to the first house again and stands at the gate, smoking a big cigar. The lover comes out to take a leak. Then goes back in. Then the woman comes out to take a leak. In walks the Mam, says 'hi!' to the lover and then, wheee, blows smoke in his face. The lover all of a sudden starts scratching the ground like a cat. He's going up the wall like a blind cat. The woman comes back into the house—the Mam has gone back outside—and cannot figure it out. The lover is running around the streets with all his clothes off, showing himself to all the women as a cat.

'Hmmmmnnn, not bad this coral tree guy,' the merchants say to each other coming home. 'He's working out O.K.' They call the Mam. 'Now, you cure the lover,' they tell him. 'Oh noooo!' cries the Mam, thoroughly pissed off. But they send him off to learn the know-how just the same.

He walks up to the lover and says, 'Hey! How come you don't have your shirt on, are you crazy or something?' And the man goes, 'Aaooorrrgh, aaaaaaaaoooooooo-rrrrrrrgh,' acting like an animal, pawing the ground, peeing on the house walls and doing all sorts of terrible things. No one had ever seen a crazy person before: *ch'ojlal* they call it: it was the first time. Then the Mam said, 'Hey, look man, everything is O.K. Don't get upset!' He lit two cigars, gave one to the man, but the man couldn't get hold of it.

Mam puffs on one cigar, blows smoke in the man's mouth and all over his face. The guy comes to, asks what he's doing there without his shirt on. The Mam: 'Well, I've been trying to tell you for half an hour, now go home and put your shirt on. But don't go messing around with other mens' women anymore.'—'Ohohohohohoho, nohonohonohonohonoho, don't worry about that!' says the man. As for the wives: they were worried about the man who looked just like their lover and they knew that something strange must have happened.

[*In most stories, the Mam turns into the lover to punish the woman and then into the woman to punish the lover. In every case the punishment is some form of craziness. Grasp the fact here that the Mam is also an* Ultimo—*as we'll see a little further on—and you do have a curious Clark Kent/Superman effect.*]

The way *Telinel* Loincloth tells it, someone like Tz'aaj is no longer a maker of Mam now but one of the cast of characters that Mam deals with:

Loincloth, 1979:

So there was this terrible woman María Magdalena. Axrom Ixtulul and his two friends wanted to get the Mam ready for her. 'Your first test is to get money away from the lover of María Magdalena,' they told him. 'Are you ready to be a bad man and a thief?' 'Sure,' said the Mam and walked right up to the hill house of Diego Tz'aaj and went right in the door. Took some money. Brought it right back. 'Not bad!' said the three friends, his makers. Then they questioned the Mam again and said, 'You are the spirit of drink, the spirit of cigar and cigarette, the spirit of poison and all intoxicating things, the spirit of everything that makes people crazy!' And the Mam acquiesced. 'We have finally found the essence of poison in this one,' said the two old ladies with the three friends, and they called him Ma K'ix: Mr. Spine, Mr. Thorn.

Then the Mam dressed himself as María Magdalena and went to sit on the knee of the man Diego Tz'aaj. Diego was playing with 'her' and fondling 'her' but: 'Before we go any further,' 'she' said, 'you should give me my money.' Tz'aaj said fine and gave 'her' a big bag. At that point, brrrrm!, The Mam turns into a young man. 'Ha! I got you that time, didn't I?' said the Mam. Tz'aaj went crazy on the spot, pacing his cave.

Then the Mam went down to the water in his normal shape and there he met with María Magdalena. 'I've just fucked up your husband,' he told her. 'Nobody does that to me!' she said, 'I have everything under control.' Then she saw Tz'aaj pacing up and down, quite crazy. 'Hey! You're pretty fancy,' she said to the Mam. 'How did you do that?' 'Oh, I have my father and I have my mother, I am an *hijo de algo*,' said the Mam. 'I am the son of a someone, I am a somebody,' he said. Then he took all the money in Tzaa'j's cave and gave it to his makers.

They tested him again with another man. 'This one lives further away,' they said, 'and he has three kinds of *itz*, of sorcery: he can turn into a buzzard, a bat, a dog. Watch it!' The Mam found it harder to get the money: the man kept on changing his form all the time. The Mam had to do so too. The man was something like a *q'isoum*, a transforming witch. But the Mam finally got him crazed and laid him down into the earth.

Finally, they put him on to María Magdalena herself. They made him turn himself into an *itz* and enter her body. He drove her crazy. She became all the things she had ever done to people: she became what she beheld. At that point, however, the Mam turned into María Magdalena and he did all the crazy things she used to do to everyone. The old ladies said, 'This guy has gone too far now and has become exactly what we were trying to get rid of!' So they called him back out of the cold.

[*So it does not come as a surprise when we find out eventually that the Mam "has two wives": an old one and a young one. The name of the young one is María Magdalena or Magdalena Castellana: the Spanish Magdalen.*]

Red Banana, 1979:
Now the Mam had gotten a little sick of making people crazy and went back up to the merchants and told them so. They told him that he could kill and cure and that that was his job on earth. So he went back and made the whole village crazy. The merchants came running back from the Coast. 'D'you see d'you see d'you see what I did?' says the Mam all aquiver. 'We told you one at a time for chrissakes! Not the *whole* village!'

The Mam was still young and learning, you understand . . . 'Well, you didn't know that the whole village was playing fast and loose, now did you?' the Mam retorted. 'They're all at each others' throats!' But they told him to cut it out right there and then and to cure everyone. So he blew smoke in all their faces and made all well.

Then the merchants told the Mam that there were girls who wanted men who did not want them and men who wanted girls who did not want them. His job from now on would be to see that all the right people ended up with each other. 'How do I do that?' asked the Mam. 'You figure it out,' said the merchants.

So the Mam goes down to the Lake waterside where the boys are watching the girls come down for water, you know how they do: they wait for the girl to go back up and then try to sweet-talk them. He says, 'Hey guys, you all want a smoke?' And they all smoke. One beautiful girl comes along and a good-looking guy gets up and goes towards her. He talks to the girl. There is this other kid sitting there and you can tell that this is blowing his mind to see the other guy talking to her.

The Mam, who knows that this kid loves the beauty, asks him what's wrong. The kid explains that the other boy is well off, has nice clothes and the girl likes him— but, as for him, he *really* likes the beauty. 'Why don't you talk to her?' asks the Mam. 'Oh! I can't do that. She hates me. She won't look at me. She clams up, she throws stones at me,' says the kid. 'Go quick! That boy is walking off. Go smash her water jug now!' says the Mam. The kid cannot bring himself to do it.

So the Mam changes himself into the kid, goes up to the beauty, smashes her water jug and tells her he is the one she should love. She tells him she does not love him: he's poor, he's uninteresting, he's this, he's that. 'She's a mean bitch,' says the Mam to the kid. 'Why on earth do

79

you like her so much?' 'Nooooooo, I looooove her!' the kid wails. 'O.K., O.K., O.K., so you're in love with this girl,' says the Mam. 'Don't worry about a thing, we'll fix you up!'

That night the Mam turns himself into a super handsome stud and wow! Stands at the corner, mmmhmmmm, you know how, and slowly lights up a cigar. He starts singing, 'Lililililililililililiiiiiiiiiii, lililileliii,' and the beauty turns *wild*. She sneaks out to 'take a pee,' runs over to the Mam and says, 'Oh, you are here, ha! Well, I really didn't know how I felt about you, but . . . who are you anyway?' she says to the Mam.

'Oh, well,' says the Mam real cool, 'I've been around and I've had my eye on you for quite some time.' 'Well, er, ou, ah, ou, er . . . ,' goes the beauty, she's falling over herself, you know, she just can't figure out what to do. She's going to go off with this stud right now, right this minute. 'Will you marry me? Will you go off with me?' says the Mam. 'I will I will I will,' says the beauty, 'I'll go get my clothes together right now!'

'Naaaah, not today, dummy!' says the Mam. 'Tomorrow or the next day, I still have to walk the town a little, don't you know, look around, check things out. . . .' She already has her shawl around him, which is ridiculous: you never see a girl doing that. He says: 'No, your father is a mean man, a very bad man: you go right back in there and keep quiet. Be ready tomorrow night at such and such a time,' he says, 'and then we'll go.' 'O.K, O.K, *fine*!' she says and goes back into the house.

So the Mam then turns himself into a super lovely girl, a real Miss Guatemala right? And he comes to the kid who is in love with the beauty. 'Honey,' he says in a high pitched voice as he sashays right into the house, 'Honey, come on over here!' 'Uh! Who are *you*?' says the kid bowled over backwards. He's a real scaredy cat.

'I've just come to spend some time with you,' says the Mam. 'I just want you to know that. I've just decided to come and live with you right away, tomorrow.' 'Er... I don't even know who you are!' says the kid. 'Wazzamatter, you don't like me or something?' the Mam purrs. 'Oh, sure, well, I, er, hmmmmm, be, ba, bi, bo, bu, you know, I don't have no place to go live for the two of us at this point,' says the kid, and 'Er . . . What am I going to do? I'm crazy about this chick!' the kid moans. 'Jeeesus!' thinks the Mam.

'Oh, my, well, don't worry about a thing,' says the Mam. 'My father is rich, we'll run away to my dad's house: you just come and pick me up tomorrow night.' 'Well, er, where do you live exactly?' asks the kid. 'O.K., you know where that beauty lives who's always hitting you? Well, I live right there.' 'No, you don't,' says the kid, doubtful. 'Yesssss, sssssirrrrr, I do, I've just kept well hidden all this while,' says the Mam. Pretty soon the kid is wrapped up, cocooned, enchanted: all he can do all night is think about this super-chick—he can't think of a single thing except going to get that marvel.

It's all very strange. That first boy down by the Lake that the beauty had liked so much: she didn't care for him at all any more, she could only think of the Mam. Poor dude! Well, the Mam in the shape of the superchick appears to this dude. Pow! The boy goes crazy: 'This is just the kind of woman I am starving for!' But the Mam blows smoke in his eyes and the dude dazes out and forgets everything. So he is out of it for right now, O.K.?

That night, the shy kid comes to look for his superchick and the beauty comes out looking for her superman. She sees this asshole kid she can't hack and goes, 'What are *you* doing here?' 'Oh! Just waiting for someone,' the kid says. Then the Mam comes in as the superchick and turns out to be a friend of the beauty's, right?

So Mam-superchick says to the beauty, 'Well, I see this

kid is here, ha! Talk to him, he's a nice kid.' *'What do you mean* talk to me? I wanna talk to you!' says the kid. They go on like this for while and the beauty tells her friend superchick that someone is picking her up. 'Betcha he don't show up! Yooo hooo hooo!' says superchick. In case you've forgotten, this someone is also the Mam. Well, eight o'clock goes by, eight thirty, no one turns up. The kid is trying to get superchick away: he's upset and furious; he's sure he's being dumped on.

Now the Mam as superchick is at the door and wondering how the devil he is going to get these people to talk to each other and what sort of invertebrates these people are anyway. The Mam says he has to go inside because 'her' father is real mean. Then he rips off the beauty's earrings, makes two crosses with them in the dust, gives one to the beauty, one to the kid and says, 'Here, grab this!' Well, peeeeeeeeeeeeiiiiiiiiiiyyyyyyyyyyyyyyyoooooooong!, both of them forget about the other parties and fall in love there and then—and right there, beauty gets her rags together and runs off with the kid.

Then the lakeside dude who thinks he's such hot shit shows up and the Mam walks back out of the house as superchick and lights up a cigar. Blows in his face once more. The dude goes crazy again right there in the road. The Mam finally gets weary of this, goes back to the merchants and complains again.

'Yep, it's part of your job on earth,' they tell the Mam. 'When there's a married woman who takes another man, you have to make him crazy, that's your job. When someone is crazy and asks you to make him well, that's your job. When somebody wants a friend and they don't have one, you've got to get them one, that's your job. When people don't get together but could and should get together, you've got to fix it, that's your job. You've got to make the impossible possible and the possible impossible. You have no mind of your own, you're a *machine*. Remember that!' This they tell the Mam.

Need I tell you we have a story also in which a girl loves a man and he doesn't love her and the Mam has to fix that up as well? So what the Mam gets himself into then is to change into a beauty and have the boys grab him and getting a kick out of it and then changing back into the Mam and blowing smoke in their faces and they all go crazy. He does the same, as a male, to the girls and then they see him as the Mam and they go crazy. 'I thought you guys had said that I was going to have some fun,' the Mam said to the merchants. 'I told you that the coral tree was going to back up on us,' one of the merchants warned.

So now they threatened the Mam and told him that he was beginning to be a liar. 'No, no, no, I never did nothing,' said the Mam. 'What do you mean, nothing? You have the whole village in a state of fright and frenzy,' said the makers. So they decided they would change things around a little bit. The Ultimo merchant held his legs down, others held his arms down, one sat on his stomach. First Merchant took his head and banged it on the ground. So they rattled his brains around a little bit. Then the Mam turned into a matchmaker nothing more, and everyone started having babies in peaceful marriage from then on.

NINE

Episodes from the Life of Nicolás Chiviliu Tacaxoy, Portrait of an Aj'kun, I

Nicolás Chiviliu, 1952-53:

O.K. This is me, Nicolás Chiviliu Tacaxoy, and this is the story of my life. The story of my life begins in Patzún over there on the other side of the Lake, beyond Panajachel.

My house had a lot of owners, all living here one after the other. This is what gave the *sitio*, the compound, and the house a lot of strength and would induce the forces of the Holy World to grant more power to the resident. The first owner was Francisco Tacaxoy, the second Yanuel Petzey, the third Gregorio Tacaxoy, the fourth Juan Acabul, the fifth his daughter María Tacaxoy—whose husband was a Chiviliu. They had two boys: my father, Nicolás Chiviliu, and his brother.

Chiviliu, 1979:

My father in Patzún is just a farmer who goes out to the fields every day and has seven daughters. In those days . . . well, even here and now in Santiago Atitlán, there are stories about daughters getting killed off at birth. If people get more than two or three daughters they simply can't hold their weight in the fields. So, my father is going berserk trying to feed all these daughters by himself. He beats his wife black and blue, she keeps trying to run away from him.

Some Atiteco, passing through Patzún on his way to Antigua with a load of merchandise, sees my father beating my mother. My father is drunk. The Atiteco says to my father, 'What's wrong brother?' My father complains that my mother is in the wrong for having had only female babies. He swears she has put the vegetable *ayote* in the fire: this plant burns the male seed and you can only have women babies.

The Atiteco says, 'No, no, no, this is ridiculous—all you have to do is go to Atitlán and everything will get fixed up!' He tells them about the power of *cofradía* San Juan. My father complains that it is far from Patzún (it isn't really all that much!) and that they have nothing to eat. The Atiteco produces some money and gives them the name of an *aj'kun* Francisco Sojuel. 'You can eat and sleep with Sojuel,' he says.

Eventually, my mother, who wants a baby boy badly, persuades my father to go. They find Sojuel at last and ask him what to do. He suggests a *costumbre* at *cofradías* San Juan, San Antonio, Concepción and Santa Cruz—this last one for the Mam. They worry about money, drinks, candles etc: Sojuel tells them not to. 'The only thing you have to remember is: when the boy is born,' says Sojuel, 'he is going to have to become an *aj'kun*.' My mother says that's fine but my father says he needs someone to help him in the fields. Sojuel says, 'That is my price. All the children born after that will be boys, but the first one must be an *aj'kun*.' This happens quite a bit when you come to ask for a boy.

My parents come three times from Patzún to do this. Then my mother gets pregnant and has me, Nicolás Chiviliu Tacaxoy. And during all this coming and going, my parents decide on staying here in Atitlán.

So I grow up here with my father and then my father dies. All these other brothers have been born. I outlive all my brothers and sisters too. I have no desire to be an *aj'kun* and, as a matter of fact, no one says anything to me about it.

Chiviliu, 1952–3:

I started very poorly in life, trying to build up a business, taking vegetables from here to Sololá and Chicacao and Coast produce from Mazatenango and San José to Guatemala City. I started doing a business from here to Sololá and Utatlán and San Jorge, yes Santa Lucía Utatlán is what we are talking about, and I also used to go to Xela (i.e. Xelaju: Quetzaltenango) through Nahualá. And then come back via the Coast. We would go from here to San Pablo, San Marcos, Santa Clara, Santa Lucía Utatlán. We would sleep in Santa Lucía, then move on to Nahualá, then to the Xela market. From Xela, we went to Zunil and Mazatenango. Finally, up through Santo Domingo, Samayac, Chicacao and home.

Chiviliu, 1979:

I am doing pretty good. I am very big for my age. I start following a trading route around the age of sixteen. I carry a very heavy load and I'm very strong: all this helps later on when I am *Telinel*. I get accosted by thieves once when I am near Godinez on my way to Patzún. I beat them all single-handedly. Another time, these thieves get onto me and I invite them all to a drink. I get them plastered and they forget about me and I sneak out through the back door. At this time, the Mam is always appearing to me in some strange form, but I am not paying any attention.

Eventually, I start getting into some money. For instance: I am the first one to own a certain kind of felt hat when they begin importing them here. You know the kind of felt hat they made in the twenties and thirties. 'Borsalinas' *(Borsalino Italian hats)* I think they were. I have a girl friend and the way I court her is: I come to see her every day, whistle her out of the house and talk to her. That's it. Perhaps I am not all that interested when you get down to it. At any rate, the mother and father are out somewhere one day, I get into the house, grab the girl and we make love there and then. When the mother comes in, she finds the two of us all bunched up.

The mother doesn't run screaming all over town because this would be bad for the daughter. She and the father agree to let me sneak out of the house if it turns out that no one has seen us. I wake up, horror-struck at what I have gotten myself into, and the girl says, 'We are married!' I sneak out and believe I have managed to get away free; a dog snaps at me but, mysteriously, no one seems to wake up. In fact, it isn't until years later that I discover the parents knew what was going on all along.

A little later, the girl's father comes to talk to me so the girl and I move into a small grass house the father builds: you cannot say it's a big marriage deal. I have an enemy who wants this girl and puts a hex on her. She is very weak. She gives birth to one boy who dies. Then another.

I am still going on trading trips but I am also sowing fields in the mountains. I'm getting to be pretty good at commerce, taking one thing and selling it elsewhere, following the prices. Meantime, I'm growing my own corn and everything is working out well. I am tougher and can do more work than most people.

Chiviliu, 1952–53:
Later, when I had built up a certain sum, I was very unfortunate: my house was burned to the ground twice. Once it was around 1943 and once around 1949. On both occasions I was very bitter and cried for twenty days and nights asking God not to let me down and give me some cash and some strength. I had some good dreams. I got a governmental indemnity of 170 quetzales at one point: that was help from God, surely. It helped me towards my new house. The house cost me 1,400 quetzales.

Chiviliu, 1979:

At some point, someone gives me a piece of land, some fifty *cuerdas* as I remember, in any event it is up on the side of Volcano-Her-Children, that is Tolimán. I get a tremendous harvest. Tremendous. Masses of corn and beans. Then, there comes a very heavy dry spell in December and the dry wind kicks up and the whole village burns down; it is a terrible mess. I am out of town. I am up in Godinez when I hear about it and come back. I had been on my way to Sololá. I find my wife is O.K. but the stored harvest is wiped out. I get drunk out of my mind. The whole village is howling, I remember: I've never heard anything like it.

So, here I am, drinking and drinking and drinking, like many other people—because I have been working all these years and now I have nothing to show for it—no house, no harvest, only one child alive. I don't know what to do. I am going out of my head with *goma*, hangover. A Godalmighty, Godawful hangover! I have a dysentery that all those who go on drinking for a week or two get regularly.

I've kept a little bit of money that I had taken with me to Godinez but that's all. I am wandering around aimlessly and this old man comes in to my house and insists I have a drink with him—but I invite *him* to have a drink. When we get to the *cantina*, the bar, the man says he wants to help me rebuild my house and gives me a fifty dollar bill. We used to drink out of big old *giraffas* (carafes: *Spanish garrafas*) in those days, with big knobby tops that you could close down over the drink. Some men are playing guitar in the bar.

There are about three people in there and I decide, what the hell, to buy them a drink; I have no money but I decide they need a drink anyway. And I've got blood diarrhea now. So I tell them to also give a drink to my wife.

Well, I go off on the road at that point, I sort of lose my

mind. The only thing I remember is hearing an owl at night, wuuuuu, wuuuuu, the owl is screaming over and over, 'Oh, we've got you now, the world has got you now!' and there are also jaguar calls. I walk into a house where a woman is grinding corn: the only thing I seem to have on is a length of cloth we call a *xtoy*, otherwise I'm naked . . . I guess I scare the hell out of that woman.

[*In another 1979 account, Chiviliu claims that, when he refused to take up his vocation as* aj'kun, *the Mam came up behind him and sodomized him. That is the point at which he went crazy. The Mam also does this to* aj'kun *adulterers or those who sexually abuse their clients. He did not see the Mam at this point since he came at him from behind. It has always been difficult to get unequivocal statements on the Mam's sex: when he appears as male, female or neuter. In this case, Chiviliu argued—of course— that he had a penis. Men see a woman, the Mam, taking off her clothes: the body has a penis: it is this that drives them crazy.*]

Chviliu, 1979:

So they find me wandering around naked in the bushes up in Chokox Aq'oum above our town, the Mam's place, the Medicine Mushroom Place. I am already something of a respected person, although I haven't done a great deal up to then, and my relatives come up to get me and see that I am safe. They bring an *aj'kun* with them and get me down from up there, wrap me up, potion me, get me warm. The *aj'kun* is a famous one, his name is Masikay.

Anyway, I am told that all this is going on because I have not heeded the call of Francisco Sojuel who had prophesied years ago that I would be an *aj'kun*. But I don't want to have anything to do with it, hear any of it; I'm crazy; eventually they have to tie me down. I'm babbling money all the time and refuse to get my mind on the right things.

The *aj'kun*, however, insists that I present myself before the Mam because the Mam is my Lord and has gotten ahold of me. I still have this 50 dollar bill I was given by the man I took to the bar: it's like a gift from heaven and it's used to buy the *costumbre* paraphernalia. The *aj'kun* Masikay is going to do a five-part affair: the Mam in Santa Cruz; San Juan; San Antonio; Santiago and the church—which is why I still do those five. The *aj'kun* is going to take out the *kii*, the poison: there is something bad lodged in each part of my body. But, in the head: that's the hardest part, only Jesucristo can take that out.

So he grabs my hand and takes me off to that part of town called *cantón* Pachichaj. He doesn't pray, he doesn't do anything much, he's not that sort of *aj'kun*. We get to Santa Cruz. He just sits and waits for the other *aj'kuna* to get done with their own *costumbres* and we drink a few more *giraffes*. I am told that I am going to have lots of dreams. I'm not even forty years old yet.

I'm ordered to make a pilgrimage counter-clockwise around the Lake: we go to San Lucas, San Antonio Palopó, Santa Catarina Palopó, San Andrés Semetabaj, Panajachel, San Jorge, Tzununá, San Marcos, San Pablo la Laguna, San Pedro la Laguna and back here. There are Mam statues in San Jorge, Santa Clara, San Pablo and San Lucas and there is a Mam head in San Andrés Semetabaj. The *aj'kun* says to me that I have to visit all these Mam statues around the Lake. On this trip I find the book which contains all the secrets of the universe.

When I get back my wife starts making trouble for me and getting on my case, saying she wants a man for a husband and not an *aj'kun*. She says she doesn't want this continence, and all these women coming in to be cured give her the creeps and she wants a quiet home life. Because, you know, it's a bit like being a rock and roll star if things get going. I tell her to hold her tongue. I'm beginning to see the light. I still haven't cured anyone or gotten my prayers together, though I've been picking up odds and

ends on my trip. That's why I seem to have so many foreign things in my prayers and why I have friends and allies
everywhere.

Things start getting really bad with my wife; we quarrel all the time. In a little time, she dies—because of all
that. You just cannot go against your nature; you have to
accept what you are: that thing in your heart has a *dueño*, a
lord, it doesn't belong to you. Her name was Candelaria
Yacantel . . .

If you follow the road of God, you receive rewards for
it: you should never harm or deceive anyone but just do
your services quietly and you will be rewarded. I think it
was after this began that I was given or acquired these 550
cuerdas of land. Anyway, at the time, I don't have a hoe or a
machete: everything had burned down. I borrow some. A
big bunch of corn comes in that year and sixty hundred-
pound sacks of beans.

The pilgrimage is very important to me. The book I
find tells me I have to remember that trip three times a
day, even when travelling, and once at midnight. I've been
doing that all my life.

One day, I'm asleep. A strange man comes into the house
and wakes me up. 'What happened to you, Nicolás? What
happened to you?' This strange character wakes me in the
middle of the night, after I've gotten all this material wealth.
There is no man there: I'm just hearing it in my ear. Someone is saying in my ear, 'Your house is on fire! Your house
is on fire! How come you are asleep?' So I'm thinking, 'Let's
go see.' I find about five hundred people suffering from
the fire. I go nuts. I start praying, 'God, why have You burned
down my house? What is my *multa*, my fine? Why do You
fine me when I haven't done anything wrong?' . . . *OH!* . . .
you know something?, I'm all mixed up: I'm talking about
that previous big fire again! I guess the fire and the call to
being an *aj'kun* go together you see . . .

Now a man from San Lucas—or was it San Pedro?—
offers me some land in his village. I have a *comadre* in San
Lucas, you know. I go to live there for a while and then I
go to San Pedro Sacatepéquez, near the Capital. I live there
three years and eat well and become rather rich. I remember well the rituals of Francisco Aguacate, Francis Avocado,
the deity of that place . . . : it had to do with multiplying
our food: seeds and animals. I come to Santiago only to do
my *costumbres* with the Mam and I bring all my customers.
I am also popular with the people of Sumpango who take
their seeds to be blessed in Sacatepéquez: by this time, I
have risen in the Sacatepéquez hierarchy. I include in my
Sacatepéquez *costumbres* a visit to Atitlán: I tell them about
San Juan and the Martín bundle and how he has the *r'k'ux*
in there—the original placenta-seed of created things—so
they leave their seeds with the Martín to be blessed.

After I've been there for a while, someone offers me a
piece of land in Santiago and, slowly but surely, I get back
here. I'm looking for another wife and I buy this little piece
of land up there, where I am now, from a man called Nicolás
Zapalu. This Zapalu decides to help me out because he
has been something of an *aj'kun* at one time and he's doing
well. I get the place virtually for free: I pay about fifty dollars over time: it's a steal. I put a house up there and live in
it with the sweetheart I've found and we have one child.

[*On another occasion, a slightly different version emerges*]:

My friend has a marimba band in San Lucas and there is
music around me all the time. I am getting fat on tortillas
and fruit and meat and I'm having a good time. One day, I
go to cut up some dahlia and bring it home to make a secret
soup of dahlia, chile, avocado leaves: it's very medicinal.
Somehow the man who is then *cabecera* sees me cutting
dahlia, commiserates with me and says, 'Why don't we

make you *alcalde* of one of our *cofradías*?' But I tell him I don't have a house.

'Well, we'll build you a damn house!" says the *cabecera* and he orders up a bunch of *cofrades* out to help me and tells them he'll have their hides in jail if they don't do well because he is the *cabecera* and, by God, he wears the pants around here. They make a house twenty yards long and that *cabecera* says he's going to check up on them every twenty days to see it gets done right away. So, you see, this proves once again that everything which is given to one is from God and not from man. That is what I firmly believe, as God is God.

Well, I'm an *aj'kun* but I can't say that I'm anything special or famous just yet. One day a woman comes in with another woman who is pregnant but the baby is not coming out. I get myself over there and the baby comes out after I've done my prayers and the woman is in good health. From that point on, my career begins to blossom and little by little it grows very well. When I get to be *telinel*, of course, my fame as *aj'kun* and my associated skills do not do any harm.

Chiviliu, 1952–3:

I was a special *alguacil* to a *mayor* in my youth [*this is connected to participation in Holy Week rituals*]. I was in *cofradías* Rosario and Concepción, and then, in succession, I became Third *Cofrade* Santiago, Second San Felipe, First Concepción and *Juez* Santiago. I became an *aj'kun* and served twelve years as *telinel* to the Mam. Now you know that *telinel* is a service but not a rank, so, in theory, you would have to start as sixth *cofrade* after being *telinel* if you had no rank. Though, in practice, you would probably jump some ranks . . . Well, after this, I was *alcalde* of San Antonio for three years and took Santiago once.

Chiviliu, 1979:

Now, I'm talking about how I get my first year as *telinel*. I have a dream in which the Mam is complaining that he has no income. It is President Ubico's time perhaps: at any rate, people who go to the Mam have to pay a fine of five quetzales to the municipality. So, after that, the Mam doesn't get much . . . or people don't come to him . . .

In a dream, a man comes in and asks me if I want a drink. I agree so he orders a *giraffe*. He drinks his part down. I drink mine. The man orders another one. I can't drink that: it is pure *guaro*, pure alcohol. I say it's time to pay but the man refuses to fork out. 'You don't know who I am,' says the man. We leave and the owner starts to call in the *mayores*, that's Spanish, in our Tzutujil we say: the *mayori*. We go up the road some ways to another bar. We have another drink and by this time we are staggering around. The man tells me he has to go to feed his horse.

I go into a house at the place where Juan Sisay lives now: at that site there used to be a *cofradía* San Miguel where the Mam was then kept. I wait but no one comes. I go to the back of the church where the Mam used to live in the very old days and all of a sudden an individual with huge boots and spurs turns up, going clang, clang, clang with the heavy spurs and asks me what I'm doing there. He says I'm supposed to be waiting in the *cofradía*. 'What do you mean?' I say. 'You have your job to do,' he says. So, I go back into the *cofradía* and realize that the Mam is not there: he is walking around in the streets some place. I tell this to the *cofrades*; they don't believe me. We go up into the rafters: the Mam is not there!

The Mam comes in—but I'm the only one who can see him. He says, 'From now on, you are going to be my horse.' He says, 'You give me my food and I'll give you yours.' So I find a way of asking for the *telinel* position; they give it to me and I start dressing the Mam the next year.

That year, there is a big robbery in Santa Cruz. No one knows what's happened to the money we've put aside for the *fiesta*. It seems to be an inside job. I get a dream from the Mam. He tells me to attach his head to his body and leave it there all the time and leave him in the *cofradía* all the time and not take him out. I do that and I pray and in a short while a big party from Nahualá comes into town from the Coast and they are whooping it up and give us a large sum of money. Within two weeks, we have made two hundred *reales*, can you imagine? It's a fortune in those days! We have a huge party. Incidentally, it is while I am *telinel* that they move the Mam from San Miguel to Santa Cruz.

I have a good many stories about misfortunes. Want to hear them? Well, there is one about an *alcalde* who steals a big hat: one of the first fancy vicunas they bring in from Italy. It's a Mam hat and the *alcalde* dies within six months. There is another one about a third *cofrade* who has forgotten to put money in the Mam box after taking some scarves—and he dies. There are poor people who borrow money from the box and they all die, even if they've paid back. You just cannot touch that stuff.

The *telinel* years are not all that eventful. During this time, my second wife dies. Some fat gets into the fire when my brother in law, Manuel Rianda, wants to be *telinel*. I flatly accuse him of being a know-nothing. Rianda goes to complain to the then *cabecera* and the office is made into a yearly one. Well, I claim that every *telinel* then dies within a year. What? Yes really! Well, it seems to me that a couple of them die within four years . . .

TEN

Stories of the Early Earth, V: The Devil's Food

Red Banana, 1979:
When the Mam had done his work sorting people out, children began appearing all over the place. Now there used to be a smoke hole in Volcano-Volcano, inside of which lived Itzel Vinaq, Evil Person—some call him the Devil. The government came to Atitlán and began making rules to the effect that each family should give Evil Person a child. To eat.

I don't know if it was every month, or every thirteen days, or every twenty days: but, each time, they had to take a child to that hole. The child was fattened up by the government and then fed to the hole. If not, Evil Person threatened to destroy the world by earthquake. The hole was at the base of Volcano-Volcano: 'under the leaning grandmother' as they say. Actually, I know a smoke hole from Volcano-Volcano even today, and one on Volcano-Her-Children, but perhaps they don't smoke any more.

So the government came with their officials, the *alcila* and *mayori*, looking for ripe children five or six years old. They would pack up the child and the wife of Evil Person would stand at the edge of the village to receive it. Evil Person would sleep in the intervening days and then would get this overwhelming urge to devour something.

There was one man, the only one ever to do it, who said he would not give his child. All his other children had died and this one was his *k'exel*, his namesake and replacement. And, even if he had to go to jail, he would not give him up. 'What are you going to do,' he said, 'kill the whole race of men because of this volcano?' 'And if we don't feed it, will it not destroy the whole earth?' they asked back.

So they threw the man into jail. A visitor friend of the prisoner came in and asked the man in jail why he did not look for a *licenciado-abogado*, a lawyer, to help him out. He knew a matchmaker in these parts who could do wondrous things. But the man in jail thought he had enough troubles without a lawyer. [*The Mam is often called* licenciado-abogado, *a lawyer with a diploma or degree.*]

Nevertheless, the visitor called on the Ultimo Merchant and asked him if he couldn't find the character who had done all that legal work before. So the Ultimo whistles up the Mam and introduces him. The visitor offers the Mam a drink. 'These merchants won't let me drink a thing,' the Mam confides, 'don't accept a thing, they said, accept nothing.' 'O.K., then, I'll fix you up later,' said the visitor to the Mam.

So the Mam's new friend took him to a bar and gave him a drink which he liked the taste of very much. The visitor told Mam the story. Well, there was one point that the Mam did not agree on. 'That lord of the hill in the smoke hole makes earthquakes!' the visitor was telling the Mam. 'Naaaaah!' said the Mam. '*I'm* the one who makes earthquakes.'

So the Mam marches into that jail dressed like a general. Clang, clang, clang. 'Well,' he says to the jailers in a stentorian voice, 'you guys are holding here my friend so and so.' 'Yeah, he's in this jail,' is the answer. 'Let him out!' trumpets the Mam. 'He is my worker—and if you don't let him out right this minute I'll hang you all one by one!' So they let the man out of jail quickly, quickly, and the man is saying, 'Who's he?' 'Shhhhhhhhhh! We're getting you out of here, meathead!' he is told in a whisper.

The man is taken home, clang, clang, clang. 'I hear they

were about to take your kid,' says the Mam. 'All you have to do now is to give me your child,' adds the Mam. 'Whaaaaaaat!' says the man. 'You have got to be kidding!' 'No, no, no, no, no,' says the Mam, 'I only want him for a week; nothing will happen to him at all and I swear he'll be O.K. I'll cut off my own head if he's not.'

In the end, the Mam takes off with the child, bags him, enfolds him, charms him, and walks up the hill. At the Mushroom Place, wwwwwwwwwhhhhhHHHHHH-WWWWWWWWWWWW, he starts up a whirlwind, a fine *silkum*. Meantime, the merchants were thinking that the Mam was becoming too clever, he could get a man out of jail now; it seemed as if his wisdom was growing. So they went looking for him to change him in some way.

Santiago came to the Mam in a dream and told him, 'You had better haul ass out of here because your makers are coming to kill you. You had better go to the volcano with us.' So the Mam gets himself up to Volcano-Volcano the next morning and calls on the Rain Angels, all those who sit up on top of the throne-trees. They all come up saying, 'Well, welcome brother, how you been?' 'Oh, fine!' says the Mam. 'But you guys have it made producing rain: all I do is match-making and dealing with crazies and it is making me nuts.' 'Well,' they ask, 'what can be done if you are of the earth?'

The Mam tells them of his plan to kill Evil Person. They tell him he is crazy: no one has ever been able to do that. 'Before me,' said the Mam, 'no one has been that powerful!' 'Ha! You red-footed little knucklehead, you've just been born and you think you are the one to do it? . . . *We* are the big guys and even we can't kill him! What do you think we make lightning for anyway? We've been shooting at this thing for centuries!'

The Mam outlines a plan and asks them for a week in order to study Evil Person's wife. Then he says to the

Angels, 'When you see such and such a day dawning, First Angel, you stand on Xokexom where the *okuy* tree blooms and you, Second Angel, on Volcano-Her-Children . . . And you on Volcano-Elbow, and you on the Mushroom Place, you on Star, you on Center . . .

'Now, when you see Evil Person coming out of his hole *don't shoot!*' 'Whaaaaaaat! What do you mean don't shoot? Anyway, you can never get him out of there by yourself,' say the Rain Angels. 'I'll get him out of there, leave it to me,' the Mam answers. 'Wait until one foot is just out of the hole and then you can let him have it. If you shoot before, you'll get me too.'

So the Mam went to the end of the village and watched the government handing over a child. The woman, Evil Person's woman, came down, she was like a *xiñora*, a *señora*, you know, curly blonde hair, very well stacked, lips painted, eyes painted, everything painted. All kinds of weird clothes on and lots of jewelry. She took the child, wrapped it up, walked up the volcano, reached the edge of the hole and called her husband. The husband said to throw the child in. He threw the bones back out. The whole place started to shake a little to show that he had 'received': she ate the bones and went down into the hole. She couldn't go down until he had eaten or he would have devoured her too.

So the Mam saw Evil Person that day: until then no one had known for sure exactly where he lived. Mam looked over the edge of the hole and saw them humping. Evil Person wasn't ugly: he was just a very strong, tough looking *ladino*, with long stringy hair. And after he had humped, snore: off he went to sleep. Then the Mam studied and studied the wife while the husband slept. Then he went back to a mirror and turned himself into that wife.

Just before the government was due to give another child, the Mam walked up to the smoke hole. He prayed and saluted all the hills round about. From each came a little shot of lightning: the Angels were ready. The Mam looked inside and saw Evil Person; he smelled a sulphurous smell. 'Hey, husband, man, *acha!*' the Mam called out: only the crassest women call their husbands *acha*. Snore. '*Acha*!! more loudly. '*Acha*!!!': still he didn't wake up. The Mam threw in a little rock and hit Evil Person on the forehead. Snore again. Bigger rock. Finally a boulder. Kioooooooongh! 'He! Eh! Hey! What's up?' says the husband.

'I've brought one of these things for you. Just specially for you.'

'But today is not the day; tomorrow is the day.'

'No, no, I brought it early.'

'I'll eat it tomorrow then.'

'Oh come on! I found it on the road. I was thinking about you. They didn't give it to me: I found it. It smells especially good.'

No answer.

'It's a special,' she pleaded. 'Take it now, there'll be another one tomorrow.'

'Well come on down then and give it over to me.'

'No, no, no, you come out here and eat it in daylight. Take a bit of sun. It'll be good for you.'

'Daylight! Ugh!' He wouldn't budge.

So she wafts a smell into the hole and he finds it very, very good—but he doesn't want the old bitch to be bossing him around. 'Don't you boss me around, you old bitch,' he says, 'come on down here now!'

'How long has it been since you kissed my mouth?'

'Oh, geeze, it's been a long, long time!'

'Well, come on out then and give me a big old kiss!'

The Mam finally manages to get him out of his hammock. 'Now how do I know that there aren't any of those water-makers out there? Any of those sons of rain, sons of thunder, sons of lightning out there?'

'There's no one out there, take a look for yourself!'

'Well, give me a hand then. I'm so sleepy, I can't get out of this hole!'

The Mam is nervous because the Angels just hate the guts of this guy and he's afraid they'll shoot on sight. Evil Person just gets his head out, no more. 'Come here and kiss my lips,' says the Mam, pulling with both hands until he starts emerging.

Krrrrrrrrr......Pyuuuuuuuuuuuuu......Grrrrrrrrrrrrrr......Yuuuupyuuuuuu.....OUOUOUOUOUOUOUOUO-UOUOOOOOOOOOOOOOOOOOOO lightning from every volcano! They fill him full of lightning bolts, full of obsidian. The hordes of Angels arrive and chase him through the clouds to the sea. Tchhhhhhhh . . . Tchhhhhh-hhhh, they are shooting at him like he was an aluminum can on the ground. He disintegrates before he even gets to the sea; he turns into pure dust.

They demolish every piece of him, except for one arm. And the thumb blows up in the air and . . . Plotch . . . drops into the Lake. The Lake starts turbulating and they realize they can never go under the Lake anymore because that is now his domain. So that's the way they get rid of him. But this *r'chbal*, this copy of part of him, starts the idea we have of the king of the drowned.

The thumb? Well, the thumb of any saint is his seat of power. 'The thumb of Jacobo, the thumb of Santiago, the thumb of Felipe Galista, the thumb of San Juan' is what you ask for to kill an enemy: ask for more fingers and you will end up killing yourself.' *(Hums to himself.)* 'At your hands, at your feet, give me the thumb of your right hand!' goes the prayer. The thumb is First, *Nabeyal*, and the little finger is the Ultimo: all the lightning, all the power comes from the thumb.

'Splendid job, old boy!' said the Angels to the Mam. 'Great shot, what!' said the Mam to the Angels and he took the little kid and blew on him and woke him up and told him to run home. Which he did and his father was very happy. 'So, from now on, you're our ole' pal; you don't belong to those merchants anymore, you are one of our crowd!' said the Angels to the Mam.

So the Mam is happy: he's got his promotion; he's made it up from the dumb *tz'ajtel* crowd to the Rain Angel crowd. This is the smart set, the ritzy crowd, the *crème de la crème*, the elite!

Now, the merchants were still looking for the Mam all over the place: by conquering Evil Person, he had added to himself that power and they would catch hell from the Original, First and Foremost Godhead if that Mam got too far out of control! 'Go to your house, stay there, don't move,' the Rain Angels had said to the Mam. The Mam said he didn't have a house. *'What!* You don't have a *mesa*, a table?' they asked in dismay. 'Well, yes, there is a sort of *mesa* where I was born . . .' 'Go there, that is your house. Otherwise they will find you and chop off your head,' the Angels told the Mam.

So the Mam went up to the Mushroom Place, which is Chokox Aq'oum, and turned into a coral tree again. He went to sleep inside it. The merchants came to look for him and couldn't find him. 'He has to show up here because he's been bought and bribed,' they said. 'We've heard his belly going slosh, slosh, slosh: he's got booze in there alright. And he smokes cigars and the people give him money and he does as they want. He always comes here to pick up the bribes.' The *mesa*, you see, is where the offerings are given.

So they waited for days and, little by little, First Merchant got mad. He hit the coral tree stub that was there and it went 'ugh!' That was the Mam's foot that was hit, and that's why he's lame. But the merchant was so angry he didn't hear him. 'I wish that goddamned Mam would come back,' they all said. But they stayed there for days in vain.

But the Mam, despite his promotion, remained a machine. The Rain Angels told him, 'When you go to your house, they are going to make a place for you and, later, they will give you a *cofradía*. People will come, burn incense and candles, give you drinks and smokes—and they will ask everything of you, both to kill and to cure. Do all of their bidding all of the time because you, when all is said and done, are a destiny machine. You are a tool; you do not decide. If you kill a man on somebody's behalf and the relatives ask you to kill the killer, then you kill the killer. Curing is the same. It is not for you to decide. You are a destiny soldier.'

Weep Wizard, 1979:
When Dust, Thread, and the Ultimo had finished making the Mam, they asked him if he was ready for a game. And he says, 'Who, me?' All of a sudden this beautiful woman who looks like the wife of Juan Poklaj turns up bringing chocolate and bread. She has a good, old fashioned clay jar full of chocolate and a loaf of the special cornbread which is made of very young corn. The bread is made by Patzún people; the chocolate is from the coast: rarely are these things made in Atitlán.

Well, here are the Power-Men enjoying this lovely woman and bidding for that food and drink. They pour out the chocolate but it turns out to be piss; they bite on the bread and it turns to shit in their mouths. The woman says, 'So, you don't think too much of me, ha?' It was the Mam. There was the Mam still lying on the ground as a piece of wood and yet he had managed that apparition. He had done his big trick on them: turning everything into decay. That's it right there: that's just where he started getting on his makers' nerves.

Which is why there is tension between Dust and the Mam as well when Dust calls in the Mam to get back his wife. I mean the Mam had already showed that he could look *better* than the wife, right? He had already screwed his own makers.

Now when the Power-Women had been going to and from the Coast, they were watched while returning to the village by Evil Person. He was peeking out over that part of town called Panabaj. One day he grabbed one of the women and started getting it on with her. Which is the beginning of all our problems in this world. Now, this woman's spirit-animal suddenly became evident: she became a *q'isoum* and started going around at night, looking for lovers. Evil Person, meanwhile, was not satisfied with just having her and was creating havoc in the village, looking for other ladies.

The Mam had already done his number with the Ultimo's wife and her lover and had driven them both crazy. The woman who got stolen by Evil Person was the wife of Dust. I should tell you that some people say it was Evil Person; some say it was Black Monster: who knows, perhaps they are the same . . . In any event, when Evil Person had taken the woman to live in Volcano-Volcano, the latter started smoking. Evil Person is with this woman and is smoking it up! The woman's name is said by some to be Bir or T'kr: she is part of the weaving kit like all those other ladies.

The Mam is called in. Secretly, some say, he wanted the job because he knew Evil Person would steal Dust's wife and he wasn't beyond fancying her a little himself. 'Do you know Evil Person?' his makers ask the Mam. 'Oh sure, great guy, drinks a lot, smokes, has a good time . . .' 'No, no, no, the idea is: he's got my wife,' says Dust. 'Aha! Ahem! Oh yes, sure!' says the Mam. 'O.K. O.K. O.K . . . I see . . . That really is too bad about your wife.' So they give him a drink and a cigar. Then the Mam says, 'What's in it for me?' And they say 'Shut up! You work for us! Don't push it!'

At this point the Mam tells them he's ready for any game in town and suggests that he invite Evil Person to a ball game. Dust and the others wonder what to do about making a ball: that is when rubber gets invented.

The Mam stands on Volcano-Elbow shouting down at Evil Person and challenging him to come out for a ball game. Evil Person comes out grumbling, throws a lightning bolt—er . . . I'm not sure he's supposed to that, I mean lightning is not his thing, but in the story . . . Well never mind—and the Mam throws it right back into his hole. The Mam tells Evil Person not to mess with lightning and to come out and have a real game with him. Evil Person doesn't know what a ball game is: Mam throws in the ball and Evil Person throws it right back. And back and forth and back and forth and back. Dust and co. are trying to sneak up to the fumarole but the Mam holds them back.

As a result of the game, the Mam and Evil Person become friends and they go arm in arm into Volcano-Volcano. The Mam takes a bottle out of his hip pocket and gets Evil Person as plastered as a bed louse. At that point, the Mam emerges with the wife, hands her to her husband who gives him thanks.

You think Evil Person likes this? Out he jumps and they have a battle royal. Wind, lightning, whirlwind, tornado, hurricane: every conceivable test. The Mam wins: his powers wax unbelievably during the battle. There are earthquakes; the volcano splits open; there is fire on all sides; everyone is going crazy. Evil Person escapes to Volcano San Lucas; they chase him to Volcano San Bernawa where he now lives. This is Volcano Fuego and it smokes, which is the sign that Evil Person is living there.

He's interesting this Evil Person because he's one entity, he has no friends, he never changes form. You can't say he's *bad*: he's just doing a job, as lord of minerals, smoke and underground things. If you say he's bad, he'll come and get you for sure. He eats people alive; he's a sort of living death. The Mam, also, in many ways becomes a living death. As for the fact that Fuego is not the only volcano smoking—there's Santa Rosa for instance—how do we explain that? Perhaps, he has several homes underground all linked up. For the time being, we have no explanation.

[*He's a lot more interesting than that. On the one hand, we seem to have a creation story, as occurs in* Popol Vuh, *where the planet is being shared out by earth forces, water forces and sky forces, and it is explained how Evil Person comes to be the underwater and subterranean force. On the other hand, something is happening to the earth's women: they are being seduced by a force they are not legally married to and the Mam is the instrument men devise to get things back in shape. The force at times is one or more "lovers"; at other times, the force appears to be Evil Person and the influence of the Biblical Devil may be conjectured.*

Something to be noticed about the Mam is that, as a wooden person, he seems to fill out a lot of what is not said about such beings in Popol Vuh. *Extremely little is said about them there, in fact, except that they were failures—a failed creation which had to be supplanted by another, more successful, creation. Certainly, the wooden persons in that book fail to worship their creators correctly: and there is something supremely disobedient about our Mam, which, incidentally, ties him in with a Lucifer we know: there is more than one hint in these stories that the Mam and Evil Person are not all that different in many respects.*

There is more. Just as, in the earlier stories, plants and Power-People turn out to be the same, it may be that the Merchants, or at any rate the Ultimo Merchant, and the Mam are the same—or of the same nature. This would explain the Mam's promotion as the newest of the Rain Angels in a system where, ultimately, Plants/Power-People/Merchants/Rain Angels are but transformations of one another for the purpose of manifesting and acting in the world.

Another thing to note is the Mam's ambivalence: he is created to cure a situation which he rapidly makes worse: he becomes what he has been created to cure. At that point, the Makers try to cut him down to size, but, in many ways, they will never succeed. Furthermore, he eventually becomes the power that gets and holds people together. No one will ever get anywhere by trying to tie the Mam down to one pole of any duality: he can only be understood in a cyclical manner: now one thing, now turning into its opposite, now that first thing again. An example is the Mam inviting Evil Person to a ballgame. It reminds one of the Lords of Death inviting the young Hero Twins to a ballgame in Popol Vuh—except that here, on the surface at any rate, it is a hero challenging a lord of death to a game.

We shall see elsewhere how easy it is to fit the Mam into one of his Christian personae, Judas. It will also be possible to offer reasons why we might take the Mam as a future Christ: that is, on the continuum, he is both Christ and Judas. We can ascertain that when we understand that both the Christ and Judas are Suns (Judas, probably a future Sun—just like the Mam is a future Rain Angel) and that, for the Maya, there is not just one Sun in this world but several successive ones according to their notion of the progress of the aeons. Ultimately, in the Maya system, the normal is only X; the supranormal or paranormal is always both X and Not-X, both a thing and its opposite. This appears to be the way in which the Maya conceived of absolute power and, in this, they were not all that different from many other archaic peoples.

Ultimately, we may arrive at the notion that there is no such thing as absolute Good and absolute Evil but only Good-Evil and Evil-Good. What is important is that all things are part of the world's energy, the world's action: now this is needed and now that. Such a view could not but sit uncomfortably with the views of medieval catholic Spain. And this is probably why the Judas personality is so closely annexed to the Mam's by the more orthodox among the Catholics.]

ELEVEN

Episodes from the Life of Nicolás Chiviliu Tacaxoy, Portrait of an Aj'kun, II

Tarn, 1952–3:

In July 1950, at *fiesta* Santiago, a Town Mayor, José Sojuel, antagonized *ladinos* by commandeering the *marimba* band they had hired for a dance of their own. The Mayor claimed simply that there were more Indians than *ladinos*. In other versions, he shut off the electric power, trying to ruin the *ladino fiesta*. The Town Secretary, sniffing mutiny, wired Sololá and some arrests were made. Apart from officials, individuals like Andrés Tzina and Nicolás Chiviliu were jailed in the capacity of 'advisers' to the Mayor. About thirty people were jailed in Sololá for three months, paying a total of some thousand quetzales in fines. Chiviliu's house was ransacked by the police who took many things, such as an *aj'kun* kit containing twenty-four divining stones. Chiviliu was still appealing to a judge in Sololá in April 1953 about a compensation case which had only just gone to the City. He had not dared ask about his stones.

By 1979, Chiviliu has it that it is Manuel Rianda who caused Chiviliu's imprisonment some time before 1950 and the story, as now told with much inflation and exaggeration, is beginning to take on overtones of the tale of persecution of a great *aj'kun:* Francisco Sojuel:

Chiviliu, 1979:

This brother-in-law of mine is so jealous and evil that he gets a petition together against all '*brujos.*' The police arrest all the *alcaldes* and the *aj'kuna* caught practicing their craft, and also the *mayori* and *alcila.* It's like some huge party. There are about 180 people there! Well, they tell me that they can't possibly feed all these people—so they send me back to Atitlán, still a prisoner mind you, to try to round up some food. I come back under armed guard and get meat from some butchers: a Zapalu, a Mendoza, a Tzina, all *cofradía* supporters. Between them, they collect about two hundred dollars and drive some cattle up to Sololá with a whole lot of other kinds of food.

The soldiers have told me that they would let me out for this service but they forget and put me back in the hole. In a week or so, they've forgotten and we all go home. Everybody feels sorry for me in fact. The Governor asks me why I'm in Sololá, and I say, 'Well, you know, Your Excellency, the paper against the *aj'kuna* . . . '

My brother in law, Manuel Rianda, still isn't satisfied. They've taken my whole kit, my divining stones, my crosses, my *r'k'ux* of this and that, all my real old things. That is why I have far less divining stones than other *aj'kuna.* This goes on in Sololá too: they get rid of everybody. It's something that the *Catequistas* and the priests have dreamed up.

So, I have just gotten back and I am weeping over all my losses, not just the house now but my whole kit. And there is Manuel Rianda plotting away and Juan Sisay, who is not really a painter yet but has a big drinking problem, is watching and all the *Catequistas* are watching. I'm with the Mam telling him my troubles. 'This man, this Rianda, has to eat bone,' I'm saying, 'because he's finished on my meat and now he has to eat bone!' And, as I'm with the Mam, the police suddenly come in, arrest me, and send me right up back to Sololá. [*Getting someone to 'eat bone' is usually considered a witchcraft activity.*]

Well, they march me up to Sololá, and this time, I'm alone, with no friends and they take me all the way up via Santa Lucía Utatlán. We get half way up and sleep at San Marcos and the soldiers ask me what I've done and I say, 'Nothing, just praying.' They take some pity on me and give me food. When we get to Sololá, they don't put me in jail because in fact they've got nothing on me. I say, 'Yes, that man hates me, it's just my fate: what can I do?' In the end, I get two days of jail and they let me go. I reckon that if I hurry back, they'll only just come and get me again so I take my time. The Colonel up there likes me and gives me a few bucks and we have a party. I visit with a few friends, people I've met on my pilgrimage, and I take my time getting home. And, meantime, there is Rianda thinking that I'm getting screwed.

I get back to the village one night, keeping a very low profile, and it's raining. But when Rianda gets to know I'm back, he has a big meeting with the *Catequistas* and that is when this whole business of the Mam's head starts up. Now: some people say nowadays that this was the getting-rid-of-the-Mam period. I think it was just for getting the Mam off the front porch of the church during Semana Santa. That's all. Maybe there were two petitions, but I think only one.

O.K. Now I'm the *Telinel* again for my last year. They make me *Telinel* when I get back from Sololá. Rianda is going out of his mind with anger. One day, I'm in Sololá and Panajachel on business. I am coming back to Atitlán and, as I get off the boat, here's Juan Sisay and his gang getting onto it. I don't remember if they had priests with them, they probably did. I ask them what they are up to and they say 'Oh, just *paseando*, moving around.'

I sort of smell that something is wrong but I don't know

what. Back at the *cofradía*, I find the head of the Mam gone and they are blaming it all on me. Very depressing. The *Alcalde de cofradía* isn't there and I'm in trouble because it is supposed to be my week on duty and I haven't been on duty.

So, now there are three *ladinos*. One is Chus Tobías, the other is . . . it isn't Fidel . . . it's one of the old Rosales brothers and the other is, er . . . Mahabran: I think that one's dead now. They are asking me what on earth is going on. I tell them. Well, they bring out the biggest bottle of whisky I've ever seen! Do we get popped! And I get the notion of asking them to send a telegram for me directly to the President of the Republic. We get a reply that it's O.K.; we can hold Holy Week; everybody can worship the Mam; there won't be a fine. Even the *ladinos* are pleased about this and I get to be something of a hero.

Now I've sent the cable but I haven't told the *Alcalde* or the *Cabecera*. In those days you had to tell the *Cabecera*. It's true now too, of course. Well, I'm asleep one night and, all of a sudden, blam, blam, blam, at the door. I get up: there's nothing. I'm dreaming. On the third knock, the Mam tells me to come to the front of the church with Third Santa Cruz and one other man. So I go out there—my wife thinks I've gone crazy—and the Mam tells me to do the one-footed dance. This is the dance I always do, holding one foot up behind me with one hand.

The Mam says, 'So, you think I don't have a head ha?' and I say, 'Well, your head has been stolen.' 'Well, my head is nothing,' says the Mam, 'and my body is nothing because I'm always present here and most sacred. Each one of these people will die year by year, beginning with the worst of them. And the rest, if they don't die, they'll pay through their children.' And it's true, you know: Rianda died within a very few years. And many others. The only ones still going: Sisay has two crippled children; Domingo has broken the same leg over and over again; Nicolás Pedro's had gonorrhea sixteen times over; everybody has been paid and even *they* admit it.

I ask him what I'm supposed to do and the Mam says that the *fiesta* has to go on and that we should go back to the *cofradía*. We don't go straight; we follow the route that the processions take, round the church clockwise and down. The Mam says he needs a *saqsuut*: one of those special, saint-handling cloths in white and purple. Then he wants twelve and I give him twelve. I'm still dreaming. So, he tells me that I'm to fold each one up in half and double it again, like this, and then fold it down this way again. Then I tie it down at the bottom. When I've done that with one, I'm to put each one over the 'head' and tie a knot at the side, until a whole ring of knots is formed.

'Then,' he says, 'you tie my mask on top of that. Then you say, "*Cabeza gavilosa, cabeza mariposa, hun di kla hiru hum bey bu pam tu dei ay San Simon don Pedro Martín aj'butayala aj'ch'ojacha, paam!*" [*Hawkish head, butterflyish head . . . (no meaning) . . . ay San Simon Don Pedro Martín, Man of Battles, Man of Wars, paam!*] That's the end of the dream and I wake up. I jump up and go running down and there is the permission telegram under the door. At the municipality, they're joking about my sleeping with my wife and so forth, because they've been knocking all night without my hearing them. So I get confirmation that I can carry on with the *costumbre*.

After this, dammit if the *Cabecera* doesn't show up and dresses me down for not having told him about my original telegram. But he's in cahoots with Rianda and co. and he dies within two years. I get to Santa Cruz, tell the *Alcalde* to leave and state that I only want Third *Cofrade* with me. I do exactly what I've dreamed with the cloths and the Mam gives me a kick, and I say, 'My! I thought he was dead and he's alive!' So I stand him up and put the head on him and say the words and the head stands right up. As soon as I go away, the head falls down. I get called back. I tell Third *Cofrade* what to do but Third has touched his wife and so cannot do it.

Holy Week comes up and everything is going fine. I pull a fast one on the village and tell them that the head was not stolen, it was something else that the priests made off with. Sisay is gnashing his teeth and everyone else is rolling around with laughter.

[*It may be that Chiviliu is conflating some elements of the 1950 robbery of the head and some of the telegram describing events of two or three years later. From other information in 1979, we gather that Chiviliu had a new head made out of* Erythrina *(coral tree, tz'ajtel) wood according to the correct dimensions. They made a spare one out of a gourd to fill the head because only Chiviliu had this trick of making the head stand up. And Chiviliu ordered a couple of masks. The head was apparently not made according to the old form (a three-pronged one), it was simply a ball of Erythrina wood.*

The original head, it is said, virtually never "came out": it was sewn up once and for all inside a number of saqsuut. *Chiviliu had seen it a number of times because it did used to be taken apart once a year, like almost all ritual paraphernalia, and he would always be the one to sew it up again. Chiviliu could, having seen the original, have ordered a copy, but he didn't. Perhaps he wanted to keep that knowledge to himself?*

It has also been said that, when the priest who'd stolen the head untied the last wrapper, trying to see what was inside, he found a paper saying, "recuerdo de Nicolás Chiviliu," *a souvenir from N.C., and he kept that. Or the Bishop did. In any event, from now on the head was kept permanently attached to the body as a way of preventing theft. The* cofradía *made a rule about it.*]

Tarn, 1954:

When he did have money, Nicolás was expansive, even prodigal. He adopted a daughter. He clothed himself and his family in the finest textiles—his wife's *xoa'* [*cofradía official's wife*] headband at the reception for *cofradía* San Juan in 1954 marked a new stage in the developing complication of headband styles. He ate fine foods and drank well, priding himself on having a good cellar. The *ladino* school principal told me once that, around 1940, Nicolás had bought a whole case of cognac from his shop as well as other liquors, especially champagne. On one occasion, he kept two or three *ladino* assistant schoolteachers drunk for four whole days. He once disparaged the twelve quetzales which his brother had spent on his daughter's funeral compared with the 75 he had spent on his own adopted daughter's death.

On one occasion, I saw him receive one hundred quetzales cash in down payment for corn. A substantial sum. He constantly visited his acreage in various parts of the countryside, had coffee and vegetable gardens down by the Lake and often went fishing for crab and minnow in his own canoe. He made good profits on pigs, poultry, and other such items sold by his wife, as well as earning twelve to twenty-five quetzales a week as an *aj'kun*. Much of the wealth was plowed back into taking on *cofradías*.

Chiviliu, 1979:
At one point, I get smart and begin associating with *ladinos*. I stop trucking vegetables and start a coffee business by buying the coffee harvests. Someone has given me a harvest to rebuild my house. With that first money, I start buying harvests all around the Lake: I have hundreds of them: in San Pablo, San Marcos, you name it. I don't own the land, of course, so I have my *caporal*, my assistant, who does the rounds and earns a good commission. People are always cheating me or trying to and I spend a good deal of time at the municipality. That is why you see a large plaza inside my compound: it's for drying coffee and I still

work at keeping it in shape. I have a tremendous coffee operation going and that is how I get to head up several *cofradías*.

My fame as an *aj'kun* is growing all the time. I have all these visitors from out of town because of the time I have spent in Sacatepéquez. They also come from Sumpango, Cobán, Cabulco, Rabinal, Tapachula, San Marcos, even Chiapas, Mexico—all over the place. When the coffee prices fall or I have an unlucky break, I put my *aj'kun* prices up. This makes the other *aj'kuna* very jealous. But I have special deals and I look after my people extremely well. I may charge them five quetzales for every *cofradía* we visit, say twenty-five for a five-part round, but I make sure everyone gets something out of it: the *Telinel*, the *cofrades*, the guitarist, everyone.

Same with the bars and candle stores and liquor stores. I blunder in any time of the day or night and always find myself a guitarist. Later, I have Prechtel as a guitarist and people love it: they say, 'Chiviliu has a *gringo* guitarist!' The *cofradías* are always agog for me to come along because I always bring a whole case of beer!

I move from being famous for midwifery to being famous for rain-making *costumbres*. At one point, there is a great drought. They go through everyone possible and eventually decide to call me. I remember that the prophet Marcos Rujuch, a successor to Francisco Sojuel, had told me that you use the red capes on the statues to get sunshine and the green ones for rain. I go into it and discover that they hadn't changed the capes at the right time in *cofradía* San Juan: they were still on red!

I then declare that the Mam also wants a cape. I put these green capes on San Juan and the Mam and do a big pilgrimage to Chokox Aq'oum and Chokoxom and Xesiwan, where Sojuel's house still stands. The rains come and

I gain fame as a rain caller. That's why they give me San Juan. All this is at the time that *cofradía* Santiago has just been moved from the home of Zapalu.

While I have San Juan around 1954 and 1955, someone manages to lose part of the *r'k'ux waya*, the small corncakes in the Martín bundle, the placenta or root of food. We think that two or three out of an original five were stolen. We blame this for the fact that two corn plantings in these parts—those of the dates of San Sebastián and El Nombre de Jesús—have become very diminished. My enemies say I sold the parts to San Juan Sacatepéquez— which is very well off for corn right now as it happens. Our lost plantings were associated with two or three colors: I think a white and a mixed were lost. I blame the loss on the then *Nabeysil* of the Martín Bundle, Tomás Chomajay, and he blames it on me. I say that the *Nabeysil* had been selling things on the Coast. The *Nabeysil* happens to find a woman around that time and that's the end of him as *nabeysil*. You know that a *nabeysil* has to remain chaste.

Then they make me *Cabecera*. In that year, there are lots of problems with the *Catequistas* but I don't fight, I'm a good *Cabecera* by general consent, try to assuage matters, keep the peace, keep everybody happy and cool. There is a problem with San Antonio, where some silver has been stolen. Always this stealing! There is a problem at *cofradía* María Entividad [*Natividad*]. No one wants to take on either of these two *cofradías*. I order that all the statues be put in the church. Eventually, I find someone for Antonio but not, alas, in time for the proper *fiestas*. I end up by merging the two *cofradías* together—this kind of thing already happened a long time ago when they joined up Sacramento with Santiago.

After putting rain-calling into my repertoire, I acquire a certain reputation for curing crazies. I cure one kid who had been in a large penitentiary for about five months. A *ladino* woman brings him from the City with shaved head— a pure cretin, a maniac. He keeps on jumping up, trying to steal, break or kill something. I remember all the guitarists were afraid of coming to my house; only Prechtel had the guts. I do all sorts of things: bite candles; bite the kid's shoulders; dance around with deer hides; get very rough with the woman, giving her all sorts of instructions. I work the Mam capes; I work the San Antonio capes. I cure that kid and the woman is still sending me donations.

Then I get this series of terrible illnesses. After being *Cabecera*, first or second time, I don't remember which. I go to the school director and to a number of others who give me shots of this and that. I have bad bronchitis. I am smoking up to two pounds of tobacco a week. It goes into pneumonia. My folks throw me into the *tuj*, the sweatbath, and damn near kill me. All my enemies are rubbing their hands with glee, hoping I am going to die. I feel I *am* dying.

One enemy is coming out of this corner; another out of that: I'm having all these battles with the enemies and, one by one, I manage to catch them and 'jail' them. But one comes out of the ground somewhere and gets inside my body and I can't get rid of him in any fashion. One *aj'kun* after another has a shot at curing me—it would make or break reputations—and fails. They're not saying my name anymore, I'm almost gone.

The man who finally cures me comes from a big Protestant family and he's a tailor. He has a dream that he can cure me. He comes up to the house with a big swab of brown cotton wool, some bicarbonate of soda and some tobacco. He chews it all up, says this strange combination of prayers: some Protestant things, some Mam things. He puts his finger deep into my mouth which is all swollen, forcing me to vomit, and pulls a wad of pus out of my throat. He washes my throat out by hand three times that day. He throws me into the *tuj* again and within two days I'm standing up. The man's name is Nicolás Quieju: his reputation shoots up and he becomes famous as an *aj'kun*. Was he himself a Protestant? I very much doubt it . . .

Another time, leading this crazy life, I'm on my death-bed again. This is the beginning of the career of Nicolás Zapalu Coche, known as Damian the Ear. He is a spy for the authorities, especially the military ones. He isn't much of an *aj'kun* at the time, just some sort of servant to me: I keep him on call to get me a guitarist when I need one and things like that. That night, Damian manages to cure me and *his* reputation shoots up. But he then blows it. He's not at all like Nicolás Quieju: he just doesn't have the *presence*. He starts asking for money when curing people, then fails to cure them; then he gets mixed up in religious politics. It's a very heavy thing in this part of the Lake where they do a lot of *costumbre* for political party big shots. *Aj'kuna* do *costumbre* for them and get big political favors in return.

Damian gets to be more political than anyone else. He starts a business carving Mam figures! One of his nick-names actually means 'Mam-carver.' He sells them to politicos at outrageous prices. Well, I get stupidly jealous and start carving a Mam. I get a Y-shaped tree trunk, carve it like a Mam, clothe it, hit it a couple of times, give it a cigar and that's it. But my figures don't sell. They refuse to be sold. They start dancing and spooking me at night, kick-ing me, spoiling my clothes, robbing me of money.

I must have been out of my mind to try to sell the Mam. I begin to regret all these efforts. So I dedicate a Mam to a *cofradía particular*, a kind of private *cofradía*, up there at the top of the town where they mess with politics a great deal. They have a mask there which had belonged to a famous *aj'kun*, Diego Quieju, and I suggest they put the mask on my figure. So I don't have to sell that Mam. This is around 1972–3. After a while Damian becomes a great enemy to me and starts preying on me. It seems to me that he is completely spurious and just wants to grab money and doesn't care a jot for what he is doing.

[*Dialogue between Tarn and Prechtel, now Primer Mayor, 1979:*

Prechtel: Well, the thing is that the Chiv would never really teach anyone.

Tarn: You're telling me! As you know, I had a godawful time with him during my first stay in the early 1950s.

Prechtel: He is very secretive. That's one of the biggest complaints about him. You can tag along with him all you like but as for him telling you anything . . . Which leads to all sorts of rumors and tales.

Tarn: Like?

Prechtel: They accuse him of flying around at night and all kinds of things. There's one rumor that the Chiv is always trying to scotch. He says, "No, I do NOT have a tail! My brother had a tail but I don't." One of the Chivilius had a tail, a projection of the sacrum, and that is very bad. It means you can be some kind of witch. If there is hair on the tail, there is still an animal element in your bloodline. Now, everybody is always saying that the Chiv has a tail and he is always pulling his shirt up to show that he hasn't.

Tarn: And, of course, they think he's capable of hiding it!

Prechtel: Of course. And then there are all the accusations of skirt chasing. His wife in the 1950s eventually died but he was accused of getting rid of her by witchcraft. See, no one really wants an aj'kun for a husband. It's hell on your nerves, on your purse; your neighbors are always accusing you of something or other. The hours you have to keep are terrible and that can end up by being bad for your health. You never get enough sleep. Never sleep properly at all. The house is always full. No time to yourself and you get poor because you don't have the time to look after your own business.

Remember: people love a nawal acha, *a Power-Person, whereas an* aj'kun *they have to use at times but do not love. It is possible that the Chiv contributed to bringing the two notions together: a matter of survival. You get to have enemy* aj'kuna; *you're always dreaming about them, getting shot at by them, having their wives come after you and getting bad prices in the market because everybody figures you're rich.* Aj'kuna *often die young: healing people is a burden which weighs you down. Chiviliu feels these days that the earth is pulling the strength from him just as it does to a plant when it is dying.*

Plus: the art is considered to be a little bit "loose" in the sense that the aj'kun's *art is thought of as being his wife and his wife is then something like his mistress. If he and she are for real, an* aj'kun's *wife is supposed to go everywhere with him. Always. The one thing she does have going for her is that she never begs for food. An* aj'kun *is the best-fed man in town.*

Tarn: I don't ever remember a wife being around during costumbre *in 1952–3. When I was following him around, we were virtually always alone.*

Prechtel: Exactly. Which is why he got rid of that wife.]

Prechtel, 1979:

Now, the person the Chiv eventually gets hold of is a girl called Thorn. That's her nickname. Her mother dies when she is young and her father feeds her, then her father dies. It's tough for a spinster to look after a parent and then that parent ups and dies. So she is a *rilaj q'apoj*, a 'venerable maiden.' The Chiv meets her and she likes *costumbre*. She also gets on very well with a grandchild of the Chiv's, his *k'exel* or name-bearer, the son of a son that drowned. She learns all his prayers—finally, he teaches her everything.

She keeps him in line: if she hadn't he might well be dead right now. She puts him in the *tuj* when he needs it and won't let him go out again after that; she takes a stick to rowdy visitors and so forth. Outside of that, she lets him run: he can even have other women if he likes—as long as he comes home. She gets to be quite a famous wife. She has one daughter who sells coffee in the market place and dies unmarried at twenty. Thorn doesn't drink much, but when she does, she always weeps for that one daughter. The Chiv cuffs her one and they have a big scramble. He comes to my house from time to time asking if he can spend the night. Thorn comes for him in the morning and we lug him home.

We are getting close to the time when I become apprenticed to Chiviliu. Interspersed with the great illnesses, there are the great toots: I guess they are inter-related. The Chiv is coming into an age now when he doesn't really have to work any more. He has two fisherman sons and all that side of the family fishes too. Two grandsons are traders with the City. Some kids have taken over the coffee business; some are just farmers. Each one gives him part of his income, crop, harvest, or what have you: he's like a real old pensioner you might say. He's always asking for money in one way or another, but it's beer money basically.

The great 1977 toot comes about because that year there is a bumper coffee crop and also the price of coffee soars. The Chiv clears about eight hundred *quetzales*. He conveniently forgets that he owes three hundred on a previous transaction and he doesn't want to look too closely at the fact that coffee prices are not going to stay way up there forever. He goes on a toot in January, anticipating the February coffee, and he's still at it in March. I'm invited to eat at his place every day; he's over at mine and I take him home a lot.

In March, we are doing a five-part *costumbre* for rain. All of a sudden, he feels this need to die. He's done it a couple of times but never as heavily as this. On one night, he does the dance of the four directions; it's a very long one; he paces all the way out to the door and the corners. In the middle of the next night, he can't talk. They call me over. Everyone thinks this is the end of Chiviliu. I'm still

121

green and think so too. So, this is really the end, the terminus of the Chiv.

He asks me to bring my tape recorder so I can tape some of his prayers. He's already asked for my machine and compared it to the one you, Tarn, had in the old days. Yeah! That clumsy, old, radio-type, wind-up thing. Well, he goes into his death-talk and starts rapping with the angels and that is where I begin to pick up the real stuff about praying. He says to me, 'Now you have my prayers, my repertoire, you have to take it. When I die, you have to keep it alive.' After the recording, he starts gurgling in his throat and everyone says, 'Aaahhhh, this time, this time he's really done it; this time he's really gone . . .' So he kicks off, he's moving, he's gone! Adios Chiv!

After about an hour, we're all there crying and howling: he sits up again. His eyeballs roll up like this; he starts shaking; it's *incredible*! Then he passes out completely, gets a kind of paralysis, all stiff as a board. What he has is a heavy hangover: he has no calcium at all in his system and it is doubling him up. The howling goes up again; it's four in the morning and people start crowding in.

And then, suddenly, he sets up a big scream, gets up, asks for another case of beer and goes out to take a leak. Everybody starts rolling about all over the floors, splitting their sides with laughter. As for him, he goes out to buy some beer on credit. His wife is ready to kill him: he's blown a year's money in three months and is up to his ears in debt.

That Holy Week 1977 is my first in Atitlán and I am drunk all the time. Most of it, I believe, he spends sober. But one night he comes in to *cofradía* Santa Cruz and dances around the crosses. He has been *tijonel*, counsellor, to Santa Cruz during Semana Santa from a long time back: they have always asked him to dress the Jesucristo. He comes in with a new black hat and a whole new set of clothes, looking fit to kill. He registers everything and solemnly declares that there's one of Jesucristo's cushions missing. The *cofrades* say they have a new one. No: he's dreamed they have to use the old one. He prays over everything: he does that every year when the Jesucristo comes out. This time, he sets up a long, loud scream: 'HESUCREEESTA, HESUCREEEEEEESTA!' he calls out to the Martín, dances again: it's a *major* production. People fall to praying rather frantically. The Chiv waits for the procession to leave. He has a beer quietly and goes home.

Around that same 1977, in June, he has a dream that if he doesn't marry in church, there will be no rain. His wife is all for it although she had been rather contemptuous of the whole idea. Father Stanley Rother, the Oklahoma priest, is all for it: he has been talking the Chiv into it for months. The *Catequistas* are delighted: after all this is part of a long standing plan of theirs to get all the *principales* married in church. They announce it on the radio. No one can believe it: the greatest *aj'kun* in Santiago getting married in church!

But out they come. She is wearing white with some bridal stuff in her hair. He is dressed like a lord and has his headcloth on; the great *Catequista* Manuel Rianda (not the Chiv's relative) is bringing up the rear; everyone is beaming and walking very tall. Father Stanley marries them, of course. The Chiv puts on a special mass and the whole village shows up. As he got married and prayed, you really wondered who he was talking to: it kind of went *beyond* Father Rother! After the service, they got back to the house and had a hell of a party with a whole bunch of chickens and turkeys the old man had killed.

Little does anyone know that the real reason he has gotten married is so that Thorn gets her inheritance. He has many sons and grandsons who are not of her blood. He has children who have turned Protestant and would sell his *Santos* at the drop of a hat.

Meantime, the Chiv is declaring to all that, with his marriage, the old world has gone and a new world has arrived—but, on the other hand, woe to anyone who forgets the old ways!

TWELVE

Stories of the Early Earth, VI: The Black Monster Wars

Weep Wizard, 1979:
Now the Mam becomes very bored again after the victory dance and eventually he leaves on a long voyage. Dust and the others resume their trading trips: the old capital of Antigua is the terminus and the Spaniards are very evil there. They accuse Atitecos of being the worst witches and sorcerers—but they are not the only ones to make these accusations.

At this time *Nabeyal* Santiago comes up to Godinez. His is another name for Dust. An old lady with a red *huipil*—we call people north of the Lake 'red *huipiles*' and south of it 'green skirts'—comes out and asks the merchants, 'Boys, where are you going?' They explain that they are on their way to Antigua and she tells them not to go. The government has a terrible Black Monster and the 'boys' are not even armed.

'At least put on pants so that you look as if you are Chimaltecos: if they know you are from Atitlán, you have surely had it.' Our decorated pants are a give-away. The lady—she is the Grandmother, the Moon and creator of all earthly life—is very worried about them, mourning that all her children have been killed by thieves and robbers. 'But we are traders,' they say, 'it is our job to go.'

So she offers them chocolate and corn bread: it does not decay in this case, but you know the Mam is going with them. The stuff puts them to sleep and they dream they have to fight Black Monster.

They awake and make for Patzún-Patzicía. They go from bar to bar, like gunslingers, listening to stories of the Monster and his fearful deeds. His body is made of pure iron; he is pure beast and he rides a huge black horse.

Dust decides to go ahead with his fish and check the Monster out: if they don't hear from him in a day they should come to get him. The Monster comes rolling out of a thicket at the place Pachebak and tells Dust to come to a halt. The Monster interrogates Dust, takes all the fish, takes also a *patin*, a fishpaste lunch, and handcuffs Dust. Did you know, by the way, that we are known as *aj'patin*, people of the *patin*, because we used to bribe all customs posts and guards with that fishpaste stuff?

In any event, Dust sees that there are twelve of these Monsters. They take Dust to Antigua on his white horse— don't forget this is Santiago Dust and Santiago always rides a white horse!—And when they put him in jail the horse trots off. So the horse, who as likely as not is the Mam, runs back to Thread and tells him all about it. Thread goes to the rescue. They all go in their turn. They all try tricks and they all fail.

Which leaves the Ultimo. The old lady begs him not to go since all his brothers are dead—but he goes back to Atitlán to fetch his weapon. A *hwit* is all he's got: a magic staff, a very special weapon. There he is, a real hero. 'But I must get some food before leaving,' he thinks, and goes off hunting.

He gets a bow and arrow and makes for Xechivoy— which is a little crazy because that's where women go to do their washing and there are no birds or animals. But he, don't forget, like all the Ultimos, is a *nikanik*, a seemingly semi-witted, half-witted Fool of God. He sees a frog and gets him in the stomach. He goes into the water to pick up the beastie, thinking of how good a frog sandwich would be, and, all of a sudden, he is not sloshing about in water, he is inside a hill.

'Hey! How come you killed my kid?' says a big tall lord of the hill. The lord shows him a little kid with an arrow in his stomach, bleeding to death. 'You better fix this, or I'll have your hide,' says the lord of the hill to the Ultimo while the Ultimo is going, 'Oh gawd, oh gawd, oh gawd! What have I done!' So the Ultimo takes saliva and rubs it on the child's wound, makes a cross sign on his forehead and the kid is saved. The lord is impressed, shows him an armory he's in charge of and lets him have his pick. The hills are full of these armories.

Has the Ultimo arranged all this in his *nikanik* wisdom? He looks at the array of goodies: obsidians, swords, lances, pikes, bows and other weapons; thunderbolts, lightning bolts, whirlwinds, and other terrors. 'Well, I'll just have one of these and one of these and one of these,' he says, helping himself. 'I think I'll change this *hwit* for one of pure iron,' he says, thinking a pure iron one will handle the Monster for sure.

Having tried out the weapons and destroyed several things in sight, the Ultimo packs cacao instead of fish and also, a tiny, wee, dinky *patin*. Coming up the mountain to meet the Monster, the Ultimo sees people from Chichicastenango and other places getting ready to sleep a night on the road. 'Here comes one of those Atitlán witches,' they all say, and they try to avoid him sleeping near them. But he is anxious to warn them that they should not sleep that night for fear of being killed.

He keeps an eye open all night; the others don't. The Monster creeps up to the sleepers and burns their feet off. He whips all those people until they turn into horses while he packs their belongings onto his own saddle. Each horse is made up of two beaten people. But the Ultimo escapes by turning himself into a small dust devil.

So, in the morning, the Ultimo gets up to where the Monster is and, of course, he is the last and the biggest of the Monsters while the Ultimo is the smallest of the brothers.

'Er . . . Care for a little *patin?*' begins the Ultimo.

'So who the hell are you and where the hell do you come from and where the hell do you think you're going and what the hell do you think you are doing here anyways?' flashes back the Monster. And all this business of the Atitecos being superwitches is because of that *patin* stuff: they would get through with that bribe whereas no one else did.

The Monster is now anxious to pack the Ultimo off to jail but the Ultimo is still talking. 'Now how's about a little game?' says the Ultimo. 'Whaaaaaaaaat? Are you crazy? A *game?*' says the Monster. Then: 'What game?' says the Monster. 'A jumping game,' says the Ultimo. The Monster laughs fit to drop his pants and tells the Ultimo to draw the line. 'No, you draw it,' says the Ultimo, 'anywhere you want.' And then they do a 'you first, no you first' number you never hear the end of. Because whoever can stay to last in any such circumstance has the best defense against witchcraft.

The Monster jumps and just about clears the line. The Ultimo jumps . . . and disappears. The Monster is completely spaced out because his prisoner has vanished, then gets even more spaced out because he comes back. There is a lot more business with the Monster wanting to leave for jail and the Ultimo wanting more games. 'How about making rain?' says the Ultimo. 'I can't do that!' says the Monster. The Ultimo claims he is beaten in advance. In the end, the Ultimo obtains one more game: a game of staffs. 'You first; no you first,' they go: you never hear the end of it.

The Monster brings out a staff and tries to hit his man

who dodges and emerges safe. Then the Ultimo has a go. He sits down and whistles. His pure iron staff comes out and slams the Monster: paaam, paaaam, paaaaaam and many sparks are flying from the two irons in contact. The Monster behaves as if he had been hit by a bunch of mosquitos. 'This is tougher than it looked,' thinks the Ultimo. He offers the Monster a cigar. The Monster refuses and offers the Ultimo one of his own. 'You smoke mine; no you smoke mine': it's a witch's trick, you know. Finally they accept each other's but they won't light up.

In the end, they do smoke; the Ultimo is very quick and manages to switch the cigars. 'Let's smoke them at exactly the same time,' he says propitiatingly. He's O.K. with his own cigar, but the Monster, smoking the Ultimo's, is in real bad shape. He's all giddy and can't move. So the Ultimo whistles up the Double-Headed Eagle with a long, special whistle he has. Up comes this *K'walk'oj* going 'peeeuw, peeeuw' above their heads. 'Grab him, pick him up!' orders the Ultimo.

Still commanding with whistles, he tells the great bird to take the monster up . . . and up . . . and up . . . until they disappear. Another whistle: 'Let him go!' In the meantime, the Ultimo has built a big *tz'alam abaj*: a square block of rock like a sacrificial altar. The Monster hits this during his fall and breaks into a thousand pieces, each piece turning into a golden coin. The Ultimo bags them up and buries the bag on the spot. The place is called Chumibaj Juyu and people still go there, looking for money.

When he had done defeating the Monster, the Ultimo whipped the Monster's horse on the rump and it turned into seven men. The men thank him for freeing them— but the Ultimo sees through those particular witches and whips them twelve times and turns them back into horses.

Many, many horses. Then he hits all the other horses and they turn into the people from Chichicastenango and other places. It turns out they have been lost for years; they were disappeared; they are all crying and weeping; they don't know where they are. He gives each one a map and tells them how to get home: to Chichi, Sololá, Comalapa or wherever.

Well, the Ultimo walks into Antigua and all he has with him is his drinking-water gourd. He begins stealing fruit in the market with the idea of getting himself thrown into jail. There, he rejoins his brothers and each brother has his story to tell. The Antigua people have been trying to execute them with all the usual methods: shooting, hanging, knifing, quartering with horses. As usual, nothing works.

The Ultimo tells them that he has brought his water gourd and they ask him why. 'So we can dance,' he says and starts banging on the gourd as if it were a two-tongued drum. So they all begin to make music and dance. They dance their asses off: the guards, alerted by the noise, rush in and try to stop them—but it is all in vain, they continue dancing.

They escape that very night and go to the marketplace where they are found eating, singing, dancing and carrying on. When the guards check out the jail, they find this solitary guy smoking a big cigar: you know who that is: it's the Mam of course! When the guards scamper off back to the market, they find no one: the brothers are back in jail!

In the market, the boys leave a huge heap of fruit, just like the Easter Holy Week monument. It has the delicious smell of Power-Women: you remember that statement in an earlier story, 'my wife is just a fruit.' The guards cannot resist that smell; they are drawn by the smell of the Power-Women. They rush to the heap of fruit and there they find a huge, hairy snake, a *x'qunq'a kumatz*, the snake with the rainbow breath, all curled up inside the pile.

Everyone in the marketplace runs in terror from the snake and rushes to the prison commander asking him what to do. Meantime, the boys are playing their gourd in prison. A water-gourd, you understand? The commander tells the guards they had better let the boys out because he just cannot think of what else to do with them.

So, as the water-gourd plays, a huge rain begins to fall, and all the tigers and mountain lions and jaguars and ocelots and wild cats and snakes and other animals start roaring and howling and hissing, and all the volcanos round about, they also start roaring and everything is roaring round about.

The rain fills up Volcano Hunajpu—Volcano Agua—and they have another *kasueel juyu*: a bowl of the mountain, like the one atop the church altar *monumento* in Atitlán during Holy Week. Then the lake inside breaks because of an earthquake. The water comes down in floods and drowns Ciudad Vieja, the Old Capital. That is how the wife of Pedro de Alvarado, conquistador, is killed. And all the palaces fall down.

Some say that the boys' ladies had arrived with the shirts of the Martín Bundle which they themselves had woven and that it is with these shirts that the boys made the rain. In this version I am telling you, three of the women turn up with chocolate: they are the clouds. Three of them are carrying Cerro de Oro, that little hill down the road from here which belongs to Atitlán, as if it was a wedding cake. Dust's wife is the main lady in this party.

Would you believe that Evil Person pops out of the woods near Tz'anch'oj, over by where Cerro de Oro stands today? The women are supposed to be re-arranging all these hills, but Mrs. Dust becomes attracted to this beautiful, handsome *ladino* and she puts down Cerro de Oro right there, where, of course, it now is. Actually it should have gone where the Center, Cerro de Burro, now stands. So, there you have another idea of what happened between Evil person and the wife of Dust.

Tarn, recording a version in 1953:
After arriving home, the boys made a double-headed eagle, a *K'walk'oj*, out of wood which they placed on the Tzutujil altar, the main altar in church. And under it, on the altar, they put a large bowl. It must be presumed that they gave the Great Bird food because, after eight or twelve or fifteen days, we're no longer sure which, the bowl was full of blood. I own two paintings by Juan Sisay showing the Bird and his blood bowl. Chiviliu says, 'But we do not know what kind of food it ate. And thus the remembrance of the Great Bird remained there. It was only destroyed when the church was heavily damaged by earthquake . . . As for the "content" of the Martín shirt, it is: tigers, suns, snakes, fruit, rains and other such things.'

■　　■　　■

We include here a final section which we might title:

THE UNDOING OF THE MAM

Tarn, 1953:
Now the figure, the Mam, began giving trouble for it was in the habit of walking about, and some began to whisper against it. Sometimes it appeared as a man, and sometimes as a woman, but whoever it looked upon was in danger and, if it should sleep with a man, that man was dead and buried within three days. The figure often used to go out into the street as a beautiful girl with blonde hair and the boys used to come up and flirt with it. But eventually the people recognized it because it only had four fingers, and they knew the danger and stayed away. Some said it should be broken up and made powerless and suggested that the head-post should be turned around to face backwards, with the mask facing forward—like the Double-Headed Eagle in a way—and this would render it powerless and unable to speak.

The head-post now used is the same one as the one the original sculptors used. The figure had a head—the one which was taken by the priests during the period of the thefts—upon which was drawn a spiral or a circle and above this, two little lines for the eyes.

Prechtel, 1979:

This is one I have heard recently: Dust, Thread and the others decide that now the world is organized and there are no more problems: it is the Mam who is making the problems they had created him to cure. They call the Mam to them but he refuses to come. They call the Ultimo who had not come that day and ask him if he would get his friend the Mam. So, off the Ultimo goes to get the Mam.

In comes the Mam with a briefcase. And a hat and a big suit—whereas, before, he had only worn a headscarf. He is a doctor now and has been to Europe. 'You have been making people miserable, turning everything into excrement,' they tell him. 'Perhaps you have been bribed just like any official.' The Mam denies all this; they tell him he is a liar into the bargain.

They decide the only thing to do is to blow mist into his eyes. After that: same power, less judgement—he is worse. They call him again, grab him, tie him up. They turn his head around: he begins to walk backward and do everything in reverse. Dust gets into a fight with him, kicks him in one leg: he not only walks backwards now but he limps.

'The only thing we can do is to cut his head off,' they say. Which they do. Which is when he starts running around without his head. They cut his legs off also: this is why he's in three parts.

And whenever they wanted to use him, they would put his parts back together. They created a place for him to sleep and they made up songs, they created a *cofradía* and the post of *telinel*.

Loincloth for a grand finale, 1979:
The two Grandmothers decided he had become as bad as the things he was created to cure. They told the Mam they would cut off his head. 'I have a better idea,' said the Mam. 'What you do is to cut me in pieces, then, when you need me, I'll come. When I'm not needed, I'll stay where I am.' The makers decided he had indeed become smarter than they since he was now telling them what to do! The first thing they did was to cut his body in half at mid-torso. Then they cut his head, his legs at the knees and his arms at the elbows.

There he was on the ground, lifeless, all his limbs quivering. The Mam's head spoke up by itself, telling them that when they needed him, they would have to put him back together. That is when they started using wooden pegs—what we call *tornillos*—when they wanted to reassemble him, they pegged on the knees, the elbows, the head. There were twelve holes and twelve pegs. The pegs were made of *tz'aaj* wood, from the *Taxicoba* tree. In the old days, there were no iron nails: all wood was pegged with that. Now, there are no more *tornillos* although we go on praying as if there were: this thing has become rotten over the years and you cannot peg it together anymore. After a while, the makers used a rope *k'aam*, to hold it together.

One time, when they had put him together again, he had started interfering with women and they didn't like that. The Mam had said, 'Well, in that case, why don't you find me a wife?' The wife should be made from his own body, he specified. So they took a piece from the middle of his body and they made his María. They made sure, however, that she stayed away from him. Because a lot of times, the Mam cannot be called, or he will not come—but he can always be lured to his wife.

He has a wife so as not to screw up the rest of the world. He can wander around while María stays still. Actually, he has two wives, an old one and a young one—maybe two aspects of the one wife—but we'll go into that another time . . .'

[*Should you wish to look into where the story of the Mam in prison, keeping the place of the brothers warm, might come from, you might look at the stories in* Popol Vuh *about the prisons the lords of death put the heroes into when they get hold of them. The heroes have all sorts of tricks for getting out of those prisons and some of them involve familiar subterfuges.*]

THIRTEEN

Episodes from the Life of Nicolás Chiviliu Tacaxoy, Portrait of an Aj'kun, III

Prechtel, 1979:

If you remember, I arrive in Guatemala some time in 1972–3. I get to live in Santiago around September/October 1976. It's said that I lived with the Chiv: he wanted me to, but my then wife, a *ladina*, was against all that. Later, when she left, I had too much else to take care of. She left about the time that Chiviliu got married.

When the Chiv marries and talks about the old and the new worlds, he tells me to study the old ways very hard. He says it's like a dog: a dog, you don't teach him things, he just picks them up. I think about that: yes, you don't teach a dog to chase rabbits, he just does it by instinct.

So I apply myself and work like hell. My Tzutujil isn't of the finest at that point, I can tell you, and it's very difficult. The Chiv tells me to come every day at a certain set time and has sessions with me. He also wants me to pray in my house three times a day and do this, that and the other. He says, 'We'll see how good you get.' His style is very original and idiosyncratic as you, Tarn, perceived in the old days. It has components from the Sacatepéquez region. Of course, you have to have permission: stealing another *aj'kun*'s praying style could kill you.

Before every festival, I have to put up the candles on the previous night and get ready for the next day's *cofradía* visit. Pretty soon, *cofradías* are calling me on a regular basis and I have to show up all the time. I'm trying to do all this while having my first show of paintings at the *El Túnel* Gallery in the City, October 6–17, 1977. My job in the *cofradías* becomes flutist: as flutist, I see an enormous amount of ritual.

Then, I become the man who cures the Chiv. It may be November 1977 and November 1978—or maybe just the latter. A couple of *aj'kuna* have had no luck: his wife comes down to get me. He won't listen to anything: the only way is to take him by the ears and force him. I push him into gargling with oregano, ginger and eucalyptus; also to drink decongestant tea and take tetracycline. It's this damned dust-kicking north wind. Two days later, he shows up at my house and I have to force him back to bed. I tell him he can't drink or smoke for a week. He says, 'Well, if I can't drink or smoke, I might just as well die.'

After this and some of my epilepsy cures, including my own wife's, I start getting quite a bit of clientele. The Chiv shows up one day and says, 'How much are you getting for this?' I say nothing. He says, '*What!* What sort of an S.O.B. are you anyway, ruining our fine art, our fine trade?' I ask him what he means. He says, 'Well, I taught you all you know and now here you are selling it for nothing! Here you are giving it away!' I tell him that I feel sorry for these poor people. '*Sorry!*' he barks. 'Are you crazy? These motherfuckers, they're killing me; here I am spending my whole life serving God and they try to kill me all the time and meanwhile you are acting as if this help is something you can just *give* away for free!'

He has a point. If you charge, the patient will feel better about it. So I get to charging for the *costumbre*, never for the remedies. It's always food and goods anyhow, never money. Some of his business is beginning to come to me. That, of course, is tricky. In the end, he comes up with 'the only thing we can do about this situation is that you send me some tobacco.' I think it over: tobacco's no good for him; vitamins aren't good to eat—on the other hand, anyone who's remained in debt to him has gotten into trouble. So I decide to make the ceremonial corn drink *maatz* and I keep on sending him *maatz* and soup.

Now, one time, Juan Sisay had made a great big statue of the Mam outside his home with a great big sign on his chest, '*Yo soy un hippie; yo soy un marijuanero*': 'I'm a dope-smoking hippie.' Somehow, we inherit the statue's mask. It belongs to students: Salvador Sisay, later a student agitator, gives it to Felipe Tuiz who doesn't know what to do with it and so gives it to us. He was with my music group at one time. I don't think much of it: it's not even made of the right wood. So, it has just been lying around there. One night, the Chiv comes to my house. He wants a guitar-player for a *costumbre* and he likes me because I know all the songs. The first thing he sees is this mask: he's drunk, thinks he is seeing the Mam and starts talking with it.

Later I get him into our musical group as *tijonel*, as consultant you might say. The whole musical group thing is his idea actually. He has a bunch of dreams and comes to me one day and says, 'Well, now, I'm going to have my own *conjunto,* my own band.' I think the idea is terrific. As far as I'm concerned, this is the Chiv's group.

If I remember correctly, the band, called *Ju'ljuuj Tijaax*, started around November 1976, at about the time I arrived in Atitlán or just before. There was a first performance at the Centro de Estudios Folklóricos of the University of San Carlos in Guatemala City in May 1977. They did it in the Casa Flavio Herrera on 14th street.

When the group goes to play the City for the first time, the Chiv says to bring the mask. Once in the City, the Chiv puts together a Mam with the mask and it looks pretty funky, I can tell you. He does an incredible performance on stage. He's putting up candles, dancing up and down, screaming and shouting: the audience is absolutely *flabbergasted*!

This is where Felipe Tuiz gets the idea of our doing performances with a mask, but these things can easily backfire. I get very upset when it turns out that the Chiv is not on our record sleeve—we make the record around November 1977—because, as far as I'm concerned, he is the cover. The record is supposed to be his message to the world. But, it is as well that it did not happen because already people are accusing him of making a Mam in the City. He is accused of selling the Mam. It is the same old story. Ironically, Juan Sisay is green jealous of Chiviliu at this time. There Juan is in his black ceremonial coat he has no right to, yet always insists on wearing—but the Chiv is the real popular hero.

Chiviliu is really coming alive with all these goings on; he starts doing *costumbres* again; he has a little army of groupies; everywhere he goes, about twenty guys with guitars converge on the place and the Chiv is walking around like a king. At this time, he is on a great eight hundred dollar binge and he is going wild. As for us, we are seeing every ritual in the book, in sight and out of sight. And we are coming out in the newspapers right left and center without having to go down on our knees for it.

What with his friends and mine, a lot of people are milling around and hanging out. I have a lot of friends from my time as a musician before I settle in Atitlán: some of them are the *licenciados*, the professional people, who have been fans of the Chiv from way back. Some are government people whose fathers he has helped.

One day, I'm in a corner bar by the church busy with a bunch of sextons about Christmas ceremonies. Peralta Mendez, the politician, is standing there. He calls me over after recognizing me and offers me a drink. I cannot remember who he is. Drink after drink. Then, he says, 'If I win the candidacy, I'm going to give you people this and this and this.' Then, another time, there is Chiviliu marching into the *cofradías* with General Lucas. Someone gives the Mam a pistol: I think it's Lucas. Another politico gives a two-hundred-dollar gold-fringed cape with a wad of money besides. So the Chiv has his walls covered with a whole lot of posters of people who cannot stand the sight of each other, all up there without distinction. The irony of the *aj'kun*'s life: he is the most hated but also the most protected.

One day, a City man who had taken his portrait blows it up into a poster: that also goes up on the wall and there is Chiviliu now, among all the presidential candidates with his own poster . . . bang in the middle of it. Of course, at some point, he is going to use one of the posters to wrap something in or he'll cut it up for the toilet: little by little the scene gets dilapidated and the posters disappear.

Pretty soon, tourists are showing up at his place. Especially, the hippies and neo-hippies. I guess I'm not crazy about this; I'm disgusted by the commercialization it is beginning to imply. I reckon I have to put up with some of it in order to get my points about cultural conservation across to someone who might be influential: after all, I have to work with what I've got! To give one example: a blonde girl comes in one day and gives the Chiv a bottle of beer and a note. The note says he has to pray to Yum Kax and Xipe . . . some strange mishmash she had concocted on precolumbian gods out of a Sylvanus Morley book.

And he is sitting there, going, 'Now, who the devil is this Yum Kax and who is this Xipe?' The *gringos* begin to feel that my presence is their passport to them coming here and 'being Indian.' I am totally unreceptive to that, as you know, but they come in droves. Chiviliu loves it: he thinks he's hit the big time. He tells them to bring so much incense and so much booze and so many candles, etc. and they do it: the cheques from home cover it.

One of the women finally asks him to do a *costumbre*

for her on some land she has bought on the other side of the Lake. He decides to go and to take me along as his guitarist. When we get to the Lake with all our paraphernalia, there is a strong wind. I tell him I'm not very happy about rowing across: in fact, I hardly know how to row. He says to get him six white candles and a bottle of mineral water. He pours the water on rocks at the Lake edge, puts up the candles and starts praying to San Lorenzo and all the Lake people, and to San Juan. In five minutes the wind stops. I'm told at the time that he's done it before; that he's famous as a wind-stopper.

We get into this godawful leaky little boat that would have drowned a cat. We do get across and we are bombed on some mescal I've brought with me. We start a fire and make a *costumbre* but we are so bombed, we don't know which way the water is. On the way back home, an opposite wind comes up and the Chiv starts praying again. He is leaning back in the canoe, paddling with one hand, holding a cigar with the other and we are speeding like a motorboat. The woman client meanwhile is going around in circles in her own canoe. Reaching shore, we hit mud, churn around in it and finally get out into it. Covered in mud up to our chins, we walk up to the first bar and get ourselves another couple of beers.

Back at his house, the place is crawling with hippies: Swedes, Norwegians, Danes, God knows, people with camera equipment, cables, lights, all milling around—and here *we* are, starving and bombed as skunks. We are supposed to have a rain *costumbre* that very afternoon; the band shows up and we straggle through what we can of the *costumbre*. I don't know how we got through that one alive!

Well, there is a girl—of Irish parentage I think. She's called Margarita here and she has a French friend who picks up the nickname of Ya Chumil, Ya Estrella that is: Star. We feel that Star is probably a lesbian. It's very complicated:

Margarita and Star are a couple—but Star has also taken a boyfriend. Margarita is furious and wants to get it on with me as revenge but I don't fancy her all that much. Star is very skinny. Margarita is immense: a local lad's wet dream.

So then Margarita suddenly starts finding the Chiv very marvelous and he is often to be found eating dinner over at her house. She is a slob and eats all the food, even her guest's; she has her man Lorenzo, who brings her food all the time but she eats it all. Margarita steals the Chiv away whenever she can. Pretty soon, he's catting around in my house whenever he gets loose and meeting the *gringas* who come over to my house and he's getting away with whatever he can. Star launches an affair with a rival *aj'kun*. It's getting pretty hot around my place.

Star and Margarita move across the Lake when their house is finished. Chiviliu doesn't really care for Lake crossings much and finds new girls at Margarita's old house. There is a Swedish photographer called Toby, a real killer, and a Ya Carib, a black girl, and a whole string of other ladies. Margarita doesn't like that one bit.

Meantime, Thorn—Mrs. Chiviliu—likes it even less. She starts sniffing the air and decides that she's going to fix their cookies. She starts doing negative witchcraft against the *gringas*. Margarita, for revenge, has started something with another man who doesn't mind making the trip across the Lake. Thorn tells this guy's wife and starts the ball rolling. Margarita goes nuts, loses her consensus, gets hepatitis and typhoid together and has to go into intensive care in the City for forty days in a row. She finally gives up her place and leaves the area altogether. Star nearly starves herself to death, anorexia perhaps. Right now she's in Colombia, I believe, and she still writes to Chiviliu. He brings me her letters to puzzle out.

All of this starts invading my life and interferes with my getting together with my wife-to-be. Also, I'm supposed to be thinking of my show at the *El Túnel* gallery in October 1977. I'm busy all over the place with this thing. One instance: Tuiz falls head over heels for Margarita but she prefers Chiviliu. Nevertheless, she manages to give Tuiz the clap. I cure Tuiz: he learns one lesson then goes on to some other nonsense. Finally, I start to feel responsible about these people and I want to get them out. I tell the Chiv I don't give a damn what he does about sex but these women are wrecking the *costumbre*. I tell the *gringas* too. They get upset, thinking I want to be the only *gringo* here and run the place. Well, as I say, they gradually flush themselves out.

The only one who keeps on coming to the Chiv is Lorenzo, an American guy, Jewish I believe. The Chiv rips off all his money. Lorenzo decides he wants to join the ceremonial life and wants to be an *escrivano*, a *cofradía* secretary. He doesn't know a word of Tzutujil; he doesn't even know Spanish; he doesn't even know where to sit on the bench. Finally, the *Cabecera* and his people clear him out. It takes the *Cabecera* in the end to clear someone right out of ceremonial life.

Sometime between Prechtel's arrival in Atitlán and August 15th, 1978, Felipe Tuiz will lend Prechtel a copy of a book entitled *Los Escándalos de Maximón* (Guatemala City, 1965) by the young French-American anthropologist E. Michael Mendelson, known as Miguel Sol to the Atitecos. This copy will be devoid of a cover. Later, Tuiz will give Prechtel a copy *with a cover*, this cover depicting the Mam mask stolen in 1950 and subsequently deposited by Tarn with a prominent European museum. Both copies will have been purloined from the Francisco Marroquín Linguistic Institute, Huehuetenango, during Tuiz's time there as a student. Tuiz will have been persuaded that the Huehue *gringos* were going to steal a wealth of Atiteco secrets contained in this book. Tuiz will not have found another copy anywhere (despite Tarn having seen at least a couple of copies in Atitlán during a brief visit in 1969).

Prechtel will wonder if the mask on the book's cover is, indeed, the stolen mask and will read the book to find out, claiming later to have formed a high opinion of the author's understanding of Atiteco religion. Prechtel will discuss fantasies of the mask's return with Tuiz while Tuiz is a member of the band.

Or, rather, it is the *head*, not the mask, which will be in question. Tarn will say, later, "But that book doesn't mention the head, only the mask." Prechtel will answer, "When that book was written, the author didn't really know the difference. When we Atitecos read 'mask,' we intuit 'head.' "

One day, Chiviliu will enter Prechtel's house and see a copy of the book, with cover. Now, he has been maintaining his spiritual contact with that head all his life, or so runs his claim. He has been prophesying that, since it had been stolen, the head would inevitably return. In fact, it would return before his death and be the token that he was now allowed to die. That event, to his way of thinking, would end the Chiviliu era. At that moment, it will have been held that the Mam, being crafty, had saved his own head and had kept it safely beyond Chokox Aq'oum, the Medecine Mushroom place, in the other world. There will be no idea as yet that anyone outside Atitlán will have had anything to do with saving the head or the mask.

Prechtel will include himself into Chiviliu's fantasies and will want that mask back faster than he would otherwise have done.

Enter Diego Sisay, a *pasado principal* and *tijonel* of *cofradía* Santiago, who will have befriended Prechtel while the latter repainted the Santiago *santos* during the summer of 1977. His nickname is "Eyes." Eyes darts about like a mosquito, full of plots and plans—his dazzling, piercing but amicable gaze on his interlocutor all the time as he explains his anxious strategies. Eyes suffers from constant gastric pains. Prechtel will have advised him to stop drinking. But how can a great upholder of *costumbre* like a *pasado principal* ever stop drinking? Eyes, who had broken a rib years before when, as Third Santa Cruz, he had helped to lift up or bring down the Mam from its trellis, will now break a few ribs after a binge and come to Prechtel for medical help.

During a curing session at Prechtel's house, Chiviliu will happen to walk in to talk about the return of the head—something he is now dreaming and talking about every day of the week. Eyes will get very excited and say, "I have the men, you get the head!" Right there, they will determine on secrecy above all and do a *costumbre* for the return. Eyes will start using Chiviliu as his diviner and *aj'kun* and they will all dream together virtually every night.

The first letter to Europe will have been dated September 3rd, 1978. We estimate that first mention of the mask between the conspirators may be dated *circa* August 15th, 1978.

At a Sunday meeting of the *Cabecera* and his *principales*, dated sometime between *Fiesta* San Nicolás (3/9/78) and October of the same year, Chiviliu will ask for *cofradía* San Juan and, perhaps as a means of demonstrating that he is not the over-aged and useless codger some take him for at this time, he will have blabbed about the availability of the head. The *principales* will not have wanted to give San Juan to Chiviliu—because of his age; because of his having had it before; because his death in mid-year would be very bad luck indeed; because rumors still persist about the Root-of-Food having been lost during his tenure.

Prechtel and Chiviliu will be fearing the man who is the favorite candidate for *Alcalde* San Juan: he is up to no good; he could sell the Martín Bundle; all hell could break loose. Prechtel will volunteer his house as a possible location for the *cofradía* and, on this basis, Chiviliu volunteers that, if he is successful, he will ask for Prechtel as *juez*.

At this meeting in 1978, or shortly afterwards, the *principales* will ask Prechtel if he knows anything about the head. Prechtel will say that he has seen the mask on the cover of a book. "Ah, yes! Miguel Sol, we remember him from way back!" some of the elders will say. And this is where it will start, right there and then, with certain elders rubbing their hands together and thinking that they will be the ones to get back the head—and, above all, to keep it forever out of the hands of the *Catequistas* and their supporters.

Note that this will be a very bad time for the *cofradías*. Quarrels are rife. Recruitment is a major problem. Prechtel will not want to say anything more at this meeting because he can see that these *principales* are split right down the middle, not just about the head but about everything in the religious organization of Atitlán.

Now here is another splendid character! Agustín Petzey Tiney (Makuxtin) is the archetypal *nouveau-riche*, fat, vulgar not to say crass, with a tendency to speak too fast and bubble as he does so. He is up one day, down the next, always plotting, always putting his foot in his mouth, always unreliable. Heaven knows how, he will now be *Alcalde*-Elect Santa Cruz (1978–79) and will still be allied at this time with pro-*Catequista* elements, though the *Catequistas* are to turn on him later.

A Damian family, with *cofradía* Rosario behind them two years running (1976–78), will be furious with Makuxtin because they want Santa Cruz. Many will think that Santa Cruz should be going to Estevan Pakay, but he will actually obtain Santiago for 1979–80. It will be hard to trust his ally, Nicolás Pedro, *Alcalde*-Elect San Antonio (1978–79), in that he had signed the original anti-Mam papers in the days of the thefts. Juan García, *Alcalde*-Elect Santiago (1978–79), will also be a Makuxtin hater, but he is aligned with Juan Sisay. Juan Sosof, a previous *Alcalde* Santa Cruz (1977–78), a neighbor of Prechtel's, is going to be troublesome in that his wife and Prechtel's wife will have been having shouting matches in recent weeks over some domestic issue. The sacristans, powerful people as *escrivanos* in the *cofradías*, will be split down the middle.

On the positive side, Diego Chayal, *Alcalde*-Elect Animas (1978–79), will accept the job again in 1979–80 specifically to aid the mask's return; his neighbor, Nicolás Ajuchan, will do the same for San Gregorio—although he'll worm out of signing the letter to Europe on the grounds that "he had watched with the *Catequistas* in times gone by." *Cofradía* San Felipe's José Yel will be in the same position. *Cofradías* Animas, Gregorio and Felipe will be among those run by committees of *pasados principales* on an emergency basis, so that the system as a whole should not collapse.

The *Cabecera* at this time (1978), José Xikay Iboy (Maxikay), will be a problem because of his unpopularity. He will be wanting to put *cofradía* Santa Cruz into Diego Rianda's house in 1979–80 when this Rianda will have had Animas only very shortly before (1977–78) and "you do not give a man two *cofradías* so close together, virtually in a row." At this point, Maxikay will have just made a land deal with this Diego Rianda, as it happens, and Rianda will have told him that he can have the land cheap if he, Rianda, gets Santa Cruz. Rianda will have wanted Santa Cruz, figuring that the head might just return a little late, during his stewardship. Maxikay will also be wanting to stay in power for the same reason: it would make him very famous and perhaps rich as well. Rianda would be taking some of his own crowd with him to become *cofrades* Santa Cruz.

From the tensions at that meeting, a virtual standstill will arise in the councils with only two or three people attending them for about six months running. A very bad business indeed. The councils will not really start operating again until Cristóbal Esquina Yataz, *Cabecera* 1979, comes into office. His arrival will be awkward and puzzling. Maxikay will be wanting to stay on for a second year. There will be terrible in-fighting between the Makuxtin faction and the Santiago/San Antonio faction (Estevan Pakay/ Nicolás Pedro).

There will also be trouble with the *mayori* who will be having their terminal squabbles at the municipality: it is during this time that certain Indian officials complain of being treated as second-class citizens and are voided by the *ladino* Town Mayor as worse than useless. *Cabecera* Esquina Yataz will find that he has already woven his headcloth of office—having accepted because there was no one else to do so and the office simply could not be allowed to lapse—and then it will seem as if he has not been named. Somehow the normal transfer-of-power ceremony will be bungled. Only four out of some sixty *cofrades* will turn up, plus the drummer and Prechtel as flutist. Prechtel will be asked to hold the staff of *Alcalde* Concepción as a stand-in!

On the next day, January 2nd, 1979, no one will show up to pick up the new *Cabecera* at his house. On the 3rd, Esquina Yataz will come to the church with all his men, complaining that no one had come to fetch him as they should have done. The party will go to fetch the *Caja Real*, the "Royal Coffer" containing the Atitlán titles, at Maxikay's house; he will be out and the keys will be virtually thrown at the new men by his people. The *Caja* will be taken to church, registered, and business will open as usual.

On January 6th, Día de los Reyes, Prechtel will learn from Chiviliu that the *Niños*, the Babes, have to be taken around the town and that there are no *alguaciles* to do so. Nor are there any drums: the old ones were somehow taken home by the last officials. Prechtel will rush to the City, buy two drums and add two of his own. He will pay four friends to go around representing the districts of the village, the *cantónes*, to help the four men who would be carrying the Babes. These should by rights be *alcaldes* but the *alcaldes* will happen to be out to lunch. In any event, *something* will be done and it will please Chiviliu and *Alcalde* Santiago as well as leading to the young *gringo*'s nomination as *Primer Mayor*. For him, there will be discomfort in knowing that it is his pocket which is holding up the *costumbre*. On the other hand, he will have proved to the old *principales* that "things do not have to die unless you really want them to."

·   ·   ·

After the return of the Maximón mask—the full account is in the next chapter—Chiviliu's life will appear to prepare itself for, and dissolve into, legend. Much of the time, he will be living in another world, full of mood swings, visions, battles with demons visible to him alone, and prophecies. Many people will start neglecting him. Despite disrespectful behavior towards him at times by *cofrades* who should have known better, Chiviliu will obviously find it hard to let go. There will be a sense that his mind is wandering: often he will be unable to remember the names of those he is doing *costumbre* for, even those close and dear to him. He will often repeat himself over and over and have to be told to conclude. He will sometimes give peremptory orders to inferiors when it is clearly no longer his turn to do so.

At the time when the mask has been asked for, he will have been hearing noises. "Ah! You hear that!" "What?" "*Primer Mayor* Prechtel and Chiviliu are going to jail for witchcraft. Watch out tomorrow morning at 6:00 a.m. You hear what the radio said about Chiviliu going to jail!" Prechtel will describe Chiviliu as suffering from terrible hallucinations and paranoid fits regarding accusations levelled at him in his younger days. Some people will have taken this seriously, because there are no outward signs of derangement. Dogs, the radio, telegraph poles, clouds: everything will seem to have been talking to him or at him.

After the mask's return, Chiviliu will be reported as having gone crazy for touching the mask and sleeping with his wife. He will climb the church bell tower and, one time, will nearly jump off. One day in Holy Week, he will say that the Sun was having dinner in the tower, had seen him walking about below and had called out to him to come and join him for a meal.

Despite Thorn's care of him, little will prevent him from sallying forth on the prowl from time to time. He will arrive at Prechtel's house, look in at the window silently, sometimes pulling strange faces and going away again, or staying, perhaps, if invited in. Tarn will also have been having such visitations. Chiviliu will no longer be calling him Tarn but Aplas (Francisco) or Francisco Sojuel.

In late August 1979, on such a visit to Prechtel, he'll declare:

An old enemy of mine in a witchcraft war—he's dead now—has left a lot of little fish in my feet. Sometimes they rise at night into my testicles and bother me a lot.

Sometimes they come out; I can catch them and throw them back into the Lake. Witch snakes and worms sometimes come out of my sides.

Sometimes I have scissors or tweezers and such things inside my legs, or arms, or armpits. They come and go. And then, there's this blackened skin on my legs—the doctors say it's an old man's disease, something to do with the blood. When I get up in the morning, the bed follows me up and my head starts whirling around. But I cannot be bothered to get up slowly like they say I should.

I've just done two groups of five-part *costumbres* yesterday: a woman from Momostenango and a couple from Zacapa.

This will seem a somewhat excessive claim. *Alcalde* San Juan will say that he has not seen Chiviliu since June . . . It may be that he is limiting himself to the church and Santa Cruz. He will have been seen doing a *costumbre* round on August 27th: clearly, he will still be active in some form. Prechtel will have diagnosed psoriasis and hoped to get him to a hospital in the City. He will refuse to go. Prechtel will have fed him on stress vitamins as often as possible. People will try to keep him off liquor which makes him crazy.

On this occasion, he will also declare that the Mam has instructed him to have a party at his house in order to make the place *alegre*, crowded and joyous, as it used to be. We'll agree to hold one for him two Sundays on and will indeed take many cases of beer up there, Prechtel's band and other festive things.

It will be impossible to say goodbye to him properly.

In April 1980, a letter to Tarn from Prechtel, soon to go into hiding because of the terror unleashed on Indian communities such as Atitlán, will announce the maestro's passing:

The last time I had talked to C was around the Fifth Friday

of Holy Week when he came to my studio on the edge of the water here. I heard his voice and, looking down the very steep and rocky cliff to the water's edge, I saw a very well dressed old man indeed. I went inside, washed paint off my hands and went out to help him up the difficult incline. Where he'd just been blinking like a white-haired badger on his hind legs: no C. So, perplexed, and looking for the old buzzard and not finding him, I went back in to continue painting. Five minutes later, I heard a weird growling, hooting and moaning outside my door; I came out and C jumped me, cackling at the top of his lungs, 'Where is it that you are alive, ha? Now I've done it to you!' So I invited the old witch into the house and we talked as usual.

When I asked him how Thorn was, he blew up into a great head of steam about her infidelity and how he'd just come back from the municipality where he'd gone to cut her out of his will. He had been sleeping alone for months by his own choice due to his guilt feeling—probably a reference to his second wife whom he had left with many children on her hands. Thorn found all of this very unfair and blamed C's enemies to whose curses he was now supposed to be succumbing on reaching his mythical 98th year. In any event, he was now claiming to be alone and to having his food cooked by a daughter: all pure invention. He told me to take care, bring him some remedies and went off. I didn't know I'd never see him again.

During Holy Week, there were all sorts of photographers in town—all of them miserable as usual. I took a liking to one called Mirella Ricciardi . . . At one point, after beers, she told me she had not yet found the one real heavy face she was looking for. I was drunk and parentally offended, thinking that it might be true that all the strong faces I was seeing were mythical; and not really obvious as such to an outsider. Anyway, I blundered with her over to C's house, to show her at least one 'strong' face, forgetting what knowledge of things here is necessary for one to understand that word 'strong.' C. was crumpled up in bed, wiped out by alcohol.

Last week, he had wanted me to go with him on a seven-part *costumbre* for a San Pedro Sacatepéquez group. He wanted me to help since he was without his wife and it would be strenuous. I was in the City and he went alone and pulled it off. In *cofradía* Rosario, he announced that he would depart within the week and wept a full hour in front of the altar, describing his life and asking for pardon.

On April 20th, he called his sons together and explained what he wanted done. At one point in the night, he went outside and started dancing alone. The next day, he stayed in bed, passing out more instructions. At 8:30 in the evening, a light, sprinkling rain started up. At 9:00 on April 21st he died in his sleep without suffering.

It wasn't until the following morning that I heard about it and my family and I went up there. C was lying in a huge coffin filled with new pipes, bowls, tobacco, enough ceremonial scarves to fill ten *cofradías* etc. etc. etc. and his head wrapped in a new ceremonial *suut*. Gifts of candles filled a huge basket. All of his children, especially his adopted kids, the numberless children he had raised—were all there weeping with the rest of us: the grandchildren must have numbered fifty and three of those already had children that were old enough to weep. The whole *cofradía* came with bell and all. Juan Sisay was there but no one paid him much attention: I think there must have been close to three hundred people in there, if not more.

The *Catequistas* got to the wake before the *Cabecera* and the *cofrades* and filled the place with their moans and groans. These Bible-droning deformed roots of suicide had even brought their super tin portable organ and its *costumbre*-hating operator. On my way up, I ran into a dozen of C's old *aj'kuna* and *cofradía* buddies who seemed reticent about all this noise: they wanted to mourn by drinking and weeping in the old manner. I pulled them in and we all wept and howled and got drunk. The *Cabecera* had been called by a senior son, Makox, and, to the *Catequistas*' dismay, the party proceeded pretty traditionally with a blend of every kind of beauty that C had loved: the *Cabecera* was not going to let any minor church regulation interfere with a four-star funeral for one who had done so much service.

This is how it was given out then, his record: twice *Cabecera*; five times *Alcalde*: Santiago; Juan; Rosario; Concepción, with one repeated; twelve times *Telinel*; once *Juez* and First, Second, Third, Fourth, Fifth, Sixth; and twenty-six times *alguacil*. So the whole thing was what C would have wanted: a huge, drunken crowd from every religion, with girls and men, *Catequistas* and *cofrades*, Hallelujahs and bums, ex-wives, children and grandchildren and great-grandchildren, all singing, howling and screaming, and rain, and violins, and funky latin.

There was not one *ladino* present or who came to visit. They had their own old man to bury: Don Lalo de León. C had told us many times that, when he died, there would be a *ladino* to go with him. Just as he had told us that, on his dying, a light rain would start up and kick off the rainy season.

The next morning the sky was clear and mass was said by the perplexed new Indian priest. After this, at 2:00 p.m., the sky clouded. After the tomb (also called *tuj*) had been closed with lime and mortar, a great rain started and since then it has rained every day.

Felipe Tuiz, of course, was one of the young pall-bearers and I bet C was heavy. I remember carrying him up rock paths when he was too drunk to walk in the intended direction.

After the tomb had been closed, one of the *ladino* pant-wearing *Catequistas* broke into his drunken exposition of what this burial was all about: absolutely no one except the other *Catequistas* listened to him. The rest of the crowd had 'buried Chiviliu' in a large tomb at the front of the cemetery and there was nothing more to say than what C had already said. The *cofrades* were invited back to the house; some went, others didn't. I and the *Cabecera*, José Sikay, went home and got popped: he wants me to help him and, in half an hour, I learned more about *aj'kun* work than I had the whole year.

One of the instructions given by our master at his deathbed was that I was to inherit all his divining tools and his saints and that I would take over his people from Sacatepéquez, Sumpango and all the others. I told the family that I was greatly honored—but I thought it best to let things simmer for a while for fear of what other relatives might suspect or of people changing their minds. All I need is to hear that I am making money out of C's death! But I was very touched—as well as realizing that this was C's way of making sure I'd pay for the *suerte* he has given me. Eventually, these objects did stay with the family.

C remembered you as 'Plas, Aplas (Francisco) Sojuel and had your picture over his altar. All the people at the wake kept waiting for you and Janet to walk in: at one point I was wishing like hell that you would. There was a certain amount of excruciating pain I didn't know where to put.

It was a great grief—and also a great relief since his life had already become a legend. Nobody would ever see the C they wanted or the C they feared: it was a different person that needed you instead of helping or hurting. His name was synonymous with getting away unscathed and having a good time while being within the boundary of blessedness. C is gone and he is no longer there for us to lean on what he knows that could defend our love for this culture. Now they have put the power into my hands to defend C's way of curing—unique and untraditional in that it is based only on the way of Food, of *Way ya'*, Our Sustenance. He had no appreciable knowledge of the "roads" of *ch'ojrik*.

He was not an *aj'kun de mesa*. His curing was by stressing the power of positive Beings rather than fighting evil, bribing it and killing the enemy. He always saw himself as more Catholic than the other *aj'kuna*. He was criticized by many because *aj'kuna* are supposed to have to serve both sides, the good and the bad—but one reason he may have stressed the good was that a persecution of *aj'kuna* under Ubico had prompted the profession to solidify the perception of *aj'kun* and *aj'itz* as two different roles where, traditionally, the two were always potentially played by a single individual. His doctrine was always that people from outside should be befriended by Atitecos. Then the outsiders would remember Atitecos on the outside and Atitecos could benefit. It was a very adaptive view and he always preached it in the *cofradías*.

His radio broke again, the one you gave him, and he wanted you to fix it. Asshole Chiv!

Love—Pretz.

An era had ended.

FOURTEEN

The Mask's Return
to Atitlán

In the Spring of 1978, Tarn pays a brief visit to Atitlán after working in Belize and Chiapas. Prechtel, about whom he has heard a
great deal—all tending to make him wonder whether the young
man is not an anthropologist in disguise—is out of town. Tarn
leaves him a message, inviting him to correspond if he wishes
and he also acquires a record made by a local musical group which
appears to be led by Prechtel.

Tarn discusses the mask with a colleague of a friend of his: the
colleague is working in Guatemala City. The friend, "Henry," is
a professor emeritus of the museum where the mask was deposited in the early 1950s. Perhaps, Tarn suggests, this colleague could
talk to Henry about the mask's return when he next visits Europe.
Is Tarn's idea of getting the mask returned to Atitlán after some
thirty years at all feasible? Back in New Hope, Pennsylvania, his
residence at the time, Tarn writes to Henry and his colleague on
May 10th, 1978, proposing the mask's return.

After the meeting of Chiviliu and Diego Sisay ("Eyes") at
Prechtel's house, some time around the end of August 1978,
Prechtel will compose the initial draft of a letter, later described
by him as "much too funky to send." He will ask a young doctor
at the village hospital to help him compose another on behalf of
the *principales*. They will type it one midnight in September. This
in all likelihood will be Document No.1 2405175, Registro
No.418507, quinquenio de 1978–1982:

Santiago Atitlán, September 3rd, 1978
Museum Director, Europe.

Esteemed Director Sir,

The undersigned wish to approach you initially with respect in order to salute you most sincerely.

We name ourselves heralds of our village, which we represent and lead, in order to explain to you the purpose of our communication. To speak historically, some twenty five years ago or so, a number of us were witnesses when a number of people, without any permission whatsoever, took away from here the principal relic—an intrinsic part of our holy image—which has been kept here from of old and which, among the spiritual values of our village, clearly an indigenous one, is still alive at the highest level of universal religious concepts.

The relic to which we refer is the head of an image which is known as Maximón by the vulgar but which we refer to as the *RILAJ MAM*, or the Venerable Grandfather, and which consists of a mask made of erythrina wood (*TZ'AJTEL or Palo de Pito*) classified scientifically as Erythrina Corallodendron. Originally, it was made moreover of a mass which resembled the head, which was given form with various lengths of cloth of different qualities and textures.

At this time, the aforesaid part of the image in its present form is considered to be a copy and this has remained the attitude of the village towards it, out of respect for the importance of the tradition and culture which our ancestors wished to transmit and communicate through the image.

We know that, on recuperation of the relic, a constitutive part of the image, this powerful spirit living latently in this culture—a culture which still vibrates and does not wish to see its values disappear into the eternity of time—will be born again.

We are informed that the aforesaid image is now in the museum of which you are so worthily in charge and this is the reason why we unite before you and, using this most viable of approaches to you, pray you hereby with all the enthusiasm of our souls to return to us the image.

We form the religious order which guides and represents our village, with the following titles:

a. *Cabecera*; b. First *Fiscal*; c. Second *Fiscal*; d. First *Sacristán*; e. Second *Sacristán*; f. General Council of *Principales*, present and past, consisting more or less of some five hundred members.

By means of what has now been said, we beg of your kindness that the aforementioned relic be given back to us and we are ready with all good will to give you back an exact copy—since, for us, as we have shown, value lies only in the original.

We remain, therefore, awaiting your answer, thanking you in advance for the kind attention you will be able to give us, with our most sincere and warm regards:

Cabecera: Sicay Yol
Principal Pasado: Diego Sisay Ajtujal (60)
    Salvador Quiju Tzina
    José Mendoza Quivak (50)
    Nic.Chiviliu Tacaxoy (93)
    Nic.Zapalu Sosof (55)
    Juan Acabul Ramírez (62)
    José Cua Pospoy (62)
    Manuel Queju (49)
    Pascual Damian Ixbalan (52)
    Nic.Ajuchan Tzina (63)

[*José Cua's is the only signature. He is listed as* Principal *not* P.Pasado. *All others are thumbprints. One age is not given. Sicay Yol is Maxicay.*]

Enter a group of three friends, of a liberal persuasion, devoted to various forms of public service and prominent in the Capital.

We shall call them the Brotherhood of Three. The second friend in age, "David," is mentioned to Tarn by a leading American conservationist in San Francisco, sometime in 1978, as a person interested in the subject of environmentally adequate technology in Guatemala. He is said to have attended a number of international conferences. The Brotherhood works from an office in Guatemala City and has projects in various parts of the country, including Santiago Atitlán.

The oldest friend, "Vicente," is more of a lawyer than anything else; the second, "David," is a doctor; the third, "Joaquín," is an amateur Orientalist as well as a doctor. One of the most remarkable sights in Atitlán during 1979 will be Joaquín's acupuncture demonstrations to the courteously friendly *principales*, often using Tarn as guinea pig. Both Joaquín and David will also be active at the village hospital, though not in any official capacity.

The day after the letter is prepared, a colleague of the Brotherhood will come to see Prechtel and will just happen to say that David is on his way to Europe. Prechtel, suddenly faced with this opportunity, will charge out of the house to collect signatures for the document addressed to the Museum Director and will then give it to this colleague so that he might get it to David. The *Cabecera* for 1978, Maxikay, here Sikay Yol but in other documents Sikay Ivoy, is the first to be asked for a signature: he will never be asked again because of his unpopularity, especially with the new *Cabecera* Cristóbal Esquina Yataz. Prechtel will be informed, however, that David has already left for Europe.

Soon after, Prechtel tries to get a letter to David. The latter will visit Prechtel and tell him he's already been to Europe and come back. He will be going again, however, the following week. The letter will have been in Guatemala City by now. Prechtel will have to tell David to collect it and will have to explain to him what it is all about. David will offer to talk to the people at the museum. There is some confusion as to which museum: several prominent names are bandied about. Prechtel will entreat David to just give the Europeans his letter and leave it at that.

David will go to Europe and stay there awhile. Finally, a note will arrive from Vicente stating that the mask is indeed in Europe but that the people in charge are going to have to have a meeting to determine its fate. The *principales* are duly informed. Eyes will come to Prechtel's house everyday for news. Maxikay and other *principales* will put on their ceremonial coats and come flying through the streets each time they hear a drumroll on Prechtel's radio. Latin American radio frequently indulges in drum rolls.

Shortly afterwards, Vicente will summon Prechtel to his office in the City and tell him that he is off to Europe in the next week. He will require another letter. Prechtel will do the same thing all over again, in shorter form but with the same signatures. On Vicente's return, Prechtel will understand him to claim that the Museum Director will have said yes, but the Government of that European country no—or vice versa. The elders will be informed. Chiviliu will refuse to believe the report and whip up another storm of *costumbre*. For several weeks, there will be silence. We are probably at the end of October or in November.

In a letter of October 5th, 1978 to Henry, Tarn refers to great changes on the lake and intimates that, to his surprise, the Tzutujil seem to see nothing but good coming from such changes. The existence of a young "counter-culture" person is reported. He has an Indian wife, speaks the language fluently, is the probable author of an LP record of local music and *Regidor* in the local municipal hierarchy—the latter a piece of misinformation given Tarn by a *ladina* acquaintance. The young man is said to be unpopular among certain Guatemalan Army elements for encouraging "localism." However, Tarn hopes that this presence will be a helpful one when he returns to Atitlán in 1979. This young man, of course, is Prechtel.

The query about the mask is then put again to Henry: the mask was originally stolen and could only be rescued on condi-

tion it was not then given back to Atitecos. There is still unpleas-
antness in the village around the subject of the mask and news of
such has even reached New Hope, Pennsylvania, via tourists and
their guides! It is said that the Europeans stole the mask. Often
Juan Sisay is named as the culprit. What would Henry think,
seriously, of giving back the mask? Wouldn't European science
derive a greater profit from such an action than by letting the
mask gather dust in a museum's stacks? Were there not prece-
dents, especially in the U.S., for such returns? One might envisage
a small ceremony, with the local colleague and Tarn and perhaps
an Embassy member, explaining to *cofradía* Santa Cruz, in returning the object, the museum's desire that all this bad blood should
be laid to rest. With a few other considerations, Tarn ends his
letter by announcing a possible visit from New Hope to Europe
around December 14th.

A young museum research worker—here called "Marie"—
describing herself as having worked for many years with Henry,
writes to Tarn at New Hope on November 11th, 1978. She
informs him that the Museum Director is not opposed to the
mask's return. It would facilitate matters considerably, however,
if the original deposit would turn out to have been made as a loan
rather than as a gift. Perhaps Tarn would be able to produce an
official letter about that. Henry writes the next day to the same
effect. On December 5th, Tarn writes both the Director and Marie
that he believes a loan had always been intended, since there had
always been a hope of giving back the mask someday to the
Atitecos. Tarn mentions to the Director the possibility that a visit
to his museum on a date unknown by a highly regarded local
painter, Juan Sisay, might have helped to originate the rumors
Tarn has heard about the mask from Atitlán.

On December 18th, 1978, Tarn will visit the museum after
learning that the Director wishes to lunch with him alone and
ask him some pertinent questions. It is made clear from the start
that a good deal of intra-mural and extra-mural academic intrigue

surrounds the relatively small matter of the mask's return but this is part of European history and should not—perhaps unfortunately since it includes a lot of entertaining gossip—be discussed here. Some will have held, for instance, that there was no need for the affair to have gone to a High Professorial Assembly, headed by a man whose estranged wife had been a friend of Tarn's briefly in 1953. (The Professorial Assembly had agreed at first, then demurred.) The whole matter could have been handled *intra muros* without difficulty.

In any event, the point will be to prove that the mask had never actually entered the State collections as a gift: for, if that were to have been the case, it could never come out again. To this end, the mask's file will have been dug out. Tarn's letter from the Legation in Guatemala of April 14, 1953, will be examined, discussed and eventually shown to have been queried from the start by museum officials as to whether a gift or loan was intended. The letter "D" in an unknown museum worker's hand prefixing the object's number—signifying *deposit*—will have been found in the file. Later, the same hand will have crossed out the D. In all probability, the passage of a great many years will have convinced some curator that the object was to be permanently housed at the museum.

The Director's object at this luncheon will be to have a paper signed stating that, in the absence of proven documentation converting this loan into a gift, the object was to revert to loan status. Various people, including Tarn, will, more or less willingly, sign the paper and it will be Tarn's impression that the paper will allow the question to be solved *intra muros* without any further external interference. The Director will assert that the object is of interest to him mainly because of its association with Nativism and Nativist Cults, a subject he had studied on another continent, and this topic will come up in another form during the lunch. As for the Director's personal interest in returning the mask, it will later be asserted by various sources that a large international agency interested in returning cultural property to Native peoples might be the source of the Director's generous leanings.

Now, something of a *coup de théâtre* will occur, revealing what might be other reasons for secrecy. On the occasion of this visit, Marie will have puzzled Tarn by such remarks as: "The Tzutujil want to give back copies of the mask in exchange for this original." Tarn, unaware of Prechtel's actions in Atitlán (Prechtel will never have taken up Tarn's offer of correspondence), will wonder how on earth she could know something like that! Suddenly, however, it will transpire that a document had arrived from Santiago Atitlán at roughly the same time as Tarn's original request, perhaps a little before, couched on legal paper in the most respectful terms by a number of leading villagers, including one Nicolás Chiviliu, said to be aged 93 years. It will seem to Tarn that the whole matter bears the imprint of the young "counter-culture" figure he had missed meeting in 1978.

At this point, the Director will reveal that the document has been brought by a young Guatemalan, whose family name will immediately remind Tarn of the young adequate technology person, David, mentioned to him in San Francisco much earlier in the year. David will have surprised Marie by speaking her language well and it will be surmised that, while sympathetic to Native causes, he belongs to the higher strata of Guatemala City's bourgeoisie.

David will have come in very modestly, keeping a low profile, begging that everything be kept as quiet as possible and that nothing ever approaching an exchange at inter-governmental level be considered. If it were to come to that, David will have declared, he would prefer no return to happen at all. For a moment, it will have been feared that the Director's approach to the High Professorial Assembly might have made such secrecy impracticable. As of now, however, Marie, for reasons of her own not unconnected to international politics, will have taken a liking to David and will have kept his initiative from Tarn until this moment because of certain promises she had made to this young Guatemalan doctor.

At the lunch, it will turn out that the Nativist Cults issue will have been brought up by David and that the Director will have gathered from him, understanding him correctly or not, that the mask was in fact an effigy of the Nativist prophet Francisco Sojuel.

After the lunch, it will seem impossible to Tarn to avoid some discussion regarding what is then known about the young American counter-culture person in Santiago. While concluding that there certainly does not seem to be anything unhealthy about his presence, "scientific caution" will suggest that care should be taken not to return the mask without knowing who is going to benefit from it: for it will be very clear that the *principales* will not have prepared this document by themselves without some sort of help. Marie will propose to contact the author of a politically radical book on Guatemala in search of further information.

At first, Marie will seem to favor February—her date of arrival on a research trip to Guatemala—since, first, the *principales*, according to David, are in favor of a reception *fiesta*; and, second, there is urgency, possibly on account of Chiviliu's age; and, third, no risk should be run by the object in transit between the museum and its destination. Tarn, at first, will have desired some role in the matter, and perhaps some credit on behalf of his projected research.

At this time, since the Director wants a museum staff person to perform the deed—very specifically Marie—and since there is so much uncertainty over the matter, Tarn will propose one) that the ceremony await his arrival in Atitlán so that he might do his part in checking out the situation; and two) that the museum party give Tarn some credit for his own initiatives; but that three) the return should be credited to the *principales* or whoever was helping them in the matter. Dates would be set up as efficiently as possible so that arrivals in Atitlán would take place concurrently.

On the next morning, weather will confuse all departures from the Continent and Tarn will miss a flight. Seizing the opportunity of calling Marie again and discussing the wisdom of all arriving together in Atitlán, Tarn will ask Marie on the phone whether she has taken into consideration the following facts: one) that the young American seems to be a shaman as well as an official in the *cofradía* system; and two) that the Catholic presence is now very strong in the village under the auspices of the Oklahoma Mission so that church and township officials might be present at any *cofradía* reception, thus rendering secrecy highly problematic. Marie will reveal that the Santiago people are planning not just a reunion of Atiteco *cofrades* but of *cofrades* and officials from the *whole Lake region*—a plan that will completely puzzle Tarn and further cause him to wonder what on earth David and his people are doing in all of this.

It will have been established on the day of the luncheon that Henry had, at one time, taken pity on the painter Juan Sisay, visiting his city on a date unrecorded, and shown him the mask. Pity, because his own people, including Nobel Prize Winner Miguel Angel Asturias, then ambassador, had treated him shabbily, put him up in a wretched hotel, failed to entertain him, and so forth. All present will agree that it is probably Juan Sisay who will have started rumors about the mask in Atitlán on his return from this trip.

An account of all this given by Juan Sisay to an art dealer in Antigua, Guatemala around this time and passed on to Tarn is witness to our painter's ingenuity. According to this, Juan had been Sacristan at the time of the Scandals and the Mam was kept in the church. Some Europeans posing as priests had asked to see the Mam. When they left, it was found that the original mask was missing. Juan had been nearly lynched by the village. On a visit to Europe, he had met Henry. He was told that the museum had a mask and he asked to see it. As a modest Indian, he had not asked for the mask back [!] but he did request a photo which he brought back and used for his painting. Some *Catequistas*, at the time of the return, said that Juan had been claiming that he had brought the mask back—but they did not believe him because of his actions at the time of the theft. Juan's popularity with the *Catequistas* at this time no longer stood very high.

■ ■ ■

Back in Atitlán, Prechtel, left without news, will have told the elders that the mask would not return and nothing new will have been heard for some weeks. Suddenly, however, Prechtel will receive a note that he is urgently needed at the Brotherhood office in the City. The date will correspond to that of San Gaspar, Dia de los Reyes, January 6th, 1979, and Prechtel, needed in the village, will not go. In the midst of the procession carrying the Christ Babes around, he will get a "strange feeling" and take his party into the tourist bar near the landing to chat up the tourists for a contribution. At the same time, they'll get some coins out of the owners who are resented because, "they make money by dressing up as Indians but never give the Indians anything." And there will be Vicente, sitting right up in front and looking very put out. A conversation between Tarn and Prechtel after the former had arrived in Atitlán reveals the rest:

> *Prechtel*: Then Vicente takes me out and says, 'What do you know about this guy called Tarn?' 'Don't lie to me!' he says when I say 'nothing'. . . looking very truculent, you know, like he was some Intelligence officer. 'Have you had any contacts with him?' he asks. 'I know you guys are working together!' I say, 'No . . . What's going on?' He says, 'Well, it turns out the mask belongs to him.' 'O.K.,' I say, 'what's wrong with that? We'll send him a letter too . . .'
> *Tarn*: Did you remember that I had left you a note in the summer of 1978?
> *Prechtel*: Sure—but was I going to tell him? So Vicente says to me, 'Well, we have reason to suspect that you guys have a plan.' I say, 'Well, yes, we do have a plan and the idea is to bring back the mask and that's all, but—as for Tarn, I don't know him from a hole in the wall.' And I

add, 'The only thing I know is that he left me a note last June and said that if I wanted to write or anything I could sure get in touch . . . oh, and that he was a friend of Chiviliu's . . .' 'Ha!' he says 'have you been fighting with Chiviliu lately?' 'No,' I say. 'Hmmmm. People say that you two have been fighting . . .' So there he is interrogating me in the street and by the time I get to *cofradía* Santiago my people have already left for *cofradía* Concepción . . .

The following week, Prechtel will go into the City and will visit the Brotherhood office where he will ask again what is going on. Vicente will pull out some kind of document, evidently written by Marie, asking what this *gringo* Prechtel is doing in the village. Vicente will claim that the Brotherhood wants to pull out of this whole business and that if Prechtel and the *principales* want the mask back they will have to work for themselves. Prechtel will understand that the Europeans are concerned that he has unclear and undefined motives.

On January 17th, 1979, Prechtel will address a letter to Marie, handwritten and in Spanish:

Santiago Atitlán, Cantón Panaj, Sololá, Guatemala, C.A.

Dear Madam,

The reason for my letter is simply to clarify my position in the village of Santiago Atitlán and my identity in this over-all matter. According to Messrs Vicente and David, who have been kind enough to transmit our petition to you, there are doubts concerning that identity.

My name is Martín Prechtel. I was born in the United States in 1951. I grew up in a Native American village of New Mexico until the age of 16, spoke only Keresan, the dialect of the pueblo of Santo Domingo. I am a painter. I came to Atitlán three years ago but have lived in Guatemala more than six years.

In this village of Atitlán, one meets with a very ancient culture, basically precolumbian albeit disguised with elements of 15th century Spanish Catholicism. Now, for very strange, or more precisely, esoteric reasons, I have been named and integrated into the traditional religious system that we call *'cofradía'* or, in Tzutujil, *r'be r'qan saq, r'be r'qan q'ij*, the Path of the Foot of Whiteness (Moon), the path of the Foot of Sun (major deity).

My position in the *cofradía* is that of he who plays the flute, *ajxul*. This implies that I have to be present at every rite and every procession and all changes of officials such as *Cabecera, Fiscales* and *cofrades* especially.

I have now worked here for two years and know the difficulties suffered by the village, its bitternesses and its secrets. My wife is a native of Santiago. I live completely tied to a variety of religious obligations and I have no desire to leave. I wish the people to learn that they do not have to remain under foreign tutelage in order to worship saints and gods which give so much to this place and the blessing of living and dying without losing one's identity in their world—*r'muxux ruchiliev*—of Santiago Atitlán.

Anthropologists have come to this place but what they do is always a professional 'game' which helps no one to eat or to live outside of those anthropologists themselves. Here children die every day and it is extraordinarily hard to survive beyond 45 years of age. But thousands of dollars are available for studying us. Thus, the theft of a head stolen from a *'santo'* some 25 years ago has become for us a symbol of the loss of traditional religion to the foreigners, or so our contemporaries believe.

The 'Mam' or 'Maximón' as it is called (Maximón means 'he who is bound' referring to the making of his body which is pure rope with a special heart or core) was originally made by indigenous prophets to combat the loss of integrity and understanding among the Tzutujil after the Conquest. Its history is a very long one.

Cofradías send representatives to my house daily, asking about the head's arrival—since everyone in a religious position has had dreams about it.

Now: as far as my own personal motives regarding the return of the masked head of the Mam, they are as follows:

1) I have no monetary or prestige interest in the matter whatsoever.

2) I had no desire to get into the business of asking for the relic back but I was asked to do so by the most respected leaders of the village, the very same who signed the paper sent to you.

3) The return of the head will enable the majority religion of the village of Santiago Atitlán to claim that it has a right to exist in the 20th century.

4) The relic will not remain with me, nor with any private individual: its fate will be decided by the Council of *Cabecera* and *principales*. The present opinion indicates very clearly that the head will eventually be guarded by its traditional guardians, the *cofradía* Santa Cruz.

5) If everything happens according to the petition which we have all signed, not a single problem will arise but universal joy will prevail.

I hope that my letter has not been too long but I wish to reiterate the completely sincere motives which govern my own desire for the return of this sacred object. I have heard that there are others who would like to bring back the piece. The *principales* would, I think, feel more than a little insulted but, in truth, Madam, it is with you that the final decision rests. Without any further comments therefore, I take my leave in the hope that *R'wa Kdta' Mam*, the Head of Our Father Mam, will return speedily to this place.

Sincerely yours,

{Signed: Martín Prechtel}

Barely four days after Prechtel will have sent this letter, conflicting reports will begin to emanate from the Brotherhood regarding an imminent return, with talk of "special diplomatic bags, or
planes, or whatever . . ." Prechtel will get the impression that the
Brotherhood has never pulled out: that they are still in the center
of activities. Prechtel will get a telegram: "Be ready on the 15th!"
They will wait. Another: "On the 20th!" They will wait.

On the 24th or so, Vicente, David and Joaquín will arrive in
Atitlán and everyone will run into the house saying that the foreigners have arrived! But whoever is down there at the landing
will not come up to Prechtel's house. Prechtel will go down to
the tourist bar and bang on the door. The three friends will claim
to be having a secret meeting: the mask will be brought very soon
but very secretly. When is the question. Very soon is the answer.
Prechtel will leave without further revelation.

A week before the arrival of the mask—at about the same time
as the tourist bar episode we have just related—Prechtel will go
to the City and call the Brotherhood office. He will ask Vicente,
"What is going on? I hear the head is back." Vicente will explode
and ask him how he knows. Prechtel will relate a dream. Finally,
Vicente will admit that the head is in his house right there in the
City. It will be Prechtel's turn to explode and to demand that the
head be brought to Atitlán immediately. Vicente will answer that
the Europeans will bring the mask on March 1st, in one week
from then.

On his arrival home, a whole bunch of *principales* will be there
dancing up and down and waiting to tell him of the head's return. "But I am coming to tell you that!" "No, no, no: we have
received a telegram!" An assistant of Vicente's, a young Protestant, will have taken the telegram to the *Cabecera*, instead of the
Cabecera getting it directly. Prechtel will be furious: now the whole
village will be in the know. It will become clearer and clearer to
Prechtel that, in wishing for a get together of *cofrades* from many
different places on the Lake or, failing that, in wanting to draw in
all sorts of Atiteco organizations, the three friends would be try-

ing to legitimize their own position in the village and pick up as much of the credit as they could.

.   ■   .

On January 10th, 1979, Marie will have informed Tarn in New Hope that, since Henry was to remain in Guatemala longer than predicted, the museum party would be able to give Tarn a little longer to get back in touch with Atitlán. The return date will now have been set for March 5th instead of the end of February. Tarn will accordingly plan a leisurely month's trip by van from Pennsylvania, visiting many museums and archaeological sites on the way, with an estimated arrival time in Santiago of February 26th. A major robbery of camera equipment will cause delays at Villahermosa, Mexico, and there will be a number of breakdowns on jungle roads.

On arrival, there will be a letter of February 2nd from Marie— a rather dismaying one in view of the times and distances that will have been involved—stating that, due to work schedules at their Scientific Mission in the north of the country, the date would now be March 1st instead of 5th. Tarn will wire Marie on February 27th but the wire will be returned on the next day due to her having sent a faulty address. Concerned and stressed about all this, Tarn will call on Prechtel for the first time around noon of February 17th and a very long conversation will ensue.

With infinite caution and diplomacy, the two parties will gradually come around to the question of the return and the virtual simultaneity of their efforts will be marveled at by both, though soon ascribed by Prechtel to "the way in which the Mam works." Prechtel will reveal that, because of some letters seen waiting for Tarn at the Post Office, he will have gathered that Tarn was bringing the head back. Tarn will reveal to Prechtel the details of the story as to how the mask got to Europe in the first place. Various other details will transpire, such as the fact that the as yet unmet-with *Alcalde* Santa Cruz, the dread Makuxtin, will have come on to the radio this very morning to announce that he

171

has no quarrel with Prechtel and that, from now on in, every-thing will be exceedingly calm and peaceful. Such will be the atmosphere in the village at the time of the mask's return.

In the absence of any further message from Marie's party, Tarn will go back to Prechtel's house at 8:30 a.m. on March 1st. The Europeans will be found to have arrived on the evening of Feb-ruary 27th, perhaps earlier, and to have called on Prechtel a little after Tarn's own first visit. Marie is in Atitlán with a man reported to be her husband and with Vicente.

The occasion or ceremony to take place will have been described as very bureaucratic, requiring that the *principales* sign all manner of legal papers, demanding copies of the mask from them forthwith and so forth. The museum party ask if it will be O.K. if an anthropologist gives the mask back and it is thought this might be Henry. Vicente will be behaving very "coolly" towards Prechtel. Prechtel will relate how he had told the *principales* the day before about Tarn saving the mask from fire thirty years before and sending it to sleep in Europe for all that time.

A new decision will have been taken by the elders: namely to make a glass case with a lock on it and place this in *cofradía* Santa Cruz. During Holy Week, the mask would come out for five days under the supervision of the *Cabecera* and the elders, then it would go back into its case. All of this will initiate a long series of deci-sions, indecisions and maneuvers by the *principales* and Santa Cruz, each side standing upon their honor like duelists or prima donnas before, months later, the mask will finally find its way back to its legitimate home.

Tarn and his wife Janet will then help Prechtel strew his reception hall with pine needles and they will return there at 3:30 p.m. at Prechtel's suggestion. There will be recognitions, rejoic-ings and gifts. The *principales* present are a small group: those who signed the petition to Europe in the first place, minus two who are "away on trips." Chiviliu will be the last to arrive: he will embrace Tarn, whom he will not have seen since 1969, but little will be said. The *Cabecera*, Chiviliu and Tarn will be seated in the middle of the *cofrades'* bench along the wall and, once again, everyone will settle down to wait.

DREAM INTERLUDE TO THE RETURN: PRECHTEL'S DREAM OF THE MAM:

When I came to this village, I had never seen the Mam. I had heard a lot about him and about that bizarre Maximón at San Andrés Iztapa, a *ladino* cult mainly I think, but never seen either. But I had a dream about him.

The first dream I had was this: There was a little guy, I guess you might call him a *duende* if you were Spanish or *ladino*. Little pants and boots, black hat, wooden face. He is sitting on a *koxtun*, a rock wall, moving his legs back and forth like a little kid. There is also a very big turkey and thirty extremely bright vermilion chicks. The big turkey keeps on killing the chicks. I have a large net bag and try to protect the chicks but, in the process, kill more than the turkey is killing. I try to gather them together and they just die in my hand. The little man laughs, ha, ha, ha, just like I've since learned the Mam does and I say who are you and he just laughs, gets off the wall and walks on. After this dream, I met Chiviliu, Tuiz and the others and saw the Mam and figured this is who the little man was.

Now, four months later, after the Chiv had told me all about the Scandals, but before I had seen the mask on the cover of Miguel Sol's book, I dreamed I was in canton Panabaj at the corner where the road splits off for Chicacao. I was waiting at the corner but God knows for what. Up comes this little guy again that I had dreamed of before. He was talking in a high pitched voice and saying to me, 'Eh! Where are you going?' I said I was going to Santiago

Atitlán. He said, 'Eh! lets go up to Pral, Volcano Tolimán.'
I asked him how. 'Take a bus,' he said. Again I asked how.
'What! Are you crazy? There are lots of buses that go to
Pral, they come along all the time.' So here comes a yellow
school bus with no one inside. No driver. 'Don't worry,
I'm driving,' the little guy says. So we get into the bus; he
sits by me and yells, 'Take him up to Pral!'

So, we go right through Chokox Aq'oum, the Medecine
Mushroom place. It's very strange this bus which is flying, although there is a road. We come to curves, right up
among the trees. Then he says that we have to walk from
there on in and that we are going to his house. 'O.K. O.K.'
I say, but think, 'That's very strange! There are no houses
on Pral!' It is cold as a witch's tit up there and we're walking along—and, all of a sudden, there is this big glass house,
modern, real modern, architecturally designed, you know,
and all of that. The little guy changes clothes—and now
he's as tall as I am, maybe taller. He's got a tweed suit on,
with a vest and a tiny little hat, also tweed. He goes on
talking like a person, although he still looks like the Mam.

Then three girls come up to us. One wears pants;
another a skirt; the third . . . I don't know. One is blonde,
another dark, the third sort of neutral. For some reason
I'm terrified of them. He tells me not to worry. I tell him I
think they are enemies. 'No, no, no, they are my buddies,
they take care of the place,' he says to me. 'Take them away,
please, I don't like them,' I say. 'They make me real nervous.' After some argument he puffs them away.

Well, we have this strange, big, glorious James Bondish
car there. He says 'O.K. Let's go to Guat City and . . . how
about a drink? Would you like a drink?' We have a drink of
some sort of booze and get into the car. Pah! Pah! Instantly
in the City. He has some mikes in a place there, the kind
they use in broadcasting studios. He's holding them tight
and, as we talk, we're in a T.V. station.

They have a stage and a kind of studio audience which is not very big . . . and he starts talking, right? As he talks, his face starts turning to metal and there are ridges on the face that go off to the side, like the ones old men have. On the side of the mouth, too. He has a very piercing, a piercing look. He starts talking, 'Well, Ladies & Gentlemen,' you know and it gets louder and louder: 'jawajawajawa-JAwajaWAJAWAJAWAJAWAJAWA', HIS VOICE IS TURN-ING PURE THUNDER AND PURE WIND! Holy Shit!—Well, all the people start running out of this pad of his, ay, ayayayaya-AYAYAYAYYYYYYYYY . . . And the Mam goes, 'eha eha eha hahahahahahahAHAHAHAHAHAHAHA!!!' you know—the way he does . . .

So he is speaking into the mike, and he says to me, in Tzutujil of course, he says, 'Turn where the Sun comes out, turn where the North Wind comes out, turn towards where our Father Sun goes down, turn yourself towards the South Wind—and with that you'll find my face, you'll find my head and you will triumph!' I can't tell right now how much of his voice was pure thunder, pure wind. And his face: when he came along, he was just an ordinary guy, you know, tanned and leathery like a Marlboro Man ad, but then he turned to pure, hard, gold: an *incredible* face. So I wake from this thing like freezing water had been thrown on me: just a very, very strong impression.

After that I told Chiviliu and he said 'O.K. Now. Now is the time.' From then on out, I was all for this thing.

■　　　■　　　■

Sits there now, once again, on whom everything depends, sunk in thought apparently, or else—his mind said to be wandering now—lost in depths beyond thought, in the dreams they talk about so much, where everything is validated, where decisions are made. Metaphor of will, of authority: I, so and so, have the age, knowl-edge, accomplishments, status, power to tell you this—and it sticks. This is the way you will do it. Who has been renowned all his life for that kind of strength, to the point of terrorizing his people, his clients, or the officers of whatever *cofradía* he had undertaken for the year—especially when he happened to switch from his favorite beers and *aguas* to the hard *guaro*, the mouth-twisting drink of the ancients. Who is ancient himself, almost no longer of this time, of this earth, nearly gone already and written into the ranks of the *Nawal Antiwal*, the Ancestors, the Power-Men, the Rain-Makers, the originals of mankind. Giving himself out to be ninety-three years old—though probably eighty-six—still pretty good for these parts. The mind has been wandering for some time now, fighting epic battles with demons no one else can see, demons he has held at bay all his long life as a master of speech, now closing in on him, waiting like buzzards for the prey to die.

Having heard through the watch that Tarn was back in town, through his own sons also going up and down the Atitlán-Tolimán road, laden with corn, shyly out of eye-corner, ah, we thought it was you (and how long this and how long that and when and where), marches late into Prechtel's building, *Cabecera* already seated there among his elders, always for maximal effect, broad smile cracking at last under the seigniorial wide-brimmed hat, toothless grin now that had been dazzling before, one tooth still, sticking out in the prognathism. Bear hug for Tarn despite the solemnity and sits down next to the *Cabecera*, more solemn than the lot of them altogether, sinks into thought, or into dream, hard to tell. Only the humor wakes him from time to time, as when Tarn speaks: "Ninety-three, eh? Well, when you're one hundred, we'll drink one hundred beers and then dance!"—broad grin, whole face crinkling up, cheeks that had been so full now sunk abyssally but filling a little with the grin, eyes half closed as was his custom even in his prime or, later, from him, when the beers had been cracked open, "Well, *meat* doesn't make friends; *tortillas* don't make friends. But with *beer*, yes! You make friends!" with that lightning fast passage from deep-absorption to joking and back again into the wrinkles. And time passes in praise of one, of the other: Tarn's praise of Prechtel; his of Tarn; the *Cabecera*'s of the old maestro; Janet Tarn's of Tarn and Prechtel to the maestro: "these are both your sons": quick grin, nod, agreement.

Tension mounts, "Where the hell are these people?" coming from all sides, some quiet, some insistent, getting louder. The museum people have gone out to get papers, legal papers, with their advisor from the City, the one whose path kept crossing with Tarn's, so that it had become impossible to untangle now whether Tarn had started the recuperation proceedings, or whether it had been Vicente, or whether it had been Prechtel quietly pulling strings in the background all the time, maybe through someone, maybe by himself: ah, and what in God's name did it all matter now, anyway, as long as the head was coming back!

But it was a sure thing that the Europeans had been in the village at least as long as Tarn had—about three days—and had been doing their own research and found out about the trouble at *cofradía* Santa Cruz and the plan for the glass case and all the rest of that stuff, although they had given Tarn the assurance that they would wait for him to find out how the land lay. As it was, Tarn had damn near missed the whole business: one flat tire or broken shock too many and that would have been it! And all those changes of dates!

So now, what were these burrocrassts doing with all those papers and why were they bringing their internal quarrels here with them, when all the people wanted was to see the head again after thirty years and to hell with papers! (Well, what they want is that all the signatories of the original document sign the receipt here today!) But what had been truly extraordinary, and far more important than all of that, had been Tarn and Prechtel's wary circling around each other for a couple of days and finding out to their diminishing astonishment that they had been both brought to converge on this place and to work simultaneously for the return of this head to Atitlán, the immemorial House of Birds!

Marie's husband arrives, a gawky, shy and awkward linguist.

He has lost the others but they'll be here soon. It takes them an hour longer. Marie enters, Vicente at her side, deadpan solemn all the way. Marie goes into a few details with Tarn, absolving herself. It doesn't wash very well at all. Now, Marie is reading aloud a document couched in legal terms on legal paper. She has asked Prechtel to translate and seems pretty impressed with him by now. Prechtel translates with charm, slipping in many an explanation in Tzutujil, getting all that burrocrasstese into human language.

The document describes how the European couple, plus Vicente, have brought the objects; how it is to be received by the *principales* in exactly the state in which it had been deposited at the museum (even a little improved by conservation); how it is to remain at all times in their trust; how, if there were to be any legal action, they would have to handle it; how they were to arrange for a copy by such and such a date named and sealed; how it was hoped that this would be a factor of union and not disunion in Atitlán—together with a whole string of other patronizing impertinences.

Then, the couple stand there nonplussed because they have only made a draft, thinking that the *principales* might wish to discuss this or that point, but the old men, Prechtel sidles up to state, have nothing to discuss. One or two elders come up to ask that another paragraph be inserted in order to thank whatever other people might, unknown to them, have helped in forwarding this matter and, then, one very sweet-talking and courtly *principal*, the great storyteller Cua, with a head like a beautiful sharp hatchet ("Hatchet" is his nickname) slips up to ask of the young woman that the paper contain an accusation against those two great enemies of the people: Juan Sisay and Domingo.

All of this is transmitted by Prechtel: it is only right that Tarn's part in saving the mask should be recorded and also that of various other anthropologists like Henry and his colleague—but whether any of this is done will always be a matter for conjecture, because the paper is no longer seen after a certain point. It has gone with all the other ancestral titles and documents into the *Caja Real*, the Royal Chest of the village, and everyone knows that, once something has gone into the *Caja Real*, it is, like all the sacred books, like the *Popol Vuh* for instance, never seen again.

So: what is this, Tarn asks himself, that he and his appeal and his research have all probably been bypassed, at some risk to his own presence here—and what is Vincent's role in all this—for instance: what is Vincent really up to on this Lake?

Another wait of an hour or more while the young woman and Vincent go to get the papers officialized. Acquaintances and relatives of the three friends arrive. Everyone goes into the courtyard for photographs, the *principales* solemn as murder and absolutely rigid because somewhere way back it was decided that this is how you stand when photographs are taken. Meantime, a group of visitors arrive. Now we have the latest "prophet," dressed entirely in white, same old-style shirt as Tarn has on with the cross over the belly-button, a red *suut* scarf over his head, looking vacantly about him, his arms, as he is led about, held by a group of drunks like a regiment of guards.

One of the guards goes into a long whisper at Tarn, the voice high-pitched and feminine: "Why have you died twenty-seven years?" "I haven't died, I was asleep perhaps," Tarn jokes. "Did you see so and so . . . (naming some of the Company of the Holy World) . . . ?" "Yes, they are all around us . . . and all well." The drunk also asks a lot about the President and Tarn tells him the President is well, thank you very much, and no doubt doing just fine in the City. Prechtel says later they are all creeps, except the prophet, who is gay, and crazy as a prophet should be—they, the guards, are all politicos who were not invited to the event—but how do you keep anyone out? Needle sticks in the groove: drunk slurs over and over: "If you see any of them, Sojuel, Rujuch, all those guys, those Power-Men, you promise to tell me?" Assurance after assurance; no gainsaying, no violence permitted. Meantime, the prophet admires Tarn's shirt and makes half hearted attempts to get it off him.

In comes another portent, youngish, obviously furious. Tarn recognizes him, fails to remember he is an "enemy": the man is polite but frozen under his politeness. He is now President of the Committee for Reconstruction of the Church, who had been a *Catequista* in his youth and is still a leading *Catequista* by all the evidence. Spies from the other side, says Prechtel: inevitable. The man tries to start a speech at Prechtel; Prechtel pulls rank on him as *Primer Mayor* and he sits down, hushed and chastened.

The museum crowd finally come back and each *principal* files up to answer his name and fingerprint the document. They go out for a moment, then awkwardly re-enter. Marie, her husband and Vincent stand in front of the table, read a toned-down version of the original document: this time the copy is to be a remembrance for their own country: for a Europe widowed of the great mask of the Mam. Tedious speech, grating accent. Finally, the husband pulls the mask out of the bag, wrapped in plastic bubble paper, places it in the hands of the *Cabecera*, covered with a purple and white *saqsuut*. *Cabecera* looks solemn enough to die while everyone files up in front of him, crosses himself or herself and kisses the bubble-paper. (Tarn: "They haven't even seen what's inside for Crissakes!") Space cleared on the table, more *suut* laid on it, package placed on *saqsuut*—and *Cabecera* unwraps.

It is immediately in front of he-on-whom-everything-depends, the old guy, the Chiv. He stares at the content intently, face motionless. Tension builds, Chiviliu stares on interminably. Tarn, on his knees like everyone else, begins to feel sick, suspects that Chiviliu is rejecting the mask. After a while, the old guy starts repeating, "Ain't there, ain't there . . ." Stares again, then again: "Ain't there." Other *principales* are muttering and comparing notes.

Tarn suddenly remembers that the Europeans had said the elders expected a whole head, something additional to the mask and positioned behind it. Prechtel whispers to Tarn, "They were expecting a wooden core, the thing that gives the doll its power, has writing on it; also three metal rings at the neck—metal so that the body can be tied to the head."

Chiviliu is looking totally stricken by this time. My God! He has given up the ghost; he has said he wanted this return before leaving the earth behind him and now, all is deception, mendacity and loss. *Cabecera*, whose immemorial function is conciliation, asks him to perform a "compassion." The mask is placed on the *suut* in the center of the table, facing the door. The *suut* is tied up by the old guy into a bundle shape, which helps hold up the mask in a standing position.

The old guy comes round to the front, lights a cigarette, places it in the mask's mouth. He has never taken his eyes off the mask (when seated, looked at it from every position, started as if seeing this or that—Tarn: "What is the old so-and-so up to, is this the old *aj'kun*'s trick-theater?"), now looks a little happier, considers it with head bent, seems to like the look of it a little better, mutters to himself that it is ancient all right, certainly ancient, very ancient indeed.

Then declares that the mask has been starving a long time, directs *Cabecera* to soak a cloth in liquor (starts with kleenex), sits down on bench cradling mask in arms like a baby, rubs away and away at mask, soaking every wrinkle in alcohol. Then, with *Cabecera*'s help, wraps *suut* as if to form a head, with mask inside it, puts this on table again in standing position. Mask holds up O.K. Music. The *son* tune of the Great Wanderer, strikes up softly and sweetly in the background, beating of the two-tongued drum—Chiviliu moves back to the front of the table and performs a short dance, his arms extended as if he were holding the Martín bundle in *cofradía* San Juan, sinks to his knees, everyone kneeling behind him and around him, starts up his well known prayer, which grows and swells like approaching thunder, deafening, encompassing the whole room, blessing all the assembled, whose names have to be whispered one by one to him as if he had been carried away and forgotten everything and everyone that he had ever known.

The Chiv, tired, says he cannot carry any more names, sits down, beers break open, all light turns to sunshine. Prechtel: "No, they're all happy now—you know the old guy, he always pulls this dissatisfaction trick, you remember how he used to go into the *cofradías* and condemn the way people did every blessed little thing. I really don't know if they believe that the head was burned with the second mask: that is another matter." *Cabecera*, the conciliator agrees that this, at the least, is a miracle, that this, at least, has survived, when it is so old after all, who knows how many years, twenty-seven, twenty-eight, that it is very, very old, perhaps much older? At one point, Chiviliu gets up and performs a short dance in front of the mask, the huge body moving like a bear around the room. Tarn, who had never danced in his youth, is moved by drink, music and emotion to dance also. He amazes himself. No one else dances for the time being.

Towards early morning, everyone has relaxed to such an extent that Tarn hardly notices that Chiviliu has taken the mask again out of its *suut* and is trying several times to make it stand up by itself. After the third or fourth try, *Cabecera* gently, almost imperceptibly, pushes a *suut* under the chin of the mask, from the back, so that it "stands." The old guy lights another cigarette, gives it to the mask.

The sessions are set: what to do with the mask; what to do about copies; what to do about *cofradía* Santa Cruz; what to do about taking the Chiv home. Everybody disperses into the night, hailing each other, more than a little drunk and yet strangely muted, quiet, a small ceremony after all, because of the quiet, the secrecy, when you would have thought that, yes, the whole village might be called out, but the *principales* wanted none of it—a whole book could be written on the secrecy alone.

But now, the world could begin again, there would be rain, there would be corn, because the Owner of the World had come back after all these many years. And all the next days, people coming up to each of us, individually, in small groups, sliding, slithering, sidling up: Is it true, is it fact that the Lord of the World is among us again? And leaving with smiles on their lips.

Tarn and Janet walking back quietly to Tzanchich'am, in that very calm inebriation which is like music, walking back right past their house in the dark, almost over to Cerro de Oro, before they realize the overshoot. Prechtel, lying awake next to his eighteen-year-old wife, poor, epileptic, woman while still a child, now "grandmother" through her husband's rank—because, for him, this is only one in an endless round of duties and wakes that will take him to the other side of Holy Week, until he can go back to being flute-player again, and painter, and rest his head.

FIFTEEN

How the Mask Went Back to Cofradía Santa Cruz

Before we take the mask back to *cofradía* Santa Cruz, we have a problem as to why the friends Vicente, David and Joaquín have interfered at all in its return. Has the Brotherhood been helping Prechtel out of kindness? Have they motives of their own? Why is an important telegram to the *Cabecera* sent, not directly to him, but through a Protestant employee of the friends who, incidentally, makes sure the whole village knows its contents? Why are the friends so intent on avoiding inter-governmental contact? Had the Tourist Ministry obtained the story, of course, everything could have turned out seedily, if not downright ugly. But is it merely this?

The Radio was originally built up by the Oklahoma Catholic Mission to Atitlán, a group of ecclesiastics who had been called in to take over the Church in 1964 and had changed it back into an orthodox Catholic stronghold. The Radio, made independent in the year 1970, has been the greatest enemy of the friends in the village. It is not that their adequate technology is bad: it is that it is not good enough. Their measures are qualified with the word "*placebo*": one can hazard guesses as to where that word has reached the Atitecos from. The friends bringing back the mask of the Mam is something like a heavy insult for certain people. All the more so, since Domingo, Juan Sisay's friend and a Radio announcer for years, has been one of the Mam's original enemies. For Felipe Tuiz, associated with the Radio at this juncture and having quarrelled with Prechtel, the latter's role in the matter is enough to cause discomfiture.

At the time of the great Guatemalan earthquake of 1976, the

friends' organization had not been independent, but was part of a nation-wide reconstruction effort with governmental backing. In order to promote their programs in the village, the organization had at first allied itself with a Radio Federation, of which Radio Atitlán was a member. The friends had offered Radio Atitlán help—not so much with building but with the services of an architect, a set of plans, some materials (cheaply obtained through earthquake-reconstruction contacts), some builders and the like.

The friends claimed that, having accepted these services, the Radio refused reimbursement or even to sign a paper declaring that they had helped them in specified ways. The issue was that the friends needed some kind of evidence that would enable them to work unhindered in the village. There were also some considerations regarding taxation.

The Radio people were manifestly very upset and it was clear that some other issue or issues must lie behind this one. These turned out to be relatively simple.

Before the friends had appeared on the scene, the Radio had been training one Sicay as a D.J. and as an announcer. Now, with his training completed and a working knowledge of Spanish, the friends had asked him if he wanted a job. He replied that he would be working for the Radio upon graduation. The friends then offered him 120 *quetzales* a month on the spot, a much larger sum than the Radio could afford. The Radio was furious at having trained the young man for nothing. Furthermore, men like Felipe Tuiz and Juan Atzip were angry at Sicay because they were older, had "been suffering" longer than he, and could well have done with that job themselves. The fact that Sicay was a Protestant, that someone was in love with Sicay's sister and other little items of such *campanalismo*, did not improve the general picture. Sicay had immediately started behaving grandly and had donned *ladino* costume: this had led Felipe Tuiz and Co. to believe that he was getting even more than 120 dollars.

It was clear that the friends wanted coverage for returning the mask. On the one hand, they had reasons for not wanting the government to hear about it too early; on the other, they were constantly trying to make the return a big Lake-wide party. Did this not indicate an attempt to corner the prestige? They had offered Prechtel money to be their ambassador at large with the *cofradías* all around the Lake. His response was that he might have been more inclined to help them had they not offered pay: this was a spiritual matter and not subject to payment.

Before the mask's return, Prechtel had stated that, should he help them it would look as if *he* were seeking credit and the *principales* would be flustered by all the public attention. In addition, no one knew exactly what the Europeans were going to give back and the matter had become far too conspiratorial. He told the friends that it looked like they wanted a "cultural revolution without bloodshed." "When they knew that I could see through their game of using me," he added, "that's when they stopped courting me."

Nevertheless, the Brotherhood felt they should forestall attempts to harm Prechtel in the City by publishing evidence of the support he had from the *principales*. On the week after *Semana Santa*, Prechtel and Eyes made a lightning trip into the City and, with the help of the friends, prepared a "Public Declaration" which was then signed by the elders at their session of April 22nd. Of the original signatories of the petition to the museum, only five signed this document: Diego Sisay Ajtujal, Salvador Quieju Tzina, Juan Acabul Ramírez, Manuel Quieju and Pascual Damian Ixbalan. New signatories included Juan Pacax (*Principal Pasado*), Estevan Ajcot (*P.P.*), Estevan Pacay (*P.P.*), Lucas Rianda Ixbalan (*P.P.* and Reconstruction Committee), Juan Tiney Tiney (*Cabecera Pasado*), Francisco Mendoza (*Alcalde* Animas, 1977–78), Antonio Ixbalan Tzina (*Alcalde* Gregorio 1977–78) and Juan Ajchomajay (*Sacristán*).

We, the *principales* of the indigenous community of Santiago Atitlán, Department of Sololá, by these means wish to bring to the attention of our countrymen the following facts:

186

FIRST: that some three years ago there came to Atitlán Mr. Martín Prechtel, North American Citizen, painter and musician who became interested in getting to know our sacred traditions and making their spiritual values evident to the world. Mr. Prechtel associated himself little by little with our community, learning our Tzutujil language, then marrying a young lady of our people, born in Santiago, and organizing at the same time with other members of the community and with our agreement, a musical group dedicated exclusively to playing works of regional folklore. These have now been recorded and made popular among all Guatemalans.

SECOND: that we, the elders of this community, impressed by the achievements of Mr. Martín Prechtel, called him to our bosoms to become a member of the Council of *Principales*. For the last two and a half years he has collaborated with us and taken an active interest in everything which favors the community.

THIRD: that, after our having learned that various holy objects belonging to Atiteco *cofradías* and stolen some years ago were surviving in various places and countries, we made an effort to recuperate these objects with Mr. Prechtel's participation.

FOURTH: that, convinced of Mr. Prechtel's positive contribution to our community, we decided to name him this year *Primer Mayor*, charging him with all the ritual that pertains to that office from the days of old and that we, as well as the majority of people here, have been highly satisfied with the organization of these ceremonies.

FIFTH: That, in making public our gratitude for the work done by Mr. Martín Prechtel, we are also glad to declare publicly that whatever other person or institution, national or international, wishes to show us his sincerity, help in concrete form, prudence and respect, with the aim of conserving our traditions and preserving the cultural patrimony we received from our forefathers will be received by us with open arms.

187

At the time of the trip to Guatemala, the notion of inserting this into some six or seven newspapers was also discussed but rejected to prevent overkill. An article did appear in the newspaper *Prensa Libre* on May 15th, 1979, giving an account by one Dina García of the meeting at which the Declaration was signed and photographs of the participants, followed by the Declaration itself. The headline was "North American named First Mayor of Santiago Atitlán, Sololá: Declaration of Appreciation made recently by the *principales*."

The architect who had contributed, on the Brotherhood's behalf, to the building of the Radio edifice came up with a proposal at this time to build a meeting house for the elders and for Prechtel in which the paraphernalia could be kept from year to year. Nothing came of this, nor of Prechtel and Tarn's ideas that a place could be kept for houseless images and other treasures in danger of being sold, such a place eventually to form the nucleus of an Atiteco museum.

■　　■　　■

It is now time to say something about the elders' own attitudes to the return of the Maximón mask.

Occurring at a period of social and economic stress, with the traditional politico-religious system in a state of disarray and experiencing great difficulties in recruitment; at a time which, with hindsight, will be seen to be the prelude to Civil War in Guatemala with its attendant Terror, the return of the head—or rather a mask—caused considerable anxiety among the responsible parties.

In February, at the time of the return, such anxiety was expressed through a good deal of questioning regarding the best means of treating the relic. *Cabecera* was thinking that it should be kept from *cofradía* Santa Cruz until Santa Cruz left Makuxtin's hands and was given over to the new *Alcalde*, Marianda, in May. The names of various elders were brought up as potential guardians. The notion of keeping everything in the hands of small committees, controlling invitations to visit and see the relic sent out to favored groups or individuals, after which a big party would be staged, continued to prevail against either an enlarging of the group of elders directly responsible or a more immediate handing over of the relic to Santa Cruz.

An outside observer could also see an open question as to whether the group was not remaining small because it could not, in effect, become any bigger: the interest and zeal necessary to joining the group not being forthcoming.

As had been the case during the Scandals, the traditionalists were always the most likely to dither. Lacking a forward-oriented program, they saw themselves as defenders primarily against a concatenation of varied evils spawned by religious division in the village, a host of political feuds and the puzzling inroads of western culture. Visibly beleaguered, they were prey to a good deal of internal division, distrust and disaffection. Yet, there were also some surprising rallies and the cause over which they had been excited for so long was to triumph up to a point in the end.

The relic itself was treated throughout as a cult object, kept in a specially made box and provided by Prechtel and his people with incense, candles and the like. At times, even when the *principales* had a meeting about some other issue, the mask was taken out, wrapped in a ceremonial cloth and placed on the *cofrades'* table with a candle in front of it. There were perennial discussions about how to deal with the copy problem. The main solution proposed involved a copy for the Europeans and a copy to be used on the Mam, the relic itself being kept in a case as a separate object. The number of copies required varied from time to time as well as the identity of the person deemed fit to carve them.

There was frequent talk of treating the mask's return as only a beginning: now that the mask was back, could the head be far behind? Little credence was given, after all, to Miguel Sol's supposition, in his book, that the head *had* been burned by the priests. Consideration was also given to the possibility of carving a new, or at any rate interim, head, possibly by Chiviliu. Anxiety about being in charge of the relic surfaced in a number of ways.

Perhaps the most graphic was Eyes' when left in charge of the mask during an unusually long absence of Prechtel's in the City. Eyes claimed to have been unwell ever since the mask entered his house. He dwelt at great length on exactly how many candles and how many "feedings" the mask had received. Above all, he pressed constantly for information on Prechtel's return—to be effected, in his hopeful view, in time for him to regain his health prior to the relic's return to Santa Cruz.

On May 19th, 1979, a session was held in Prechtel's house and *Cabecera* kept it waiting for five hours before showing up. Makuxtin's Santa Cruz was reported as being in yet further trouble: the First *Cofrade*, later to become the *Primer Mayor*'s Second *Mayor*, had left his post as a result of quarrels. The *cofradía* found itself accused of having started "business" again by charging nine *quetzales* for bringing down the Mam. The *Escribano*, usually considered a friend of Prechtel's, had decided that the mask would be returning on January 15th, had ordered beer and had been clobbered by Makuxtin when the mask failed to show up. Understandably, he continued nursing a grudge against the *Primer Mayor*. Another session of the elders was scheduled for May 26th.

On that day, *Cabecera* was sent for at 11:00 a.m. and his wife reported him out and not due back until 4:00 p.m. The *principales* were ill-disposed toward accepting his excuses. They were now caught in a protocol problem between *Cabecera* and Santa Cruz. At this point, they argued against the proposal to create a *cofradía particular* for the relic. Each man would have to take a week's responsibility in turn; it would be impossible to avoid accusations of graft; the strain on the *Primer Mayor* would be too great, etc. etc. At 11:00 a.m. the great "politician" and fine-talker Hatchet was sent out with Juan Ajcabul on a mission to Santa Cruz. They came back with the inconsiderate message: "Bring it back, or not, as you please." There was a great deal of talk about the insult suffered.

Nothing, however, could be done without *Cabecera*. After a break from 12:30 to 4:00, he was summoned again at 5:00. Excuses again. There was much talk of breakdown of group solidarity: Juan Tiney, an ex-*Cabecera*, decided to pull out for the time being. On the previous evening, the mask had been taken out, talked to and consulted; now it was brought out again and approached with many anxious questions as to whether *Cabecera* will not have gone over to the enemy. Two rounds of beer cheered the elders up and they retreated into the telling of stories about bygone days.

Cabecera eventually turned up at 8:30, explaining that he had gone to *cofradía* Santa Cruz the week before and gotten insulted and, for this reason, had not come today. He undertook to turn up fully dressed with a document relating to the mask's return. By this time, however, the *principales* had veered around again and favored the idea of a privately owned and run chapel, a *cofradía particular*. To meet every fortnight, not weekly. To make an exact copy of the mask for *Primer Mayor*'s own miniature Mam and to put the relic itself in a glass case for public visiting. To name a *telinel* so that *Primer Mayor*'s marital life would not be interrupted. To write up a legal document, ensuring that everything would be above board.

This plan was not adopted and matters vacillated weekly all the way up to August. It was felt that Juan Tiney's exit may have been due to the defeat of his proposal to give the mask over to the Reconstruction Committee, a body enjoying the status of *persona juridica*. This in turn had arisen out of *Cabecera's* effort to get this relatively ecumenical body behind *Primer Mayor*'s assumption of his role after the dissension surrounding the return.

At 5:00 p.m. on August 31st, the *principales* held yet another session on the return of the mask. Prechtel and Tarn held their peace about a visit to Santa Cruz in the course of which they had been treated very meanly by the then Third *Cofrade*, not much respected for his religiosity as it turned out, who had stubbornly maintained that no one from Santa Cruz would go to a conciliatory meeting with the elders.

Cabecera stated that there was to be no more pussyfooting around: the time had not been ripe; they should see if it would be ripe now, if the Mam wanted it now. "Santa Cruz is now under its new leader Marianda—Diego Rianda Ajtujal—things should have improved." A visit to the *cofradía* came about.

This Marianda is a very large and broad man wearing flashy clothes, his mouth full of gold teeth, with expansive and expensive habits: the picture of a *nouveau riche alcalde* who has never done much in the way of service before.

At the *cofradía*, a long story of misbehavior on the part of the *Telinel* Matchajpin was recounted. For some time, he had been very jealous of anyone approaching the Mam, systematically contrary to visitors and *aj'kuna*, showing favoritism in the distribution of privileges and making profit from offerings. The *Alcalde* Marianda claimed he had been going easy on Matchajpin, not wishing to be accused of being like his precursor Makuxtin. Also: "A *telinel* is lord of the Mam. What Mam wants at any given time, the *telinel* manifests it. Even if he is out of hand. The *alcalde* is only the lord of the place, the *cofradía*, not lord of the Mam. *Telinels* get away with murder!" And: "When a *telinel* misbehaves, it is a sign that Mam, the omnipresent, is not there, has chosen not to be there. He is dissatisfied with the village and it is everyone's fault. This happens often with a *telinel* if he does not have the great power he is supposed to have in order to handle the Mam. The *telinel* has to handle and carry the weight of the position; of the Mam itself; of all the sins which go into the Mam's body and of the constant contact with the dead which the job involves. He has to be able to wag the tail, not let the tail wag him."

In any event, this *Telinel* Matchajpin is to be blamed for refusing to take the returned mask back out of sheer contrariness. Marianda has tried to calm him down by pointing out to him that he was fond of drink and that the *principales* would certainly be bringing a healthy amount of it. At this point, the *cofrades* up and accuse Marianda of just wanting a party, informing *Cabecera* that they feel insulted for good measure! Things are not helped by Marianda's obvious enjoyment of the little luxuries of life. In the meantime, Marianda has purchased his own supply of liquor against the coming of the elders and he now contrives to become insulted by his own *cofrades!*

To dispel this great load of insult in the air, everyone strives to judge the imbroglio one large misunderstanding, caused by "having a *telinel* at their throats," literally: stuck in their throats and impeding speech. There is also the fact that some visits of Marianda and his First *Cofrade* to *Primer Mayor*'s household have coincided with the latter's absence from town (caused by the prolonged illness of his first son) and this circumstance has added to the bad blood.

The strain of *fiesta* Santiago at the end of July, with its constant stream of visitors, will not have sweetened the *Telinel's* sour disposition. Things will boil to a head in the case of one Machinouy, an old side-kick of Nicolás Chiviliu's, to whom it will have fallen this year to "bring on the whores." These ladies, standard attendants at all titular *fiestas*, will visit the *cofradía* daily as great devotees of the Mam and of his "whore" wife María Castellana (a devotion nation-wide, it is said). On July 23rd, satisfied with his financial take, Machinouy will have bought a large quantity of beer and brought it to Santa Cruz.

Telinel will manage to alienate Machinouy by keeping him cooling his heels while allowing other visitors to precede him in doing their *costumbre*. Marianda will have tried to soothe the party by taking the ladies and Machinouy out to lunch—during which time Matchajpin will have found occasion to put away much of the beer. Marianda and his *cofrades* will have gone to the church from their lunch, as well as other sites where their duties called them, and Matchajpin will have handed the remaining beer back to the ladies at the *cofradía*. In Matchajpin's wife's presence, Marianda will have told Matchajpin to shape up. The wife will have immediately proceeded to run through town shouting to all that Marianda was just another feisty Makuxtin.

On July 24th, matters will come to a climax during a ceremonial dinner held by Marianda in the *cofradía*. Matchajpin will refuse his food. He will say that the food is witched. This will be an incredible thing to say to *cofrades*! It frightens the *r'k'ux*, the root or placenta of the sacred in any place, and can kill it. A deadly calm will settle over the *Alcalde* and his people. The *Telinel* will continue to refuse. Marianda will say to him, *"All right, you rest now."* He is out on his neck.

Matchajpin will start ranting and raving and stalk off with Third and Fourth *Cofrades* (they are usually his assistants), praying and witching at the door, at the entrance and on the road. Third and Fourth think better of it and turn back at the entrance. Shortly after this, there will be a large session of all the town's *Principales*. *Cabecera* will be out of sorts and in no mood for nonsense since, at the transfer to new *cofrades* of *cofradía* Santiago on August 2nd, he, a "poor man," will have fancied himself insulted by a "rich man," the new *Alcalde* Santiago. The ex-*Telinel* Matchajpin will arrive to question Marianda's right to evict him. Marianda is not then in *Cabecera*'s good graces because of a rumor that he had been insubordinate. At the meeting, Marianda will demonstrate that it was Matchajpin who had made the offensive remarks.

The *Principales* will vote unanimously to have the *Telinel* out and, by July 25th, Santa Cruz has a new one. This man, Malvex, our storytelling friend Loincloth, a good-hearted, strong and temperate *aj'kun*, will have been *Telinel* already some three, four or even five times. *Cabecera* will have to go in person to Matchajpin's house before the latter will allow the María icon (a representation of the Mam's wife) and other *telinel* appurtenances to be taken away from him.

After these explanations, talk will turn to the relic and Marianda will declare general dissatisfaction with a mask offered by himself to the *cofradía* on assuming it, a mask made by Felipe Tuiz, or perhaps his brother. (*Primer Mayor* will allege that this brother will have been perpetually snooping around his place to try to see the museum's relic.) Tuiz will be rumored to have incited Makuxtin against *Primer Mayor* and given him a chance to "talk against" Prechtel on the Radio. Tuiz is considered a rival of Prechtel's, claiming to have been the one to initiate him into traditional ritual (*pace* Chiviliu!); to have launched the idea of musical *conjuntos*; to have a right to the *primer mayor* position, to the mask and so forth.

In any event, the relic, Marianda states, would now serve as the original for all future copies, thus guaranteeing authenticity. In some ways, this will justify one of *Primer Mayor*'s ideas: to have a permanent meeting place for the *principales*, where the *primer mayor* of the year would keep his paraphernalia and which would serve as a proto-cultural center and proto-museum where old treasures could be protected against vandalism and sale.

The final discussion will center around the timing of the return of the mask relic to *cofradía* Santa Cruz: how to get enough leisure and attention for the ceremony, as well as discretion. This in view of the problem of visitors. The elders will vacillate to the very end between making a big thing out of it or being discrete. In the end, 5:00 a.m. on September 2nd will be decided upon.

The group assembles at *Primer Mayor*'s house between 3:30 a.m. and 5:45. After some discussion regarding what would be given to the *cofradía*—Prechtel to keep his box and Eyes his ceremonial cloth—*Cabecera* will perform a muted *costumbre*, consisting of laying the relic on the heads, breasts and hands of all those responsible for the return. Now: how to carry the relic? Eyes will get *Cabecera* to put his ceremonial black coat over his head, hold the front fringes over his hands and receive the mask in the front folds that way, the cigar alone jutting out of the arrangement. Offerings of candles, liquor and incense will be arranged and paid for.

Brisk walk to *cofradía*, via church inevitably, meeting only with a San Nicolás *cofrade* on the way: he will be allowed to kiss the relic. At the *cofradía*, party performs six direction signing, salutes Xoa', enters, aligns on bench. *Cofradía* produces ceremonial cloth, places it in front of *Telinel*'s bench position; relic placed on that.

The mask will then be much admired and discussed with the *cofrades* looking on like children delighted with a very special new toy. Stories will be rehearsed about the Scandals, the original masks, and head. *Primer Mayor* will give a mind-boggling and very graphic description of Tarn plunging his hands into the fire to pull out the mask ("It'll be too tame otherwise; they'll never credit it!"). There will also be much talk of Makuxtin's misdeeds.

The general attitude will be summed up as, "Who knows how many thousands of years old it is; it is from the beginning of the world; it is from one hundred years ago; it is at least thirty years since we have seen it, half a lifetime ago, and there is nothing like it in the whole universe!" With drink befuddling the issue, every part of the Mam will have gone to Europe; maybe even been made in Europe; in any event the Mam's reputation as a great traveller will have been amply confirmed. All through this, the desire to put the mask on the Mam will wax in intensity.

After a while, *Telinel* will go up into the trellis with Third and Fourth and stay up there some forty-five minutes. The Mam will then come down feet first, wearing the mask, with everyone agreeing on his splendid appearance. It will be conceded that only this *Telinel* can stand him on his feet facing the door, in front of the *cofradía* table, without his tumbling or even shaking at all. Meantime, *Telinel* will take the opportunity to show off his *savoir faire*. Observing that the mask, consonant with its antiquity, has no mouth aperture, he will "test" it by giving it a drink. A small cloth bib is placed under the mouth; the figure is dropped back at an angle of some forty-five degrees; the drink is poured and imbibed by the bib as well as the wood: another sign of its great age.

Cabecera will perform a thanksgiving *costumbre* again and Tarn will recount a dream about being naked in an academic conference, grabbing at his wife and being told by someone that he was always into that. The interpretation will be immediately forthcoming: the Mam is naked without his mask, will lunge to accept it: the mask, as all that covers flesh, is, of course, female. Then: a ritual meal offered by Marianda in the course of which the most elaborate salutations by rank on the part of everyone present precede and follow the meal to the great exacerbation of everyone's hunger.

Visitors will begin to come in: *aj'kuna* with their clients. A very powerful—or, in any event, very theatrically-gifted one, Mabernadin, will put on an extraordinarily elaborate performance. Preceding the meal, *Telinel* will have danced the Mam three times, followed by Third and Fourth.

Mabernadin will court trouble by petitioning to dance the Mam. *Telinel* will tell him roundly that, the mask having just come in, only the present *cofradía* officials are entitled to dance the Mam at this time. He will be very obviously jealous and tense but courtesy will be preserved. While Third and Fourth guard the Mam, one at each side, a couple of *principales* will join the fray and Mabernadin will find himself ejected as graciously as possible (later to be seen down the road, drinking heavily).

From then on, the congregation will have the good fortune to be left alone with the day developing into a royal party. Case after case of beer will be produced. Everyone will go through heavy weeping fits; even the elegant *Escrivano* Pascual Mendoza. *Cabecera*, who will have been drunk all night as a *tijonel* counsellor elsewhere, will have been sweet-talking the ladies prior to passing out. Before the collapse, Pascual will be playing some fine, muted guitar music while *Primer Mayor* and *Telinel* produce a whiny and nasal singing in honor of the Mam.

The men urinating outside will shower a small black piglet who keeps shaking himself at the honor but does not move out of the way. Eyes, on the wagon with orange juice, will leave quietly at 2:40 p.m.; the others will steal away around 3:30, with more beers on the road and, eventually, sleep. Tarn's notebook says, "Hangover for two days, perhaps three."

Many months later, while taking his leave of the village at the beginning of the Civil War, *Primer Mayor* will be saying goodbye to an old man, the new *Escrivano* Santa Cruz. The old man will say he is glad that the head of the Mam has been saved and is now in the village. *Primer Mayor*: "But, we don't have the head; it was only the mask that came back!" The old man: "Oh, we know that it is with you. As long as we know that it is safe in or near the village, or even somewhere in the world, we are quite happy.

We know you will protect it. It is enough for us to know that it is safe somewhere!"

Which is the way myth refuses to die. Which is the way myth refuses to be killed. Which is the way, one cannot help praying, the Maya will eventually overcome oppression.

SIXTEEN

Understanding the Mam and the Martín in the Nineteen-Fifties

We'll deal first with the Maximón and then with the Martín. At the beginning of Chapter One, Tarn described the wooden core and composition of the Maximón icon together with the way in which the core was dressed by a *telinel* for worship by Atitecos and visitors from the outside. The following continues his description and analysis as he understood the icon in the early 1950s:

Tarn, 1952–3:

The wooden core of the Maximón is said to be made of *palo de pito* or *tz'ajtel* but accounts vary as to form: one had it that the core was forked so as to provide legs. A persistent rumor that the core contained a little 'idol' could not be checked: some spoke of a gold or silver figure, pagan or Christian, others of a silver cross; one person of an ear of corn. Some denied the 'idol' altogether.

The 1952–3 *Telinel*'s distrust always overcame suggestions that I should be allowed to see the upper side of the roof trellis. The core seems to be kept in a mat tied by a cord, perhaps considered umbilical, to the central roof post, possibly related to the idea of a central world tree. Near this there is a wooden case with a glass side-panel, about three feet long, in which a blanket covered bundle reveals only a Maximón mask at one end. This is sometimes brought down for pilgrims to worship and there is evidence that it is a recent innovation, possibly copied from the *Santo Entierro* or 'Holy Burial of Christ' case kept on the main altar. The sides of the upper trellis bear some fifteen bundles of pilgrims' gifts of clothes: nothing of Maximón's should ever be destroyed. Recent gifts are kept in a box at the back of the *cofradía*. They are aired and the box is danced with at *fiesta* time.

The first modern mask is said to have been made by the 'prophet' *Nabeysil* Francisco Sojuel some fifty to seventy years ago. The *nabeysil* is, roughly, an equivalent of the *telinel* and looks after the Martín Bundle in *cofradía* San Juan. Sojuel then asked a certain Esteban Ajcot, also a quasi-deified ancestor, to make a second one since his was too small. While Nicolás Chiviliu was *Telinel*, around 1945, he asked his brother, an Esteban Chiviliu, to make a third. One mask, probably Sojuel's—said to hold to the head without strings—is never shown. The two others were those taken by Catholic priests in the raid of 1950. In 1953, one mask was found in Guatemala City and placed in a museum abroad. At this time, in Santa Cruz, there seemed to be again two masks in use: one for the glass case and one for the icon to wear when dressed.

It was said that many years before, the Maximón had enjoyed a *cofradía* of his own in the sacristy close to the Santa Cruz altar on the left side of the back of the church. Here there was also a sweatbath or *tuj*, where *aj'kuna*, the 'sons of Maximón,' used to gather and pray. This might have been an original *cofradía* San Miguel, staffed by sacristans, which by 1946 had been transferred to a private house. After an earthquake, *cofradía* Santa Cruz became the home of the Maximón. In 1952, *cofradía* San Miguel no longer appeared to exist and Santa Cruz alone celebrated the *Fiesta San Miguel*. But a little stone head carved at the apex of the sacristy dome was still pointed out to me as being the Maximón's. The double-headed bird *K'walk'oj* and a large snake are also said to have lived there.

While respects are paid to the Maximón all the year

round by *aj'kun*-guided pilgrims from all over the Highlands—especially San Pedro Sacatepéquez—the figure is only dressed, up on the trellis, on *Fiestas* San Miguel (September 29th) and San Andrés (November 30th) and, on the floor, during Holy Week. During this Easter Week, a little-known, somewhat-private series of rituals of the Maximón is carried out at the same time as the public ritual of Jesucristo at the church.

During the Fridays of Lent, 1953, groups of boys paraded in the night with imitation Maximóns on their shoulders. On Holy Monday, April 30th, a midnight washing of the Maximón's clothes took place in the Lake on three special stones kept each year with the previous year's Third *Cofrade*. There are indications that the washing water may have been drunk in the past for certain medecinal purposes. In my time, I only saw women drinking the water of the monthly washing of the Holy Burial's clothes. 'Clean' water from the middle of the Lake is used for the latter.

The clothes dried out on Tuesday morning in the compound of a house which had belonged to Francisco Sojuel. In the afternoon, an eight-foot-high wooden post was planted in a hole on the church porch floor, about a yard to the right of the main entrance (candles had been lit at this spot on the nights of the Fridays of Lent).

On Tuesday night, in the presence of the *Cabecera* and various officials, took place the most solemn dressing of the year: The *Telinel*, crouching in the middle of the room on a very large mat whose sides were held up by *cofrades* to shield him from sight, worked sitting astride the shawl-covered core. When the icon was dressed and raised, all present filed up to it and prayed—and some later danced three *sones* holding it in their arms—but the respect shown to this figure, especially by the *Telinel*, who slapped it on the back, calling it 'brave': and 'pretty boy' and keeping its mouth filled with cigarettes and cigarillos, was not as fervent—on this occasion in any event—as that paid to the Martín bundle in *cofradía* San Juan: when the Maximón once fell over, the *Telinel* was very leisurely about picking it up.

On Wednesday morning, the *Telinel* carried the Maximón on his shoulders—said to be a supremely difficult task—to the municipal building or *juzgado* where the icon was laid to rest in the middle of large piles of fruit brought from the Pacific coast and later used to adorn the main altar *monumento* in the church. At noon, the Maximón was carried to the post on the church porch, now decorated with leaves. It was strung up by Nicolás Chiviliu. The figure remained here, constantly attended, prayed to, incensed and candled until, after the exit of the dead Christ in procession from church on Holy Friday, it joined the end of the procession, then breaking off to go back to its *cofradía* and be dismantled.

In this context, the Maximón is said to be Judas Iscariot—but he is not, as elsewhere in the area, reviled in any way or destroyed at the end of Holy Week. One Atiteco had it that the present cult of the Maximón had begun only in the time of Francisco Sojuel. Before that it was a Judas of straw which was thrown into the cemetary, only the clothes being kept. Sojuel had decreed that it should be made of wood like the other saints.

All others consulted held that the Maximón had been created 'in the beginning of the world' and for most of them the association with Judas was tardy or irrelevant. [*They told the kind of origin stories which are being recorded in this present book.*] They claimed that it was the Maximón who called *aj'kuna* to their jobs and punished any refusal with illness or even insanity. To this day, provided he has the 'power of prayer' without which the Maximón would crush him on Holy Wednesday, a *telinel* is said to have certain powers over the icon to be used against sexual offenders.

There are also indications of the use of adverse magic.

Maximón magic, chiefly the curing of fever and madness (often connected with illegitimate sex: some say that the Maximón fathers cretins) is claimed to involve an *aj'kun* stationing a partner outside a house and speaking, when invoked, in a high, plaintive voice. In former times, boys are said to have done their courting disguised and in a high voice and there are rumors that Maximón impersonators likewise obtained the girl of their choice.

The Maximón is held to be a 'great traveler and walker.' He has a 'whore wife,' María or Magdalena Castellana— an echo of Mary Magdalen?—whose *fiesta* (October 7th) is held by Santa Cruz. In the early 1950s, this date fell outside my stay.

Atitecos calling the Maximón *rilaj acha* (the old, venerable man) and *Mam* affords a clue to the way in which an ancient Maya deity may have become associated with Holy Week.

FIRST: the ancient Maya had a deity called *Mam* whom they feasted on the *Uayeb* days marking the passage from one year to another. Both the following quotations from Spanish colonial sources appear in Alfred Tozzer's monumental edition of Diego de Landa's *Relación de las Cosas de Yucatán*, published by Harvard in 1941:

They had a piece of wood, which they dressed like those figures of boys made of straw that are used in bullfights and placed on a stool on a mat. They gave him food and gifts during the feast known as *Vayeyab*. When the feast was finished they undressed the idol and threw the piece of wood on the ground without troubling to reverence it any more. And they called it *Mam*, grandfather, whilst the offering and feast lasted. (Cogolludo)

The Indians feared those days, believing them to be unfortunate, and to carry danger of sudden death, plagues and other misfortunes. For this reason these five days were assigned for the celebration of the feast of the god *Mam*, 'Grandfather.' On the first day they carried him about, and feasted him with great magnificence; on the second day they diminished the solemnity; on the third they brought him down from the altar and placed him in the middle of the temple; on the fourth day they put him on the thresh-old of the door; and on the fifth, or last day, the ceremony of taking leave (or dismissal) took place, that the new year might commence on the following day . . . (Pio Pérez)

SECOND: there appear to be certain parallelisms between Atiteco Holy Week ritual and the *Uayeb* rites, among others: in the timing (a short week of five days) and the anti-clockwise processions to four temporary chapels in one case and the movement of idols to four corners of the town on the other.

THIRD: basing ourselves on a myth recorded by the French scholar Guy Stresser-Péan in the Huasteca of Northern Mexico, there is the possibility that the *Uayeb* rites are a ritual summary of a waning and waxing agricultural cycle, symbolized by young godlings who, after fertilizing the earth by union with their females, become old and degenerate, being later reborn after a drunken sleep. The last days of the year would naturally be ruled over by the old aspect of these gods, whose dying and subsequent rebirth, expressed as a crisis, could be associated with the Christian crisis of death and rebirth at Easter—often, in peasant societies, symbolizing the death and rebirth of crops.

There are other Catholic aspects of the Maximón. He is also said to be San Pedro, San Andrés, San Miguel and Pedro de Alvarado, Conquistador of Guatemala. Peter and Andrew are brothers; Peter was the first apostle; Andrew was the first called and Michael was the first of the angels. In the Yucatan, Michael is the leader of the *Chac* rain deities; in Atitlán he is patron of the *palo volador* dance (though this has not been performed for some years). As a knight, Michael may have been the link with Alvarado, or else the name Pedro.

The confusion of personalities appears to hinge a good deal on the name Simon, an interesting fact given the present-day etymology of Maximón as *Mam-Shimon* and frequent mention of Judas as Simon Judas. Peter is, of course, Simon Peter. Peter in Rome fought Simon Magus: a San Pedro Mar or Magro figures in church ritual during Holy Week and we find that Peter, a great healer, is, according to Ruth Bunzel, "holder of the keys of heaven and hell, identified with the masters of the medecine bundle, patron of diviners and sorcerers" in Chichicastenango. We should also remember that Pedro is the patron of Atitlán's sister village of San Pedro la Laguna. Don Pedro and San Simon are the names most frequently used for the Maximón by Atitecos, though, interestingly, *cofradía* Santa Cruz pays little attention to the feast of San Pedro.

St. Simon and St. Jude Thaddeus share one feast day and there is evidence of confusion between Jude and Judas in popular Catholicicsm. Guy Stresser-Péan, speaking of a feast of the hanged in the Huasteca, apparently associated with the old Maya hanged goddess *Ixtab,* recalls associations of the hanged Judas with Jude in Huastecan belief. Finally, "Judas, son of Simon" is a frequent reference in the New Testament. Add to all this the fact that, in the iconography, Peter, Andrew, Jude, and Simon are usually represented as old men and also note that Peter, as well as Judas, "betrayed" Christ. All of this should afford clues to the Atiteco reference to the Maximón as First Apostle, *"Primer Apóstol,"* and to resentment at the *Catequistas*'s insistence on treating the icon as Judas and nothing more.

Nicolás Chiviliu, perhaps confusedly, perhaps not, stated that, during Holy Week 1953, the visiting Catholic priest had spoken of "three Simons: 'Simon Sametaya' [*Thaddeo?*] in Paradise; 'Simon Peda' [*Pedro*]; and the Maximón who was the adornment, image or *representante* of the Simon in Paradise." The fact that the Maximón was only a representative—i.e. not a live god and therefore guiltless—was constantly used as an excuse for him during the events of 1952–3 and a number of *aj'kuna* even claimed that he was hardly dangerous in that "he did not talk any more."

There is a story that the "prophet" Francisco Sojuel was once saved from prison by the Maximón taking his place and sitting there, smoking cigars. There may be a connection with St. Peter's liberation from prison by an angel. Another connection may be with the story in the great pre-Conquest Maya text, the *Popol Vuh*, wherein the hero twins smoke cigars in the House of Gloom to mislead the Lords of Death. Of course, the Sojuel stories tend to be modeled on stories told about the ancestors (with a lesser possibility that ancestor stories were modelled on "facts" in Sojuel's biography or hagiography). See the story of the Power-Men merchants' escape from Antigua prison told here in Chapter Twelve.

The Maximón, then, is obviously a complex product of the mixture, at several levels and at various times, of Maya and Roman Catholic ritual and beliefs. Historical reconstruction is hampered at every step by lack of sufficient information with which to bridge the gap between the 16th century Spanish Conquest of Guatemala and the present day. Is the equivocal and ambiguous character of the Maximón already present in his precolumbian antecendents or is it entirely a product of the mixture of beliefs, in part agreeing, in part at odds with each other? Bisexuality; mono-polymorphism (*Mam-Mamlaab*, etc.); indeterminate moral status where "good" (youth) and "bad" (age) tend to be associated with the waxing and waning of crops, are all to some extent characteristic of many Maya deities.

It is difficult to unravel the strands of Maya and Catholic content in the fertility rites associated with the Martín Bundle and the Maximón. For instance: is the chastity required of the young fruit-bearers of Holy Week, without which the fruit will arrive unripe from the Pacific Coast, an example of Maya ritual chastity at times of great religious importance or is it a product of Catholic abstention? The Maximón breaks the sexual order which he has been created to set up and defend. He is ambiguous in witchcraft, attacking adulterers and *q'isoma'* witches whose main crime is adultery in bestial form but also living with a "whore" and seeming to connive in elopements and even rapes. Is all this the product of a specifically Maya dilemma or of Christian ethics confusing a fundamentally amoral (because linked to the birth and death of plants, animals and humans) Maya attitude?

The confusion was obviously abetted when the Maximón, whether in the time of Sojuel or, more probably before, became ritually Judas. In 1894, Brinton was already pointing out that "*nagualists' sodalities*" (his term, one believes, for groups of *aj'kuna* with animal familiar spirits) were dedicated to Judas and Pontius Pilate out of hatred for the church: it is probable that Sojuel, around the turn of the century, was a nativist *aj'kun*: that is, one who rebelled both politically and religiously against the *ladino* authorities, whether planters, municipal officials or priests.

When the Maya and Catholic dying and rebirth rites were blended at the time of the Conquest in the Holy Week ceremonies, was the *Mam* made into Judas by the Indians or by the priests? Both, perhaps, may have collaborated: the priests for obvious reasons; the Indians to mark their opposition to the God who had either destroyed the old religion or forced its deities to assume such debased new shapes. Frequent Atiteco references to a "death of the world" during the conflicts of 1952–3 always harked back to a blighting of the powers of ancient prophets and magicians, a diminution of sacredness in the life of the village, ever more increased by the continual disappearance of the old ways of doing things and the inroads of foreign intervention. No doubt such inroads began with the Spanish Conquest, four centuries before.

The idea at this time then is that part of the Maximón's ambiguity, if not all of it, is due to his being the vortex of a clash between two different religious solutions to the problem of disordered sexual activity. In one, such activity temporarily weakens nature but bypasses "sin" because it fertilizes the earth (Mam as part, or an aspect, of the natural force known as Martín) and another in which it irrevocably weakens sinful man in his relation to God (Mam-Judas). Continuing conflict over the Maximón as late as this, 1952–3, suggests that this agreement to disagree in a vital aspect of belief still underlies the peace, apparent only, of the continuing Conquest situation.

■   ■   ■

"The natural force known as Martín." It is hard to even begin to fully understand the Maximón without knowing something about the Martín:

Tarn, 1952–3:
It very soon becomes clear, in Atitlán, that not all *cofradías*, are equally important. A major one is clearly *cofradía* San Juan. Like Santa Cruz, it has an extra official beyond the *alcalde*, the *juez* and the six *cofrades*: in this case the *nabeysil*.

The *cofradía*'s room also has extra features. The ceiling trellis is not only hung with tropical leaves and fruit: it also features some twelve to thirteen stuffed raccoons. On a shelf near the door are disposed some thirty older stuffed animals, mostly racoons, plus odd bits of animal skin. A table opposite the altar bears several complete old deer skins, some with skulls and horns attached and two or three old jaguar skins. Under the table lies a two-tongued drum of pre-Conquest pattern: only *cofradías* of major ritual importance have these: Santa Cruz, San Juan, San Antonio, Santiago (the patron saint) and the Virgin Concepción. The altar bears three statues of San Juan—the largest and smallest holding a Bible surmounted by a lamb. There is also a little Virgin in a painted box. Two wooden cases on each side of the altar are rarely opened. One of them contains a bundle known, not as *San Martín* but as, simply, the Martín.

Cofradía San Juan celebrates two *fiestas*: San Juan's on June 24th and San Martín's on November 11th. San Martín's is also celebrated by *cofradías* San Antonio and San Nicolás, both of whose altars bear statues of San Martín on his horse. *Cofradías* San Juan and San Antonio are related in many ways: they share with *cofradía* Santiago the honor of performing extra ritual details in the transfer of power to new officials ceremonies at the end of the year. Both little San Juan and his corresponding Little San Antonio take the lead in all processions of saints to and from the church.

A dance of the Martín is performed in San Juan on seven major *fiestas*: those of San Juan, San Martín, Santiago, Holy Week, Todos Santos, Corpus Christi and New Year. Thus, San Juan is busy all the year round. The Martín is the only icon present in more than one *cofradía*: it is also found in two private houses, called *cofradías*, by extension: *cofradía* San Martín Particular (which has a bundle) and another which has a statue: these appear to be hereditarily-held cult places. [*In 1979, as one might have expected given the relationship between the two saints: patron of wild animals/of domestic animals, the equivalent of a bundle was found in* cofradía San Antonio.]

The official in charge of the Martín Bundle in San Juan, the *nabeysil*, is, like the *telinel* in Santa Cruz, an *aj'kun* and wields considerable power in the village as an intercessor. Like the *telinel*, he should have a special power (*nuwal*) or feeling for the job without which he could not lift the Bundle. Like the *telinel*, he should remain chaste in office but the office, ideally, should be held for life. He is responsible for the dance of the Martín. The word *nabeysil* is usually held to mean 'first (*nabe*) throne (*silla*).'

The dance was the most esoteric element in Atiteco ritual: in 1952–3, no village *ladino*, however old a resident or well-versed in Indian custom, seemed to know of it and most young Indians had very woolly notions about it.

Tarn, 1952–3:

On the evening of November 10th, 1952, *fiesta* San Martín, the *cofradía* was full of *cofrades*, members of the *Alcalde's* family and visiting *aj'kuna*. A marimba played behind the drum table. On the altar table, in front of the statues, lay a rectangular bundle, some twenty-four by twelve inches, covered in red cloth, slit horizontally along the top. On the narrow slit lay five small flat rectangular cakes of hardened corn meal. On the bundle's left lay a small apron of old, distressed cloth with little wooden, colonial-style *putti* faces sewn onto it.

A half hour before midnight, the *Nabeysil* gave the signal for the rite to begin. Four young men seized the skins on the drum table. Two put on *masat*, deer costumes, composed of a head-to-ankle length back piece bearing the skull and horns decorated with a criss-cross pattern of green and red cotton ribbons and a square, waist-to-knee apron piece, tied with string to the shoulders of the back piece and held primly out in front of him by the deer while dancing. The two *bajlam*, jaguars, wore back pieces only and each carried a stuffed squirrel in hand. The marimba played and the four dancers moved in circles, hopping from foot to foot and swaying from side to side, occasionally whirling round in one spot. The jaguars emitted long low whistles and sharp cries and pawed the backs of the deer with the squirrels. Four times, the group knelt abruptly, one behind the other, and crossed themselves, thus saluting the four cardinal directions at three to four minute intervals in the dance. They then went into the courtyard, performed again, returned, kissed the drum table and lit a candle in front of the drum, took off the costumes and danced again, this time saluting eight directions.

All the while, one individual said to be the leading jaguar and 'very wise in the dance' swung an incense burner over and around them. This man, with one assistant, now repeated the dance as the deer and, in the courtyard, a real battle was enacted, the deer striking with his horns and the jaguar assistant with teeth and paws. Eventually the deer died, climbed onto the jaguar's back and was carried into the *cofradía*. Costumes were taken off and the leader danced once again, alone, more leisurely, with knees flexed, the legs passing alternately in front of each other, arms held out, palms straight and facing inward.

At midnight, the *Nabeysil* ordered the doors and windows of the *cofradía* to be tightly shut, approached the altar and knelt before the Bundle. From under the corn cakes, he extracted a short beige shirt covered with designs resembling conventionalized tongues of flame. This he put on while lit candles were distributed among the now silent congregation. With much deliberation, he then danced in a similar fashion to the jaguar 'leader,' motioning people out of the way, his eyes closed as if in a trance. After dancing to the four corners of the room, he stopped with his back to the drum table, leaning slightly against it, arms outstretched sideways, legs crossed at the shins, head lolling on the right shoulder, face (constantly wiped by attendant *cofrades*) anguished— as if crucified. Only one person, when asked, associated this with Christ's crucifixion, stressing the fact that the right leg should be over the left. He was from the *cofradía* San Martín Particular, whose dancer observed this pattern. The San Juan *Nabeysil* was inconsistent.

One by one, *cofrades* in the lead, the congregation knelt before him, crossing themselves and kissing his belly, hand and feet. One man kissed the belly as altars are kissed: centre point, point to the left, point to the right. A *cofrade* began beating the two-tongued drum and the marimba, silent during the homage, joined in. The congregation then kissed each altar saint—as is the custom in all *cofradías* after each ritual—while the *Nabeysil* went back to the Bundle, took off the shirt, crossed himself to the four directions and repeated the performance.

I never witnessed the 'crucified' position again though, on other occasions, I saw the *Nabeysil* carrying the corn cakes or the whole Bundle. Usually the dance is done some three times during each *fiesta*, as close to noon or midnight as faulty watches and general inebriation allow. The deer and jaguar dances usually precede it and their dancers, said by some to be *aj'kuna* in training, also precede the *cofrades* to church when they inform San Juan on his altar there that they have taken his *cofradía* in charge for one year.

On one of my last evenings in Santiago, I saw the *Nabeysil*, very drunk and reluctant to dance, drop the Bundle. After a moment of stunned silence, all present rushed to the altar, knelt and prayed frantically. The *Nabeysil* was then held up by the *Alcalde* and the deer-dancers until the dance was over. I knew that the *Nabeysil* had recently asked the *principales* to relieve him of his charge—in vain . . .

What is the meaning of all this?

First, note that the Indian belief in *dueños* (lords), the supernatural owners of the various aspects of nature, blended satisfactorily, in the *cofradía* system, with Catholic belief in patron saints. While San Antonio is the Atiteco *dueño* of domestic animals, San Juan looks after the wild ones, said to be "of God": their skin can be sold and flesh eaten but their bones must "go back to the hills from which they came." Hence the stuffed raccoons and skins brought in by successful hunters: *cofradía* San Juan may well be conceptually "the inside of a hill."

The deeper one pries, the more *dueño*ships are found to drift from the control of ordinary *cofradía* saints into the hands of Martín, until one finds him as the head of all the *dueños* who act as subservient "angels" at his royal command. In this context, he is usually called *Rey* Martín, the King. It is believed that only at noon and midnight can the Bundle be safely opened: otherwise all the winds would break out of it and "wreak havoc in the whole world." In any case, doors and windows are shut during openings and the bottom shirt, being the most "powerful," is never brought out. When the Martín emerges at these times "he must walk about over the hills and volcanos and all the Departments to give orders to his angels. The houses of the angels are in the hills and valleys and clouds where they work and give the plants and food and the rain." San Martín is patron of Cerro de Oro, a small volcanic hill with a village near it which is a dependency of Atitlán's: many hill *dueños* live, own treasures and hold *fiestas* in there. Some older Atitecos voiced a belief in "about three or four or six huge volcanos, situated in some other country or part of the world which, at noon or midnight, become the resting places for the throne of heaven." This begins to sound like the ancient Maya *Bacab* which stood at the cardinal points to hold up the sky.

The dance, in the *Nabeysil*'s words is "a kind of confession, not of sins, but for the asking of beans and corn since we Atitecos are poor people." Seed corn, indeed, is often blessed in the *cofradía* before the box of the Martín Bundle.

For Nicolás Chiviliu, the Martín was "the *dueño* of the whole world, older than any other saint and father to all of them. Each village might have its Martín but it is also true that never in all my travels have I seen a Bundle like ours and therefore it is true that Atitlán is *r'muxux jap*, the navel of rain, and *r'muxux ulew*, the navel of earth, the center of the world." He also enumerated, among the hosts of heavenly beings, twelve principal Martíns, twelve Marías and twelve Angels. The numbers twelve and thirteen derive from Maya calendric day names, as well, it appears, as the twelve Apsotles—thirteen when including Christ. While this might have arisen from an *aj'kun* rhetorical device in prayers—citing a basic name, then making a long list by repeating it with secondary name attached—he did produce lists for me of this "company of the Holy World": a heterogeneous crew of Catholic angels and arch-angels, saints, Maya calendric day names, wind names, ritual object personifications (god-incense; god-candle, etc.), personages from Spanish-Indian *fiesta* dances (kings, soldiers, demons) and, this is most important, certain dead human beings who turn out to have been dead Atiteco *nabeysila*. Subsequently, such lists seemed fairly widespread among Atitecos.

213

The Marías appear to be subordinated to the angel-faced cloth, kept in the other box in the *cofradía*, which represents *Yaxper* (usually María Isabel or María Ana), "a very old woman of ancient times, crippled and bent but still powerful who opens the path for children" and is prayed to by the *iyoma'*, the midwives, female equivalents to the male *aj'kuna*. Some called the cloth a representation of the "insides of a woman" (*las tripas*). Sick children are sometimes clothed in little red and green shirts contained in the box for a while by *iyoma'* or *aj'kuna* called in by their family. The association of human, animal and vegetal fertility and well-being, so strong in all Maya ritual, is thus consecrated in *cofradía* San Juan.

During one dance of the Martín, some *cofrades*, usually impervious, pointed out that thunder could be heard and rain could be expected. The nature of this performance as a rain-making ritual appears most clearly in accounts of dead *nabeysila* said to have lived some fifty to seventy years before Tarn's time in Santiago: "In those days, whenever the village needed rain, Santiago, San Juan and San Antonio were clothed in green 'cloaks of rain.' The Bundle was brought out and various tricks were performed such as lifting the *cofradía* table into the air by going up to it and making as if to bite it. Then there were processions which brought on the rain. There was also another custom after the rain to ask for the sun back and at this point red cloaks were worn by the saints."

The colors of these capes suggest a meaning for the deer antler ribbons, the shirts in the *Yaxper* box and the procession saint-carrying stretchers found all over the Guatemala Highlands. Today, in Atitlán, a rain-making ceremony is performed by the main *aj'kuna* at the mid-point of five official sowing-of-maize dates on *fiesta* san Felipe (February 5th), but Tarn found no trace of a sun ceremony: perhaps this is no more than a rite to stop floods. The respective positions of the San Juan and San Martín *fiestas* suggest the possibility of a connection to the equinoxes.

Finally, there are the twelve ancestor figures, the "merchants" from our stories of the creation of the Maximón. Some of the names of these ancestors reappear in the lists of twelve *dueños* used by *aj'kuna*, strongly suggesting that the *dueños*, angels and ancestors are transforms of each other. One part of a story is particularly interesting. The ancestor brothers are locked up in an Antigua prison after killing an enormous monster with the aid of the Double-Headed Hawk, the *K'walk'oj*. Their sisters or wives or female aspects bring them the shirts of the Martín. Putting them on, the brothers dance and arouse a great storm which destroys Antigua and sets them free, an event witnessed by all the great cats in the land gathered on a mountain top—perhaps the animal familiars of the brothers. A similar adventure is said to have befallen Francisco Sojuel, the most famous of recent "prophet" *nabeysila*, and led to the creation of the Bundle in one of the *cofradías* San Martín Particular.

What of the designs on the shirts? The "flame" pattern on them resembles closely the pattern on the conventionalized fleece (actually camel hair but fleece to Atitecos) worn by statues of St. John the Baptist and may represent this. Perhaps the Baptist's preceding of the Christ and living in the desert associated him with the old gods of the wild. Another anthropologist suggested the shirts might be related to the cape shared with a beggar by the original Saint Martín.

Various elements in the Martín cult suggest that the shirts might be connected with the precolumbian custom of wearing sacrificed human skins by priests of Xipe Totec, the Flayed God. This is not a Maya divinity—but the Maya of this region were affected by Central Mexican ideas. Historical literature refers to dances not unlike the deer and jaguar dance here—though featuring other animals as well—taking place as late as 1620 at Mazatenango (Town of Deer), a town closely linked by trade with Atitlán and also, one suspects, by religion: many of the "angels" of the Martín are patrons of villages in the Mazatenango area. The great Mayanist J.E.S. Thompson has felt that the Mazatenango dances were "almost certainly" associated with Xipe Totec.

Further back still, the precolumbian *Popol Vuh* gives the deerskin as a symbol of a major god Tohil, associated with rain, thunder and human sacrifice. Tohil was the god of Jaguar Quitzé, first of the Quiché ancestors (of which there were four, the last, in some accounts, unmarried) who, upon dying, left to his sons a *Pizom Gagal*, a "fiery bundle of Majesty" as a "symbol of his being." In Dennis Tedlock's translation, the passage runs as follows:

> And then Jaguar Quitzé left a sign of his being: 'This is for making requests of me. I shall leave it with you. Here is your fiery splendor. I have completed my instructions, my counsel,' he said when he left the sign of his being, the Bundle of Flames, as it is called. It wasn't clear just what it was; it was wound about with coverings. It was never unwrapped. Its sewing wasn't clear because no one looked on while it was being wrapped.

A few pages before this occurs, there is an interesting account of how Tohil and two other ancestor gods, or their visible familiar spirits, go to bathe in a river and are tempted by two daughters of enemy chiefs. The chiefs tell the daughters to bring back a "sign" that they have seen the three gods. Then, it is said, Tohil and the others plotted with the penitents and sacrificers and were told:

> 'You must draw figures on three cloaks. Inscribe them with the signs of our being. . . . they'll go back with the maidens who are washing. . . .'
>
> After that they drew figures for all three of them. Jaguar Quitzé drew first: his image was that of the jaguar. He drew it on his cloak.
>
> And as for Jaguar Night, he drew the image of an eagle on his cloak.
>
> And the one who drew next was Mahucutah, who drew the images, the figures of swarms of yellow jackets, swarms of wasps on his cloak.

When the girls take the cloaks back to the chiefs, two lords try on the first two capes with delight and without harm. When a third lord tries on the *last* cloak, he is violently stung and "defeated." Subsequently the enemies of the Quiché Maya often succumb to wasps.

In a note on the *Pizom Gagal* (our *Q'aq'al*) bundle in his *Popol Vuh* translation, Adrian Recinos refers to the Conquest-period writer Torquemada's mention, in his *Monarquía Indiana,* of a Central Mexican bundle, the *Haquimilolli* made of the mantles of dead gods in which they wrapped some sticks with green stones and the skins of snakes and jaguars: this was their principal divinity.

It is clear from precolumbian data that some relation was thought to exist in ancient Maya ritual between a god, his sacrificial victim (human or animal substitute) and the priest who impersonated the god, especially when wearing the victim's skin. Clearly too, there is a relation in modern Atitlán between the dead *nabeysila* and the gods in the forms of the Martín's angels. Can we also see an equation between the living *nabeysil* and a victim whose symbols might be the *nabeysil* himself or the murdered "deer" of the deer and jaguar dance, or the shirt/skins worn in the Martín dance? At no stage was the *nabeysil* said to be the Martín, but the observed ritual and the respect shown him, taken together with the belief that the great *dueño* comes out at noon and midnight certainly suggests an impersonation.

The Mayanist Alfred Tozzer, quoting his colleague Ralph Roys, tells us: "Roys points out that Crucifixion was associated with the worship of the rain gods and the *cenote* [*deep sacrificial well found especially in the Yucatan*] cult and that . . . one of the first missionaries reported that the Cross was adored as a god of water and rain." Early "Nativistic," that is anti-Spanish, movements among the Maya featured crucifixions of children and adults as part of rain ceremonies, a fact which may afford a clue to the origin of the apparently "crucified" position of the *nabeysil* in the dance.

Finally, note that the *Nabeysil* described here had a shrivelled leg and limped. The great Conquest commentator Sahagún, among the Aztecs, writes about disease and the rain gods (*Tlalocs*): "The various diseases for which they made promises to the *Tlalocs* were the gout . . . also contractions of the tendons in any part of the body. . . . or contractions of any member, limbs or arms, or for paralysis. . . . They also said that if anyone suffered from a shrivelled hand or foot. . . . all this happened to him because the *Tlalocs* were angry with him." Whether the modern rain priest of Atitlán's impairment can be linked to this or not, Tarn was not certain.

An interesting observation was made by Ruth Bunzel when studying the Quiché Maya village of Chichicastenango:

> The vegetative aspect of the earth is worshiped under the name of Diego Martín, a name arbitrarily chosen when the first missionaries forbade the use of the names of the ancient gods. By verbal analogy he is identified with San Martín, who thereby has become *dueño* of the earth, and his day (November 11th) is observed with ceremonies at mountain shrines. . . .

San Juan, in Chichicastenango, is "identified with the forces of destiny that rule men's lives." He is apparently the giver of familiar spirits and of the "*suerte*" or fate of each individual, and each child must be presented to him at birth: something familiar to us from the Yaxper rituals within *cofradía* San Juan.

In summary, it would seem that some beliefs apparently as old as any obtainable today in the Maya area have both reacted upon and been influenced by the deeds of certain native priests, *aj'kuna* and *nabeysila* of the turn of the century, like Francisco Sojuel's when, borrowing a shirt from the Martín Bundle he created *cofradía* San Martín Particular after supposedly escaping from a deluge and a fire and the hands of his enemies. The older the Atiteco, the more he sees an equation, or even an identity, between the *dueño* gods, ancestors and a long line of *nabeysila* who have come to the rescue of Atitlán in times of great need. Today, unusual, crippled, retarded, or eccentric individuals are still sometimes granted miraculous powers and Atitecos are constantly on the look out for such characters, despite many young peoples' assurances to the contrary. Even Tarn, after participating in certain rituals and helping with the return of the Maximón to church, was referred to as "the son of Francisco Sojuel" and occasionally referred to—friends told him—as Sojuel himself and as a "god."

The beliefs associated with the Martín, then, represent a survival of a cyclical view of history in which both problems and those who solve them recur in a similar fashion time after time. Similar but not identical since circumstances are bound to change, these problems always involve a mechanism of salvation based, in the last resort, on the original model of the rain priest's salvation of natural abundance through his own special "power" or "destiny."

■   ■   ■

In 1952–3, puzzling as to how to make sense of the Maximón and the conflicts surrounding that icon without neglecting the possibly older Martín complex, Tarn tried to argue that the Martín aspect of Atiteco world-view would conflict with the Judaeo-Christian tradition of history seen as a purely linear succesion of discrete events. That conflict would express itself in terms of a third view, sharing the repetitive nature of the first but also the linear nature of the second—in a "death of the world" afflicting natural and human powers whose origin may well have been the trauma of the Conquest itself. The dualistic Maximón would be the symbolic vortex of this third view.

Tarn also wondered, thinking of the Maximón and sexuality, whether the fundamental crisis in the coming together of the Indian and Spanish world views did not occur when a theory of sin brought about by disordered sexual behavior, yet somehow neutralized by the consequent fertilization of nature clashed with another theory of sin similarly incurred but only expiable through a divine moral law at odds with any pagan salvation through fertility.

There were many problems with this. One was that it neglected the extent to which Folk Catholicism too was cyclical, especially as it might have expressed itself in its 16th century ritualism. More importantly, Tarn did not yet appreciate the extent to which the Maximón himself was a *dueño* in the old style. This begins to be shown in the story, first heard in 1979 and told in Chapter Ten, of how the Mam became the youngest of the angels. But there is a great deal more to it than this and it will need another book before the whole tale can be told.

SEVENTEEN

The Primer Mayor's Tale: I

Prechtel, 1979:

Well, you know that with the ever-accelerating growth in the importance of a money economy, people are unable or unwilling to take on religious responsibilities. The result is that people are elected to *aj'kun* positions who want them for the wrong reasons. You get senior positions filled by people who have not gone through the ladder of services. They have no idea how to behave. They behave like *nouveaux riches*; they have no manners. There are all sorts of scandals and quarrels and complaints to the *Cabecera* and the Council of *principales*. A great deal of distasteful political behavior was associated with all this: individuals had to have a *Cabecera* who would suit their needs.

So, all of a sudden, you had this hateful and hated man Makuxtin in charge of *cofradía* Santa Cruz. Perhaps as few as two of his people had any previous experience. He kept on having problem after problem, hiring and firing *telinels* by the week.

Now at this time around the end of 1978, I'm in the *cofradía* to do some *costumbre* and Makuxtin announces he has a man who has promised him the Holy Week fruit— the fruit that are put up as ornaments on the huge wooden *monumento* in church. . . . It's that structure built with old colonial pillars and architectural bits and pieces that covers the main altar statues at Holy Week. There is no need for anyone to do anything more: he will take complete charge.

The tradition is that the young *alguaciles* go to the Pacific

Coast and bring the fruit home on their backs, abstaining from intercourse with their wives all through the arduous proceedings. But Makuxtin has decided to modernize! The fruit is going to come up by truck; the ritual of the Mam 'sleeping with the fruit' in the municipality building before going to the church will not be done: the Mam will go straight to his chapel and the fruit is going to come the same day with the *corozo,* the great flower of the Cohune palm. 'What about the cypress?' says I. 'Oh, any fool can bring the cypress,' he said. 'Anyway that's their problem!' 'Theirs, who?!' says I. He did not answer. Then he wanted a *marimba* and I pointed out that the Mam was not supposed to have one at that time . . . well, he had it all figured out and figured out dead wrong.

Now. *Alcaldes* Santiago and San Antonio, who are of the same ilk, are teamed up together against Makuxtin because of personal problems: land quarrels and such. Makuxtin's Santa Cruz had not attended any of the *Cabecera*'s Council meetings for six months and had not participated in procession or done duty in church allegedly because the Committee for Reconstruction had taken the *cofradía's* alms from the Santa Cruz box in church—which is what Makuxtin is really upset about. Then the Committee tells Makuxtin that, if he looks after the fruit, he'll get the money back. He's happy.

This is now January 1979 and the Council is deciding where Santiago and Santa Cruz are going to go. There is a lot of friction because the latter, after Makuxtin, is going to Marianda, someone who has just had a *cofradía* when you are supposed to rest for at least a year. The proposed Marianda is accused of having bribed for this—which happens to be true. So now Makuxtin, who would like to add Santiago to his laurels, is felt to have no money for his own *costumbre* and still, despite *his* lack of rest, to want Santiago which is the most expensive *cofradía* of the whole village!

At this time, there was also a lot of politicking around as to who would be *Cabecera*. Some wanted the old *Cabecera*, Maxikay, Mr. Stick, who had been responsible for allowing the ranks of *alcila* and *mayori* to be abolished at the municipality; who had thrown everyone out of Concepción after a big fight so that Concepción had no *cofrades*; who had gone along with the Committee in their seizure of the alms and had also taken a lot of bribes. There had been some three-way land deal going on between Maxikay, Makuxtin and Marianda and everyone thought this was a terrible way for *cofradía* people to behave.

The person they ended up by getting as *Cabecera* was Cristóbal Esquina Yataz, a man who had made an enemy of the *Catequistas* for some action against them years before. This Cristóbal Yataz happened to be a friend of Eyes and a friend of mine. This got Felipe Tuiz and some of my other enemies and rivals mad. Felipe Tuiz is the young man who was in my musical group and was trained as a linguist by the *gringo* Huehuetenango School of Linguistics. Little by little, for very complex reasons, he became my rival and enemy.

The election of Esquina Yataz looked planned to these rivals but actually it was coincidence: the *Alcaldes* Antonio and Santiago had put him in against Makuxtin who had wanted Maxikay. These two *Alcaldes* had been terrible to Maxikay with the result that no one, but *no one*, came to the Council sessions . . . So Makuxtin is glaring at everybody out of his crazy yellow eyeballs, mad as hell about Yataz and everything else.

Meantime, all the *aj'kuna*, including Chiviliu, are going to other Mam icons around town, saying that the Santa Cruz one no longer has any power or has left Santa Cruz to live elsewhere. Well, *Alcalde* San Antonio begins to say there is no way Makuxtin can be trusted with the fruit business. Makuxtin's donor should simply hand the fruit over to the *principales*. Then the Committee starts getting grand illusions and their president, pompous old Nicolás Chávez, decides that he could be *primer mayor* and get a lot of public political acceptance that way. He and his Committee decide that the alms money they had taken could be used for that. But where would they put the fruit and how would they bring it? They still talked of trucks because they couldn't imagine anyone bringing it without being obliged to, as they had done in the old days.

For my part, I was thinking that, with my little *conjunto*, I could at least do the cypress part properly: I had been with the cypress parties a couple of times and knew what to do.

One day, I run into *Alcalde* Santiago (not Makuxtin yet, of course!) at the hospital and tell him about that idea. He perks up and starts saying that there is nowhere for the fruit to go. At this point, I say that I have a big room in my house, in a separate building, and think my landlord would approve because he is a *costumbrista*. *Alcalde* Santiago perks up some more: 'Oh,' he goes, 'can I tell *Cabecera* about that?' and I say, 'sure,'—which is the right way to go: you tell an *alcalde* and he tells the *Cabecera*.

A week later I get called by the Council and repeat my offer. No this was *not* a bid to be *primer mayor* at the time: it was just a question of offering the house. And the Council certainly said nothing. They told me to be at the next meeting, which corresponded to *fiesta* San Felipe around February 4th. I come to this huge meeting: there must have been some seventy people there, unusual at the time: even *Alcalde* San Antonio is there! Well, I'm just standing against the wall, listening to everything and they call for Makuxtin.

In he came, flashing his eyes and chewing his gum and popping and snapping about. All of a sudden, *Alcalde* Santiago says, pointing to me, 'Well, I think this guy should be made *primer mayor.*' Now he was doing this to mess up Makuxtin, you understand, not because he had any great love for me! And everybody said, 'Yeah! it's a great idea!' And I said (Makuxtin glaring a hole into the back of my neck), 'Well, look . . . ,' and there was this tremendous silence.

So the formal way for this to happen is that the *Cabecera* stands up and says, 'This is how we could do it. What do you think each one of you?' and then each one stands and says his piece. But, here, everyone stood up together and said, 'fine': I had done them each many a little service, you know, and I guess that it all, over time, added up. So they went through the big spiel: 'This guy has not killed, has not thieved, has not robbed, has never spoken badly, has never gone to jail, has never mixed in politics etc. . . . all in all, this guy is fine!'

Then, suddenly pompous old Chávez pops up and says, 'Well, we were thinking . . . but seeing we have a new member, our friend . . .' (he would never say 'our brother' of course), 'and he comes from another place and has a good heart and is going to help us out with our problems . . . ,' which, translated, meant 'to hell with you but O.K., we'll take your money,' and everyone knew that. As for Makuxtin, he has already ground his teeth to dust by this time.

So I got up and made a long speech about the honor . . . : 'But we are so close to the time already and what about the *alcila* and the materials . . . and my wife is still a child,' and so forth. Whereupon *Alcalde* San Antonio told me not to worry: he had pots, dishes, poles—I could have them all; the Committee promised help; *Alcalde* Santiago said he had been *primer mayor* and would give me all the counsel I required plus two of his men who had been *mayori* and two others who could help with the fruit—but, note, they were all still thinking the fruit would come by truck.

Then I made a ceremonial speech which they like to

hear because it lifts all of this off the mundane level. 'What I don't want,' I said, 'is to make enemies. Because I've got plenty of those already,' and I made a joke of it, 'this urinated white-assed *gringo* who is not an Indian,' and everyone cracks up and says, 'Well to hell with those who speak against you, we run this town and have the say-so.' To avoid hard feelings I suggested it might be good for them to take my house and get someone else to be *primer mayor*.

At that point they asked Makuxtin what he thought. He said, 'No! there's no way you can give this honor to this outsider because I've already had dreams about it and all this was born in my house: the truck idea and the fact that this donor gave me the fruit and what have you.' So the principales asked, 'What donor gave you the fruit?' This had never been clarified. Then they tried to tell M. very patiently that no one could do two *costumbres* at once and, 'Look, where are you? here you are without even a *telinel* and you want to do the Mam and also to be *primer mayor* and it's very rare even for a *primer mayor* to do it all because it is so difficult . . . and having these two things in the same house, come on! It's impossible!'

So M. walked out. But the terrible thing was that, as he walked out, his pants' zipper had come undone and there he was, er . . . hanging out and everybody was holding their heads from the *Cabecera* on down while his penis was going up and down and finally *Alcalde* Santiago said, 'You'd better zip up your pants because there's old Estrada Cabrera sitting out there sunning herself,' (the idea being that he might get a hard-on with this old *ladina* lady you understand . . .). So there is Makuxtin zipping up his pants and stomping out more rabid than ever.

What had happened about the fruit was that the little donor on the Coast who had made the offer had had a dream some twenty years before that, if he promised to give the fruit, he would get a large harvest. This worked out. So, now came time for the 'payment' and he came looking for the *mayori* who should have been nominated (but for those ranks having being abolished) on the *fiesta* San Martin in the previous November. Actually: he would look for the second *mayor* who is in charge of the fruit, the *primer mayor* being in charge of the whole *costumbre*.

This man, Second *Mayor* 1978, had suddenly become a Protestant and told the donor that there would be no *mayori* in 1979. So the donor went to the *Cabecera*. But the *Cabecera* was in trouble then. Finally, he goes to Santa Cruz and falls right into the jaws of Makuxtin. Now Makuxtin pretended to the Council that he had bought baskets and *kakaxtes*, carrying boxes, and all sorts of equipment—this turned out to be untrue.

What had happened now is that I, basically, had been named *Alcalde* of a *cofradía Frutas*, with Chávez and the Committee finding the young helpers and everything else! Ridiculous! I was going to put in two members: they were not to be called *alcila* because Nicolás Chávez was trying to prevent my being called *primer mayor*. Chávez's plan was to put in himself, another friend and *Alcalde* Rosario who had land on the Coast. So we all decided to go to the Coast to check on how much Makuxtin had actually spent and also to talk to a *marimba* group.

The day that Makuxtin had walked out, my rival Felipe Tuiz went to him and warned him against me. Makuxtin went to the Coast with a friend and made all sorts of accusation against 'the *gringo*.' So I sent to the Coast the man who would be *primer alguacil* if I got in and two guys who would become *corozo* palm *alcila*, to find the fruit donor. After explanations the donor said he would give to us and only us and come to a Council meeting in Atitlán to confirm this. The *marimba* people stated that, yes, they had been given fifty dollars—but it was for three *tocadas*, sets of music, only, whereas a *primer mayor* should have six.

Things were getting very complicated with Tuiz and co. At that point, Makuxtin comes on the Radio flinging accusations right and left. Everyone is saying, 'They won't even let the *Cabecera* on the radio; how come this Makuxtin is allowed in?'

'Ah,' I said, 'it's Tuiz . . . He's president of the Radio and he's using this old Santa Cruz dog Makuxtin to have his own say!' Then the Radio speakers pitched in, telling the people that Makuxtin would give the fruit and not this damned *gringo*, etc. In the end, I said, 'Let Makuxtin give the fruit; it's not worth all this trouble!' But the *principales* said, 'No, no, no. We are not going to let this clown do the *costumbre* after insulting us so terribly!' So we talked to the *Cabecera* and he started wising up. We proposed a bunch of ten *alcila* who would go for the fruit and suggested we need not bother with the use of the Radio at all.

Well, the 11th of February comes and we are all waiting for the people from the Coast. I had gone home on instructions from the *Cabecera* to take off my black wool *mangax* coat worn as flutist because we were now on probation. I was having problems with getting a show of my paintings together in Antigua; people coming in for cures; my wife saying she wasn't ready to be a Mrs. *Primer Mayor*; her father saying he didn't want hassles in the house. The suspense was killing me. I went to the church before the call and there was no one. But, in the meeting hall, there was every *cofrade* I had ever seen in my life plus two national and two town policemen in case anything sparked out. Then, with some three hundred ex *mayori* and *alcila* looking on, in walk Tuiz and the Radio people with Makuxtin right out in front. They sit down.

Then it turns out that the fruit-giver has not shown up on the bus. But, all of a sudden, there is this little barefoot guy in front of the church and someone is yelling, 'There he is! There he is!': He had missed the bus and taken a truck and walked into the church to do a prayer. Makuxtin clapped eyes on him and ran out. Everyone shouted, 'Hey! we're in session, where are you going?' and that's when everyone really started hating the man: 'What kind of a clown is this guy anyway? Just like a woman, you know, getting mad all of a sudden when nothing has happened yet; no dignity whatsoever, etc. etc.' And his *cofrades* are hiding their faces because he was making fools of them.

The *Cabecera* gets up and orders Chávez to tell what happened on the Coast. Chávez gets on his soap box and tells everyone where things are at. Well, he no more than gets three words out and Makuxtin starts bubbling, 'Ehbbblllbbbblllbbbbbblllllll,' you know, 'Bbblllbbbblll-bbbbblllll,' and everybody says, 'Aw! For God's sake, we haven't said anything yet to anybody, so for Christ's sake shut up!' but M. would just not shut up. And M. was stomping about there, backwards and forwards, going, 'Er, yes, er, yes, er, no, err, grr,' losing his *mangax*, on and on, and the *Cabecera* saying, 'No, we speak one by one here to see what each has to say and what each has decided,' and Makuxtin getting all the time more and more violent. Then the *Cabecera* got up and said, 'Look! I'm the *Cabecera* here and you, you bloody well sit down!!!' So Makuxtin went on a full half hour growling and gnashing his teeth and his people were trying to hold him down and finding it incredible that anyone could keep it up for that long!

Finally *Alcalde* Santiago gets up and starts tearing into Makuxtin. Goes through everything wrong that M. had ever done, and M. turns more and more colors. Tuiz is whispering to himself, 'He just doesn't stand firm; he just *doesn't* stand firm!' then all the *principales pasados* let him have it one by one, because they haven't even gotten into the nub of the subject yet! But M. keeps on shouting that he has lots of money and there is no need to give the fruit to that idiot *gringo*: 'What do you want with him? Tomorrow or the next day, he's out of this town because I've given him a *puub-chay*, a lightning-blood...'

'Oh, so you're a witch are you, ha, well, if you're such a good witch you must have witched your own grandson and killed *him*. And if you had so much money why did you borrow my tables and pots and pans when you did in Santa Cruz?' Insult after insult and, 'Why did you buy a woman's sweater in the market and why are you wearing it back to front?': They hit him with absolutely everything they'd got and we thought he would explode or have a nervous breakdown there and then or a heart attack, and 'Argh, argh, arrrrgh, arrrrrgh,' he's screeching, and the crowd starts yelling, 'Throw him over the church steps! Throw the bum out!'—I've never seen anything like it before or since—'Throw him out of Chukumuk! Bash his head in!' and all the ex-*mayori* got up and were going to grab him and throw him over something or other you can be *sure* and people were telling him he only wanted the *costumbre* to make money out of it and *ad infinitum*!

So the *Cabecera* roars for everyone to stop and desist and the poor little guy from the Coast is asked what his mission is and the words do not come out. After a long while the words start rolling: 'Well, because God is in the sky and because . . .' and the others: 'Oh, Hell! we know where God is! Let's get this shit over with!' and he's going on about the whereabouts of God and M. is going, 'Bbbbllll, er, bbbbbbllllllll,' so the *Cabecera* finally says, 'Look! we'll make it easy for you: this is what we heard and this is what we want to know and . . . are you going to give the fruit or not and, if you are, then to whom?'

Finally the people are screaming, 'Give it to the *Cabecera*! Give it to the *Cabecera*!' with everyone holding M. and his guys down—they were mad as hell now, they were going to kill M. for sure—and *finally* the little man says, 'I will give it to the *Cabecera*' and a roar goes up from the people and M. is trying to leave with his usual way of walking out backward, his sweater turned back to front, screaming and yelling until we thought the air would go out of him! The little kids chased him and stoned him all the way back to his *aj'kun* and there he was, having insulted me all week on the Radio without my doing anything, and suddenly the people had revolted.

This had been a victory and so we sat down and had something to drink. And after a while the speeches began again: 'Well, if you are going to be *primer mayor*, you are blind, you haven't been born yet, you haven't seen the light,' and all of them were promising indoctrination and help. When the question of the trucks came up, I said that I wanted their permission to ask for volunteers and *not* to use trucks. At this point pompous old *Chávez* starts turning colors. So I did my big speech about this being for God and anyone who had been a *mayor* before could do it again and then sat down.

There was a tremendous controversy. But I said to myself that, as far as I was concerned, I was going to paint my house. They could get on with the fighting but I . . . I didn't have any *alcila*, I didn't have any *mayori*—but I was going to paint my goddam house. All this tremendous amount of preparation that has to begin on that day.

Then, the *Cabecera* shows up and says that the Europeans are coming on March 1st with the head of the Mam. So I realize I can't paint the house; I can't paint period; I have to do the *primer mayor costumbre*. But I can't go to Santa Cruz because of this lunatic Makuxtin . . . and then I start to ask myself, 'I have no idea what I'm supposed to do. How, for instance, are we going to make *maatz*?'—you know, the ceremonial corn gruel—How on earth do I make *maatz*?'

From then on, I had three sessions every day for twenty

days. One session with the *Cabecera* in the morning. One session with my volunteers. A third breaking them up into parties to go and find more volunteers for the various jobs. I proposed to the Council that all these preparations should be done early every year and that it be organized like a kind of *cofradía* with the *primer mayor* being used only for sacred things not for guarding *ladinos* or tourists or playing soldiers or anything else *but* opening the roads at Holy Week, duty at Santiago and Concepción, and the like. Everyone agreed.

We put the plea for volunteers on the Radio once but we got nothing but flak and gave up. We went from house to house. I reckoned that the sight of the boys on the road with their ceremonial whips would be the best propaganda and it worked out. We talked to about fifteen potential *mayori* and got four, while two more came of their own accord. And *alcila* came rolling in. I only had one hundred dollars and it was going to cost eighty dollars to send this lot to the Coast.

So we broke them up; I named four guys *mayori*: one for the fruit; one for the *corozo* palm etc. We did not yet have a second *mayor*; only a third: he had once been with the *corozo* party as an *alguacil* and seen the job: this made him third. The *corozo*, as you know, is that huge, long flower of the cohune palm tree—yeah!—something like a Brancusi sculpture you're right . . . The potential *alcila* would come in and I'd say, 'Sorry, we're full-up!' This made them all the keener. Then we had to get the girls who would cook food all night for these boys to take in the morning. All of a sudden, these boys are calling me '*Ta*,' father, and starting to call my wife 'mother' just like they'd done it all their lives: all of a sudden everyone snapped into it.

The night before they were supposed to go on the first visit, we went to ask the *cofradías* to open their road. We even went into Santa Cruz and managed to take the head of the Mam in there secretly so that he should see the place of his origin—the museum party had come by that time. Makuxtin was calm and gentle but we told everyone not to take anything from him: no drink, no smokes, nothing. We were not going to risk any witchcraft! *Cabecera* was the *costumbre* maker—he is a great *aj'kun* specializing in spiders and snakes (that's why they are always saying, 'Why can't you take the venom out of Makuxtin?'). I stayed up all that night to oversee the women making the tribute that had to go to the Coast. There are two *patin* (fish sauce paste dishes) for the sponsor; two for the man who actually has the fruit on his land; two for the *corozo*-donor, then one for each of the *alcila*. Usually, it's one big *patin* each to the first and third *alcila*. Then you divide the Atitlán produce into three parts: five pounds of tomatoes each, a bit green so they don't rot; five bunches each of onions; one pack of candles each, plus *ocote* (kindling), *pom* (incense) and, of course, tortillas.

You always give surplus so that half comes back: that is a symbol. Only the *alcila* go: they are the 'dogs' of the *mayori*. First, second and third *mayori* have their personal *mayori* and *alcila*; the other *mayori* just have *alcila*. So this was the strategy: to make the *costumbre* better than before and let everyone witness that—including the Coastal people. The *mayori* didn't want to carry their whips: I insisted they do so.

On Wednesday February 28th, we sent them out at 6:00 a.m. You line them up and say, 'I am borrowing your hands, your feet; your heart; I am borrowing your body, your Sun—your Day—watch out for your company because you are *nabeyal*, first child; don't jump to anything; always wait and consider; don't say anything harsh; whatever your company says *always* be patient. When you get to Xokexom, kneel and pray. Same at Mesebal. When you get to Chicacao, go see Machiquival, whose house you must sleep in; he knows all the *costumbres* and you can consult him on anything because he lives at the crossroads of all these important places.'

You speak to each *alguacil* in turn. After first *alguacil*, you speak to second because he leads on the return. Among *mayori*, second takes the going; fourth the return—in this case fifth since we did not have a fourth, I forget why. In the old days, individual *mayori* were responsible: the *primer mayor* did not have to pay for everything. The idea is that the lead man goes first but gets help from his second on the way back when he is tired. Collaboration is of major importance and it comes in pairs. The men going have to say their prayers and dance with their boxes (not the ritual carrying *kakaxtes* on the first trip) if there is a guitar.

To the third *alguacil*, you warn him to place his candles properly, right there where the *corozo* is and nowhere else, make sure that they are in the earth because that is what is eating the candles and you tell him not to be afraid when he sees the Mam—the Mam is there throughout this whole business, much more than on any other occasion, and there isn't an *alguacil* on any of these trips that doesn't talk of seeing the Mam in dream or vision or whatever.

After goodbyes and taking them to the doorway of the road they are off. Our people are saying, 'My God, they are really going after all.' I come back into the house for special prayers and I'm supposed to remember the travellers at noon, in the afternoon and at night. The next day: incense three times. Candles must burn right through Holy Week, fed day and night. The *primer mayor*'s house is like a spiritual central house that they relate to, go from and come back to: it is their link with the *r'muxux*, the navel or center of the earth. As yet, there is no adornment in the house, only light and fire. The house isn't really born yet. It is not until Palm Sunday that adornments are put up.

So they are gone. On Friday March 2nd they all come back. They had all had a good time on the Coast. One of them had done something wrong but realized it in time so he didn't cause trouble from craziness. When the fruit guys got to their destination, a lot of fruit had fallen because of wind. When the *corozo* party got there—they go on further at Chicacao, then link up with the main party back there for a joint return—the donor was sick.

They say an old man came out with rope and asked to help. He took them to the *corozo* palm trees, showed them how to mark the base with a big white cross, climbed up, chopped fast and gave them the flowers. They figured this must be the Mam so they put up their candles. When they came back they got lost in the rain but this old man was sitting at a corner and put them right. The Tzutujil down there were coming out bringing food and offerings: they were so happy: they had heard the *costumbre* had died.

Having slept in Mesebal the night before, the boys came in between 8:00 and 10:00 in the morning. I had been to bed at 5:00: we had been doing the mask ceremony that night. A dream of the Mam woke me up in time and I incensed the house: you are supposed to do this the minute you wake up every day of Holy Week.

You can't ask the boys anything before they've eaten. You incense them and their boxes and sit them down and feed them. Then they drink. Then you ask the first *alguacil* for an account. He takes out the fruit and explains in detail how each piece was acquired. The tale includes many epic ramifications, as well as confessions of misdeeds and punishments (like happening to see a pretty girl in a house doorway without meaning to). Second *alguacil* then gives his version. There are several such accounts, about the fruit, the donors, the adventures. Then you open a *corozo* palm flower and hang it in the house.

Then I look at the fruit to see how much has come: two

dozen bananas; four cacaos, four *pataxtes* (a large inferior grade of cacao)—no *melocotones* (big squash-like fruit), they weren't ripe yet. Then the fruit are divided: one of each kind goes up in the trellis in the center of the house. Some go to the bringers; some to me; the rest to Santa Cruz. This is the beginning of adornment.

There are little episodes at Santa Cruz. Their people had come to fetch us; we took them back. Makuxtin accuses them of 'loading this poor *Primer Mayor*' with bad stories about him and of being badly arrayed compared to 'these fine people of the *Primer Mayor*.' The Santa Cruz *Juez* tried to insult us over the small size of the *corozo*, but Makuxtin made him apologize. The *principales* later figured out that M. is now being nice because he still hopes to get the Mam head. We do another *costumbre* for having delivered the fruit.

More volunteers started coming in and the meetings increased. Felipe Tuiz sent in spies and was more angry even than before when they told him how well things were going. On the 6th, we met with all the *alcila* I had to date: some fourteen I guess. My *conjunto*, my musical group, declared they didn't want to be *alcila*: the First *Alguacil* was Hatchet's son and was in this band: the others found him too violent after drinking. That left me in a fix. Another problem: I got everyone together and we went to *cofradía* San José Particular. They hold the church *monumento* paraphernalia and they were cross because the ritual called for them being asked one by one. They wanted calls on the first, third and fifth Fridays of Lent. I said there were not as many *alcila* as in the old days. They insisted. I could not do it: there were twenty-seven people to be called on! A lot of strategy and diplomacy were called for!

The *Cabecera* was in trouble finding apostles—little boys who represent them at a ritual feast—because of the First *Fiscal* having left and there being no Second. Eventually,

Tuiz's uncle, a major *aj'kun* and friend of the *Cabecera*'s, turned up and took the *Fiscal* job. Second Friday went by and I had a show of paintings in Antigua. Before the next visit to see the fruit, we went to Santa Cruz and the church. Santa Cruz wouldn't take the Mam down so we went up into the trellis. The Third *Mayor* lost his mind, seized the Mam and shook him; we had to pull him off because he got glued. It was a sign there would be a fight when the boys next went out.

There was. Third *Mayor* had told the Mam to hurt certain people. His wife and kids got deathly ill. I told him not to witch people because he was not an *aj'kun* and just to ask the Mam to open the road again. He was Miguel Pablo, the little jaguar dancer from *cofradía* San Juan, a poor man trying to do us a favor. I was sorry for him. On the 21st, we had the second trip to 'see the fruit': it matures very fast right now and you have to watch that it isn't rotten (black) or unripe (green). The boys messed up though: they came back on the 22nd instead of the 23rd and I wasn't ready. At that time, there were some nasty characters who came to try to steal the mask.

As we went to Makuxtin to give him his second lot of fruit, the First *Alguacil* went crazy. It always happens: from the tension, the walking, the fatigue—somebody loses it. The *Primer Mayor* 1978 had attacked his father and done him damage. I told my man he was already inside this *costumbre* and didn't belong to himself until it was over. He went on misbehaving and, at Santa Cruz, attacked the Second *Alguacil*. So we realized he had done something wrong and gotten caught by the whirlwind. He was packed off to rest at his house. We had more problems at Santa Cruz, refusing to smoke each other's cigars (in case of witchcraft) and Makuxtin's wife refusing to drink my liquor. That time, we gave Santa Cruz the biggest *corozo* flower

I'd ever seen. But a lot had gone wrong and I kept wondering whether the guys hadn't just sat and drunk beer in Chicacao . . .

We got home from Santa Cruz. Traditionally, the *primer mayor* receives the boys with drink and male words; his wife with food and female words. The First *Alguacil* had come back. He bridled, believing my wife was going to upbraid him, when all she wanted to do was to 'receive' him. Well, she gave him a very long, flowery speech and he broke into tears. The old *principales* from my mask group said this meant that there would be fights on the last visit (there were: they had three). In the old days, there were three visits 'to see the fruit': on first, third and fifth Fridays. Because we were on a shoestring and each one of the visits cost about 130 dollars, we did it on first and fourth and left sixth for the final run. So we had two 'viewings' instead of three. The three coincide with the three callings because when they go to see the fruit, we call the others to duty—the *monumento* people et al.

One fascinating aspect of this is that the men are married but cannot have sex, whereas the women who cook the food should all be *merkani*, women who have had husbands but do not have any now. It has to do with the building up of desire, rather than purity as such (which is what's talked about when you're stressing the men). Atitecos don't believe that virgins have desire: they have not yet been 'opened' or 'seeded.' The *merkani* share something of the image of the Virgin Mary who has no husband and who has lost her child. Now they are preparing the food for the men and all this food is, conceptually, female.

After the problem with the *Primer Alguacil*, a lot of young men came to me and said that, if I would get another different one, they would all come with me. I said that he 'already had the words and the roadness on him' and that you cannot take a man out of a ritual just like that.

There were so many meetings and so much coming and going (to the municipality for all sorts of licences, to Antigua for my show of paintings, to Guatemala to buy kitchen equipment, incense burners etc.), that I cannot remember it all. We did not have enough *alcila* to make up the *corozo* party. On April 1st, the *alcila* brought baskets of corn to make the *maatz* and lots of other people, many older ones, sent corn, beans etc. as gifts because of delight in the thing actually taking place. On April 2nd, we spent the day bringing all the *metates*, the corn-grinding stones, and pots and so forth into the house and marking them so as to know where they should go back.

On April 3rd, we had a big meeting of all the *alcila* (about eighteen now) the *mayori* (we had six out of a desirable twelve) and all the advisor *principales*. There were difficulties with the numbering of the *mayori*. The traditional pattern would have been something like: First (stays home with Eighth); Second and Fourth with fruit; Third and Sixth with *corozo*; Fifth and Seventh with cypress; the rest apportioned according to need. In this case, we didn't yet have a 4th and those who should have been Seventh and Eighth could not be because they had been Fifth and Sixth before and could not be demoted. Something like that: I forget the complexities. We were trying to run a big ship with half a crew.

The Second *Mayor* was there and also the guitarist who had been going with the fruit for something like twenty years. We went to the church for *costumbre* and to Santa Cruz where Makuxtin was irritated once again, mainly I think because here were all these *mozos*, boys acting as servants, doing things for me for free whereas he would have had to pay his *mozos* had he done the fruit—and also my *conjunto* came in to play which made him feel worse. As on other occasions in Santa Cruz, my head felt speedy and weird, from *silkum* probably: from whirlwind witchcraft.

Then I stayed up all night for the *encomiendas*, the gifts to the fruit-donors, the exchange of Highland produce for the Coastal fruit. These were much more complex by now: there were two very big *patin* for each of the top *mayori* and *alcila*; six smaller ones for the other *alcila*, plus two for donors (Chiquival and the little old fruit-giver), plus another eight for the *alcila* because I really wanted them to eat well. On this day alone, by the way, the *patin* is made from meat seasoned with lemon and salt: not fish. Incidentally, here as anywhere else, you never throw away food wrappers or food that's gone bad: you bring it back and give it to your wife to throw away.

Then there was three half-gallons of liquor (we drank one half in the house before they left); twenty-five pounds of incense and two burners, twenty-five packages of candles, and all the vegetables and tortillas. So the Second *Mayor* divides all this up. There must be a candle lit, by the way, wherever they go: even while walking, it's the first *alguacil* who has to carry it and that's why he comes back covered with wax.

There are supposed to be twenty *alcila*, the eighteen plus the personal ones of the First and Fifth *Mayori*. The first *alguacil* then lines up the boys according to rank—they call themselves *arilleros* from *guerillero*, the warriors, or *aj'ch'oja* and *aj'chayi* in Tzutujil, whereas the *mayori* are called Mam: so the *alcila* are the warriors of the Mam. Then I had to give out money—let's say, taking *quetzales* and bucks at par: $25 for mineral waters, incidentals, repairs etc.; $15 for meat in Chicacao; $5 for coffee and other small sums totalling about $65; then there was $60 for the other *mayor* who came back. Traditionally, a lot of this should have been paid by the second *mayor* who also gets the *alcila* to give from two to five bucks each towards the costs but in this case it was the Fifth *Mayor* who spent about $120 of his own and I footed the rest of the bill.

Traditionally, the only thing the *primer mayor* asks for from the *alcila* is a contribution to the *marimba*. I'm not sure I did in this case. I also gave fifty dollars for fruit in case the fruit-donor went back on his word for any reason—which would be disastrous. The accusers who eventually wrote the 'Bulletin of the Revolutionary Sorcerer' criticizing my tenure as *Primer Mayor* [*see Chapter Twenty-One*] may have heard of something like this or even seen it and misinterpreted it as giving and taking money: they were so dumb and ignorant they could not have judged anything rightly: some of them were even calling me *Primer Alguacil!*

There was one little guy, about thirteen, an orphan they called Chicken Louse who had a field of his own on the Coast to and from which he used to travel all by himself, and he kept bothering me for weeks because he had dreams about fetching the fruit and I kept telling him he couldn't go. In the end he said that he would go whether we liked it or not and would play the *matraca*, the big wooden whirling-rattle, all the way and that we should give him his *patin*. So we did.

Then they all put their packs on after long admonitions and stand in a kind of S-shaped line and have to go through all the goodbyes to the *Xoa'*, in this case my wife. The traditional pattern is that the major *mayori* are at the back, carrying the road, and the minor ones are between the *alcila* with their staffs guarding the road and with the first *alguacil* opening the road. Then, they all go to the municipality to take leave of the Town Mayor (he has been informed and 'called' the day before). Traditionally, each *alguacil* carried a credential: this year I have to get a blanket document for them to be carried by the second *mayor*. It is really quite a sight with the *matraca* grinding up and down the streets; the guitar—actually he goes first, 'carrying' the first *alguacil*, and 'opening the road'(he played from 6:00

a.m. all the way to Chicacao); the incense which has gone before (it burns all week until Holy Wednesday non-stop). There are supposed to be two lines of ten *alcila* each, with the first taking the right and the second the left. They are told to go real slow so that everyone can have a good look at them. The whole school comes out: the teachers had lost control; there is a big crowd, some delighted, some jealous; lots of old ladies kissing our hands . . . At the last moment, a kid who had just gotten back to town, insists on coming with us: we fit him out with the *kakaxte* of a missing *alguacil* back at my house and rush him back into the line. The *mayori* have to fetch their *maletas*, their travel bags containing personal belongings; at this point, they can only do that with their personal *alcila*, their faithful 'dogs,' and they take forever over it.

Now, when the boys get to Chicacao and the house they are going to be in, they plant a candle and pray. Then they go to the person who is acting as Lord of the Fruit (or 'Lord of Our Little Maidens') and put a white candle in his house. He gets gifts, a speech, etc. Then the boys are taken to where the fruit is. First to the bananas. They put candles underneath, pray, light incense, drink, then begin to cut, but in a special way.

The bananas come off usually in groups of fives because each *alguacil* carries fifty, no more, no less. They have to be green and in a certain condition which people who've done it before know about. The bananas are put on a mat, with candles in front and they are prayed to. Then liquor again on both sides. Then they go to the cacao and the *pataxte* and do the same. Eventually, there are three mounds on the mat. Then come the *melocotones* for a fourth mound.

Then the *mayori* look after the packing. First they make a 'nest' out of *muxan* leaves (it's like a banana leaf) all around the edges, then torn-up real banana leaves packed into the bottom. Then two groups of five bananas are put in with their top ends outward and their bottoms facing inward. Then a *pataxte* because it is the hottest, then the next bananas facing inward. Then a cacao. Then bananas outward. Then one *melocoton*. Then twice again. So on top there is always a *melocoton*. There are usually three cacaos, *pataxtes* and *melocotones* per load. All of this packed in with banana leaf which, as it dries, casts a strange white powder over everything. On top of the load, they put flowers, on the outside. Then the *kakaxtes* are lined up and incensed. From then on, those *kakaxtes* are always guarded and always incensed.

With the *corozos* palm flowers, there's less packing of course, but the Third *Mayor* has his thing with the rope. He carries, or his *alguacil* carries, long ropes for lowering the *corozos*, also shorter rope for the carriers, a special knife to open a little window in the *corozo* husk etc.

During that day, when the party has gone, the women, who spend the whole week at my house—they don't go home at all—were getting their act together; the remaining *alcila* I had (there were about twenty-two over the twenty who had gone) were bringing in more stuff left over from April 2nd and we started the full adorning of the house. I had sent two guys to cut reeds (they didn't know and brought the wrong thing and had to be sent back out again with an expert) and others to get *pexlak*, the ornamental plant that goes into the trellis but there were problems with this: my in-law relatives wanted to get paid, whereas unrelated people had done things for free, out of religious faith.

Anyway: suddenly this old man comes in, with his son—I had never seen him before and they were carrying the most beautiful lot of *pexlak* I had ever seen. They stayed with us the whole day, helping us (the old man gave us twenty dollars and a liter of heavy home brew) and the *corozo alcila* who had not gone yet helped also. Hatchet brought in thirty canes needed for the roof. There is a great deal of work to prepare the materials used in the roofing: soaking the cane for instance, or tying up hundreds of little bunches of *pexlak*.

Meantime, I was going all over the place for police permits: for a *marimba* permit; an electricity permit (we put it in that day); for my shoes . . . Everyone is still turning up offering a bench, a chair, a load of firewood . . . That night, we set off a *bomba*—a very heavy firecracker that makes a huge noise but no great display (we're all popped after drinking all day since all these people have to be given food and drink). There comes a point in the ceremonies when you cannot set the *bombas* off—because, from the Christian point of view, it's a time of sadness. Then we went to call on the priest, Father Stan Rother, to see if he would help with the *marimba* because we had nothing big enough. But he kept telling us his truck wasn't big enough either.

Well, we were fed up being in the house and went marching around the *pueblo*, completely popped, asking for the prices of hiring various trucks. Little did I know that we were going to be up all night drinking again! Then my father-in-law insisted on going off to fetch the *ramos*, the palms of Palm Sunday—we had a lot of old guys who had been making those for years: each *cofradía* has to make its own. There was some strange character who called me out and started reciting witchcraft incantations over me and told me he was going to blast me out of town as a lousy *gringo* tomato—but I told him to come in and sit down and have a drink.

Because the whole idea is that if, in spite of all the drink and stuff, you can go right through without fights, then you have truly succeeded and truly carried your burden, your *carga*. In the end, my father-in-law had to be called and bashed the strange character on the head and threw him into the street and the police took him away. It was all this tremendous tension that builds up over a thing like this.

The *marimba* arrived and Father Stan only charged me five bucks: he had very kindly fetched it after all from San Juan la Laguna. So we set up the *marimba* and had to drag the players out to salute the municipality and inform them that the *fiesta* had started. They played about an hour; we took them back, fed them and plugged them in. That was when the *fiesta* really began. You cannot imagine all the gifts and money coming in: I must have done about forty thanksgiving prayers that night. Then I bought ten gallons of really strong stuff which normally cost five dollars a gallon but the liquor seller gave it me for four. He was the *Ch'eep Alguacil*, the junior of the *corozo* guys and he kept coming back: I bought a total of fifty-five gallons from him. Normally people dilute a lot but I gave them the full strength stuff and everyone loved it.

We had also sent out the Third *Mayor* to *cofradía* San Nicolás to get the big drum: he came back dead drunk after about three hours: they had opened several bottles of wine and three bottles of aguardiente! Normally, the *mayori* stand in the yard and keep people out, but, that night, there was no way—hordes of people came into the house; it was an extraordinary succession of events . . . Well, you remember the party well enough!

EIGHTEEN

The Primer Mayor's Tale: II

Early the next morning, there were another few liquor-induced fights but we tied people up and let them cool it off. I had some nineteen women doing the grinding all night and about five house servants, a total of twenty-four, not to mention the relatives. The *maatz* came out and we drank that. As soon as that was done, they had to prepare the food for the boys, coming back, as well as their wives. We used about one hundred pounds of meat and the family mostly held back: even that wasn't enough.

At about five in the morning, the wives of the *mayori* turned up all decked out in their finest and we were still in our rags from the night before. The drummer was a lot the worse for wear: he had been playing solidly for about four days and nights: we gave him a good stiff drink and more food and that gave him back his spine. The wives of the five leading men were supposed to bring two bottles of liquor each and hadn't done so—so I had to fork out the equivalent, plus my own four bottle *costumbre*, and take it along. Well, perhaps some of them didn't know . . . but most of them were probably just letting me do it. I also had to send the wives of the *alcila* out to buy incense which they should have brought (the wives of the *mayori* don't: the *alcila* wives become the 'servants' to the latter.)

As you know, it takes forever to get the girls out of the house, so I was nudging and pushing and shepherding them along because the elders and *their* wives were already out there, and the drummer, all of them waiting. The emotional side of this for them is that they and their husbands are recently married; they might well be pregnant with their first child who will give their *alguacil* husband the right to be a *mayor* (yes, you're right, it does seem as if abstinence might coincide with the last stages of pregnancy . . . . Well, we finally got going. A big crowd followed. But when we got up to Puruwachabaj, behind the cemetery, no one had come with us that far.

So we heard that the fruit boys were about one kilometer down the road having a beer with someone. There was the tremendous suspense of waiting. We had already sent some emissaries with food and liquor the day before to meet them as they were coming back and now we were sending these out again from time to time. It's a sign of respect. And the *principales* were telling me what I should say in the greetings speech and I was wishing we had prepared for this the day before.

You are supposed to bring them in. There's an invisible line somewhere (some senior person decides where it is) which you have to bring them over. The boys have to stay on the other side and we on this side. The boys put their packs down and the *alcila* from this side, the *corozo* party, have to take care of the packs. Then there are interminable speeches to the *mayori* and answers to the speeches along the lines of 'Thank God we see your mouth, we see your face. Thank God you gave your hand, you gave your foot, you gave your heart. You've guided your daughter your son (this is to the *mayori* for guiding the *alcila*) across woman earth, across woman hill, across woman plain; you withstood the north wind, the force of God (i.e. rain: you can't say you were able to tolerate rain, that would be an insult to the Sun whose liquid form rain is), the force of the Sun . . .' Then you ask how the man is and he starts telling his story at great length.

This exchange establishes a kind of relationship. You become *compadres*: the term used to address in-laws or the parents of a godchild. When you've done this with all the *mayori*, you start on the *alcila*: it's always the same speech, with modifications according to rank and duties. All this takes place in a big circle until you come back to the beginning and then the women start in: these are the wives of the *mayori* who receive the men; the *alcila* wives do not. The tension is extraordinary at this point—of course you have to remember that everyone is exhausted *and* bombed—but: the *mayori* were near to tears, the First *Alguacil* was actually crying—and a lot of the receivers weep, especially when they see the men and boys first arrive.

At this point, too, rumors start to creep out about why so and so is looking weird, or has a scar or whatever . . . but I'm not supposed to tell the *principales*, it's all hush hush. Then we go through the whole palaver with the various bottles and everybody downing liquor and reciting thanks. I cut that a bit short because more drink had appeared and I didn't want the place to become a madhouse. After that came the business about going to be received by the municipality (the *Katbal tz'ij*—the 'arbitrators of the word'). Each *alguacil* is given a helper from the house-side to help him put his load back on and hold him up so he does not fall.

What they are supposed to do is to *dance* into town but that rarely happens (when they get to the house, they have the *marimba* so it's easier). When the *mayori* see the church, they take off their hats and pray. We have to have the Second *Mayor* by the arms, bringing him into town: I'm on one side, the other *mayori* on the other. Well, at the municipality, the Town Mayor, a *ladino*, just thanks us for keeping up the *costumbre* but makes no speeches. We just get the drinks, that's all. I make a very long, big, flowery speech thanking every possible person and thing that could be thanked. That must have shown them how to behave!

We send the *marimba* on in front to be ready to play for

us as we arrive and I go in front to be at my house first. The *marimba* plays the *sones* tunes of the Mam and the three *recibos*, the receiving tunes. The Mam mask is there and we have the same situation as we had tried to prevent elsewhere: the Mam and the fruit in the same place too early. But what are you going to do? I had to bustle about like mad, because of the huge crowd there, getting the boxes unloaded, guiding drunks to their seats, serving food—many could not eat, simply couldn't take anything more into their mouths.

I had had to get a lot of banana leaf wrappers so as to make doggie bags for the food because God help you if those guys don't get their food! I had to go out with another party to get the Town Mayor and his people, bring them to my house and give them *maatz*: it turned out that the *only maatz* which went sour the whole time was the stuff we gave them and they drank it so as not to embarrass us! There are two *kakaxtes*, carried by the last guys in the rows (they are meant to give heat to the rest), which are supposed to have ripe fruit in them and these you take out and distribute to all the people, two fruit each: you start with bananas and then go on down—you and Janet got *melocotones* if I remember right.

Then I have to invite them all to dance. The *Primer Mayor* dances with each *mayor*. Then it goes on down. The *alcila* couldn't care less about the dancing but the wives seem to love it because there is a *marimba* there and all—often their parents have to come on out to drag them home. Then a bottle of rum showed up which had been for the Town Mayor—but he had very rudely left without saying goodbye.

The rum went into us and I knew nothing more until I was woken at seven in the evening. The *marimba* was leaving and had to be paid its first installment. Everyone else had been asleep too. So we did the 'cuenta,' the accounting for the fruit, around 10:00 p.m. with all doors closed. It's a fine art to see what stage the fruit is at; how much of a blush or slight sweat it has on it: the Second *Mayor* was very good at it and another *mayor* got jealous as hell: it's a big honor you see to check the fruit.

Now Second *Mayor* got hold of me and told me very quietly that I might hear all sorts of rumors but should pay no attention to *anything* until we were out of this ritual. The implication was that some of the fruit might be green—although it is taboo to use that word. The Second *Mayor* said, "There will only be one Judge, our Father God, and He will let us know with His colors, with His heat (i.e. the degree of ripeness) but we are to say nothing.' All this is in the context of the fruit-donor weeping around the village for days (he was not obliged to come up to Atitlán but he wanted to and did) because somebody had upset him down there on the Coast and he couldn't forget it.

He had paid some forty-two dollars for the fruit, a big sum for him, but someone had accused him of 'living off the *gringo*' and this made him crazy. There had been various incidents with one *alguacil* going nuts (like one on the previous trip had tried to throw himself off a cliff and had to be pulled back) and taking off all his clothes and trying to make it with a table and hitting the Fourth *Mayor*. Whereupon the Fourth went crazy and wanted to hit the Second and then Fourth 'lost the road': they found him sleeping in the middle of the path seven kilometers away all passed out. The Second never lost it nor did any of the others but kept going.

Well, when we looked at the fruit, all of it was fine except four *kakaxtes* that were 'cold.' So we started incensing those fruit like mad so that they would get to be ripe. That night, a lot of trouble makers came to the house and had to be thrown out. Saturday, everyone got sleep: the *alcila* were still in the house. On Palm Sunday, *Domingo de Ramos*, we checked the fruit again: one box looked as if it was catching up. The *mayori* were supposed to go to church for the service but Third and Sixth (who had never been *mayori* before) wanted to go for the *corozo* early in order to get back that day—so I sent my personal *Mayor* (it should have been Eighth but was one of the Fifths, we seem to have had two . . .) and the Fourth to the church with the palms.

Now the *corozo* party has to get its equipment and its food-gifts, but these are less substantial because the *corozo* guys don't have to overnight as much as the fruit guys: they walk all day and all night and go further than the fruit guys but do not sleep over. Actually the old colonel who has a plantation with a lot of cohune palm trees likes his liquor rather than food: he has been giving *corozo* for years and not charging. They do have to carry *petate* mats to put the *corozos* on. Now no one wanted to carry the Sixth *Mayor*'s suitcase because, of course, it's much more flashy to carry the *corozo* but we got a little adolescent who wasn't even married yet and he became a sort of hero of this deal.

So these guys leave, walk all day and get to their destination at about 10:00 p.m. The next day, they cut the *corozo* and come back the same day and walk all night again and rest at Mesebal. Before dawn they come down to Xokexom and arrive at Puruwachabak in the early morning. They have very little sleep: they go as far as where they can see the Pacific Highway. The main reason for this haste is that the *corozo* flower goes bad very quickly: if it lasts a week you are doing good. The boys had to discard four *corozos*: they had brought forty but arrived with thirty-six.

We noticed one thing: that it was very difficult to get *corozo* people and that those who went were strong traditionalists. Usually, no one actually wants to go for *corozo*: they prefer to go for the fruit which is more fun and considered more glamorous. Surprisingly, this year the *corozo* fetchers were volunteers. The reluctance is in part because of the fear of the snakes (never called 'snake' but 'woman child of the hill' or 'woman's headband of the hill') that are supposed to be curled around the *corozo*. They are related to the Rainbow snakes and all recent reports give them white-yellow hair and beards. They can scare the soul out of the body; sometimes they breathe on you but you don't know it and afterwards you feel sick. This is why they use servants whom they pay to climb up the tall palms and cut the huge long flowers down and lower them slowly on ropes. Also why they put candles in there, to feed the Mam and the spirits so that no damage ensues.

So we sent them off and went back to the house. The people came back from mass and we all had food and drink. Second *Mayor* and the *alcila* all stayed around, did not change their clothes and behaved themselves: but Fourth *Mayor* did come and go, did change his clothes—which is taboo—and went a little nuts as a result. You are not supposed to change your clothes or wash until the fruit has been decorated with gold on the Tuesday night. You must sleep on a mat in front of your fruit and not leave it in any way. I kept them pretty busy around the house—army tactics you know—so that they would not get bored.

At 6:00 a.m. and at noon and again at 6:00 p.m. (every six hours) you look at the fruit, having closed the doors—like when they perform the Martín bundle ritual in *cofradía* San Juan—and fill the place with smoke; you kiss the fruit and encourage them, calling them 'little girls, little virgins': they are still not ripe yet. A second *mayor* is like a technician: he notices that one basketful is not coming along as well as the others and he tells the *alguacil* responsible to incense it even more. He tells him how to do it, where to apply the smoke, how not to interfere with his neighbor's box which may be ready.

In the evening, the Second *Mayor* announced that the First, Fifth and *Ch'eep Alcila* all had unsatisfactory bananas. First was very upset: he was of good family; he was very proud and then there had been something which had happened on the way. First was in tears. Normally, he would come to *primer* and second *mayor* and we would go to Santa Cruz to do a big *costumbre* with the Mam and to confess to the Mam what he had done wrong. And there was Fifth *Alguacil* also with green bananas, but not too worried. I looked at his and figured he must have done something wrong. I said to him, 'Hey, you aren't the one who said to your friends when you were recruiting, "Let's go and screw (*chingar*) the bananas," was that you by any chance?' And he said yes and I told him that one single word wrong like that could mess up the whole venture.

Well, around one a.m., when we had taken the last look for the day, the Second *Mayor* told me we should have something to eat and go into another room and he began saying that he could not tell me anything because *mayori* are not supposed to but that Second *Alguacil* would and Second began telling this endless story about First *Alguacil*. On the first night's sleep, as they lay down, First had begun to criticize and make fun of some of the other guys. That's when it started. When they got to the bananas, First wanted to hurry the proceedings and the others wanted to eat and rest first. He started down the road by himself and the others said he had gone crazy.

When they got to Chicacao, they wanted some liquor but the money for that had run out. There was still fifty dollars fruit money they were supposed to give me back if it was not spent. I had told them it was O.K. to spend out of that if they ran out. So they drank and First begins telling the fruit-donor that he is just 'living off this *gringo*.' Then Fourth *Mayor* started criticizing Second *Mayor*, after which he said he would buy everyone a drink and went off to the *cantina* and got lost. They were supposed to be there for the night and get up for the return at 3:00 or 4:00 a.m. Then the First *Alguacil* got after the Second *Mayor* and wanted to hit him. The others all pulled him down and he passed out.

At this point, the *Ch'eep Alguacil* took all his clothes off and tried to get it on with the table and with the little old lady of the guy who owned the house: they were all losing it you see! And to make it worse, the house-owner is symbolically the Mam for that night! It really gets hold of you that stuff: which is why you have to *think rain and not women*, and all sorts of good thoughts, and constantly be praying and keeping your attention awake. The *Ch'eep* went to sleep persuaded that he was in jail and was still crazy in the morning and they had to throw him in the river (despite the no washing rule) and hold on to him all the way.

Then, First *Alguacil* lost his temper yet again on top of the mountain when they suddenly found Fourth *Mayor* passed out on the road. So First *Alguacil* got mad and hit Fourth *Mayor*. Second *Mayor* kept at them saying that if anyone wronged any one else, that other should not reciprocate, not 'return the *k'exel*,' i.e. should not wrong him back. So the fighters were pulled apart; they prayed, put up candles and kept going. *These* then were actually the guys whose bananas were green!

Well, all the *principales* who had brought seven cases of beer the day before had gone home by morning when we looked at the fruit again. Fifth *Alguacil*'s was O.K.; the other two were still in trouble. Now *Ch'eep* who had lost it and run away, and had done no incensing—we had decided to do it for him—all of a sudden shows up. This was the day for putting up the *monumento*. So we left some to sleep and some to incense and took about twelve *alcila* with the Second *Mayor* up to church. The people from San Nicolás in charge of the Cross hole in church had come by to remind me. We went to *cofradía* San José Particular to pick up the materials. They were angry because no one had 'called' them: the *Cabecera* had obviously forgotten. We *needed* them to put the structure up.

Incidentally, most of the San José people—they are chosen for that—are canoe makers and carpenters: José is patron of cultivation on the Coast (which is where the canoes come from), of cutting down trees in the slash and burn activity before agriculture can take place and so on. These guys are real heroes, real monkeys you know! We didn't really have enough men to carry all the stuff at once so I began, as *Primer Mayor*, to grab people—which is tense when you are a *gringo*—but they came and were very sweet about it, although most of them were *Catequistas*. So we watched, ready to give things they might need.

A *primer mayor*, for instance, is supposed to provide two dozen San Pedro size ropes (three *varas* long) and so on down. Now, in the old days, a first *alguacil* would have climbed to the top and put up this enormous earthenware pot, the *Kasueel Juyu*, at the top. But the *Catequistas* had cut the thing in half and put it up on a structure carved by the Chávez family as a sort of permanent *monumento* of their own. They could not, however, manage to kill off the old *monumento*. Anyway, they made the real *monumento* a little small this year, also they only had eleven of the twenty-seven makers working, thinking we would have less fruit when, in fact, we had three times as much as the structure would take.

Yes, the old white-bearded guy that you saw in the 1950s as the *Dueño del monumento* must have been José Mendoza Ajuchan (he was an incredible *ajkun*), *Alcalde* San José, father to the present *Alcalde*. We are not supposed to even touch the *monumento* until the fruit arrives. There are, of course, people responsible for all the other *monumentos*—arches decorated with fruit—that are put up on the procession road, also on this Monday. It is when the main *monumento* is made in church that I have to give up my staff and the *alcila* their whips: now we use *pacaya* plant stalks, which is what San Juan Carajo's headdress is made of. The idea is that the Christ-killers use wood or metal weapons; the deities use vegetal weapons. Our *pacaya* sticks stand for divine wind: they are used also for flagellating people on *Sabado de Gloria*, Holy Saturday.

So they are putting up a network of tied ropes, a little house as it were, to symbolize the big house, the *Kasueel Juyu*, and the whole thing has a cross on top which, in the old days, was put inside the upside down pot representing the hill. The cross, inside, represents the sprout of maize, the sacrificial tree and all those things. *Only* a first *alguacil*, as first, bravest, warrior, can touch and put up the pot and cross. In the old days, he would not have a ladder but climb up the trellis. It seems he is symbolically linked to the younger of three brothers in one of the creation myths: a young brother who is turned into a monkey when told by his elders to fetch fruit for them in a tree.

After this we had my offering of drink to the *monumento* builders, the *cofrades* cleaning their altars etc. We had a big meeting. But *cofradía* Santa Cruz, who were supposed to bring the cloth for the apostles' table, the clothes for Jesucristo and other things had not yet come. At this point, half Santa Cruz did show up, including the *Escribano*, saying they could no longer hack Makuxtin and were resigning! *Escribano,* by the way, is the father-in-law of Second *Alguacil*. They had gotten into trouble with Makuxtin on Palm Saturday because the parents of the *alcila* are supposed to bring drink to a *primer mayor* on that day. The *primer mayor* is supposed to look after those *alcila* from the start, to be super-sensitive to everything and to catch the smell of the fruit coming back in the air as a sign that they are returning safely.

Now, the Council told me that Makuxtin's fruit came on the Saturday and that he was going to try to build his own *monumento* in church—at which point I should call the Commissariat and have him arrested. But the dumb thing was none of the fruit he had brought was of the type that should go on the *monumento*! Also over half of it was green and had to be trashed: you can imagine the magic in that! They 'froze up,' they were picked too young and died. To add insult to injury: those that made it and ripened, he ended up by selling in the plaza market!

Now I had to get going on the cypress: to get the boats ready and to send boys up to cut the cypress beforehand and give it its *costumbre* so it would be ready for pick-up when the boats got there. So two *mayori* and five *alcila* went to do that *costumbre*. The boats by tradition go from Chini-mya; the *costumbre* party goes by road. The drummer had to go with the party in the boats, drumming the special beat that he has when over water. Two men had to be sent for the *marimba*: it was raining that day and everybody got wet. So, here is another *fiesta* night with crowds and a lot of booze being received! No *maatz* today but the women are working very hard all day to feed the guys who come back from the cypress. Also you have to feed the *corozo* party returning and their wives, and, believe it or not, the wives of the fruit party also.

Then the guys, around 10:30, said, 'Let's go and see the cypress come in,' and I told them they were crazy because I'd never seen it come in before midnight. Well, we went to the shore and waited endlessly and at about 12:30 they showed up. They have to be received: a first *mayor* gives drinks, then a fifth, then the first again. We cut it a bit short because the same guys who went for fruit went for cypress and there was no need to kill them! Well, on our way to the municipality, we get this incredibly pure, strong smell of *corozo* on passing near the Sixth *Mayor*'s house and we figure the *corozo* party must be approaching Atitlán. We get to the municipality and they aren't waiting for us but we get the doors opened, drop the cypress and go back to the house.

All the women except my wife were drunk; my father-in-law was angry because my mother-in-law was dancing with another man, albeit a relative, and my wife's ex was there too: so I threw these two buzzards out on their backsides. I told the *marimba* to stop at around 2:00 or 3:00 instead of 4:00 or 5:00, so that I could catch an hour's sleep.

Now we had looked at the fruit and everyone seemed as if they were going to make it; even the *Ch'eep*'s—he in the meantime had come back and was sound asleep. Well, I knew my father-in-law was out drinking and I got all the house doors locked from the inside. An hour later, he showed up and started tearing us and himself apart so I called the cops to get him into jail and keep him safe. We had trouble in the morning because he had smashed all the eggs and tomatoes and things and how were we going to get other breakfast food at 4:00 a.m.?

So we went through the whole business again of going out to meet the *corozo* party at Puruwachabaj. These men were far more wiped out than the fruit ones; they hadn't slept at all. I'd sent them food and liquor in the morning but they had not been able to touch it and had brought it right back on their backs. They were much more long-winded than the previous lot; Third *Mayor* especially talked a blue streak and looked very irritated but I couldn't tell why just yet. Sixth *Mayor* was also irritated but he was a zombie. There was so much liquor around that we got roaring ripped again. Some of the *alcila* were not even able to pick up their loads: the little boy had had his carried back from Xokexom by the man I'd sent out that morning with the food and drink. Usually no one bothers to come see the *corozo* but this time there was a huge crowd. After the *alcaldía* reception, the whole party staggered back, each one with his helper so that the *corozos* wouldn't poke anyone's eyes out. They danced into the house. *Corozo* count revealed thirty-six, there had been forty. Four had gone bad (last year there had only been twenty). We split the husk of a big *corozo* and hung the flower up. We gave them to eat. Two passed out as soon as fed and slept a day and a half.

Then we get the municipality, the Reconstruction Committee etc. for the definitive opening of the fruit. The *Cabecera* is drunk and nowhere to be found. Second *Fiscal*, Tuiz's father, stood in for him and the Committee said they would do the gilding in lieu of the municipals who obviously didn't want to. The fruit were opened in no order with no names mentioned, just in case, one after the other. Then we sent out presents of fruit to all the important officials and personages in the village, even the enemies of this particular event. Finally we all drank to get drunk and were dancing around like bears.

Second and Third *Mayori* filled up some twenty-two baskets of fruit now gilded and adorned. Nicolás Chávez discovered his *mangax* had been stolen so I told him mine had gone the day before, and my clock in the night, etc. etc.—so we were all even! I told all the guys to go home and get some sleep and be there on the Wednesday morning. That night we had a big party again; I bought more liquor and Second *Mayor* came back to stand guard all night and let me have some sleep. The *Telinel* was supposed to come after a visit from *Rox Mam*, Third Mam, i.e. the Third *Mayor* who had taken him a *corozo* and a basket of fruit. Well, we waited through the night but he never came. He was probably under orders from Makuxtin.

The *principales* came in on the Wednesday morning and the *Cabecera* warned me that we would have police protection and if anything happened with Makuxtin we had every right to bang him on the head. I gave an eight-bottle *costumbre* in the house and it was getting late: the Mam should go up at noon and it was already 11:30. We got the line of *alcila* up with their baskets and then the fish came in for the apostles. The crabs never came in and I suspect the *alcaldía* had made off with them. In the last five years, no one had brought fish so I have the record of three pounds of fish—which is ridiculous because there's supposed to be fifty pounds! A couple of guys showed up, one with carrots, one with some other vegetable: quite unorthodox but they wanted to do their thing for the apostles.

Now I had to walk in front to bring everyone in: quite a change after always walking *behind*. We get to the municipality, put down our fruit, set up mats and candles etc. (which should have been a *cofradía* Santa Cruz job). Then we race like mad to Santa Cruz for the struggle to be head of the line when the whole thing comes back and the Mam is brought to the municipality. I notice that Santa Cruz has put the Mam down facing the wrong direction! I tell my people not to touch him. You are never supposed to touch the Mam when he's dressed until he's been hung—because he's so full of power and energy. The fruit-donor wanders in drunk and starts kissing the Mam and we figure he's going to have a lot of trouble. *Cabecera* is still away drunk; *Fiscal* Tuiz comes in and I say, 'Let's get the Mam out of here.' The *Telinel* is shaking all over already: I advise him to get hold of himself.

All sorts of stuff happens in the confusion: Makuxtin swears at me for not giving back the Mam mask and tries to grab me until his headcloth falls off; Fourth Santa Cruz, muddled, puts it onto the Mam; a policeman keeps on trying to grab one of my *mayori* and I have to dissuade him over and over; *Telinel* is sweating and straining and Eyes says to me, 'This guy has got wind in his brain.' We feel he's going to fall down any second. We say, 'The Mam is carrying him,' because, when the Mam comes from the *cofradía*, symbolically the *telinel*'s coming from thousands and thousands of miles; he's coming as wind. The Mam is pulling him. The horse of the Mam is wind and the Mam is pulling him through stones, bushes, thickets, obsidian, lava, what have you. You see a *telinel* but he isn't there; he's some other place altogether.

We get to the municipality and lay the Mam down and all is cool except that the Santa Cruz guys have forgotten the candles. I come up with mine. Those candles are the symbol of the Mam consuming those fruits: as the candles get lower, the fruit is being 'eaten.' Then the *cofrades* start making the two bottom panels of the *monumento* with the cypress which has been left there and with two or three *corozos* and the *ramos* palms and corn husks: those belong to Santa Cruz; the rest of the *monumento* to the *mayori*. The *Cabecera* is supposed to go to church and check that the Mam's pillar is ready etc. etc., say a prayer, return and order departure. The first three *alcila* had gone off to get a coke and were not there to carry the fruit up—which pissed me off. I had to grab another bunch of people as carriers.

We go. The *Telinel* is shaking more and more. He's supposed to go to the door of the church, kneel to the four directions and then take the Mam to his pillar. All my men are like pulled along following the Mam and that's not where they're supposed to go—yet every year it happens like a magnetic force. In fact, one basket and one *corozo* are supposed to go to the *monumento* on the esplanade *in front of* the church and the boys had taken it to the Mam by mistake so I had to sort that out. The rest go to the church. The main *monumento* then gets adorned and all the *alcila* help—after the cypress panels have been tied by the *cofrades* with reed ties made the day before by Committee and *cofrades*. We have our liquor; I set a guard over the whole thing and we go back home with all the baskets and stuff.

We rest some in the house and then nominate who is going to guard various places and who is going to man the *rondas*, the check-up marches round town that we have do to at the rate of two per night. I cop the first *ronda* from 9:00 p.m. to 1:00, so I get to sleep from 1:00 to 6:00. You go to the church and see that the *monumento* and fruit are O.K.; then you go to where they are cooking the food for the apostles and see that kids don't run away with the food; check with the Mam and his guard; make a round of all the external *monumentos*.

I desperately wanted to go to sleep but had various visits—*Juez* San Nicolás wanted to borrow a flute for their all-night Wednesday ceremony; an ex-*Alcalde* Santa Cruz wanted to inform me that my *mangax* had been taken (by mistake?) by *Alcalde* Concepción; I had to go with a senior (Eyes as it happened) to borrow money from a rich ex-*Alcalde* Santiago . . . and by the time of the *ronda* I had not slept. Well, *Fiscal* was at the church and gave us some terrible mixture of alcohol and Kool-Aid! Sugar: we were instantly drunk. I found the poor Mam people without their Santa Cruz *Alcalde* or *Xoa'*, just *Telinel* and the poor little Fourth, and without food: so I went out and got them some food: a quarter's worth of fish from the apostles' fish!

After this, we found the San Nicolás *cofradía* people in front of the church and I pleased the *Alcalde* by taking over the flute for a couple of sets. Then *Fiscal* sent a notice that he was getting tired of watching the fish fry at the apostles' place and would appreciate hearing some drum and flute, so we went over there. Got home, and there was my wife who'd been snoring all afternoon, still at it. I crashed and actually slept.

Thursday. I guarded the fruit. The *Catequistas* had sabo-
taged the *monumento* event for years and elaborate rules had
been made up to deal with any offender stealing fruit: *Catequista* to the *Catequista* President; *alguacil* to the *primer mayor*;
cofrade to the *Cabecera*; plain citizen to the Town Mayor, with
a fine of ten dollars. I said, 'Nonsense, the thing is to guard
day and night.' We didn't lose any: just a few to our own
boys who got hungry guarding sometimes for eight hours
at a stretch. We did have one incident of an *alguacil* who took
down a *pataxte*, ate the sweet inside and put it back up again
empty. Something empty to God! A terrible taboo break!
He could ruin the rainy season with that one thing. So we
let him have it verbally and he cried a lot.

Then Eyes came in and said, "Let's go get your *mangax*.'
But no one was at Concepción: they were with San Nicolás,
waiting to help them bring the *santo* to church. Well, by
protocol, the whole of Concepción had to come back to
its own place and we shot the breeze for a while . . . So:
Juez Concepción pipes up and says that it's not lost, he has
it in his house, but he'd been so busy, etc. and all his *cofrades*
are looking at him and he's miserable. At his house, he
gave drink and he started crying and saying he was a terrible thief and I said no, because he was giving it back: if
he'd been a thief he would have cut the round hole in it
for the head. *Mayori* are the first rank to get a *mangax* but
they wear it slung, without the hole which is for higher
ups, for 'cooked,' mature, people.

Then we took him back to my place to give him the
one full of holes he'd left behind, and the *k'exel* drink (the
reciprocity) and some food: marvelous food, the first I
remember *eating* in the whole week. I ate a whole half turkey by myself: my patients had brought a lot of food in for
this day and Thursday is the day you eat turkey. Even the
military commissioner, Martín, with whom I'd been bit-

ter enemies for two years, decided to be friends and sent
me a big hunk of bread.

I get back to the church; the apostles have arrived and
crowds are showing up. I start running around again, seeing to everything, especially as the *Fiscal* is drunk and out
of it. The Second *Mayor*, with Fourth *Mayor*, is in charge
of the *alcila* who serve the little kid apostles and all the
alcila have to be placed according to rank again. I stand guard
over the table. Well we had all our problems with that
magazine journalist and the photographer—you remember: we saw the whole thing together so we don't need to
go through all that.

Fiscal's wife was very happy because it was us who gave
them all the baskets etc.: they had nothing (*Alcalde* Santiago
had promised a bunch of plates etc. but didn't show up—
they were all asleep, the clowns!) and we helped them out
greatly. They invited us in for the leftovers. Then I went
back to the *monumento* because of a sneaking suspicion that
someone had abandoned his post and I was right. That
morning, someone had given us a live squirrel to put under
the *monumento* and there he was, the darned little thing, all
tied up and not doing anything in particular but not looking unhappy either . . .

I guarded till 4:00, then went home looking like death.
One of the Brotherhood gave me a massage, which was
good: if I'd slept, I would have been finished. At 9:00 I
was back at the *monumento* and then decided to walk around
the town counter-clockwise through the external *monumentos*, just to see it all a little and to enjoy it. Which we did
and we kept on saying how beautiful the world was and
how well everything had gone . . . and all talking together
in the flowery ceremonial language, you know, each one
of us with our little personal *alguacil* in front . . . you've
been through that, you know how beautiful that can be . . .

I went in with the Mam and there was Makuxtin. I

greeted him ceremonially and he didn't answer. So I said that it seemed that someone was mad at us guys and there was no place to sit, so we got ready to leave. *Telinel* ran out, still happy with his fish, begging us not to leave. So he presses this dollar on us to get cokes for the *alcila*: he feels real bad that the *mayori* are not having their usual great bashes with Santa Cruz. And I tell him that you cannot ever have it all and let's be happy with what we've got.

Back in church, the experts are tying the San Juan Carajo statue to his stretcher and we have to keep all the drunks off San Juan because everyone wants to carry this guy. The men who aspire to carry have to pay; it's a kind of auction, it gets up to something like five dollars maybe . . . The money used to go the *Cabecera* to buy liquor for *cofrades* and *principales* but now it seems to be the Committee that is collecting . . . We get the saints going and the carriers do the procession route, at a run which they shouldn't do, and we have lots of trouble keeping the *santos* from getting bashed. Then everything starts falling to pieces; my *alcila* are drunk and whirring *matracas* with San Juan Carajo, or having coffee at the apostles' place: no one is guarding the fruit, etc. etc. I set up the fruit-giver to guard the fruit, get home at 4:00, crash an hour and there are the San Nicolás guys, telling me to be ready for the Cross ceremony. This is *Viernes Santo*, a Holy Friday the 13th!

My *Alguacil*, without whom I can't move, comes in and, with two more, we go to the church: the fruit-giver is still there and no *alcila*. I go over to San José because at this point I have no help and am responsible for putting the great Cross up and taking it down: it needs at least ten boys. San José tells me not to worry. We go back to the church and they are doing the Cross-hole *costumbre*, putting candles into the hole and so forth. You know well how secret and holy *that* thing is, the very entrance to earth's womb! They told me not to let any little children watch this. Then they instructed us how to bring over the Cross which we did without problems as well as the native bamboo forked poles to lift it with. They are called *axkaal*, which means 'corner post,' just as in house-corner posts and the four corner-posts of the world.

Now the hole is covered with a *saqsuut* and *cofradía* Santa Cruz is supposed to be here, in charge of the Jesucristo who is placed on the Cross. Sacristans were needed but, as usual, they had gotten drunk during the San Juan Carajo races because they have to sing through the night at the races when San Juan Carajo is run time after time between a standing Christ and Andolor, María Dolores, taking each of them 'news.' We found one sacristan and then sent ten *alcila* with *matracas* to get the clothes from Santa Cruz, together with the *Cabecera* who had finally appeared and *Fiscal* and *principales* and also Nicolás Chávez. Well they took ages, so one sacristan began and the Christ was taken out of his case, washed and prayed over on that table they put up in front of the hole.

They sewed the flowers onto his special cotton *vex*, his loincloth, just like they do when anyone dies and then made the headdress which, instead of thorns, is really of flowers. 'Oh ten, one thorn, one hand, Flower Man': there's a Martín Bundle prayer which relates to this thing: the thorn sacrifice, the flower, the one hand, the ten: for ten deities that relate to the measurement of the sky: it's all very archaic stuff and we don't even know exactly where it's from— plus, don't forget how the ancient Maya used to bleed themselves ritually with thorns . . . Then we come to the three nails, the *clavos rayos* (lightning nails) and I remember that I always play the flute when they put those in. Each nail has a special flute and drum tune.

At this point Juan Sisay, whom they'd forgotten to invite, walks in and wants me to move aside so he can help—but there's really nothing much left to do. So he gets a nail and waits his turn. Then he starts criticizing my flute and asks me why I don't get one from Coban. I say, 'Are we in Coban? This is a local flute!' I tell him I don't like fancy things from foreign places, I like things born and raised here in Santiago, but he always goes looking for something better. I get pretty mad. Then they tell me to get the Cross up, which we do, and get its bottom end into the hole and drive in the wedges; then the two ladders go up and get tied with white belt cloths by the sacristans.

Father Stan came out and asked what had happened with Juan Sisay. And what was this bird in the *monumento*? I said it was a squirrel and animals in the *monumento* represented the eaters of food. He liked that and said I should get him a squirrel. We had to change the canes (four now, in the old days twelve, I believe: they represent the corn sprouts coming out of the *monumento)* and also the candles—I think I used up forty pounds of those during the three or four days or so. So, you've seen how glorious it is when that huge Cross goes up and all the fat ceremonial candles are lit up! [*Tarn recalls that as perhaps the most beautiful thing of his whole stay in the 1950s.*]

Home for food and back to find the place strewn with pine needles. We slept happily until the end of mass. They went through the whole business of taking Christ down and putting him in the famous Juan Sisay donated urn with the recording of a bird singing inside it and the generator under it to keep it going. All I was supposed to do now was to clear the way.

At this point, I'm at the orders of the *Cabecera*. For instance the procession is getting on its way very slowly, very ponderously, and a *cofrade* San Juan who is doubling at *cofradía* Animas runs over to tell me that 'my sons, my daughters' will not carry the statues of María Andolor and San Juan Carajo. Now this is the first time I really get into doing something that doesn't pertain to me—and it gives you an idea of why a *primer mayor* is not always popular; there's a policeman aspect to it.

We were out there nervously grabbing people and both *Catequistas* and Protestants, for instance, would get very upset if asked. We finally got about eight people—María Andolor was already moving, mostly little old *cofrades* who shouldn't be carrying the saints, so I took them out and put in the new troops. The next job was to put the Cross back in church. Which is not easy. First: the whole place is full of wax, so you're slipping and sliding around; second: the Cross has to be wrapped with its cover and rope; third: the thing weighs a ton, plus everyone is drunk. The rope is sixty-nine meters long! It has a special way of crossing in the middle of the Cross which is very complex. That takes about forty minutes.

When the *alcila* got the *axkaal* to put them back, they had lost their strength and were shaking like babies. Then the old guy responsible for the Cross put the cement block back on the hole. Then the ladders went back. Then, everyone connected with the Cross is supposed to receive a *costumbre* drink from the *primer mayor*—which pleased everybody because it was said that for the last four years or so no one had done that and the *mayori* had not helped with the Cross.

Things were starting to cool off now, so we decided to stand guard over the fruit all afternoon: we invited Father Stan, who didn't want liquor so we got him a beer. Well, we heard that Second *Alguacil* was in my house talking with my wife, which I didn't like because of being tired and jealous; then we heard he was eating which got us all mad because we were so hungry. When I sent for him, he didn't come: he went to his store to sell more liquor. It was doing well that day! Actually, it turned out that he was interested in one of the *mozas*, the servant women: a lot of men go preying on these ladies without husbands. I went home, got fed and came back to the church until the procession came in around midnight. There is great emotion when people have done this whole procession with those huge ornate candles. The traditionalists go leave the candles in various places: often with San Juan, sometimes where Sojuel lived, and so forth. The more *Catequista* inclined types leave them in the church.

The *Catequistas* came and asked me to put out the candles; I did not want to since the expectation is that they burn all night. 'No, we are going to close and lock up.' I said I would not put out any candles and not leave until *they* were out because they were banana eaters too! Well, in the end, Nicolás Chávez was the last one out: he had snuffed out most of the candles but I left about twenty of them going.

I had a drop of liquor left and we sat down by the esplanade cross and finished it off. Exhausted, we went home. I wanted to be back when they opened the church. My personal *Alguacil* stood guard all night and ran to me when they opened. The church was in total darkness. I lit candles and a couple of *Catequistas* told me to put them out. I sat back of the fruit, waiting for the first sunrise of the year which this literally is. Well, at one point a guy crept forward saying, 'Let's do something about those bananas.' I struck a match and there was this guy who, the night before, had been screaming at me that I was uppity about my bananas!

In the old days, they lit the new fire with flint and cotton but now Father Stan came in with a big candle and they all lit their candles off that one. Nor was there the traditional beating of people after the mass to get rid of sins which you saw in the old days: the *Catequistas* would not let them do it. But people did it in their houses: people, trees, animals, household implements, tool etc., all their 'servants' in fact. In the old days the church was supposed to be closed with the people in it and then the light was brought in the morning. We stood guard again all day and at night until they closed the church around 10:30.

Sunday was dismantling day: taking down the *monumento* and giving back all the various component parts. We gave out the fruit: to Father Stan, to San Jose, a whole basket to the Committee which, strangely enough, was very thankful. Then a *costumbre* again: more drink. Finally, the last procession back to the house, with the fruit that was left in their baskets. I said I'd run out of money but I got one case of beer all the same. Everybody drank and started crying, saying goodbye, and the *alcila* started out with baskets of fruit, taking it to the various people who had helped us—as far as we could remember anyway. We had a little party with the *principales* and the *alcila* brought me a present of a couple of bottles of liquor plus beer for the old men. Then we had three *alcila* take the old men home and put them to bed. I personally took Eyes home.

On Monday my wife had a *costumbre* for the *mozas*. You offer them money which they refuse. They give back all the pots and pans and sort out what belongs to whom. Then they have a dinner made by themselves. I give them a little drink and it is all over.

There is an eighth day *costumbre* for the participants but they did not come: only Second and Third *Mayori* came in. There is also a fortieth day reunion for the *mayori* and, at some point, we have duties at *cofradía* Santiago.

I guess that's it. But I still have a list that I made of my expenses; perhaps that would be interesting . . .

■   ■   ■

EXPENSES OF THE *PRIMER MAYOR:*

Before March 28th:	*Dollars*
Party to convince Fourth and Fifth *Mayori*:	7.40
Trip to contract *marimba*	7.00
Down payment on *marimba* hiring	10.00
2 size-five *lienzo petate* mats	9.00
6 pots	13.00
24 Sta.Clara baskets	9.60
32½ *arroba* baskets	3.60
Metal cans for corn cooking	7.60
Plastic washtub for washing corn	1.90
3 smaller tubs	1.50
2 *kasueel* earthenware pots	13.50
Clay coffee jugs	2.00
2 baskets	1.30
Lime for corn cooking	2.50
24 bowls	24.00
100 lbs. incense	58.00
100 packs white candles	25.00
2 incense burners	5.40
Tortilla cloths	12.00
1 cloth	5.00
12 gourds	2.50
3 *comales* (flat clay dishes)	3.75
2 small pots	3.00
Head cloth	6.00
Pants	20.00
Shoes	10.00
Wife's shoes	12.00
Ocote (kindling)	.50
Wife's accoutrements	40.00

Basket	3.00
8 *tareas* (work-loads) firewood	80.00
12 ropes	4.80
1 ball nylon string	2.00
4lbs bailing wire	2.00
50 lbs. yellow candles	112.00
Hat	29.00
Suut (head-cloth)	28.00
Cloth	11.00
Pot	20.00

February 28th: Costumbre to the Mam
for first trip to Coast:

1 liter alcohol	4.00
Moonshine	1.50
2 packs candles	1.00
Incense	.50
Alms	2.00

March 1st: First trip to Coast:

25 lbs. tomatoes	5.00
Fish	2.00
Wrapping leaves	3.00
Corn	2.50
Onions	1.60
Cilantro	.25
Chile	.15
Cabbages	.80
Coffee	2.00
Sugar	.50
Cigarettes	.60
2 packs white candles	1.00
Firewood	2.00
Incense	1.00
1 liter alcohol (8 *octavo* bottles)	4.00
2 boxes	.40
2 mats	2.50

For Return Home:

10 lbs. meat	10.00
Tomatoes	1.50
Corn	2.50
Cabbages	.50
Chile	.50
Lime	.10
Cigarettes	1.00
Coffee	2.00
1 liter alcohol	4.00
Incense	1.00
White candles	1.00
Beer	.90
Firewood	2.00

Second Trip Preparation:
March 20, Costumbre with the Mam:

Candles	1.00
Incense	.60
Liquor	1.50
Alms	3.00

Second Trip to the Coast: March 21:

Very similar to First trip but more:	51.90

Third Trip to the Coast ("for real"):
Palm Wednesday:

4 gallons Moonshine	20.00
4 large *patin*; 2 small	7.00
25 lbs. incense	10.00
Meat, *tortillas*, coffee, etc.	35.00
Fifth *Mayor* expenses	25.00
Second *Mayor* expenses	25.00
Fruit	50.00
Tomatoes, cabbages, onions	6.00
Coffee, sugar	6.50
18 Gallons Moonshine	72.00

Adorning house, etc.: Palm Thursday:

Food	12.00
Electricity	1.50
Electric goods	11.00
Cigarettes	2.00
Brooms	1.00
Cane for tying trellis ornaments	2.00
Corn	24.00

Arrival of marimba, etc.: Palm Friday:

Food	30.00
Liquor	5.00
Mineral Waters	7.50

Palm Saturday:

Food	50.00
Tomatoes	10.00
Coffee	30.00
Sugar	5.00
Rum	3.25
Beans	2.00
Marimba	20.00

Palm Sunday: Corozo trip to the Coast:

3 gallons alcohol	18.00
10 lbs. meat	2.00
Coffee	10.00
Expenses for Boys	6.00
Third *Mayor* expenses	22.00
Sixth *Mayor* expenses	20.00
Coffee, sugar	10.00
House food	10.00

Holy Monday: The Monumento:

10 gallons alcohol	18.00
Food	40.00
Patin for cypress party	4.00
Patin for Xokexom	2.00

Holy Tuesday:

Food, meat	120.00
Supplies	45.00
Two cases mineral waters	3.60
Golden paper	3.00
Glue	.50

Holy Wednesday:

16 gallons alcohol	64.00
Food	10.00
Marimba	230.00
Marimba transport	7.00

Holy Thursday:

7 gallons alcohol	35.00
Food	10.00

Holy Friday:

7 gallons alcohol	35.00
Food	8.00

Holy Saturday:

Food, cigarettes, etc.	15.00
Transport money lost	5.00

Holy Sunday:

2 cases beer	15.00
2 gallons Moonshine	10.00

Monday:

Food for *mozas* (women servants)	15.00
Pay for same (those accepting)	13.00

TOTAL EXPENSES $ 2004.00

NINETEEN

Understanding the Mam and the Martín in 1979

This chapter deals with a deepening of Tarn's and Prechtel's understanding of the two great icons in 1979, as a result of which Tarn's interpretation in 1952-3 now appears shallow.

Let's start from the Holy Week expedition of the young *alcila* to the Pacific Coast which *Primer Mayor* Prechtel has just been describing.

We had suspected for some time that the coastal trip had something about it of an initiation. *Alguaciles*, typically, are young men married in the year previous to service. They are clearly sexual beings. But they abstain from sexual activity before the trip, the heat retained being transferred to the fruit they carry so that they ripen. If the fruit, on unpacking, proves unripe, the *alguacil*, traditionally, used to be severely punished. The welcome given to the young men on their return—one of the most emotional moments of the Atiteco year—is heroic. They are hailed as "warriors" (*achijab*), incensed by their wives, cherished by the assembled elders, and taken back in triumph to the center of town. After the unpacking, they are licensed to drink, clown, be irresponsible, beg for drink money, and, of course, renew contact with their wives.

As they do so, immediately after Holy Week, the first plantings of maize occur. This also launches the wet season, ruled over by Jesucristo as solar deity, resurrected as maize on, or within, his Cross. At this time, the Mam, principally the deity of the dry season, is said to return to sleep.

The Atiteco year, like that of many agricultural societies, is thought of as cyclical. Its principal divisions are wet season (Holy Week to All Saints) and dry season (All Saints to the next Holy Week). Two principal starting points to the year are conceived of: the Jesucristo/Sun's birth at Christmas and his rebirth, or "planting" for the Christmas birth, nine months later at Holy Week. The period from Christmas to Holy Week (dry) covers the Sun's youth; that from Holy Week to *fiesta* Santiago (wet), his maturity; and that from *fiesta* Santiago to Christmas (wet and dry), his old age. We can see from this ternary pattern, imposed on the binary pattern of wet and dry, that the Sun's rebirth or planting at Holy Week is in fact a passage from youth into maturity.

The life and death principles associated with these cycles are inclusive of each other in the acts of planting and harvesting. In order to plant anything, it is necessary to kill or, more precisely, to bury the seed. Seeds are often called "little skulls": there is an echo here of the skull tree in *Popol Vuh*. The act of harvesting implicitly heralds birth in that food is produced, yes, but also seed-corn. We'll find that, at work inside the binary life/death opposition, is a dynamic ternary element acting as a catalyst or transformer, moving a thing from one state to another without itself being affected. The main structure involved in this process is an all-embracing metaphor involving the equation CORN/ MAN/SUN as passing through identical successive stages from birth through maturity to death and from death to rebirth.

Study of the precolumbian Maya or Mexicanized Maya worldview in the *Popol Vuh*, reveals the belief that normal work among human beings—the growing of maize, squash and beans—is invariably flanked, on the one hand, by the exuberant and undisciplined play of youth (often thought of as "still animal, not yet human") and, on the other, by the fading, retiring, non-work of old age. These in turn are linked with normal adult sexuality, bracketed by presexuality, on the one hand, and by postmenopausal lack of sexuality on the other. Both pre- and post-sexuality are associated with magic and/or sorcery, a sorcery, in turn, closely linked to "the arts": principally adornment, music and witchcraft.

We suspect that all of this might be related in turn to a relative weakness or impotence of the Equinoxial Suns (young Sun/dying Sun) versus a strength of the mature summer Solstice Sun which fertilizes nature and makes it ready for work.

This ternary view has many echoes in the social set-up. Among them would be: grandsons/husband-and-wife/grandparents or *alguaciles/mayores/principales*, etc. It is most important to realize that only stage two, maturity, is truly fertile. Stage one is thought of as extremely sexual but sterile, disordered and socially unchannelled. Stage three is menopausal, non-sexual and, in that sense, also sterile.

The complex iconography of the three principal figures in the Atiteco world-view—the Martín, the Mam, and Jesucristo—now begin to look as if they might be similarly organized. The Martín Bundle, paired with a María (single or multiplied) is associated with the concept of "normal" maturity: food corn, working farmer and Sun at its most fertile in the form of rain—the liquid aspect of the Sun. Jesucristo, in his resurrected form at Easter is the Martín or, perhaps more precisely, the matter or substance with which the Martín works.

The Mam is "paranormal," both immature and over-mature. As immature, the Mam is the deity of unbridled sexuality, lust and disorder—often translated as hermaphroditic, bisexual, homosexual, clothes-crazy, loving song, music, adornment, in love with love and linked to one or more unbridled females, associated, among other things, with that which produces adornment, namely weaving. As an over-mature deity, the Mam is the Old God, probably associated with the *Uayeb*, the five days of passage from old year to new which might have passed from the old Maya calendar into the Catholic calendar at the Easter week.

The Mam, both young and old, is mainly associated with the dry season and the dry Sun and other aspects of creation, seen by Atitecos as "negative," such as femaleness, night, left, dryness, south, west, death, coldness, etc. At the same time, however, there is some kind of close link between the Mam and the very positive Martín. In the stories, the Mam eventually appears as the youngest Martín in a plurality of Martín forms: that is, when the Martín is seen as 12 or 13 Martíns. He is created by the 12/13 ancestors (earthly transforms or *nawal* of the Martíns) to guard their wives while the ancestors are away on buying and selling trips. Incidentally, it looks as if the dry season Martíns are understood to be merchants, the wet season Martíns to be warriors. Interestingly, there are merchant-warrior castes in traditional precolumbian Mesoamerican society.

Now the youngest of any set of divinities is always potentially powerful in that s/he is also the seed, i.e. the *oldest* of the next set. This ambivalence takes a variety of forms. Thus, the "youngest Martín" is the shirt or cape buried deepest in the Martín Bundle, the one which can destroy the world if it gets loose. Thus the Mam, once made and set up as "the guardian of the earth," defeats Evil Person (*Itsel Vinag*), assumes his characteristics and becomes the very danger he has been set up to guard against. Thus, following the *Popol Vuh*, the youngest is often represented as a very wise monkey who, in turn, is frequently associated with previous creations, producing an equation of wooden men/monkeys/the arts still active in the present creation. In this respect, the Mam (made of wood, of course) is occasionally associated with monkeys and may be to Jesucristo what a previous creation is to present creation: the dry Sun as a wet Sun-to-be.

For similar reasons, the end of an era or judgement (*juicio*) may be merely the end of a given solar year or it may be the end of a Sun. Here it is worth looking at a story frequently told in Atitlán. This is one of a number of versions (there is never any such thing in Atitlán as a fixed, unchanging story):

Tarn, 1952-3:
According to the ancients, the angels have the right to visit women every fifteen or twenty days. There was one angel

who disobeyed this order and was tempted by a woman into seeing her in the intervals. One day, after committing such a sin, he saw in a field the fruit of the tree *kuxin*, took off his angelic clothes, lay down his angelic weapons and climbed the tree. While he was eating, there came through the air a huge snake. . . . which curled itself around him and started sucking blood with its tail. The angel screamed for help. A merchant from Chicacao, happening on the scene. . . . was told by the angel to put on the angelic clothes, take up the weapons and shoot the snake. The merchant was somewhat inept but finally managed to do this. Out of the weapon came a great bolt of lightning and the snake fell to pieces. The angel also died and turned black.

At this point, the merchant was caught up into a great cloud, and this, since he did not know how to drive it, flew at great speed toward the sea, with terrific rains which lifted the roofs of houses and changed the courses of rivers. The king of the angels, alerted, called his other angels from their resting places in the hills and told them to catch the cloud before it fell into the sea—otherwise the world would be destroyed. They finally caught the merchant and his cloud and brought them to the king. The king told the merchant he would beat him but the merchant accused the angel who had made him do what he did. Whereupon, this angel who had come alive again was beaten too.

Thunder and lightning are most often described as caused by angels agitating their ornaments and weapons in the sky. Clearly, we have here echoes of syncretism with Catholic stories of the Judeo-Christian Fall and, perhaps, the Deluge. But Atiteco myth seems to turn on another kind of fall: that produced by a deity— or possibly an aspirant to divine status—taking on, sorcerer's apprentice or Icarus-like, a task into which he has not been properly initiated and ordained such as carrying the Sun or flying a

Martín cape. In the latter case, he will be driven into the sea. He thus creates a judgement (*juicio*) in that only a full Sun-being can fall into the sea (the West): all the merely human Atiteco dead normally retrace their steps back up the Sun-path eastwards.

Breaking history into periods is a task puzzling to the Atitecos. But, as we shall see in a while, there is evidence for history, following precolumbian patterns, being seen as a series of eras or "Suns": as few as three and as many as five. What is often confusing—and what may have been permanently blurred by syncretism—is whether the process of succession is cyclical or linear.

If it is linear, we look at versions in which each Sun retreats to a "hidden deity" position (*deus absconditus* as it is called in theology). This is sometimes said to have happened to "God the Father." If it is cyclical, then much evidence could lead us to believe that a dry Sun, or Mam, could eventually become the true wet Sun. A similar ambivalence afflicts the contrast between young and old angels. The young ones are the warriors wielding the weapons of "war"; i.e. the weather which produces both men and their food: cloud, rain, lightning, thunder etc.: you meet this in the story of the killing of Evil Person. The old ones, concentrated at Cerro de Burro, the "Center of the World," on the south rim of the Lake, "govern" the young ones but are thought of as *pasados*, reflecting the sexually sterile but socially powerful status of over-ripeness. Their rains, defined as urine, are from the young if strong, from the old if weak and drizzly. Sometimes, both old and young are known as Martíns, sometimes they are distributed between the Mam and the Martín.

Do the old angels disappear linearly or do their "souls" return into some kind of stock from which the young are reproduced again? Both views are touted. One thing, however, becomes clear. The dual youth/age status of the Mam (we saw it in Chapter Fifteen in the Stresser-Péan Huastec story) qualifies him more than any other for the role of the "transformer."

When conceived of as binarized, or we might say "polarized," he is more dry than wet. When non-polarized, he works in the sytem at large during both dry and wet seasons as the force which makes babies into youths; youths into *alcila* (young Mam); *alcila* into *mayori* (Martín); *mayori* into *principales* (still Martín); *principales* into *pasados* (old Mam); *pasados* into deities (angels); perhaps gods into babies again. Much will become clearer when we look, soon, at the female aspect of all this. But one thing can be said now. When polarized, the female principle works primarily with the Martín in the wet season. When non-polarized, it functions both with the Martín and the Mam. This explains why, sometimes confusingly, the Mam also has a María and why she is dual: both young and old.

The Mam is lord of many dry things such as dust and the powder on the wings of butterflies and moths. His wood, *Erythrina*, has red flowers and seeds, indicating heat. His "sleeping place" and the roof of a sweat bath (on which he often stands in the stories) are built of red *Taxicoba* (*tz'aaj*). As lord of earth-fire, he cooks, ages, ripens and rots. The Mam works at night when the Sun rests and sleeps during the day. A child needs the Mam's heat to be born as "First Sun, First Dawn": the Mam separates fruit (baby) from stem (the umbilical) by ripening it so that it "falls" into life (planting). Thus "dawning" is "planting" as it is in the *Popol Vuh*.

The Mam as the dry season, ripens the world for the wet season and the planting of Corn/Sun/Jesucristo. His hanging himself from the wet dahlia tree appears to symbolize his turning himself off, or going to sleep, during the world's day. *Erythrina* storing water and acting as a shade tree for the cacao plant indicates that the dry season hides, guards and protects humidity rather than destroying it. In the wet season, despite the Sun's heat, the earth is green/cold because the Mam sleeps. The humidity/rain/sex, i.e. the Martíns into which the young Mam has, or (if plural) have, grown, matures our food. On waking, the Mam brings back the dryness required for the harvest. Thus humidity concerns life;

dryness concerns birth into, and death out of, life. In another set of stories we will need another book to tell, the sweatbath originated, through a "grandmother's" death, as a primal womb from which all humanity was born.

Our food/sex life is made what it is by the Mam as "crazy lust" (*ch'ojlal*): exquisite and unavoidable pleasure-pain. Our life is "sin" (*il, mak*) itself. At death, all souls pass through the Mam's sweatbath to burn off sin as a child must cleanse itself of "filth" (food/sex/dying) before meeting its father. When the Mam is dressed, he is treated just like a dead human. He takes the dead on their trip back east toward the Sun. The body is planted in the Sun's village—the cemetary—and, as a seed, will produce namesakes perpetuating the lineage of the dead person. Sin is burned off in the sweatbath. The rest proceeds to God.

One above the other, behind the back wall of the church building in Atitlán, stretch the Mam's original altar or residence (before he moved to *cofradía* Santa Cruz): the old disused town cemetery; the origin tree of the Mam at Chokox A'qoum, the Mushroom Place; a place of the Sun's crucifixion and death of which the main church altar is a transform, and, beyond that, all the foreign locations that are not part of the "navel of earth and sky" which is Atitlán. The Mam's place—there is some confusion between the residence and the location of the tree—is thought of as a sweatbath, a hill, a sulphurous mineral spring, from which, at night, issues a steamy, hot, skunk-smelling wind which cools by dawn. It is here, in Chiviliu's Words that the Mam works at night as "captain, jailor, warden, night *mayor*, lawyer, advocate, justicer of souls."

The Mam's night work is considered hyper-sexual and perverse. He lives with a harem of women who love sex and tie themselves to him before death. People who do not "pay" and atone for sins through ritual are dried by the Mam and taken to his sweatbath, tied (*xmon*) like prisoners or loads of firewood. Indeed, one reading of the term Maximón goes *Mamxmon*, the Old Lord who is Bound, this refering also to his core being bound by rope and, as we shall see in a while, to his relation with weaving. People who wish to avoid the fire pay substitute "hot" fines, such as alcohol, tobacco, incense, clothing, and tallow candles.

To look now at the Mam as a transformer through the act of initiation, we must make our way back to the Holy Week proceedings.

We have precolumbian evidence that the *Eythrina* tree was a major shade tree for the cacao plant. Cacao, in turn, is together with *pataxte* (*Theobroma Bicolor*) and the cohune or *corozo* flower (*Orbignya Cohune*), archetypal of the tropical produce which is brought, at Easter, from the coastal Piedmont to the Highlands. When we talk of things brought in that direction, it is hard not to remember that this was the direction of tribute from Highland possessions in the Lowlands, with the flow continuing on, at times, from the Tzutujil people to overlords of theirs further to the North or East.

Another essential piece of information here is that the produce is thought of as essentially female and essentially *munil*: a category of edibles signifying not-real-food (*waya*: corn-water) but food-in-addition, food-as-enjoyment, dessert, surplus, excess. The fact that the word "*munil*," in Quiché, as well as in Yucatec, has the connotation of "female slave" adds evidence to the tributary nature of this "fruit" from the "female" southern regions. Connotations of "vice" also need exploring.

The *alguaciles*, remember, must go down to the Pacific in a state of abstinence. They go as warriors. The terminology suggests that capturing a victim/copulating with/eating/sacrificing are all included in the paradigm of things that the *alguaciles* do to or with the fruit. So we find ourselves asking whether the *alguaciles* are abstaining from their wives in order to have relations with the fruit: their task is to rain on, or ripen, the fruit. However, the fruit, as mistresses, concubines or secondary wives, are brought back and presented as a tribute to the political superiors and overlords of the *alguaciles*: the *mayores*, the *principales*, the Mam and Jesucristo. Might it be that the *alguaciles* are, as it were, "training" with Coastal concubines, being initiated that way into sex, so as to be able to attain true maturity in the beds of their own true wives? Or is it something other than this?

After unpacking, the fruit is presented first to the Mam in the political headquarters of Atitlán, i.e. the Municipal building. The Mam who has been carried from *cofradía* Santa Cruz by his *telinel*, is laid on the floor and the fruit is disposed of in a circle around him. Something very mysterious is supposed to be happening at this point and Atitecos are extremely loath to talk about it. The principal idea is that the Mam is "eating," "sleeping with" (that is "copulating with") the fruit. Only after this, is the fruit taken out to be hung on the *monumento* while the Mam goes to his special chapel to be hung on what is thought of as a dahlia tree. Note now that Jesucristo, when he is finally taken by his enemies—Jews, Romans and so forth—after a very long and complex saga, is captured while hiding in a *corozo* palm tree and, some say, "as a *corozo* flower: the most female of all the *munil* virgins." Note also that the Mam, in his Judas persona, is alleged to have sinned above all by one) "eating before Jesucristo at the last supper"; two) selling Jesucristo to his enemies for pieces of silver—also called *munil*; and three) killing Jesucristo because of a type of "desire" or "lust" identified with jealousy of a person in a higher state than one can ever attain to oneself. Etymologically, the words for desiring/eating/copulating with/sacrificing/victimizing/doing someone a bad turn—or as we might say "screwing" someone—are all part of one paradigm. Note finally that, while it appears as if the fruit is going to the Mam first and then to his overlord Jesucristo, it is actually the Mam who enjoys the *jus primae noctis*, the Indian deity that is, rather than the Christian one.

Now: if the Mam is lying with the fruit and "eating" it, he is also lying with and eating Jesucristo as the *corozo*. It would seem that Jesucristo may have to be thought of as female, or more probably, bisexual. At his crucifixion, however, he becomes male by shedding his blood (associated with sperm) onto the ground and onto the fruit of the *monumento*. While the cross-hole, a "womb," or "navel," of earth, is in the floor of the church building, it is also held to be located at the top of the *monumento* in the *Kasueel juyu*, and, cosmically, on the volcano back of the origin tree of the Mam. From the two higher locations, the blood/sperm can indeed flow onto the fruit. And Jesucristo also finally "eats" the fruit in this manner.

Could it be possible that the "mystery" of the Mam and Jesucristo involves a sexual assault—perhaps not dissimilar to that which the Mam inflicts on a potential *aj'kun* who refuses his vocation—in the course of which the Mam "eats" the femaleness out of Jesucristo and thus matures or initiates him out of youthful bisexuality into full maleness exclusively? So that, at this point, he can deal with his own female or females, María and their multiples, the female Martíns? And that this, with the so frequently found equivalences of "mother" and "wife" (or an elision of "mother" in the stories, leaving the "grandmother" as the only true maternal figure), might be the grounds for the sexual relations alleged to take place between Jesucristo and María Andolor (de las Dolores) before the Crucifixion? And is there in turn a relationship between what happens to the *alguaciles* and their fruit as the boys are made into fully mature men, eventual *mayores* or Martíns (and the fruit into ripe rather than unripe fruit)? Something of this kind must lie behind the notion that the *alguaciles* must be abstinent because they have to go out to the Coast and "not make love but make rain."

In such a case, the passage from an immature state of bisexuality to one of unisexuality in which mature, fertile, "married" sexual union between male and female can result in the production both of human kind and its food would be revealed as the initiatic transformation which the Holy Week ritual represents. The Mam, as the lord of the *mayori*, and as an almost Gnostic Judas in some Maya "Gospel of Judas" represented as essential to the enactment of Jesucristo's *agon*, would be the *initiator*. The young Jesucristo, Manuel, as the eternal boy, abstinent as the *alcila* are (or as the *telinel* when dealing with the Mam or the Martín Bundle's *nabeysil* permanently), is the *initiated*. This may be the ultimate signification of that strange involvement of the Mam with sexual magic which could only be noticed in the early 1950s but not resolved.

For when, in the stories, the Mam seems to be turning his job topsy-turvy and becoming the breaker of sexual rules which he was created by the ancestors to protect, it may, in reality, be something else that is happening. While there is no end to the delight produced by stories of the Mam's "misdeeds," a significant number of stories have the Mam breaking the rules so that those who should not be joined together should be sundered while those who should be together should be united.

Thus the Mam appears in another role he is known for: as the marriage broker, the old man who opens the way to a matrimonial union from which the child of the lineage is born, once again helping with "the New Day, the New Sun." Sterile himself/herself—because, as we are about to see, the Mam, like all true Maya deities is essentially and indissolubly male/female—the Mam opens the way to cosmic and human fertility. Static itself, the Mam is the transforming power keeping the world in motion. And, in the last resort, in that game of mirrors which all cyclical systems end up by instituting, the eternally recurrent cycle of birth, life and death ensures the ultimate identity of the Mam, the Martín, and the Jesucristo, whose Christian drama has been so brilliantly assimilated into a Maya world view.

One other complication might be mentioned. There is much in Atiteco lore which sees the Mam as a powerful *ladino*. The question of the Mam's *jus primae noctis* could then conceivably have another sense: that in which plantation owners and rich *ladinos* in colonial times, most of them located on the Coast, often took advantage of Indian women. This would involve looking further into the identification of the Maximón with Judas and the complexity of Judas's treacherous relation to Jesucristo. But this seems to us to be a subtext of the major text which is the Indian view of fertility.

There will be a good deal more to say on these mysteries in another book.

TWENTY

The Deities When Female, 1979

Very little was found concerning the female side of the pantheon in the early 1950s. A great deal emerged during 1979 and it is vital to a full understanding of our triad: the Martín, the Mam and Jesucristo. It will be connected to an apparent paradox in the field of belief. On the one hand, divine female identity tends to be constant when compared with the shifting nature of male identities, especially in relation to age. On the other hand, the behavior of divine females is thought of as inconstant, fickle and irregular. Tarn got used to talking about this under the heading "Constant Inconstancy."

A few general principles first:

Atiteco thought conceives of male and female as aspects or facets of one original living unit and no living unit can be other than both. Certainly, nothing completely fulfilling its function in the world can be other than both. Thus, a man cannot take office before marriage and all offices have complementary tasks for the husband/wife pair, whether they function together on any given occasion or not. By extension, what we might call "units of function" stand in male/female relation to each other with the "female" element standing as "assistant" to the "male." For example: the second *fiscal* (with his wife) is female to the first *fiscal* (with his wife)—the *cabecera*, at the top of the system being male to the whole village—or the *juez de cofradía* (with his wife) is female to the *alcalde de cofradía* (with his wife). Some even say that the Martín is "wife" to the *nabeysil* as the Mam is wife to the *telinel*—although one might think it would be the other way round . . .

On arriving home from the hospital one day, our friend Eyes

kissed his corn, his beans, his woodpile and the earth of his compound, then smiled at Tarn and Janet and said, "I have just kissed my four wives." A man's body is his wife—everything concerned with the mind and wisdom being male and everything concerned with the body and beauty being female. Water appears to be essentially conceived of as a female substance in the power of a male activity, although we'll find there are male waters and female waters. Eating is male, the substance eaten is female. Clothing, as concerned with adornment and beauty is female. Surprisingly, the penis is held to be female in that the urethra is a small vagina; the clitoris does seem to be male.

The corn plant is female, although often divided into male stem and leaves and female flowers. The corn itself is the baby and the farmer is male to these, abstaining from sex while planting. The human race, taken as a whole, is female to God, thus explaining various human criminal interferences with God's power to fertilize. An apparently harmless act such as Judas's "eating first" before Jesucristo at the Last Supper is the Mam's awesome arrogation of Jesucristo's powers in the cosmic drama of "eating the fruit." That definitions are primarily male weighted and oriented goes without saying and the belief system is far from completely logical. Are any belief systems not so?

Such principles are at work in the "history" of the cosmos. We'll find here that any unit of function can be transformed into any other when it is a male/female creative unity that is being discussed. Put another way, the primordial couple, say, is defined as the First Sun (and his wife) where *history* is concerned, but can become any of the succeeding Suns, including the present one, when *function* is discussed—or vice versa up and down the scale. Because, relatively speaking, Suns differ "historically" more than Moons do, any confusion arising out of this will be greater in the lunar case than in the solar.

The full study of Atiteco cosmic history must be left for another book but we can illustrate by hearing one of the simpler and more cogent versions of the creation:

Cristóbal Esquina Yataz, Cabecera 1979:
At the very beginning, the first *Tetixel* was the world, the *Mundo*. Nothing had blossomed yet. When he died, he split into two and became male and female: that is *Tetixel* the male Sun and *Tetiej*, the female Moon. [*Note that the* Tetixel *is often called Eternal Father*—Padre Eterno.]

When a god dies he becomes the Sun and Moon just as, when we die, we become the Stars. That first *Tetixel* was the First World; the second *Tetixel* became the First Sun and his *Tetiej* was the First Moon and they were the Second World.

The First Sun and First Moon have three children. You know the story of how the first two children kill their grandmother by shoving her in the sweatbath and then they become the Sun and Venus. In this Sun and Venus pair, the Sun is the Second Sun. The third child, also male, becomes the Lord of the Hills. There are also two sisters: one becomes the Moon and the second the Moon's Star.

The Second Sun, Lord of the Third World, marries María whom we call Water. The *Tetixel*, the First Sun, is conquered. He goes to outer existence; he is no longer visible. He becomes the Remembrance of the power of the *Tetixel*.

The Second Sun and María give birth to Manuel, who is the first *Nawal Antigwal*, the first ancestor, the first prophet. It is he who is going to make our world, the Fourth World. It is he who fights the enemies left over from the previous creation. It is he who teaches his mother María; he who makes the world we live in out of the bones, which are rocks, of the previous Sun; he who brings us the corn etc. He becomes the Third Sun at his death and resurrection when he is called no longer Jesucristo but Cristo Salvador. It is he who makes the Fourth World which is this one of ours.

He has brothers and sisters. His brothers are Santiago, our village patron, who is Venus; Juan Martín, the North

Wind; Diego Martín, the South Wind; and San Juan, the Lord of the Hills. The Moon is the same one as before. [*In answer to a query*]: Yes, I guess she is Manuel's sister.

There are much more complex versions with up to four or five Suns and/or worlds. The major thing here, for us right now, is to notice that, whereas usually the storytellers are relatively clear about the numbers of Suns and worlds, the Moon remains rather problematic. While she seems to be the *mother* of the First Sun, she appears to be more like a *sister* to the next Suns. Or she seems to be one of a sister pair (the Moon and the Moon's star), not necessarily relating to the given Sun and his brothers (the Second Sun, Venus and the Lord of the Hills).

It is often said that the Moon "doesn't change." There is a confusion in the aside of the storyteller: when the two brothers kill their grandmother, that grandmother is in fact, in that story, their mother. It is often said that the Sun's wife is also his mother: a mother-wife. The generational pattern in its female version is often confusing: grandmother, mother, daughter can take each other's places; a mother can be a wife and vice versa. This may be due to original Maya views; it could also be tied to complex perceptions of Catholic versions of a Virgin Mother-Wife. Or, indeed, both.

Most frequent of all is the assertion that the Moon is a grandmother, an old woman with flowing white hair—and this in spite of the fact that young, middling and old Moon stages are also talked about. The elision of the mother here may well be related to the fact that the Atiteco ideal of domesticity is linked to the older woman past child-bearing, secure in her knowledge and crafts, her lineage and residence—whereas the still actively mothering female remains a potential breakaway from the domestic unit, still a danger until she is older. Other beliefs suggest that the Moon's identity is more permanent than the Sun's, although her behavior is fickle: she runs with other stars and planets, she is "such a traveler" that she has to mark time in relation to them and so on.

In Yataz's version, the Second Sun's wife is María, described as Water—though it is clear from much else that earth/standing water/Moon are closely related, as indeed they were in the precolumbian pantheon. The fact that the Catholic María icon stands on a moon is helpful. On the Catholic side, Manuel, of course, poses a problem: he does not marry. There are, however, those assertions about intercourse at the time of the San Juan Carajo races during Holy Week, with Andolor, i.e. the María de las Dolores, and here we come again upon the theme of the mother-wife.

There is much more on the Moon:

> *Cristóbal Esquina Yataz, 1979:*
> The Moon, our grandmother, the *Iyom Pak'lom*, is the great power here in Atitlán. She brought everything out of her belly. She gets big and swells and gives birth to the months. Each month is born out of her: these are the Twelve Marías. [*For Eyes, 'There is one Sun-day which is our year: he is born, lives and dies. The Moon does it 12/13 times, the Sun does it once.'*] She is like some bitch-dog who gives birth to puppies all the time. She gives birth to the Sun also and she creates *il* and *mak*, our pleasure-pain sin. She is into *mak* herself so she comes and goes.
> The first child of the Padre Eterno, the *Tetixel*, and our grandmother was not made from a sexual union because, really, there were not two people. They felt each other and the child was born—but through *her* womb, her vagina. Only in the time of Jesus was this different: here the Sun's wife is a virgin who delivers the child into the hands of the midwife (*iyom*) Yaxper, who is María Isabela.
> The Moon lives on top of the twelve steps (*kablajuj q'amuq*) of which she is the *ajaw*, the (female) lord. The steps stand on land which goes up when there is a *juicio*, a final judgement. The land stands on a tree with roots somewhere underneath. When the *juicio* flood subsides, the land

goes down again. It is on these steps that she greets the Sun when he comes in from work and from here she sends him off again.

Looking at the deities we find on the ground today, this account seems to relate mostly to the female of the Martín in *cofradía* San Juan. She is called María and sometimes *Iyom Pak'lom*, most frequently seen as a variant of the *Tetiej-Tetixel*. Sometimes she is *Yaxper*—although most people say that *Yaxper* "came after" the *Iyom Pak'lom*, is merely "an imitation" or "image" of her, or, again, that *Yaxper* only concerns the Third Sun, Cristo Salvador, as his midwife (*iyom*) Elisabeta or Isabela. Implantation of a root (*r'kux*) in a woman by the *Tetixel-Tetiej* is clearly distinguished from the "receiving" of a child by the midwife *Yaxper*. Eyes said: "*Yaxper* just gives birth because we are flesh. But that is like a dream. The spirit is put in there in a flash by God. The grandmother receives and grabs the child and sets up its Star." The Martín either is divided into 12/13 entities—the 12/13 Martíns— or has 12/13 sons. Attempts to fill out lists usually fail to produce such numbers, until you realize that 12/13 means "totality." Again this might be Maya or connected to the 12 apostles, 13 with Christ. Or both. There is also evidence for lists of 12/13 sacred places around the town of Atitlán. The *Iyom Pak'lom*, on the other hand, is or becomes, the 12/13 Marías. In many stories, it is clear that the First Martín is Cristo Salvador and that there is an overlap between a set of Martín brothers and a set of *santo* brothers to the resurrected Jesucristo.

These 12/13 Martíns make themselves, more or less subsequently, manifest on earth in the *apparently human* guise of the 12/13 *nawal taq achi*. In virtually all versions, we have these divided into male and female (*taq exji*), but the constellations vary: 12 male and 12 female; or 6 male and 6 female (totalling 12). The gendering of these presents difficulties for people. For one friend, these *nawal taq achi* and *taq exji* were male/female facets of one unit of function, though they did have human husbands and wives. The problem is to some extent appeased by the statement of another friend: "a *nawal* doesn't have or not have sex: he or she *is* sex." When Cristóbal Yataz tells you that "they only have sex every twenty days" and you know that the traditional Maya calendar has twenty days, you begin to suspect something important about the identity of these versions of the Martíns.

Remember that, in the stories of his creation by the 12/13 "ancestors," yet another term for the *nawal taq achi*, the Mam is either a thirteenth Martín originally or becomes one by virtue of this creation and his deeds of valor. As such, he can be talked of either as the youngest (*ch'eep*) of the present set or the oldest: the boss of the next set of Martíns. This apparent contradiction is clearly linked to the calendrical cyclicality of the whole system. In any event, the *ch'eep* of any set is always an extremely powerful being. That the Mam also overlaps with Jesucristo is clear, often seeming to be a transformation of that figure. The definition by separation of the three icons in the early 1950s now seems shallow. The unit is undoubtedly separable from one perspective, and inseparable from another. It is regrettable that the traditional calendar is in such sad shape in Santiago, precluding further identifications.

Christianity always remains a complicating factor. It is hard to know whether the non-wived, or abstinent, nature of certain figures is Christian, Maya or both. Manuel Jesucristo's bacherlor-hood is a problem, but it fits with some Maya notions whereby the young have to abstain at certain times, especially when, as young Mam figures, they avoid human sex in order to make cosmic sex in the form of rain. The Atiteco tendency is to wive Jesucristo, overtly or covertly, in one way or another according to the unit of function principle—just as the Mam and the Martín are wived.

■ ■ ■

The María box in *cofradía* San Juan contains a piece of cloth which can only be handled by the *alcalde*'s wife, the *aj'kuna* and the *iyoma'*. The three little colonial period *putti* faces on the cloth represent "the three corn girls": yellow (on the right facing the cloth); white (center); and black (left). Nicolás Chiviliu called these "the three faces of the three navels" or "the first navel (*r'muxux*) of man" and claimed that there were also three faces in the box which, like the last shirt of the Martín, were never taken out. The María faces are also called, respectively, Yamri (María); Yachon (Concepción); and Yaxuan (Juana).

An *aj'kun* can place the cloth on the belly of his female client, faces downward. Whatever "looks at the child will give it its face." The cloth will give the child the propitious face of one of the three corn-colors. Ribbons attached to the cloth represent umbilical cords and the tendrils of plants and human lineages (*sejutay*). Under ribbons at the base of the cloth, there are two small round, very hard cloth bags. No one has seen their contents. There is speculation that they may be hardened leather or—perhaps more likely—old ground corn paste. These are named *yuxa*, "divine twins." One male, one female, they are the original placentas, the original seeds of the human race. They are called *r'k'ux ak'ala* (root of children), *nawal taq iyoma'* (first midwives), and *nawal taq alaniem* (first birthmakers). The whole object is said to represent a womb.

Someone said that "each object in the world has a different father, but an umbilical links it to this single large womb-root," which he also called a "tree-root" in the sense of lineage tree: this provides another reading of the "constant" aspect of the divine female. Because the María box is associated with the Moon, it is hung from the ceiling rather than placed on floor or table, the same being true of a leather case associated with the Mam's María in *cofradía* Santa Cruz.

The earth aspect of the Martín's María is evidently represented mostly by plant images which are in themselves also male/female. Remember the fruit of Holy Week: the Mam is said to "shoot his wad" with them when, representing all the *nawal taq achi*, "he takes the smell of the fruit: they don't have faces and they don't have arms but they have a smell and they are beautiful." When this Martín's María appears as the 12/13 Marías, it is mostly in vegetal terms: María *tiney* (dahlia); María *tul* (water reed); María *muuch'* (*chipilín*, a vegetable green) etc. María *pop*, the mat, is often referred to. When, in ritual, the *Cabecera* says, "I have my father, I have my mother," he points to the reeds that mats are made of. There is one reed (*tsok*) that is associated with María Agosto. Men are said to have eaten reeds before they ate corn. In precolumbian times, the mat was a throne.

While María Entidad *[de la Natividad]* in *cofradía* San Gregorio is thought of as the patroness of the Lake, it is stressed that María in all her forms is mostly the Lake and all standing water, which is female, as opposed to water falling from the sky which is male. When people see sunshine on the Lake, they say "Oh! our father with our mother," or even "Oh, our father reflected in our mother."

Of the Moon's stages, the first is often called "little girl," "child" and also "water Moon": anything planted under it matures slowly or not at all. The Moon contains the water that is rained. She slowly turns up sideways toward the rainy season until the water spills out. A Moon tilted over Ch'umil Volcano and turning red signifies rain soon; she is bathing in the ocean. The Moon picks up water, pours it over her body, whence it falls to earth again. As a new Moon, she is shy of water and so tilts away from it. Both the Sun and Moon bathe: rings around either signify rain. Rings around the Moon are associated with snake-rainbows (related symbolically to the grandmother's headband). Another image has the Moon sending the first water up to the sky for evaporation and being also the lady of stored water, as in the domestic water jar. It is often pointed out that the feminine prefix *Ya* (Ms., Miss, or Mrs.) is the same word as water.

There is a very great deal more to be said about the Moon and water, and about the Lake and its produce, but this must be kept for another occasion.

■　　■　　■

In *cofradía* Santa Cruz, there are two Marías. One is Jesucristo's and represents his clothing. It is in the care of an *escribano*, a sacristan of the church who is also the *cofradía*'s secretary or record keeper. The other María, the Mam's, is kept in his own house by the *telinel*. This María has the appearance of a small Maximón-like figure, lying down in a wooden box with a glass window front. The body is invisible, wrapped in a scarf or bed cloth, but the head, mask, hat, boots, and cigar are like Maximón's. Eyes told us that this María has very long white human hair which is an actual female scalp from "long ago." The hair has something tucked inside it which might be a fistful of lake reeds. The main body is hidden in a *suut* scarf and he infers from *aj'kun* practice and from the terminology that it is most likely a weaving stand.

From the origin stories concerning the grandmother killed in a sweatbath, the association here is with an old woman who combs her hair (the weaving stand) with a comb (the batten), producing corn cobs which fall onto the ground. For Eyes, this process is parallelled by the original Marías' weaving of natural earth products and creatures into the original earth mantles: these are represented by the capes in the Martín Bundle. They wove their children: birds, snakes, jaguars, and so forth. A series of metaphors connected with "feeding the loom" link cloth and children; also the way in which a loom is rolled up and carried about like a child. The "food of the weaving thread" follows a sinuous line which is compared to the hidden way of the earth (the "hills and valleys" in the precolumbian Maya formula) and contrasted with the straight path of the Sun represented, for instance, by the central orange band of a cofrade's head-scarf. Cloth thickness and child fleshing are both due to "food."

The cloth is also like a year, conceived of as moving upward toward the loom's tying post associated with the original world tree. The 12/13 Marías, as parts of the loom, are also the first twelve months of a child's life, with María Batz'bal, who is probably not too different from Francisca Batz'bal, as the thirteenth. Also, before a child is one year old, the question will be "how many Grandmothers (Moons) does the child have?" The cord tying the loom to the post is known as the umbilical and the extremities of the warp beam are called *tioxa* (divine twins). The Mam is known as *suutin ala* (*suut* boy), from *suut* which is primarily a weaving stand full of cloth. The imagery here is clearly linked to that of the Martín's María in *cofradía* San Juan.

Confirming much of this, Nicolás Chiviliu had it that this Mam's María had "three layers on which she sat or rested: the batten, the shed stick, and the heddle." In a similar vein the 12/13 Marías, when referred to in this context are called by the twelve main parts of the loom.

We have talked about the young (presexual), mature, and old (postsexual) aspects of Maya deities. The young and old aspects of the María are most clearly displayed in the Mam's María. As in the case of the invocation to the Mam (*ay! nawal ala, ay! nawal acha*—boy/man), so here the invocation to María in songs is to *ay! nawal q'apoj, ay! nawal ixoq*—girl/woman. In her old form, her preferred name seems to be Francisca Batz'bal which is the name of the grandmother figure in many of the stories. In the cycle of the Mam's creation stories, it is she who primarily calls the Mam into existence. He is her child until he stands up, then, after she dances with him, he is her husband: another example of the mother-wife theme. As Francisca, (Yaca), she is associated with the grinding stone, an archetypal image of the female sexual organs. She is also associated, under other names, with the original corn plantings made by primordial deities, with death and with witchcraft.

In essence, Batz'bal is the spindle, the thread-maker. The Mam is the thread (*batz'*) that she spins. He is "wound" as well as "bound" (*xmon*—Mamxmon—Maximón) with rope (*k'aam*—Maximón *K'aam*). This, in turn, is part of an extended set of metaphors in which the Mam can embroil humans in traps set by witchcraft with the use of—among other things—thread, rope, poison and drugs (*Erythrina*, *Datura*, tobacco and alcohol, the earth-warmer). Some prayers suggest that the Mam's head is a spindle, although his wood, *Erythrina*, is apparently not heavy enough for spindle making.

Batz'bal can make people crazy with spinning; she can drill holes into muscles and bones; she ties off the extremities of cloth, and other objects, in order to kill; she is particularly connected with epilepsy. An intention to witch can be expressed as, "I'm going to tie you up with thread," or "I'm going to tie you from ear to ear," (i.e. slice your head off). Human witchcraft is sometimes connected to leaving weaving instruments in the Mam's clothing box, a large box "full of pain and sickness," which then afflicts the bewitched victim. Witchcraft began in the creation-story cycle as a divine way of ordering the world—but humans got hold of and perverted it. This makes the Mam into the archetypal human, the link between the Martín deity complex—the *nawal* ancestors—and subsequent Atitecos.

In her younger form, the Mam's wife is called María Castellana, or Castiliana, and she is very much a contrast to María/Francisca Batz'bal. Whereas Batz'bal is an old Indian lady, past menopause and a great sorceress, the young María Castellana often seems to be a *ladina* and she is promiscuous, loquacious, noisy, outrageous, flirty, playful, and detests work. For some she is the "whore wife" of the Mam. All this links up with the Mam as the "plaything" of the *nawal taq achi*: he is a toy and he plays; his very rich clothing is, lexically, associated with play. It also links up with the Mam as a rich *ladino*—a fertile theme throughout Guatemalan folklore.

Whereas Batz'bal is vicious, Castellana is described as "just crazy." She is sometimes called "the virgin-whore" and described as barren as a mule. One friend associated her with women who had been rejected by their husbands as barren: they are passed from hand to hand and hence "promiscuous." Castellana is the lady of bright clothes, ornaments, song, flowers, all the delights of love. With one of her sister-forms, María Sarabanda, the many-breasted *marimba* woman, "she sings to the Mam and makes everything move." Many Atitecos stressed the Mam's popularity with prostitutes in Guatemala City: "They keep images of him in their rooms and call him their best friend." It is also said that women who "become accustomed to *il* and *mak*" ("sin") ask the Mam to take them at death to his underworld sweatbath. As for Sarabanda, she, with her sisters, sang the Atitlán church from Cerro de Burro, the world-center, to its present position in the village.

▪   ▪   ▪

Looking back at the stories of the creation of the Mam—and, especially, at the version by Loincloth featuring a María Magdalena, we begin to come to a number of conclusions.

Remember, first that all the Mam creation stories involve the Mam in: one) being made to put order into the world's disorder, created by witchcraft, sexual sin, adultery and so forth, usually on a woman's part; two) turning himself into the disorder he is supposed to have been made to cure; and three) being taken to pieces on account of this and being used sparingly. This may reflect an attempt to deal with the differences within similarity of a unit of function that governs two radically different seasons—the wet and the dry. It may also, insofar as it seems linked to themes in the *Popol Vuh* (creation of the wooden men), be connected to an ancient Highland Maya creation cycle.

Furthermore, in his adventures, the Mam is a male to women and a female to men. It is in fact almost impossible to tell whether he is originally male or female. Tzutujil though strives to pin him down (Loincloth prayed to the Mam's María box as, "You the woman, you the man, you the woman that turns into a man" etc.), but we clearly have here one of the best examples of a male/female as well as young/old unit of function. The latter age principle is well illustrated by the grandmother-wife/lover facets of the Batz'bal/Castellana pair. Christian influences are also manifestly present, as they are everywhere. Frequently, the original sinning woman is "the devil's wife." The Mam has to change into her in order to lure the Devil out of his volcano so that the Martíns can kill him—at which point the Mam becomes the 13th Martín. We cannot help noticing the presence of the "sinner" Mary Magdalen as well as a creation from the Mam's body of the Castellana figure in the style of the creation of Eve. There is a chance that the Mam's relation to the fruit is more than a little connected to the apple of Genesis. It seems curious, on the face of it, that no one talked to us of a marriage between Jesucristo and Magdalena.

The relation of the Mam and the Marías to childbirth, and of childbirth to the whole process of creation, is worth going into in a little more detail. In the story of the grandmother killed by her two grandsons when she is entombed in the sweatbath, the grandmother becomes a *güisquil* plant (*Sechium Edule*). From this plant grows the tendril (*siljutay*) which will bear all created things. In the creation stories, the Mam is often shown as standing on top of a sweatbath while preparing his tricks and transformations. This is a complex image. Francisca Batz'bal/steambath/world-womb has a roof (her "back") made of a very hard wood, one of the original *nawal taq achi* forms: the *tz'aaj* of Diego Tz'aaj—seemingly the Red *Taxicoba*. The Mam stands on this roof, reminiscent of the back of a precolumbian earth monster. He also abides, "sleeps," on the roof trellis in *cofradía* Santa Cruz made of the very same hardwood: this is his *warabal* or sleeping-place. There is thought to be a relation between the womb-steambath and the sleeping place.

While the Mam works all the year round, he is, in his privileged form, Lord of the Dry Season and is conceived of as guarding, storing and shading the Sun-child slowly being cooked into existence in the womb as well as the water and produce of the wet, fertile season which are—not destroyed—but preserved inside the earth. As such, he is the *cha'jalniel* or *cha'jalbe*, the guardian standing in the middle of the house. He is called there by the midwife at childbirth or in case of child disease. In the dry season, he is naked or flaming red with flowers, awake and hot—an image from his tree *Erythrina* whose trunk is full of water during the dry season but dry during the wet one. This Mam keeps the unborn child warm with his heat.

When the Sun is born, the Mam shades the earth from the scorch with a green leaf cape, a cape of clouds and fog (*suutz' muyew*), at which time he is, relatively, asleep. This image is related to the role of *Erythrina* in shading the cacao tree. Battle with the Devil, in the stories, is thought of as the battle of earth-water with fire, causing clouds. Another analogy, based on the analogy Sun-birth/Child-birth/Plant-birth, has to do with the Mam guarding children while the *nawal taq achi* and *nawal taq exji*, equivalent to rain and cloud forces, are away "at commerce or at market." Yet another analogy makes the Mam into the old marriage broker, the sterile power which can arrange for fertility and the lineage sequence.

The child is asleep in the night of the dry/dark season owned by the Mam. The formation of the child in the womb has analogies with the dressing and "forming" of the Mam within the *cofradía*. The child, born head-down, has to be "turned" with head facing up, an action also performed on the Mam by the *telinel* during dressing. The child, before birth, is with his Fire-Star (*q'aq'al*) in the night womb of the other world. The Mam opens or "breaks" his road as *k'amalbe* (guide, road-opener, marriage-broker); parting the cervix bones as the child comes onto his road. At birth, the Star-soul stays in the night of the other world as the child moves into "His Sun/His Day" of the wet season. The child is bound with his father's belt so as to decelerate the separation of the soul and so that the child feels warm and safe. The mother is given steam baths to replace the heat lost in birthing.

Clearly, the Mam has a role in forming the child in the "night and darkness" and has some control over the child's fate. There is a relation between the use of *Erythrina* seeds in divination (they represent man's testicles) to "knowing one's Sun." Remember that the Mam, like the wooden men in the *Popol Vuh*, is made from the divination tree. In some Maya areas, the Mam is pluralized as a set of calendric forces.

At a birth, the midwife receives the Mam in the center of the house with incense and candles, and the quality of the reception and duration of offerings will determine the ease of birth. When the Mam is installed, the *ixoq ajawa*, the "women lords," also known as *cha'jalbe winag*, the "guardian persons," undoubtedly the

Twelve Marías, make their arrival. They come to receive the child and are very much feared. There must be six to twelve candles for them at all times up to the last day of sweatbath treatment. Should they go out, the child will die. If the mother has been "condemned" for any reason, she can be killed by the *ixoq ajawa*, at which point she is immediately received by the Second Sun in his Catholic form as father of Jesucristo. Perhaps she becomes a new *ixoq ajaw*. It may be that these *ixoq ajawa* are ultimately related to the western sky women of Nahua myth who, dying in childbirth, accompanied the Sun in the afternoon and into night.

To get a complete picture, we would also have to look at the María or Marías of Jesucristo (involving a number of different Catholic female saints) and then look at the very rich relations between the Marías and the Female Principle in precolumbian Maya and associated peoples' beliefs. This, however, would go beyond the scope of the present book. Here is a last look at some thoughts on the whole Martín/Mam/Jesucristo system:

We have been dealing with duality of sex and age in various aspects of the Maya belief system. Also, with the alternation of wet and dry seasons in the life of a Sun, or Sun-year, and their role in the birth (youth), life (maturity), and death (old age) of Sun, human child, and plant child. These matters are variously stressed in the three sub-system: those of the Martín, the Mam, and Jesucristo.

In the Martín sub-system, it is the sex and age duality in the middle, mature generation that is stressed. There is a wealth of information on the lives and ages of the Martín Angels which must be left for another time. Martín and his María have to do with the natural—the animal and plant world—which brings life about, matures it, sustains it and feeds it. Above all, the Martín/María are food: *waya*: food-water.

The Mam sub-system is associated with things other than *waya*: everything to do with heating, building and other matters involving wood and tools on the male side and everything to do with weaving, the loom, thread and other female tools on the female side. The Mam and the Martín, while dry and wet respectively in many senses, function together throughout the year as aspects of each other.

As for the Jesucristo sub-system, it appears as a branch of the Martín sub-system principally, with Jesucristo as the Sun and the Sun's products (food) generated and manipulated by an assembly of Martíns and Marías. Jesucristo seems to serve as a link between the concept of the First Martín and that of the First *Nawal*, understandably in view of a four-hundred-year Catholic stress on Christ's dual divine/human nature. To this sub-system, the Mam appears principally as a traitor—in the form of Judas—when he kills/eats/copulates with Manuel Jesucristo in the process of making him, through sacrifice, into what he needs to be, the next, mature Sun-year. It is only an apparent treason however—for outside consumption as it were—since the Mam is only fulfilling a seasonal function of the dry: to care for the wet while the latter is unborn/asleep and to go on caring, as shade, even when the Mam himself is asleep. In this sense, as well as in that where he suggests Christ in his position as 13th Martín, a whole paradigm gradually appears in which the Mam is an alternate form of the Sun, the "dead" Sun of the dry season. Some evidence suggests that, in the creational pattern, the Mam might be the *next* Sun in what would, in effect, become our Fifth World.

Only the mature stage of life is fully sexual, while the immature stages share qualities of both youth (oversexual) and age (undersexual/menopausal). Much of the Mam's sexual ambivalence comes from the fact that the Mam is married either to the grandmother or to the daughter, or both, but *not* to the mother. The grandmother is a constant function, the daughter is an inconstant one, and the "mother" as the only "balanced" function is denied to the Mam.

Could this be because, in Maya belief, the mother is preempted by the male in the Martín sub-system to such an extent that she, outside the Martín system, becomes in version after version, *elided* or, we might say today, *disappeared*? In ritual terms, the mother of the Mam is in *cofradía* San Juan and not in *cofradía* Santa Cruz where the Mam resides. In the same vein, the Mam is a grandfather and a grandson but not a father/son. Another way of putting this would be that mature sexuality is so totally dual in nature that any remnant of divided sexual identity has to become located in the "youth" and "age" poles primarily.

Something of this is suggested by what happens in the Jesucristo sub-system. In Christianity, the mother, the Virgin Mary, is of the utmost importance. What we see in Atitlán, however, is a picture in which most of the various Virgins known to Atitecos constantly move up and down the kinship scale in such a way that they successfully *avoid* being the mother of Jesucristo. Another aspect of the Jesucristo system is that we may always be left in doubt as to whether non-sexuality is a Maya mark on the divinities or a Christian one—now indissolubly linked by four centuries of Conquest.

On leaving these topics, we notice that the mythical material from Atitlán gives us the impression of occasionally adding to the picture we have in *Popol Vuh* and other older texts. Perhaps the fullest available *Popol Vuh* needs to be presented in concordance style, adding to the *Popol Vuh* as it stands all the mythical materials from the various *pueblos* studied in the Maya area. In that way, materials which may conceivably have been lost from the *Popol Vuh* itself might eventually find their way home.

A final note. To look at the mystery of the Mam's name further, check out Dayley's *Diccionario Tz utujil* (*xiim* to *ximon*); Saenz de Santa Maria's *Diccionario Cakchiquel* (*xim* to *ximon*) and Edmonson's *Quiché-English Dictionary* (*ximoh*). This should wind and bind together the word for "bound" and the name Simon!

TWENTY-ONE

Contemporary Forms and Causes of Conflict: Change in Atitlán: 1950–1990

It is time to come back to present-day Atiteco religion and, indeed, to come closer to it than we were ourselves during research on the spot—since that ended around 1980.

To get to the present in Santiago Atitlán in order to have an idea as to why the Maximón, of all older religious figures, is still the one going strongest, we have to look at very complex changes in the life of the community. Many of these changes introduced new causes of conflict into Atitlán during the two decades preceding a time when the place would be engulfed in a much more widely-based and more destructive struggle.

The casual visitor to Atitlán in 1979 might not be too aware of these changes—but they were profound. By this date, Atitlán was facing a land and population crisis which showed very little likelihood of improving due to the Guatemalan government's political stance. Other anthropologists than ourselves, especially Robert Carlsen, have specifically studied socio-economic change, and the rest of this book will have to rely heavily on their work.

During colonial times, the Atitlán area had remained Indian and the traditional method of agriculture was still that of the slash-and-burn corn field. It was not until after Independence that the coffee boom brought much good Tzutujil land into non-Indian hands and the *ladino* big plantation system with small native land parcels for Indians came into being. By 1928, only some 20% of Atitecos were free from some form of working off interminable debt. The transformation of communal lands into alienable private

SCANDALS IN THE HOUSE OF BIRDS

holdings under the dictator Barrios had not improved the situation. There had been no positive land reform. The Atiteco land base strictly limited by geography—the surrounding lake and volcanos—became less and less sufficient—a situation made worse by a population explosion. In 1940, the population as recorded in the Fifth Census of Guatemala was just over nine and a half thousand. By 1979, it stood at over twenty thousand.

In recent years, infant mortality had declined considerably as access to medical treatment increased. Since Atitlán was moving toward less agriculture, one might have thought that fewer hands would be needed. However, children would still be providers for old age and the petty industries replacing agriculture were still labor intensive. Atiteco women were found to be little interested in birth control. Initial, relative Protestant success with mercantile pursuits were overwhelmed by rapid increase in Protestant numbers. Also, in the 1980s, prices had increased way above wages.

As late as 1940, Atitlán was still the region's largest exporter of maize. It was not long before Atitlán became a net importer. In 1965, only a third of the population grew fully enough corn to live on and this number went on decreasing. Projects of an American Catholic Mission arriving in 1964 did not seem to improve the agricultural situation a great deal. Many Atitecos, in their strategic position between Coastal and Highland areas, had always been traders: it looked as if commerce in one form or another would be the majority economy of the future.

Approaching the town in 1979, tourists coming up from the lakeside would get a different view of the place than they would have had in the early 1950s. While Santiago itself cannot substantially expand, lands to the north of the town had gradually been alienated by sale to Guatemala City residents and foreigners, mainly American. The jealousies and backbiting provoked by these and other land deals could fill a book by themselves. By 1979, the municipal records gave a figure of 168 *chalets* extending from Cerro de Oro to Xetuk. In 1952–3, almost all Santiago houses were of stone, with walls of cane and a straw roof, capped by a ceramic pot. New styles— new materials: by 1979, the old pot-roof house appeared to be a rare antique.

Roads and transportation also grew. In 1952–3, a proper link between Santiago and San Lucas was a *ladino* dream. By 1979, trucking and bus transportation had grown enormously and road travel was a serious rival to lake travel.

The growth in the numbers of businesses is also suggestive. In the early 1950s, Atitlán had fifteen businesses, all *ladino* owned. By 1979, it had 226 businesses, a considerable number of which were Indian owned, especially those dealing with textiles and crafts.

Robert Carlsen in 1991 found that a quarter of the population were now *comerciantes de fuera,* outside traders. He also found that traditionalists in religion tended to own more land and be involved in more cultivation than orthodox Catholics and Protestants and saw the move toward mercantilism as a major reason why an agriculture-based traditional religion might be losing ground.

The decreased use of the magnificent native costume would be another noticeable change, as elsewhere in the country. In the 1950s, approximately 1% of men would not be wearing costume with less than a ½% of women. In the 1970s, some 25% of men were not wearing costume with the figure for women not having changed, a factor for them of maintaining Indian identity. But there has been a move from a fairly uniform set of colors worn by everybody to something like a riot (expense-provoking into the bargain) in which lavish new details had caused the "old" costume to virtually disappear. The use of *jaspeado,* or woven tie-die thread, seems to be the major destroyer of traditional patterns in swamping out other elements of design.

Tourism has grown tremendously over the years. In 1952–3, Santiago was already part of the regular national tourist route. There was one small boat a day, carrying an average of eight to fifteen tourists. By the mid-1960s, there were up to two or three boats a day—with more at *fiesta* times and with the tourists still following the same route. Atiteco-defined "corrupt" behavior by sellers became more noticeable in the 1960s and 1970s: by then there was a regular tourist's cafe near the boat landing and the whole progression up "*Calle Gringo*," *Gringo* Street as it was now called, had become something like running a gauntlet.

By 1979, there were six and one half times more tourists on average than in the 1950s. Boat companies mushroomed between the 1950s and late 1970s when there might be over sixty boats a day arriving from three hotels in Panajachel. The number and size of native-owned boats plying between lake communities had also visibly increased.

We also have to take account of a "return of the missionaries." In the 1950s, Atitlán had been served, if at all, by occasional visits from outside priests coming in for baptisms, marriages and major ceremonies. In 1964, everything suddenly changed.

On the first of March of that year three priests from the Catholic Diocese of Oklahoma, U.S.A., arrived in Santiago and radically altered the religious balance of power in that town. The establishment of the Micatokla (*Misión Católica de Oklahoma*) had been inspired at the Diocese of Sololá in the early 1960s in response to a call from Pope John XXIII and was based on a contract to last initially a solid twenty-five years.

The leader of the three priests was a Father Raymond Carlin whose special interests were linguistics and liturgy. From January 3rd, 1964, to December 1st, 1975, five more priests arrived at different times, of whom two stayed until 1979, as well as seven sisters and some experts in agronomy and engineering.

The Mission's projects comprised the following:

1. The rehabilitation of the church and neighboring buildings This task was completed in January 1972.

2. The setting up of a local Radio station to give talks on agriculture, health and welfare and the provision of fixed frequency receivers in the homes of a number of trained local teachers so as to form sub-classes of the Radio school. This was to grow into the "Voice of Atitlán" with a long and checkered history.

3. A co-operative with a membership of some 350 responsible for various projects.

4. A credit union.

5. A medical clinic.

6. A children's malnutrition clinic.

7. A crafts project.

8. An electrical generator for church and convent.

The fortunes of these projects varied considerably.

The literacy situation in Atitlán had always been extremely poor. Tarn, during the Arbenz regime in the 1950s, had taught Maya history to a very small graduate-type class under reformist impulses but it did not reach out to a large public. 1966, William Douglas found the illiteracy rate among heads of households to stand at nearly 91%. By 1973, statistics suggested an illiteracy rate of 84% for *municipio* children between the ages of seven and fourteen, with the rate climbing to 88% for persons of eighteen upwards. Only some 10% of children attended the local school.

Though the school had always been *ladino* staffed, with *ladino* objectives and a mere one-year Spanish training (*Castellanización*) program for Indian kids before first grade, *ladinos* in Atitlán were not perceived by Indians as having achieved a great deal by attending school.

To remedy this, one of the Mission's principal objectives was concerned with both child and adult education. Out of the initial budget, four thousand dollars was invested in a Radio station and materials. The program started on August 19th, 1968, with a formal inauguration on August 25th. The Bishop of Sololá, and various radio officials from around the country were in attendance.

Classes were located in teachers' homes, the teachers gathering students from family and neighbors. A program was devised in Tzutujil by native speakers to teach basic literacy and arithmetic as well as problem-solving in Atiteco and Coastal contexts, this as a step to understanding basic technology and toward integration with regional and national systems. The goal was gradually to make teachers independent of the Radio and capable of creating their own programs. The Radio itself was encouraged to seek its own development and autonomy. Eventually the directors took over the partial financing of the radio school, to the tune of 20%.

By 1973, there had been two sessions of the school of eighteen weeks duration each per year. A broad listenership had grown outside the student body: the Radio claimed to have received about one thousand letters. By July 1979, it was announced that the Voice of Atitlán had thirty-nine schools; sixty teachers and six hundred and fifty students—mostly over fourteen so as not to compete with the local school. Twelve supervisors oversaw radio work emanating from the Voice in all the municipalities of the lake area. The Radio had become an areal organization with considerable power.

There was, however, jealousy and constant backbiting over radio jobs, especially between the Reconstruction Committee and *Catequistas* on the one side and the Radio on the other. All the radio people were related in one way or another and nepotism, insolence to old and young, and corruption were said to be rife. They were much envied and the monetary affairs of the radio were constantly under attack.

As an example: Domingo, Juan Sisay's old side-kick, was accused of having obtained his job because a one-time President of the Voice, a married man, had made his daughter pregnant. The job was his for keeping quiet. Domingo was accused of self-serving here just as he had been when he had worked at the municipality and charged people for services which were supposed to be free. When in the Radio, he had parted company with Sisay, "not needing him anymore." (He once managed to say to Tarn, "Yes, Juan Sisay the painter, I am sure you must know him": this after thirty years of our working together!!!)

By 1991, Robert Carlsen found that the overall literacy rate for heads of households had jumped to nearly 27%. By that year, school attendance had escalated to 2,056. However, the picture was less rosy when it was found that the drop-out rate between first and second grade was worse in 1991 than in the mid-1960s. Nearly half of all students dropped out by second grade and no significant cultural capital could be formed by the community. These high drop-out rates were the main cause of continued illiteracy in Atitlán.

Doubtless, the most successful project of the Mission was the medical one. Major problems encountered were: traditional native medicine affording very limited help; high birth and death rates and low life expectancy; poor nutritional standards and sanitary conditions (getting worse by the year as the lake, the only source of water, had become more and more polluted with huge quantities of raw sewage and detergents); and the most rudimentary toilet arrangements in the vast majority of compounds. Major problems included: parasites; anaemia; diarrhoea; tuberculosis; ulcers; a variety of coastal tropical illnesses; as well as infectious and malnutritional diseases.

The Mission began trying to improve services immediately. Some rather grandiose plans for a downtown center with adequate technology bells and whistles had to be shelved. A May 1965 press report claimed, however, that $120,000 in medical equipment, including a complete X-Ray laboratory and a complete kitchen set-up had already been given; that four plane-fulls of 35,000 pounds had already arrived with another 8,000 pounds to come. The Tinker Air Force Base near Oklahoma City was involved, and truckloads, driven from the United States, arrived at various times over the next few years.

In midsummer 1967, the *Oklahoma Courrier* described a new drive for $100,000 on behalf of the clinic launched by the wife of the Governor of Oklahoma. Only $35,000 so far had been obtained. It was clear that funding was a major problem. A new Board at the Oklahoma Diocese had decided against too much municipal help lest the land eventually revert to the Guatemalan government. Accordingly a piece of land in Cantón Panabaj, some three kilometers from the town center, had been donated by a private Guatemalan citizen. Though $50,000 short of their goal, urgent need in Atitlán prompted the Board to implement a multi-stage building program.

On August 2nd, 1969, readers of the *Courrier* learned that the hospital had been open two weeks. On January 29th, 1972, the *Oklahoma City Times* announced that Fathers Stanley Rother and Jude Pansini had reported the building stages of the clinic completed together with those of the Mission.

But outside help was needed. A private Project Concern, founded circa 1961, quartered in San Diego, California, finally took over completely on September 1st, 1975. The staff consisted of: an American administrator and wife, a physician and a registered nurse from the U.S., plus two Guatemalan doctors and other local workers.

From the start, Project Concern sought cooperation with the Guatemalan *Ministerio de Salud Publica y Asistencia Social*, the Ministry of Public Health and Social Aid, which invited the Project to take over all existing health institutions in Atitlán. Out-patient services were moved into town and joined to the *Ministerio*'s *Puesto de Salud* clinic which, with very limited resources, had been seeing some 100 patients a day. The new *Centro de Salud* opened on June 20th, 1976.

The actual hospital—*Clinica Santiaguito*—enjoyed seventeen beds, catering to an average of ten patients but able to handle up to thirty; a laboratory; an X-ray room; a surgery theater; an emergency room; a dentist's room; a kitchen; and a lecture hall. A Guatemalan doctor was resident full time and also supervised the town *Centro de Salud*. The radio was helped financially by Project Concern to broadcast socio-dramas on health and nutritional themes.

After the earthquake of April 2nd, 1976, the hospital distributed large quantities of helpful materials all over the country, set up a clinic in a Patzún suburb on the north side of the lake and brought fifteen patients by helicopter to the hospital, caring for them and sending them back to Patzún. This is a list of the main contributions only. Costs to Project Concern for the fiscal year September 1977 to August 1978 were reported at close to $91,000.

Atitecos saw the use of the hospital as an extension of services provided more expensively by local pharmacies. By and large,

Atitecos did not see Western and traditional medicine as antago-
nistic and would oscillate between the services of doctors and
aj'kuna—applying to the latter in cases clearly perceived as per-
taining to ailments they alone specifically dealt with. Western
medicine generally was narrowly understood as providing very
specific services, injections above all.

As one might have expected, friction did exist between Guatemalan and American medical personnel. Other sources of
trouble for local American doctors were said to be linked with
Project Concern. In 1979, someone came from the Project to
announce that it was "changing its philosophy" and would probably close the in-patient hospital, keeping the out-patient and
nutrition services!

From the indigenous viewpoint, a *Catequista* official told us in
1979 that, originally, Atitecos had been very satisfied with "these
American priests who cared about poverty, health, education and
so forth and who said hello to everyone whatever their religion
might be." They sided with the Americans against the local *ladinos*
who were very jealous of them since many of their little trading
deals had been upset by American generosity. It was the *ladinos*
who swore that everyone would get contagious diseases if the
hospital were built in town, forcing the hospital out to the edges.

It was true that there had been a lot of confusion among Indians over the changes involved in the move from management by
the Mission to management by Project Concern. Indians thought
of Mission help as funded by charity money and held that medicine should therefore not be sold, at least not at high prices. Efforts
to explain the change and its implications had been minimal.

It was also clear that contention between *ladinos* and the *padres*
often involved land issues. Local plantation *ladinos* were then being
accused of extracting a lot of shoreline land from Indian owners
so as to monopolize the building of *chalets* for rent to outsiders
and foreigners and to achieve control of future shoreline businesses. There were problems between church and municipality
over church land and some over church locales between Atitecos

and doctors. Father Rother had been called in to talk to the doctors but, accoding to one Atiteco, "Father Rother and the doctors had never really gotten it together."

This should give some idea of the major moves made by the Micatokla Mission in Atitlán. As for the overall costs, we come up with a total in round figures of some $300,000 or even more. It was a substantial investment.

Among the many changes in Catholic organization effected by the Mission, Father Jude Pansini's cantonal restructuring of the *Catequistas* ranks high in importance. Pansini adopted the traditional procedures of the elders in appointing officials and organized standard election procedures for cantonal groups. He had everything done legally so that they would be able to take money and decide how it should be used. These *Catequistas* were the sons and grandsons of the original *Catequistas* of the Maximón Scandals period, the founding generation. They comprised about six hundred families led by about forty officials in all.

A movement was afoot in 1979 to get the *Catequistas* to "look after everybody regardless of religion" but this was hard to push since *Catequistas*, on the whole, felt that "the Protestants have systems of mutual help which are far more efficient and better off than ours." The *Catequistas*, however, had evolved a variety of interesting tactics, such as the idea of purchasing a house secretly in every canton which could be offered to a *cofradía* or to a *primer mayor* or anyone else in need of help—this with the thought of gaining merit while also keeping tabs on *costumbrista* activity. One such form of control was that they would, at times, decide that such and such a custom was "heathen" (for instance, a special kind of funeral for *Principales pasados*) and would withhold communion from such "heathen" practitioners.

It may certainly be said in the future that, from the point of view of Catholicism, the Micatokla Mission arrived just in time. Fundamentalist Protestant missionaries had begun their work in the lake area around 1920, and the first conversions are recorded for 1922. Until 1935, a strong Catholic censorship obliged the

Protestants to remain hidden but, in that year, the first chapel of the *Iglesia Centro-Americana*, the Central American Church, was founded in Panajachel. Very soon there were a number of sects.

Protestantism was not part of Tarn's concerns in 1979, though he was amply made aware at all times of its decibel potential. Anthropologist William Douglas's figures for 1966 were: traditionalists 31%; *Catequistas* 13.8%; and Protestants 8.6%. He saw some 46.5% of people as being only nominal Catholics or not interested in religion. Around 1990, Robert Carlsen was suggesting the percentage of Atiteco Protestants as 34.9%; "Catholics," including *Catequistas* and Charismatics (a new development) as 45.6%; and the rest, including the traditionalists and the unaffiliated, as 10.7%. This last figure, however, shrank to an alarming 2.5% when current or occasional service in *cofradías* was asked about. The final 8.7% said they had no religion—but it was found that while they were sometimes *cofradía* visitors, they often belonged to families split between religions and found it more comfortable to say they had none. In the following account, Carlsen's work is the main source of information.

It was already clear to Tarn in the early 1950s that becoming a Protestant freed someone completely from the system of traditional belief, ritual and service—allowing that person to concentrate on his own family's wealth and on purely political channels of advancement. This freedom had permitted enterprising young Protestants during the Maximón Scandals to exploit the gap created by the *Catequistas* between themselves and their traditionalist brethren to the great discomfiture of the *Catequistas*. With this process, what remains of the deepest levels of Maya culture is very largely abandoned. Aesthetically, the caterwauling noises set up by Protestant loudspeakers in all parts of town—often strategically timed or placed in order not only to draw in new converts but also maximally to annoy Catholics—was amply in evidence in 1979. *Catequistas* were finally beginning to see that the "enemy" was not the *costumbristas* but the Protestants.

The situation ten years later, however, is more serious. In 1989,

Carlsen writes: "With some exceptions, the Protestant mission-aries in Guatemala constitute an extension of the fundamentalist wing of America's religious right." Since the mid-1970s, the American Right "commenced a program of massive Guatemalan missionization in response to Guatemala's political situation."

While the Catholic Mission was and is, on the whole, apoliti-cal (though aware of the fact that many *Catequistas* are affiliated with progressive organizations) and mostly medical and educa-tional, the Pentecostals preferred to bypass the improvement of material conditions, putting all the stress on conversion and assuring new converts that the new religion would bring them, of itself, new prosperity—this apart from the all-important doc-trine of the prompt second coming of Jesus Christ. It is a decisive fact that the Assembly of God alone has over one thousand churches in Guatemala but only ten clinics.

To some extent, there is competition between private Protes-tant schooling and the local government school; recently a Dutch donor presented a *Centro Americano* school with a large gift of clothes for each child: native for the girls, completely *ladino* and uniformly designed for the boys. Carlsen has mentioned to us a *Templo Bethel* movie showing how a young boy, after conversion, began to pull up quantities of fish from the lake, whereas beforehand he had only been able to catch small handfuls of minnows.

One of Carlsen's most telling points is that the American Right, or its affiliates, heavily finances these missionary ventures. Reli-able sources, outside Atitlán but on the lake, witnessed that a very large sum indeed by Guatemalan standards had been invested there by one of the most prominent of U.S. tele-evangelists. Another sign of the presence of the Right in Santiago is the arrival of the "Moonies'" Unification Church. Carlsen found they had very ambitious lakewide interests.

Protestant missionaries are extremely ambivalent toward Atiteco culture. Good/evil distinctions are rigid. All traditional-ism is "pagan," "witchy," "evil." The old prohibition against alco-hol now also includes listening to any *marimba* music at all. The

Elim and the Alpha and Omega groups even prohibit the remembering of any traditional myths. Additionally, the worst religious factionalism in the Atitlán of the 1990s is between Protestants. Elim in particular has caused much trouble by raiding other Protestant groups for members, taking over converts to those groups for their own organization.

Carlsen concludes that by such processes the Indian village is being pulled into the expanding economy of Guatemala and beyond that the late-Capitalist economy, while the "huge ecological and structural problems" of Santiago are being ignored by those who do the pulling.

For Carlsen, religious conversion here is "a change of magic systems. In desperation, these individuals have embraced the missionary promise that through religious change 'all things will be added.' " What takes place when the local Protestant small entrepreneur gets gobbled up by expansion from Guatemala City, as is beginning to occur with transportation and trucking companies for example? What emerges when the divine blessings fail to materialize? Carlsen has begun to notice a "nativistic" strain in Atiteco Protestantism based on disappointments suffered by Atitecos who had moved to the city and the revealed impossibility of the promises made by U.S. fundamentalists being fulfilled. In recent years, Elim, for instance, has begun to stress that only Atiteco members would be saved in the final judgement, not the whole Protestant body in Guatemala.

We can now better understand another facet of this whole problem: the difficulties that the traditionalists have in recruiting members. In 1980 we gathered available information on twenty-eight sets of eight officials each, a total of 224 positions in the system during 1977-80. The problem was acute: not enough people were joining up; too many ranks were unfilled.

A few examples: In none of twenty documented cases, was a sixth *cofrade* nominated: yet this rank is the gate to the system of service. In only five out of twenty documented cases was there a fifth. Only twelve out of twenty-four cases produced a fourth. In the three higher ranks—third, second, first—nearly a third were vacant. In the totality of positions above sixth, twenty individuals had no previous experience when they should have had—if only as sixth. In twenty-six cases, men were holding the same rank in the same *cofradía* as they had held the previous year. This showed that *cofradías* were staying in the same hands for more than a year.

The *Principales* tried to palliate this situation—mainly by expanding the position of councillor to a *cofradía*. It was now often taken by a *pasado* as a way of remaining active and enjoying the benefits of *cofradía* routine without doing much work for it.

There are other, somewhat conspiratorial, aspects to these processes. In October 1979, we were told that the *Cabecera* for 1979 had frozen all the *cofradías* for the coming year: in essence, he wanted to be re-elected to the job another year and for this he had to keep people favorable to him in power. The *Cabecera* previous to him had served three years, and he had leaned to the *Catequistas*: he was always drunk; it was under him that the religious organization had lost the *mayori* offices and he had allowed Rianda to buy *cofradía* Santa Cruz.

It was predicted that, at the big *Todos Santos* meeting in November, *cofradías* Santa Cruz, Juan and Antonio would be decided on. People would come in saying, "We have so and so and so and so." *Cabecera* 1979, who had gained prestige by his political savvy, would block this with, "You are not going through the proper channels." The proper channels would mean *him*.

He would get *Alcalde* San Juan to stay, keep *Alcalde* San Nicolás because he was his *compadre*, and move Santa Cruz out of the *Catequista* camp, possibly by giving it to our friend Eyes. Other *cofradías* had been successfully frozen back in September. Then, if he were re-elected, he could give Santiago, Nicolás and Rosario to friends around January 6th. There were also factors relating to political parties in upcoming municipal elections. *Cabecera* '79, it was known, would lean against one of the candidates because of his *Catequista* connections.

Robert Carlsen has told us that, from 1982 to 1988, the major *cofradía* San Antonio had been immobile and that community funding (help from the Council of *Principales* probably) had ensured the holding of the main *fiestas* only. The *Alcalde* had stated that the *santos* could stay at his house but that he was unable to perform any celebrations on their behalf. A Carlsen list for 1991 shows that *cofradías* Concepción and San Francisco only had an *alcalde* and a *xoa'*; San Francisco had these plus one female official (*tixel*); San Nicolás these plus a *juez*; San Gregorio, these plus one *cofrade*. San Antonio and San Juan were without *alcaldes* and looked after only by a *xoa'*. Only Santa Cruz and Santiago continued to change hands on a yearly basis. By 1992-3, *only* Santa Cruz—the *cofradía* in which Tarn had found the Maximón to be the vortex of everything conflictual in the Atiteco world-view of the early 1950s—was still going strong. Correspondingly, during this period, Carlsen found that there was much more *church and chapel* attendance by orthodox Catholics and Protestants.

Anthropologists had argued in the early 1950s that political competition—by its nature unending and part of everyday normal existence—was beginning to replace religious conflict in the context of crisis in Atitlán. The Protestants' stand on behalf of the Maximón was a defining moment. Thirty years on, traditional values continue to be endangered by ever-increasing politicization and secularization, some of it still wearing religious garb. But the garb wears thin and a whole way of life is in the balance. In that no satisfactory substitute for agriculture, the basis of the traditional world-view, has been found, while the outside world with all its downturns continues to oppress Atiteco life, the future may yet be grim for Atitecos—as for most indigenous peoples on this planet. Atitlán may continue to need the Mam as mediator and joker in the pack for a good while yet.

We must now go back for a moment to the Oklahoma Mission to understand the fate of Atitlán during the Civil War beginning in 1980. It may seem inappropriate to dwell on the fate of non-Indians when so many Indians suffered so badly during the Terror, but the Mission's personnel were so involved in Atiteco adaptation to change that some attention to their story is unavoidable.

By 1979, Father Stanley Rother seemed to be following a policy of minimal interference, to be attending *cofradía* rituals when invited (including the Maximón dressing during Holy Week), and to be continuing the program of enriching church ritual and liturgy. His troubles began in 1980 with the onset of what can only be called "The Terror." His letters to his superiors are eloquent of the changes in Santiago. They are contained in Father Henri Nouwen's *"Love in a Fearful Land"* published by Ave Maria Press in Notre Dame in 1985. On September 22nd, 1980, Rother writes of the Army visiting the town in force, of strangers asking many questions and of precautions taken at the Rectory. He expresses fears for the people in his charge:

> I am aware that some of our younger catechists are working with those that are preparing for a revolution. They are young men who are becoming more and more conscious of their situation and are convinced that the only option for them is revolt.
>
> I am not in as much danger as he [*Father Bocel, the only other priest present*] is, because I am a foreigner, and I hope they will give me a chance of leaving if they want me out. They haven't killed an American priest yet. . . . [*He adds that he wants to get Bocel out to safety.*]
>
> Two days ago a young man from the neighboring parish was taken in the middle of the night. He is a cousin of one of our nuns. He is not expected to be found alive. . . . If I get a direct threat or am told to leave, then I will go. But if it is my destiny that I should give my life here, then so be it. . . . I don't want to desert these people, and that is what will be said, even after all these years. There is still a lot of good that can be done under the circumstances. . . .

The letters continue in this style until his death.

A few days after a massacre of Chacaya Plantation workers on January 7th, 1981, a friend of Rother's was informed by a government source that the priest's name had been seen on a death list. Now that a direct threat had appeared, Rother was back with his family in Oklahoma on January 29th. Father Pedro Bocel was also out of the country and the two did some activist work in the States and Mexico. In the course of this, it appears that he had made some comments interpreted as leftist by certain informers.

In late February, the same source told Father Rother he could return and he was back in Santiago by Holy Week. On July 11th, Rother reported that *Catequistas* were paralyzed by fear and that he had had to give *orders* that classes should continue.

On July 28th, 1981, at about 12:30 a.m., three men tried to kidnap Rother from his bedroom. To avoid torture, he provoked them into killing him on the spot. On the next day, thousands of people gathered in the church.

The news spread very quickly: Prechtel called Tarn from Arizona to New Hope, Pennsylvania on July 29th. Father Rother's heart and a piece of blood-soaked gauze were buried behind the main altar in Atitlán (and moved to the front of the church around 1990); the body was taken to Oklahoma. From the beginning, candles have been placed regularly at the grave. Robert Carlsen tells us there is continued reverence for Rother and a big memorial service at which his open coffin draped with his head-scarf figures in the annual church ritual.

Nouwen's book and most other sources place the blame for the murder clearly on the Guatemalan Army. Benjamin Paul and William Demarest, in their exhaustive study of death squad operations in neighboring San Pedro la Laguna, mention suspicions that the worst military commissioner in that village had had a hand in it.

As far as Father Rother is concerned, our experience in 1979 was that he was an honest and dedicated man doing a difficult job to the very best of his abilities. On the other hand, it cannot be denied that he was also feisty and pugnacious, with a reputation for authoritarianism at times, for picking fights and for attacking tradition head-on when diplomacy and patience might have been better advised.

That foreigners were *always* under suspicion was an endemic reality of life in Santiago. That they might be standoffish was less frequently reported: we heard several times (before life became dangerous) that Father Rother spent too much time cloistered in his rectory or repairing and maintaining his equipment and not enough going around the village to visit his parishioners.

A couple of documents are eloquent. On February 11th, 1975, a letter was addressed to Bishop Angelico Melotto in Sololá by Cristóbal Esquina Yataz, *Cabecera del Pueblo*, fourteen *Principales* and the *Alcalde* of the San José *cofradía particular* with seventy nine other signatures, some six to ten of which were womens'. Juan Sisay was heavily involved.

The complaints were as follows: one) that Atitecos did not know under what conditions the American *padres* entered into Atitlán; two) that the *padres* did not carry out *fiesta* ritual as expected traditionally by the town and said mass in their own way "contrary to church custom"; three) that much money had been sent from the U.S. which had not benefited the town in any way and that the Americans were merely drawing their salaries and doing nothing for the people; four) that the Americans had set a bad example in that four (named) priests had left and married; and five) that the Americans were bringing about the entry of *los jipis* (hippies). They should therefore be replaced by Guatemalans or Spaniards.

The arguments about money, which continued during this time in many other forms, concerned the extent to which money spent, buildings and material, belonged to church or laity. During 1979, there were many searches, with and without lawyers, by many parties for deeds and titles and the Mission was pressed for accounts.

On April 14th, 1975, Bishop Melotto answered the accusers to the effect that the Americans had come in under contract and knew what they were doing; that Catholic rites had changed in recent times; that everyone in the Mission was honestly earning his living; and that local priests would serve the people the minute someone had graduated from the Seminary in Sololá: to date no one had. He refuted the "calumny" that one of the priests named had married and pointed out that hippie invasions were a universal phenomenon. On the 15th, the Bishop sent all the documents to President of the Republic Kjell Laugerud who had obviously become involved, stating that the American priests deserved nothing but gratitude.

In late 1979, Atitecos still maintained that the one priest in question had married the daughter of the Civil Registry official at the municipality—and that this *ladino* gentleman had gained a two-story house out of it. There was irritation still alive against ex-Father Jude Pansini for having "sent his wife to Antigua while continuing to say mass at Santiago"—this despite explanations to the effect that "intended wife" would have been a truer description. People were wondering, according to this channel, when Father Rother himself would finally marry (a scurrilous bulletin going so far as to wonder whether he "was a man" in view of his being the only non-married priest!).

Another document, an *Acta* no. 20, of 12/3/78, goes into more detail about Father Rother's alleged insolence. After "insulting" people at the meeting, he "stated" that the Panabaj plantation (a Mission project) did not belong to the Atitecos but to the United States and that, when he left Santiago, he would take all the machinery and equipment with him, that everything would be sold and he would leave with a lot of money in his pocket. The other *padres* there at the time would leave also. Meanwhile, the people assembled were to yield up all the books and keys. He would depart the village with the church locked.

A typical grudge by an individual involved Juan Sisay. He had supposedly been offended because Rother had blessed his spectacular mansion with water from a tap instead of using what Sisay would consider "special" water. Rother had told Sisay he would not bless the house if Sisay was going to be "idolatrous about water." Juan initiated a legal document with Juan Mendoza, an ex-Town Mayor. It was clear that Sisay and Rother were in a running battle.

Criticism of later priests ran high among the *Catequistas*. Father Adán, a Guatemalan *padre*, was held to deal mostly with *ladinos* from whom he could derive direct profits. He was said to be the main American watch supplier for this area and to act as a pawnbroker and loan shark. He was also felt to be uninterested in education and over-interested in women. A diabolically complex story involves Adan's affair with an Indian girl (on the "usual" pretext that he would leave the priesthood) who was also sleeping with a leading *Catequista*, a married man (working at the hospital but anxious to become a radio announcer). She was also alleged to be sleeping with yet another man, the president of the radio association. Adán was forced to leave at the end of 1979 and was transferred to Sololá. He was replaced by a Sololá Indian, no doubt the Father Bocel of Henri Nouwen's account.

Given the expectations surrounding the eventual arrival of an Atiteco native *padre*, the case of Gaspar Culan, whose father had been a famous *aj'kun* and whose grandfather had been renowned as a storyteller, is important. Culan had completed school, fifth grade in Santiago and sixth in Chichicastenango, then went to the Sololá seminary where his ordination was retarded because of some alcoholic misdemeanor. The Bishop of Sololá had sent him back home to cool his heels in Santiago. Father Rother gave him the job of preaching on Sundays because of his literate and exciting use of his native tongue. The Bishop then gave Culan twenty days in which to decide between the City and Honduras. It was at this point that Culan decided, by himself, to leave church service: we do not know whether he was ever ordained or not, but doubt it.

Culan's ideas appear to have been too far advanced, theologically and politically, for his flock. He was ambivalent: against idolatry but attached to the traditionalists as "sincere and lovable people." After an episode in which he talked of chopping up *santos* for firewood since they were being treated as idols, Juan Sisay who had been indirectly accused of making money out of restoring them in church (this type of accusation haunted him for life), attacked Culan in documents sent to Cardinal Casariego and others. The Cardinal, very angry, called Culan in and told him to shape up—even though he personally agreed with his anti-idolatrous positions.

Culan then had his problems with Rother as well as with the Bishop. Though *Catequistas* voted to keep him, Culan suddenly resigned without further consultation. When forced to leave in this fashion (as he saw it), he took a wife, had children (the temptation to marry may have been present for a while), and continued to give his fiery sermons over the radio, despite complaints from Rother and Adán. It was felt by many that he might have become a religious force in Santiago although he would have had to develop some *savoir-faire*. However, he was dragged out of his house by a death squad on the 25th of October, 1980 and "disappeared." The files and equipment of the Radio were subsequently broken into.

An equally dark aspect of Mission history is the record of Father John Vesey who began his ministry at Micatokla on July 25th, 1984. His complex story can be read, with a favorable interpretation, in Henri Nouwen's book. The story seems to suggest the possibility of American Embassy participation in the Guatemalan Army's operations in Atitlán, an involvement inimical to the human rights of the native population. Other authors have since taken up this matter.

Something remains to be said about changing *Catequista* attitudes to the traditionalists.

Undoubtedly, at this time, the *Catequistas* were beginning to realize that their "enemy" was not the traditionalist party but the Protestants. They began to manifest a change of heart. At a meeting set to discuss the return of the Mam mask in August 1979, *Catequistas* contrasted a previously held view that *santos* were a bunch of wooden posts imported by Spain (to which Indians should react by simplifying their religion, adoring one God only so as not to be exploited through idolatry, etc.) with a new view that the Spaniards had told the old stone gods they would now have new jobs as *santos* and be made of wood, this new view being more favorable to the traditionalists.

Catequistas were also playing down the concept of heaven, knowing that traditionalists made great critical use of the theme that it would be absurd to go up there beside the Sun, where souls would fry. In adopting Father Pansini's hierarchical organization, the *Catequistas* tacitly gave up the egalitarian views with which they had hammered away at the traditionalist hierarchy, acknowledging that various levels of wisdom were possible among groups of individuals.

Even the older *Catequistas* were changing in this direction. An interesting case is that of the Reconstruction Committee which made itself into a kind of ecumenical bridge between senior *Catequistas* and *Principales pasados* who found it a good place in which to continue to exercise active leadership. The Committee members are often found as go-betweens in the 1970s because of their possession of *persona juridica*. There were, of course, struggles between various *Catequista* and *costumbrista* factions for control of the Committee.

As the 1980s progress, the rapid evolution of political thought in Santiago and the history of *Catequista* political allegiances, often radical, is best left in obscurity for some time owing to prevailing political circumstances.

We should, however, look at an aspect of ethnocentrism among Atitecos and self-nominated defenders of the Atitecos. This concerns Prechtel's presence in the native hierarchy. The Brotherhood and the Radio were not the only ones to be influenced or upset by this.

First the non-Atitecos: Tarn and Prechtel had heard, through friends, of the imminent arrival of an American journalist, proud owner of an M.A. in anthropology and working for an internationally famous geographical magazine. The journalist arrived for

Holy Week and, without any claim to expertise beyond an alleged reading of the Miguel Sol book, immediately began to air his opinions and utter comments on all village matters.

It was then discovered that one) this journalist did not work for the famous publication mentioned but for another of roughly the same kind, European in origin but just launching an American office; two) he had been asked to read a European text for the American edition and had found it wanting, thus landing himself with the job of writing a piece, either with the original European pictures or with pictures by a well known Guatemalan photographer; the latter was as well known for his right wing views and army contacts, be it added, as for his art; and three) he was critical of Miguel Sol's hypotheses concerning the Mam, claiming that the great Mayanist J. Eric Thompson had denied the Mam as a syncretistic figure and defined him purely as an "old deity." He had persisted in this view even when informed that Sol's ideas had arisen out of Thompson's work and had subsequently been confirmed by Thompson.

On the afternoon of Holy Friday, awaiting the big procession not far from the chapel where the Mam was hung, the Guatemalan photographer suddenly asserted loudly that many people did not support Prechtel's position in the hierarchy. Left alone with Tarn, the journalist made a point of disassociating himself from the photographer's views, asserting that the latter had not merely heard but had gone on to elicit anti-Prechtel views in the course of the previous evening's session in a local bar. It became clear that he had sat with *Catequistas* in Atitlán's one gay bar near the plaza.

The journalist's stance, however, was not all that different from his colleagues' despite his ostensible desire to appear as the impartial observer. He adhered firmly to the view that Prechtel was in fact an anthropologist, had married into the village in order to ingratiate himself, had won over the *principales* by various innuendos concerning his own magical powers—in short, that he would "do a Castaneda" and then leave the village. All of which was in the highest degree unethical. Despite Tarn's assurances that, whatever Prechtel's talents, he was not an anthropologist and his asseverations of Prechtel's good faith, the journalist persisted in considering that "any participation in fieldwork is a mark of anthropological bad faith." The alleged M.A. in anthropology was obviously being wielded with the force and precision of a blunderbuss.

Moreover, the man insisted, Prechtel had been unpleasant to him and had "tried to prevent him from earning his living." Prechtel's account, given later, was that the individual had bothered him at very crucial moments in his extremely complex role as *Primer Mayor* and had refused to be put off by tact and kindness:

Prechtel, 1979:

I finally told him that he had made two mistakes: one) by asking me who would give me back the money spent on *costumbre*, refusing to believe that religious work could be done altruistically; and two) by bothering me without having done sufficient homework, especially when I was very busy. When I quizzed him, he had no idea of how many *cofradías* we had or anything whatsoever about the politico-religious hierarchy. He was trying to get some questions in with the Second *Mayor*; the Second deferred to me and I said, half jokingly, 'No, we don't tell anything to this kind of guy.'

A second occasion arose on the night when the journalist and the photographer allegedly got their information about my supposed unpopularity. I had come to visit the Mam in his chapel—as I was supposed to do as *Primer Mayor* while guarding the church and nearby places—and the chapel is near that bar they were all in. One of the party followed me and told me that those men were asking all sorts of questions. He asked me if it was O.K. to answer. I said, 'Sure, but are you aware that the journalist is taking your words away with that little hidden recorder of his?' That did it right then and there.

As for the photographer, look, those men make their living out of purveying 'pure' visions of the Indian scene and they sure don't like seeing my curly blonde mop in there!

There had been something else. During the Apostles' supper, the photographer had abruptly and rudely taken a young man's hat off and thrown it to the ground when it blocked his view taking a picture. Prechtel had told his officers to discipline the offender and this was promptly done.

The journalist made himself more pressing and finally had to be told that, if indeed he was an anthropologist, there were good reasons for a little diplomacy on his part. His reaction, as might have been expected, had very little to do with science. He ended up "earning his living," substantially no doubt, by telling as much of the mask's return story as he could in the first issue of the new magazine without a credit to his sources or sending a copy to anyone concerned. Unrepentant, the gentleman was seen— in Tzutujil clothes!—at the Holy Week ceremonies a year later, at a time when only Prechtel remained in the village. So much for parasites.

It was interesting to find that the Oklahoma Mission people, in contrast, remained very calm. On Holy Monday, at the ceremony of the dressing of the Mam in Makuxtin's very depleted *cofradía* Santa Cruz, the Mission Director Father Rother told Tarn he had heard the mask had returned and asked him whether he had had anything to do with it. Tarn stressed that it had been mainly a matter between the *principales* and the Europeans. Someone, he added jokingly, had finally read Miguel Sol's *Los Escándalos de Maximón* book carefully and found out the whereabouts of the stolen mask. Friendly relations with Father Rother appeared in no way to have been altered by the episode.

Concern about the activities of the young North American painter were reflected in the City press on a variety of occasions. In June 1979, an exhibition of abysmally undistinguished "pyro-engravings" on leather by a young Argentinian resident in Atitlán was attended, on a basis of friendship, by Prechtel's second musical group. The occasion produced a piece by one Eugenia Gordillo in *El Imparcial* for 6/23/79. After paying some compliments to the Instituto Guatemalteco-Americano for holding the show and some undeserved attention to the objects displayed, the article continues:

> The second aspect of the evening's program was a 'show *típico*' [*sic*]. For many years, we have had groups of *ladina* girls presenting such shows and let it be said, modesty apart, that they were better presented, although learned and not based on ethnic affiliation. My models took more trouble in making seem natural what for them was contrived. This group of pseudo-natives, that are native but have been commercialized, offers a sad spectacle deforming as they do the Guatemalan tradition.
>
> Its director claims to be already a *principal*: an impossible claim in that tradition does not let a Guatemalan *ladino*, let alone a foreigner, ever be a *principal*. A native swung an incense-burner mechanically while the four interpreters of popular melodies maltreated a Spanish guitar and sounded a flute and a *chirimia* with a native drum (*tun*) as base—but not the *tun* of Miguel Angel [*a reference to novelist and Nobel Prize winner Miguel Angel Asturias?*].
>
> I know that neither the blond-haired boy nor his pretty wife, in her costume adulterated with silver and gold thread, lacked good will in presenting their 'show,' but Guatemalans have an obligation to respect our ancestors: that of keeping alive our traditions. Commerce—the father-buyer of many things—is capable of doing great harm to our customs and, because of this, we must be vigilant about events in the course of which folklore is presented.
>
> There are various authorized Institutes qualified to assess, without cost, the value of such presentations. Such are the *Instituto Indigenista Nacional* under the direction of the great artist, scholar and leading figure in Maya culture

Maestro Jose Castañeda as well as the *Instituto de Asuntos Folkloricos* of the University of San Carlos, under the distinguished leadership of *Licenciado* Celso Lara, folklorist and researcher on folklore. Without any desire to criticize but with a strong desire to present our patrimony as the daily acts of a pure race, and not mere theater, I would like to suggest to the group that they should request such an assessment because, in truth, they very badly need it.

In many countries, folklore is mere legend. If it was ever lived, it is not so now—as it is lived in our case when our natives continue their traditions year after year and celebrate rituals and their *costumbrismo* day after day as part of their quotidian life and not as a show for cameras, lights and television.

With all possible courtesy and with the experience of his great scholarship, *Maestro* Castañeda approached the group and stressed his disagreement with their lending themselves to such a *costumbrista* farce. He begged them not to adulterate the rich traditions of his race and offered his services so that, when they would have the time, they might come to his office to obtain the necessary instruction and guidance.

We associate ourselves with this plea and, in order to stress our protest and clarify it, we question part of the text of the invitation: *Rilaj Mam* (in Tzutujil) is the Old Man; *Ucoj Maximón* (in Tzutujil) is the Old Man; *Ocoj Maximón* (in Quiché) is Mask of Maximón. *Rucoj Maximón* (in Cakchiquel) is also mask of Maximón: what then did they mean? [*We do not know what this display of linguistic 'expertise' refers to.*]

To the *I.G.A.*, our gratitude for their exhibition which presents our national heritage and, in this case, for a very good, although not extraordinary, exhibition. Our commentary exempts them completely from responsibility for a lack of same on the part of some artists who, God willing, will soon receive the necessary instruction for the presentation, without falsehood, of a true MASK OF Maximón, corresponding to reality and not to commerce.

However much one might understand the running sore of wounded nationalism, and whatever one felt oneself about the "show"—the term was not used by the *conjunto* itself—the self-presentation of these particular *ladino* individuals as experts in Maya culture is farcical. The sanctimonious nature of the piece and the astonishing ambivalences regarding "*their*" Indians manifested by a certain class of Guatemalan *ladinos* can hardly be better illustrated, nor can the rip-off involved when *ladina* models dress up and go through simpering simulacra of "Indian" ritual. We doubt that much justice was done here to the scholars of the Indigenist Institute.

These sentiments are even present, of course, together with the full range of babble emitted by such *ladinos,* in a vein of sentimental exaltation of the picturesque whenever the Indian countryside is evoked, in articles *favorable* and beneficial to Prechtel. Examples of this can be found in *Horizonte* for July and August 1978, a Sololá publication, with articles by J. Enrique Maldonado. These, replete with lyrical clichés about the lake, potted histories of the Highland Maya and biographical details about Prechtel, make the point that Guatemalans should be grateful to such young men for helping them preserve "*their*" traditions and hope that others, but of *local* extraction, should be born to continue the work. There is a hint of recognition that the music discussed contains nativistic claims for Indian liberation which should be heeded—but this is rapidly dissolved in Liberal goodwill and cordiality.

For those wishing to study a Yankee equivalent of all this, there is Marjorie Harvey's piece in the *Boston Sunday Globe* for June 25, 1978. The intent here is clear in one paragraph particularly:

> As he talks on in the half light, we feel our usual view of reality slipping away, as it did for Carlos Castaneda in the hands of his Mexican Indian sorcerer, Don Juan.

Truth, indeed, is stranger than fiction!
Now comes the question of Atiteco attitudes to Prechtel.

Another reason for taking precautions was the hostility of the various *Catequista* factions during Holy Week. The *principales* and *mayori* complained of harassment by *Catequistas* concerned, like the *mayori*, with guarding the church: both parties trying to be the last to leave the building—"you go first and we'll lock up!"—and the *mayori* claiming to have caught *Catequistas* stealing fruit from the *monumento*, that same fruit the *alcila* had taken so much trouble to bring up from the Coast. The Radio was rumored to be angry with the elders for pulling off the fruit *costumbre* without their help after strong rumors that the Radio was planning to boycott them. The Radio people suspected that the Brotherhood had turned to the elders when they, representing the younger element in the village, had failed to make their payments to them.

A particularly acrid battleground turned out to be the Committee for the Reconstruction of the Church (a hold-over from earthquake reparations) composed both of *Catequistas* and *principales*. At one meeting, Lucas Rianda Ixbalan, a member of the *principales'* group and a very respected elder, had slapped a *Catequista* for impertinence and said that it was about time older people should be listened to again in Santiago.

Juan Sisay's main discomfiture during Holy Week, directed in good part against Prechtel, was to find that he had not been called—as was the habit—to the dressing of the Crucified Christ in church on Holy Friday. On arrival, he had found that Lucas Rianda Ixbalan had done the dressing.

On the same afternoon as the confrontation with the journalist, Tarn had gone round the village to take certain photos of small chapels, one of which happened to be stationed right in front of Juan Sisay's house. Sisay was "very busy" but offered a beer, then, suddenly, burst out with, "All this business about the mask: you know about it I guess." Tarn became evasive: visits to Juan Sisay's house were not easy at *any* time in 1979. "Well," Sisay went on, "it is not the one they had at the museum: it must be some copy that those museum people made; I have seen it over there at the Chapel where he is hung and it is *not* the one!" Thunderstruck for a moment, Tarn then remembered that, of course, the returned mask was not *on* the Mam: the outburst, however, seemed to indicate that Sisay was ignorant of the fact that the mask had not yet been returned to *cofradía* Santa Cruz.

We can give a taste of the gathering violence of feelings among certain sectors about the whole question of foreign interference by looking at a bizarre little mimeographed bulletin titled the *Aj'itz Revolucionario* or "Revolutionary Sorcerer" which appeared anonymously in Santiago around mid-1979.

This bulletin begins by claiming inspiration from the ideas of such "defenders of the poor" as the assassinated national politician Manuel Colon Argueta and attacks a considerable number of local targets for corruption, sexual abuse of women and girls, illiteracy, persecution of Indian folk etc., naming names official and private.

Cofrades are attacked as a group for endemic drunkenness.

There are specific accusation against one candidate for Town Mayor of helping Prechtel ("that exploitative thieving *gringo*") with the Holy Week *costumbre* as well as harming the poor by conspiring to deprive them of lands. Prechtel, "who claims not to gain a cent from helping local *costumbres*, is in fact getting money from home and was recently given $1,500 by an anthropologist." The attack is larded with heavy insults about his marital life.

All of this eventually becomes Prechtel "earning thousands of quetzales through the sweat of our brows" and being advised to leave town "because we no longer want *gringos* and mixed bloods here who are ridden with syphilis, gonorrhoea and the famous 'flower of Vietnam.'" The "other *gringo*," Francisco Rother, has doubts cast on his virility and is accused of possibly being a spy [*an ear: oreja*]. He has also claimed that all Mission property would go back to the U.S. if he were forced to leave.

The priest Adán, is described as a "ratman" and *marijuanero* embezzling everyone in Sololá at this point as Director of Caritas and getting a fine colonial-style house out of it. He is accused of being a "musical specialist in women, teaching *marimba* in his bedroom" and the details of his adventure with a girl [*we have touched on this*] names the names of all involved. The Radio people are sinful as well as ignorant of their own language; soliciting correspondence which is then never read, let alone answered, and so forth. The then Director and Gaspar Culan are both named.

Juan Sisay is brought into play as local leader of the right-wing party C.A.N., using the hated right-wing politician Arana Osorio's money and pushing road-building with the help of the *chalet* owners. Among his named partners is our friend the Protestant Pedro Ramírez Mendoza—the latter described as so bemused by money that he forgets all the principles he once upheld as an elder of the Centro Americana Protestant church.

A list of some twenty named people to be attacked in the next issue is then previewed. It includes our Domingo, "falsifier of documents"; a chief of the military commissioners who makes thirty to fifty dollars out of grabbing men of all ages for the army; three "ears" of the government; a thief and seller of INCAPARINA agricultural products donated to the town; a seller of communal lands; the people of the landing stage tourist cafe as dealers in marijuana and women; a *ladina* making profits out of the nutrition programs; "a Somoza *(the Nicaraguan dictator)* in Atitlán"; as well as some locals living in situations of incest or homosexuality. The paper ends with renewed demands for the resignations of the whole municipality; the expulsion of Prechtel, all priests and pastors; the disappearance of all *cofrades* who are selling Atitlán to foreigners through their alcoholism; and the construction of a school rather than the San Lucas road which will only be of use to the *chalet* owners. Tarn was forced to wonder "how he alone escaped" unless he was intended to be the rich anthropologist!

It was reliably reported later in the year that the people behind this bulletin were Juan Sisay, a prominent person in the Radio organization and a *Catequista* leader, as well as some Protestant individuals: accusations against themselves had been thrown in to minimize suspicions. A report we consider more reliable claims that the Bulletin was masterminded by a radical student, a rival of

Felipe Tuiz, who is alleged to have firmly believed that factories should be built in Atitlán in order to foster a "proletariat!" This man had his own reasons for being jealous of Prechtel. We do not know if he is still alive.

The brilliant, complex and tragic Felipe Tuiz, with his constantly shifting allegiances, is reported to have been killed by the Army around the end of 1982 or beginning of 1983 in Chacaya, wearing a guerilla uniform. Some soldiers had been killed by guerillas in this area at the time. Tuiz's and three other bodies were rowed back to Atitlán and buried there. Thus ended the life of a man who took a great deal of time to make up his mind.

We are not aware that another bulletin ever came out: the authors are said to have been disappointed that the bombshell effect they expected did not materialize. Privately, however, there was a great deal of astonishment at its outspokenness.

TWENTY-TWO

The Terror and a Memorial
to the Dead of Atitlán

The rest of this book, covering a period during which we were not in Atitlán, could not have been written without the contributions of Robert Carlsen based on his recent extensive research in that place. He told us, in September 1990, that Army bases remained in Atitlán—though the soldiers made themselves scarce during tourist hours. The Army evicted Carlsen during the summer of 1990 and he was unable to finish that season's research project. He has been back since.

The question of who the Army was fighting remains somewhat obscure. Carlsen records that the guerilla Revolutionary Organization of the People in Arms (*O.R.P.A.*) came to recruit in Atitlán in June 1980, promising justice and land. At first, they obtained satisfactory responses from Atitecos who had heard a good deal on the radio about labor strife in the Capital. In the month after this visit, plainclothes police officers asked many questions in the locality. The Army came in forcefully in October 1980. Two weeks later, two disappearances occurred and by early December ten individuals had been lost. Various sources cite material on *O.R.P.A.* and their continued presence in the volcanic foothills before their removal elsewhere around 1988. *O.R.P.A.*'s activities during 1980-88 scarcely endangered the locality, let alone the country. Carlsen doubts that most of the attacks attributed to *O.R.P.A.* since the end of 1988 were in fact carried out by them and sees these incidents as Army instigated provocations designed to justify its continued presence.

The story of the Army's occupation of Santiago Atitlán is told in the records of the Guatemalan Human Rights Commission U.S.A. (G.H.R.C./U.S.A.), the other source which was indispensable to this chapter.

The following text is from two reports entitled *Santiago Atitlán, preparation for a massacre*, G.H.R.C./U.S.A., March 1985:

For several years now, the Army has unleashed a wave of repression against the inhabitants of Santiago Atitlán. An enormous number of illegal executions and forced disappearances have taken place. During 1980, the illegal executions and forced disappearances of Indian peasants, *Catequistas*, traders and farmworkers began. In February 1980, the Army set up a military base on the football field in the village of Cerro de Oro, near Santiago Atitlán, and another base on the parish farm in the village of Panabaj near the hospital in July of 1980 [*other sources date this as of October 1980*].

In July 1980, during the annual festival of Santiago Atitlán, about one thousand army soldiers surrounded the town, restricting comings and goings and demanding the identity papers of anyone wanting to pass by. During the night the soldiers went into town and detained a number of individuals.

During the month of October, forces of the National Police and judicial officers arrived in four trucks, surrounded the building housing the Radio station 'Voz de Atitlán' and began asking for several individuals, particularly the heads of the various radio programmes. Failing to find them, they left. Between the 18th and 20th of the same month, another member of the church disappeared.

On October 25th, State troops again barricaded Santiago Atitlán and abducted the head of the Radio station, Gaspar Culan Yatas [*Yataz: this is the Atiteco Indian Catholic ex-priest mentioned in the context of the Oklahoma Mission's story*]. He was brutally beaten in the presence of his wife and children; taken away unconscious to the military camp, and never seen again.

By night the soldiers would burst into homes, beat the

inhabitants and ransack the house. The people were terrified and, by the month of November, the majority preferred to spend their nights in the Catholic church or the twelve Evangelical chapels of the village, taking it in turn to keep watch and warn of any sudden raids by State troops.

On November 15th, five members of the Radio station were abducted: the president; the night watchman; a member of the board of directors and two others. Three of them have not been seen since. Diego Sosof Alvarado, reappeared in San Lucas Sacatepéquez, in the center of the country. He had been tortured. His eyes had been put out, fingers and toes mutilated; he had burns on his chest and had been castrated.

In January 1981, the village was again barricaded by State troops.

In the same month, the peasants had gone to work in their fields. When one of the peasants shot a wild duck one day, the Army reacted by shooting indiscriminately at the peasants. Several were killed and another eighty were arrested by the soldiers and later tortured in the coffee fields. The majority were later freed on the condition that they speak to no one about the torture they had endured. Eighteen of the peasants were not freed. Their bodies, bearing signs of torture and mutilation, were later dropped from a helicopter onto various open fields. One of them was the Evangelical pastor Pedro Ramírez Mendoza. The population organized the burial of each body as it appeared over the next two or three days. The Army went to the cemetery, warning the peasants that the Army was fulfilling what it had to do. During the month of March 1981, the detentions and disappearances continued.

The reports then outline the warnings received by Father Stanley Rother and his eventual assassination. One Atiteco stated some time ago, and before the case of the insurgent leader Comandante Efraín Bamaca became an important issue in the U.S. in 1995, that the alleged C.I.A. agent Colonel Julio Alpirez was in charge of the Atitlán base at the time of Father Rother's death. After this:

> During 1982 and 1983 the illegal executions and forced disappearances continued. Many local people were threatened and many women were raped by the soldiers; several of the women became pregnant. In 1983 another priest came to be with the people and to celebrate Mass. He, too, was threatened, as were the sisters who were staying in the parish. The priest left.

It was also in 1982 that the Civil Defense Patrols (*P.A.C.*), a creation of Efraín Ríos Montt, were instituted in Atitlán as elsewhere in the Highlands, forcing Atitecos to patrol the town and outlying settlements in search of "subversives." These *P.A.C.*s were a source of unbelievable amounts of abuse throughout Guatemala, often involving the settlements of private vendettas and the satisfaction of illicit desires, especially by the chiefs of these patrols. Atitecos obtained their disbanding in 1986 but, on a later occasion which Carlsen places in 1990, the Army made great efforts, visiting all local leaders, to try to re-instate them. They were only very partially successful.

The reports continue:

> In 1984 the Army closed its base in the village [*cantón*] of Panabaj. However, they returned frequently with greater control over the population due to the forced participation of the peasants in the civilian patrols, which the Army has called a 'self-defense' measure.
> During July of 1984, another United States priest, Father John Vesey, known as Padre Juan, took charge of the parish at Santiago Atitlán. He also has been threatened.

In 1984, the town municipal buildings were attacked and burned down—the work, it is generally agreed, of *O.R.P.A.* This action destroyed a great many documents relating to local residents

suspected of subversion. It also did away with others relating to
election procedures and, finally, with a great deal of precious demographic information constituting a major loss to future historians.
The reports continue:

According to investigations carried out by the Human Rights
Commission in the area during March of 1985, the Army
and security forces have increased their pressure and intimidation against the people, as a prelude to unleashing an even
greater wave of terror. During March the Army began a
census of the population throughout the area of Santiago
Atitlán. This usually indicates the first steps toward establishment of a 'model village.' This one would be located in
Nahualá [which seems to confirm other rumors heard at
the time], in which there will be an effort to concentrate
survivors and displaced persons resulting from the government plan to 'clean out Santiago Atitlán.'

At 10:00 p.m. on March 29th, 1985, soldiers in civilian
dress, from a military post near Panabaj, violently removed
Julio de León, Pedro Damian, and Nicolás Cali from their
homes in Panabaj. They have been 'disappeared' along with
Juan Coquix Ratzan and Diego Tacaxoy (treasurer of the
Village Betterment Committee) who were also 'disappeared'
that day. The Army is exercising strict control over the entire
zone and many abuses and threats from military commissioners have been reported.

From the 26th to the 30th of March, 1985, the Army within
the "framework of its counterinsurgency program operations in
the area" burned down large community forest areas.

Another report was issued by the Human Rights Commission from Mexico City on September 18th, 1986. It stated that
international intervention had been successful and that "faced with
such international pressure the military regime was forced to halt
the widespread repressive operation planned against Santiago
Atitlán." It went on to record that on "April 3rd, 1986, thousands

of Atitlán residents took to the streets to demand the dismissal of the Mayor Antonio Cumes for incompetence and because he ordered the illegal detention of a man known as Juan the salesman, who had been tied up and detained by the Army." On May 28th, "large numbers of local authority workers in Atitlán were dismissed by the local council, presided over by the Mayor Antonio Cumes."

The text then continues:

Information received from a sub-office in Quetzaltenango, marked urgent, reported that on 28th and 29th August, fifteen hundred soldiers arrived in Atitlán in twenty-nine lorries, escorted by three tanks and with air force and artillery back up. There is already a permanent base in Atitlán with two hundred soldiers.

Following military occupation of Atitlán, the Army have initiated a campaign of intimidation and threats against the residents. One high ranking officer in charge of the operation informed residents that they would suffer reprisals for any past or future guerilla attacks on the Army in that area.

The report launches a second international appeal on the basis of these imminent threats pointing out that the danger to Atitlán is "taking place at a time when the Christian Democrat government is striving to project an image at an international level of a Guatemala where human rights are respected and safeguarded."

On September 15th, 1986, residents of Chicacao reported Army bombings of town outskirts and mountain villages. 20 military trucks arrived in town. Soldiers had faces painted black to terrorize the people.

On December 17th, 1987, General Hector Gramajo, Minister of Defense, announced that the Army would continue pressure on Atitlán until the end of the insurgency.

On January 9th, 1988, some ten schoolteachers of both sexes having served from fifteen to twenty years in Atitlán declared that they had received death threats and left the town. School teachers had been among the most conscientious and outspoken critics of Army behavior.

On January 10th, 1988, the Commission announced an Army occupation of the *pueblo* since the beginning of the month with aid from the G-2 Intelligence branch and the judicial police. Curfews were imposed; soldiers with painted faces stole and killed animals in private compounds; military commissioners menaced people with accusations of helping the insurgents. Town surroundings were mined. The Army took control of food sales.

On February 3rd, 1988, more teachers were said to have received death threats.

On the 26th of October, 1988, the *G.A.M.* Organization of the Disappeared accused soldiers in Cantón Panabaj of persecuting villagers to drag them into military service. They were said to catch them in streets, fields and other workplaces.

On June 10th, 1989, armed men broke into the home of Salvador Ramírez, Municipal Secretary General of the political party Unión del Centro Nacional (U.C.N.). They damaged part of the house and told his wife they would be back.

On August 7th, 1989, Antonio García Peleu, a teacher from Atitlán was walking on a street in Guatemala City near Congress when anti-riot police tried to capture him. He ran into the nearby building of the "Centro Socio-Educativo Rural." He was followed, taken, stripped and beaten. He was conveyed to the Red Cross for treatment of multiple wounds.

On September 4th, 1989, the brothers José, Salvador and Antonio Ixbalan Cali were taken and tortured. Salvador Caj Tzihuina, his younger brother and seven other agricultural workers, all from Tzancaj, Atitlán, were also taken. Neighbor pressure obtained their release from the Army camp.

On October 4th, 1989, in El Plano, near the Monte de Oro plantation, five workers from Panabaj, Atitlán were taken and beaten. Their machetes were confiscated. Soldiers threatened them with death if they should talk.

On October 25th, 1989, it was reported that persecutions and death threats had forced hundreds of workers to leave their bean and corn fields in "Sakbalche, Tzanknak, Perwac'xom, Poplan, and the area around Matzabal" (sic) in the municipality of Atitlán. Many workers were not allowed to cut firewood.

On November 2nd, 1989, a communique from the national Committee for Campesino Unity (*C.U.C.*) announced that continual military control and curfew were in effect in the Atitlán settlements of Panabaj and Tzanchaj from 7:00 p.m. to 5:00 a.m.

The forced recruitment of youth, mainly indigenous country people including minors under eighteen, for military service began throughout the country on November 4th. On November 1st, 6th and 7th, 1989, the Army entered numerous homes in Atitlán and forcibly recruited young men into its ranks. They also went to a Protestant church, turned out the lights and took away five young men. The minister later managed to get these released.

In a report on his 1989–1990 work in Atitlán to the Guatemala Scholars' Network and the *Report on Guatemala* which eventually reached the U.S. Secretary of State, Robert Carlsen mentions and analyses a number of 1990 abuses (murders, tortures, rapes, robberies etc.) claimed by the Army to be the work of guerillas but, in his opinion, manifestly masterminded by the Army itself.

As 1990 came to an end, the anger and frustration aroused by these persecutions erupted in a way which aroused national and, furthermore, international concern.

On December 1st, 1990, five soldiers in plainclothes, including two armed, from the Panabaj garrison had been drinking hard in a local bar all afternoon. The five included the garrison commander. Around 7:00 p.m., they moved to another bar where three of the soldiers beat up a few clients. They then wandered about the streets, abusing people and beating them up. Around 9:00 p.m. four of the men went to the house of the local merchant Andrés Zapalu Ajuchan and tried to pull him out of the house.

Responding to his cries, neighbors ran up. The soldiers got away but not before wounding a nineteen-year-old Atiteco.

People went to the church and rang the church bells for over an hour while others went through the streets waking the Town Mayor, Delfino Rodas Tobías, and the Mayor Elect, Salvador Ramírez Ramírez. The Mayor went to interview the wounded man. Several thousand Atitecos gathered in the town plaza. The crowd, informed by the Mayor and Mayor Elect, decided to march on the Army base. The two Mayors asked them to put down sticks and stones and to walk armed only with white nylon banners to demand an explanation.

Salvador Ramírez tried to talk to the sentries but got no answer. As the Mayor then tried to speak, a soldier fired in the air. Other soldiers immediately fired directly into the crowd. Eleven people were killed on the spot, including three children, and seventeen were wounded. The wounded were taken to the Sololá hospital where two of them died. A paralyzed seventeen-year-old was eventually taken to a hospital in Oklahoma City.

National reaction was, given past history, amazingly prompt and thorough. At noon on December 2nd, the Guatemalan Human Rights Ombudsman, Ramiro de León Carpio, went to Atitlán and took testimony from the Mayor and Mayor Elect and others. He examined the bodies of the dead, noted that there had been a full moon on the night of the 1st with excellent visibility and ascertained that the soldiers had tried to detain Zapalu Ajuchan illegaly.

On this day also, a crowd of reporters, including Amilcar Mendez, president of the national Council of Ethnic Communities *Runujel Junam,* (the *C.E.R.J.*), went to the Army base, found the commander removed and were informed by a temporary commander that the crowd had fired first. When told the crowd carried no guns, he refused to comment further and referred the group to the Army's Office of Public Information.

On the 4th, more legal officials met in the Municipality and heard from eleven Atitecos and two *ladinos*. They also visited the

Sololá hospital. A document was obtained from the Military Zone commander. On the 5th, testimonials were taken from the wounded in hospital. Also now on hand was a document addressed to the President of the Republic, signed or fingerprinted by some *fifteen thousand* Atitecos, demanding justice and an Army withdrawal. To these was joined a report from the Office of Human Rights of the Guatemala Archdiocese and several press communiques: some fifty reporters had attended the mass funeral of the victims. At one point during these proceedings, the Mayor and Mayor Elect went on national television to explain that the massacre had been the culmination of a decade of oppression and killing of thousands of Atitecos.

At a town demonstration on the 5th, Francisco Co Mendoza, "the head of the *cofrades* of Atitlán," called for non-violent resistance to any further Army presence. Unions and popular organizations contributed three thousand *quetzales* to the victims' families.

The Ombudsman reviewed an Army declaration of the 3rd accusing the Atitecos of attacking the military base. This was followed by assertions from the same source that, if responsibility there were, it was only the base's not that of the whole Army. All of this was categorically rejected by the Ombudsman.

The Ombudsman's report, issued on December 7th, began with lengthy considerations on the importance and uniqueness of his own position as nominated by the Congress of the Republic following Guatemala's adherence to international Declarations of Human Rights. This was made necessary by the Army's overriding predominance in national affairs. The report then went at length into analysis of the word "genocide" to conclude that there had been such, perpetrated by the Army against a "specific ethnic group, the Tzutujils" both as to murders and to a ten-year history of intimidation, abuses of authority, oppression, rape, theft, coercion, terrorism, and interference with the peoples' means of subsistence. The Army, far from working for the security and good of the people, had become the guarantor of *insecurity* and internecine conflict in this area and was hereby publicly censured.

The Ombudsman then went on to name the guilty soldiers, a lieutenant base commander and two sub-lieutenants, as officers responsible to be dealt with by pertinent authority. Finally, the Ombudsman called for the evacuation of the Army base from Atitlán.

The base commander and a sergeant-major who had fired on the crowd were eventually tried and sentenced. It was reported in November 1991 that the former was given four years and the latter sixteen. The commander might be given more. Critics maintained that several other soldiers had gone free and that the Army's investigation had been very lax.

While the Ombudsman softened his tone somewhat in subsequent interviews, Congress, faced with an international outcry, withdrawal of U.S. military aid and outspoken criticism of the Army by the U.S. Department of State, called for the military to leave. Some days after the massacre, the U.S. Ambassador, in a meeting with President Cerezo and General Juan Leonel Bolaños, Minister of Defense, demanded an Army pull out. Soon after the massacre, the German Government was reported to have cut off all technical and financial aid to the Guatemalan security forces; Ambassadors of the European Economic Community recorded their vehement condemnation; and the Guatemalan Embassy in Washington had to issue a message to the international community.

On the 14th of December, the European Parliament was reported to have condemned the massacre and urged that the responsible officers be tried by civilian and not military courts. On the same day, a delegation of the Communities of People in Resistance (the *C.P.R.*) met with diplomats, churchmen, media people and trade unions to protest the massacre, congratulate Atitlán on its resistance and target the Army as the secret instigator of disorder in the Highlands.

On December 20th, the Army took six hundred soldiers out of Atitlán, relocating them at Base Number Fourteen in Sololá.

Robert Carlsen points out that Guatemala was in the final days of closely watched political elections. Atitlán, as a prominent tourist destination, lying across the Lake from the famed tourist town of Panajachel, was very much, at all times, in the public eye. Of great importance also was the fact that Army crimes, usually attributable only to "unidentified armed men," had now been openly seen by thousands of witnesses.

For some time after the event, black flags and ribbons were seen on many houses and commercial establishments. A photo display of the victims of the decade's terror was set up in the Municipal building. At the old Army camp site, a peace park was set up with a marble plaque citing President Cerezo's decree. On the second day of every month, people from all denominations began coming together for commemorative meetings (*concentraciónes*) which were also town forums. On one occasion, the Mayor declared that there were no longer any religious conflicts in Santiago. A twenty-five square kilometer zone around the town was declared out of bounds to both Army and guerillas. A Committee for Security and Development was instituted, comprised of members from most Atiteco institutions, to create and organize nightly security patrols (*rondas*) carrying only whistles and white banners. An offer of participation by the local branch of the National Police was summarily rejected and an effort was made to evict the Police in the same way as the Army had been. It was stressed that there should be no replacements: everyone from top to bottom of the society should do his service. It was also noticed that increased mobility in agriculture meant a return to customary work and better harvests.

On January 4th, 1991, five policemen from neighboring San Lucas Tolimán, claiming to be looking for escaped prisoners but driving a vehicle associated with abuses, were disbelieved and nearly lynched by an Atiteco crowd. The Atiteco Chief of Police had to use tear gas against this crowd. The Ombudsman Ramiro de León Carpio arrived at 2:00 p.m. in an Army plane to issue a reprimand. He announced that he would return to visit Atitlán on the following week. The National Police Chief responded on January 10th by naming "selected" officers to increase the force in Atitlán. On January 27th, a drunken policeman shot at a group of people and wounded José Mendoza Tzina. Again Atitecos demanded the departure of the police. Again they were ignored.

In May 1991, on two consecutive days, well-armed Army patrols came into Atitlán, one of them getting to within two kilometers of the town center. They were met by groups of unarmed civilians, some one hundred strong, and told in no uncertain terms to go back. In the meantime, Army spokesmen tried to project an image of goodwill as well as continued strength in claiming that Atitlán was still a "zone of conflict" and should be protected by them. Carlsen does tell us that, by December 1991, Atitlán's attention had turned back to older problems. One faction of Protestants refused to attend the *concentraciónes* which they characterized as a "cult of the dead." There were unseemly threats by a prominent leader, in the midst of political conflict, of "bringing the Army back" in case of defeat. In July of 1993, Salvador Ramírez who had left the position of Mayor on the 15th of that month, complained that he had been getting death threats on the phone. It appeared as if factionalism might be back and might stay, barring a resolution of Atitlán's real demographic and economic problems.

On October 9th, 1993, Atitecos published an advertisement in the City press reporting continued repression by the Army. They asked De León Carpio, now President of the Republic, to restrain the security forces. In response, on November 11th in *El Grafico*, the Army claimed to be still pursuing the *Javier Tambriz* Front of *O.R.P.A.* and that Atitecos obviously sympathized with these terrorists! In March, 1994, the Atitlán Mayor again reported that disguised and face-painted Army personnel in an identified truck beat up two residents in a group that confronted the invaders. On May 23rd a travelling Atiteco, Antonio Ixbalan Cali, was beaten and threatened with death by soldiers while on the road. In October, twenty families in Cerro de Oro, under threat of expropriation of land they had held for a century were threatened and oppressed by police.

Eloquent of Atitlán's ever evolving problems was the growth

of crime in Atitlán. As part of the Army's provocation, young men, conditioned by a decade's upbringing under martial law, were set against their own people. In 1994, there was an escalation of violent robberies, mainly by masked young Atitecos boarding buses as they returned to town with merchants and their earnings. There were brutal, sordid and apparently arbitrary beatings and killings. After one of these, in October 1994, the Development and Security Committee under the ex-Mayor Salvador Ramírez, attacked the suspected leader in Cerro de Oro and other individuals given away by him, eventually delivering the whole gang to the prison at Sololá.

It must be admitted, however, that after the December 1990 massacre, the number of extra-judicial killings reported by the Human Rights Commission dropped dramatically. Atitlán, though not the rest of the country, appeared to be relatively safe for a while. A memorial is placed into this book so that the dead of Atitlán may have a place to rest in the story of their home on earth before the Terror. A number of the dead here remembered are people who figure largely in this book: Salvador Sisay Petzey; Juan Sisay Sisay; Pedro Ramírez Mendoza. Some of the names have not been officially recorded but we know they are gone: one is Felipe Tuiz. Most of the documentation is recorded through the care of the Guatemala Human Rights Commission/U.S.A. operating in monthly reports out of Washington D.C. with the help of the *Comisión de Derechos Humanos de Guatemala* in exile in Mexico.

The abyss into which the Highland Maya have fallen—Atitlán is but one home town among hundreds—has been and continues to be one of the worst known to man since the end of the Nazi era in Europe. We guess that only the sufferings of Cambodia, Ruanda or Bosnia equal or exceed those of the Maya.

To work with the files of the *Comisión* is to bathe daily in torture, decapitation, quartering, castration, mutilation, rape, and death. It is also to realize that the names of the recorded are few compared to the unrecorded and that to pick out the names of

Atitecos is to select from thousands of dead among the indigenous communities suffering at the hands of an allegedly democratic regime in Guatemala.

Names of people and of places have been kept here as recorded in the *Comisión* files: understandably, given the extreme difficulty of obtaining any information at all under circumstances of repression, transcriptions fall short of the exactitude one would wish for. We have suggested some corrections of names where these seemed fairly certain and merely queried others for future reference.

Occasional data are available in the publications of Amnesty International. Another good source is the monthly information sheets of the *Centro Exterior de Reportes Informativos sobre Guatemala (C.E.R.I.G.U.A.)* based in Mexico, which has been running, as far as we can tell, since about March 1986. This source also records insurgent activity in the country, including the Atitlán area. We have abstained from going into the latter in that it would only make true and full sense in the context of a future history of the Guatemalan popular Movement.

In recent months there have been reports of successful talks between the Government of Guatemala and insurgent parties. It is too early to say what effect these will have on the future of the Higland Maya.

RECORDS OF THE DEAD

7/80
An unknown number. About one thousand soldiers entered the area during the Santiago titular *fiesta*. A quantity of people were spoken of as detained and the impression is that some may have been killed.

10/25/80
Gaspar Culan Yataz, the Atiteco Indian ex-priest.

11/15/80
Diego Sosof Alvarado plus three unnamed members of the Radio.

1/5/81
Father Rother's "most sought after Catechist. " This is presumably Diego Quic, snatched from the church porch by armed men in a car while Father Rother looked on helplessly.

1/8/81 and 1/9/81
Pedro Sojuel Mendoza (age 32)
Julio Melgar (24)
Diego Chajchoj (17)
Car (sic) Velasquez
Pedro Mucuy Yax
Angel Alfredo Rodríguez Lopez
Jacobo Galindo Barrios
Juan Sicay
Pedro Ramírez Mendez (sic: Mendoza)
Salvador Tuy Pablo
Augusto Yaxen Rodríguez
Gabriel Ramos Chayun
Martín Sapalu Pablo
Pedro Sapalu Pablo
Plus four persons unnamed
The Army was attacked by guerillas on the 7th. Following a shooting episode in a field already mentioned in a Commission report, the Army entered houses on the two following days and killed people in cold blood. Families fleeing by boat on the lake were machine gunned by helicopters. Tortured corpses of eighteen people were thrown from helicopters. Among these was that of *Pedro Ramírez Mendoza: friend of the authors, 1952–3, 1969 and 1979.* Fifty-two or more persons were released after torture.

7/28/81
Father Stanley Rother
friend of the authors, 1979

7/5/82
Angel Augusto Tobías
Taken while fishing and 'disappeared.'

3/29/85
Julio de León
Pedro Damian
Nicolás Cali
Juan Coquix Ratzan
Diego Tacaxoy
Plus one person unnamed ?
These were violently taken from their homes and 'disappeared' by soldiers in civilian dress. They were reported tortured in the basement of the local military base.

4/29/85
Manuel Antolin
Plus four persons unnamed
'Disappeared' by the Army.

6/25/85
Salvador Sisay Petzey (51)
Shot by unidentified men in the presence of his family at his drugstore at 8:30 p.m. *Salvador Sisay: friend of the authors in 1952–3, 1969 and 1979.*

7/31/85
Carlos Ramírez Arteaga
Owner of the "Las Ninfas" buses. Shot dead by unidentified raiders at his home.

11/26/85 and 11/28/85
Salvador Mendoza
Nicolás Pop
Diego Xiquibal
Plus three persons unnamed
Detained and 'disappeared' by an operation group of Army Intel-

ligence, G-2, who came into town to scout around on two occasions in two Toyotas, one blue, one red.

12/27/87
Dolores Pospoy Ajcabal
Barbara Ramírez
Two "artisans" shot to death at night. 5.56 mm. bullets prohibited to civilians were found near the corpses. The Army attributed the deaths to the guerillas but the Commission attributed them to the Army. Amnesty International Urgent Action paper UA29/88, 1/28/88, reported that B.R. aged 32, embroiderer, and D.Pospoj (sic). A., weaver, were found naked, raped and shot on the road between Atitlán and Tzanchicham where they lived.

1/23/88
Jose Mecia Hernández (34)
Antonio Mecia Hernández (24)
Detained by unidentified men in olive green clothes in Tzanchicham with death threats. The brothers' bodies were later found.

1/28/88
Diego Sisay Sapuluc (24)
Gaspar Yataz Pablo (25)
D.S.S. was detained by the Army in Panchinchay, Atitlán on the 25th. His tortured body was found at Kilometer Eight of the Atitlán-Tolimán road. G.Y.P. was taken by unidentified men at Pachitulul off a bus to the Coast: the "Fuentes del Sur" bus, plate C-287451. His tortured body was found also at Kilometer Eight on the same road.

2/2/88
Mariano Xoch Tzorin (39)
The president of El Triunfo Residents' Committee was found killed on the La Vega Estate in Panajachel. He had worked to help widows in the area and was taken from a bus on January 23rd by heavily armed unidentified men. His nine-year-old son witnessed this. Tzorin's parents had been killed by the Army in 1982.

13/15/88
Cristóbal Ramírez Sosof
Shot to death by unidentified men at his house. Presumed a guerilla. Official information was given that insurgent tapes and documents were found, plus military uniforms.

5/4/88
Not identified (50)
Bullet riddled body of an unidentified man found in an Atitlán
street.

5/5/88
Bernardino Pospoy (67; elsewhere 76)
Shot dead at dawn by unidentified men in Cantón Panay *(sic:
Panaj?)*.

8/2/88
Setum Lopez (20)
Juan Manuel [?] Setum Lopez (14)
Fermin Pablo (20)
Shot dead by unidentified men. [*Data unclear: three or four people?*]

10/20/88
Juan Chojpen Cajtin (36)
Shot dead in a mountainous place [Choacruz] by unidentified men
on his way to construction work. His companions Cruz Pop Quieju
and Victor Canij [*elsewhere: Caniz*] Chicaj escaped safely.

1/31/89
Felipe Coche Damian (33)
Killed with bullets and machete while out fishing according to his
wife Nicolása Coc Tzina. His body was found in a wood of Cantón Cuchicaj [sic: ?]

2/26/89
Nicolás Ramírez Culan (26)
Gregorio Ramírez

Juan Damian Coo
Diego Ixtite La Savalu [sic: Ixtetela Sapalu?]
These four went out on work-related errands on the 23rd and never reappeared. María Elena Salvalu [sic: Sapalu?] and Rosario Culan made a deposition with the Police.

4/21/89
Juan Sisay (68)
Shot dead while walking to his house by unidentified men. Archbishop Prospero Peñados del Barrio recorded that Sisay had told him of death threats. Internationally known painter. *Juan Sisay Sisay: Friend of authors 1952–3 and 1979.*

9/11/89
Andrés Samuc
Martín Samuc
Taken by soldiers on the road to Patulul [Coast] and transported to the military base in Huehuetenango. Not heard of since.

9/12/89
Andrés Quic Ajuchan (19)
Baltazar Quic Lacan (21)
Taken at an Army road block while travelling to Guatemala City. Not heard of since.

9/19/89
Gaspar Coche Sisay (24)
Found murdered on the slopes of Tolimán Volcano. He was not specifically identified as an Atiteco but it is probable from the name.

10/6/89
José Ajtujal
Cruz Ixbalam Ramírez
Hailing from Tzanchaj, Atitlán, they disappeared from hills near Chicacao on the Coast while collecting fruit. Soldiers were seen in the area at the time.

2/90
Juan Ixbalam
Telinel at the time. Shot down by three masked men as he was
walking home from the *cofradía* (Carlsen).

3/20/90
Pascual Petzey Ramires [sic: Ramírez?] (28)
Body found in an isolated area of Santiago Atitlán.

5/20/90
Felipe Ramírez (53)
Francisco Coche Coche (39)
Were attacked by several armed and masked men in Santiago
Atitlán.

5/24/90
Fidelino Raúl Tobías Aparicio (41)
Miguel Angel Rianca [sic: Rianda?] Sicay (44)
Gregorio Ramírez y Ramírez (42)
Juan Pablo Quiejuy [sic: Quieju?] (48)
The bodies were found on the Oro [sic: Cerro de Oro?] hill in
Santiago Atitlán: strangled, tortured and shot. Residents reported
that the men had been picked up separately, at the same time,
by armed men in military clothing two days earlier in the villages
of Xechiboy, Pamacoj, Achichoy and Cheritay [sic: ?] in Santi-
ago Atitlán.

6/13/90
Diego Ajcabul Catu (17)
Guillermo Ajcabul Catu (13)
These brothers were shot by four masked men wearing olive green
clothing in Cerro de Oro, Santiago Atitlán. Seriously injured, they
were taken to the regional hospital.

6/22/90
Gregorio Quiej [Quieju]
Shot to death by several men in olive green clothing on Cerro de

Oro in El Pacayal, San Lucas Tolimán.
Corrected in a later report to: Gregorio Quieju Quebac was dragged from his home by ten soldiers in the village of Chaguajal [sic: ?] Santiago Atitlán on June 21st. The body was later found on the public thoroughfare. G.Q.Q. reportedly opposed forced recruitment into civil patrols.

7/21/90
José Mesis [sic: Mesias?] Petzey (28)
Gaspar Mesis Petzey
José was shot to death by unidentified men who attacked him and his two brothers in Panoj [sic: Panaj], Santiago Atitlán. His brother Gaspar was wounded; the other brother was uninjured.

8/21/90
Antonio Silverio (35)
Detained/disappeared as he was traveling on the road from Guatemala City to Santiago Atitlán. Four armed men in a white jeep intercepted the truck in which Silverio and Oscar Raúl de León Alvarado were travelling, threatened to kill Silverio and then forced him into their jeep. De León Alvarado reported the crime to the police.

9/12/90
Juan Ixbalan (53)
The body was found with bullet wounds in a hallway of the municipal building in Santiago Atitlán.

10/4/90
Antonio Pacay (19)
Miguel Sosop [sic: Sosof] Vásquez (22)
They were shot to death by unidentified men in Pazamay [sic: ?], Santiago Atitlán.

10/15/90
Salvador Sosof Vásquez (20)
Baltazar Pablo Mendoza (25)

They were shot to death by six men hidden by knit face-masks who arrived on foot and broke into their home in Cantón Panul, Santiago Atitlán. Relatives of the victims say that the killers acted quickly and silently, giving them no opportunity to intervene.

10/23/90
Martín Quic Ratzan (50)
He was shot to death by unidentified men with blackened faces while attending a *cofradía* meeting of Santiago Atitlán at the house of Nicolás Quiej [Quieju?]. The men walked directly to Quic Ratzan, shot him with automatic weapons and fled. (Carlsen reports him as *Telinel*, sitting next to the Mam at the time. The Mam's mask's nose was also shot off . . . but according to hearsay the nose grew back. Setbacks to the Army have been attributed by many to this shooting.)

12/2/90
Juan Carlos Pablo Sosof (20)
Pedro Mendoza Cotu (18)
Francisco Giron Chicajau (10)
Juan Ajuchan Mesias (15)
Salvador Damian Yaqui (50)
Felipe Quieju Culan (53)
Nicolas Ajtujal Sosof (47)
Pedro Crista Mendoza (14)
Gaspar Coo Sicay (18)
Pedro Mendoza Pablo (29)
Pedro Damian Vásquez (45)
Plus at least nineteen wounded
These are the confirmed casualties so far in the massacre of December 2nd, 1990. Two more names of the dead are given in a report a week later: Manuel Chiquita González and Salvador Alvarado Sosof. The following are given as wounded, with those starred listed as critical and taken to the Roosevelt hospital in Guatemala City.
Diego Ixbalam Rianda
Pedro Sicay Sapalu
Antonio Rianda Coche

Antonio Aju [sic: Ajau?]
Francisco Mendoza Mendoza (12)
Pascual Mendoza Tiney (15)★
Nicolás Ratzan Sapalu
Diego Chavajay Coche
Antonio Pablo Taj
Cristóbal Tacaxoy
Nicolás Tzina
Pedro Culan Sosof
Gaspar Tzina Tiney (18)
José Sosof Coo (17)★
Antonio Chivilin [sic: Chiviliu?]★
Plus at least one other unidentified.
The next report lists Salvador Diaz Sosof, wounded, as now dead on December 5th in Sololá.

12/21/90
Juana Coche Tacaxoy (52)
José Pospoy Mendoza
They were shot to death by unidentified men in a building at Kilometer Fourteen on the road between Atitlán and San Lucas Tolimán. The husband and wife are believed to be related to victims of the December 2nd massacre.

3/16/91
Unidentified
Human bones were found in a bag buried in the former Panabaj Army base in Santiago Atitlán. Residents asked that excavations be continued.

2/9/92
Miguel García Julaju (50)
Antonio Sacalxot (38)
Esteban Coche Xicay (46)
Francisco García Chingo (30)
Felipe Petzey (10)
Plus one unidentified.

Nine individuals were listed as wounded plus the bus driver and another unidentified man. At least four of the victims killed were believed to be Atitecos. The incident took place at Pochuta (site of a military base) between Patulul and Atitlán. On 5/10/92, a bus from Mazatenango to Atitlán was held up and robbed. Two women from Tolimán and one from Miramar were raped.

There are no further killings reported up to mid-1995. The relatively few names here are those recorded among a very much larger number killed with estimates ranging from a total of five hundred at the conservative end to two thousand at the highest. Some of the names recorded for surrounding communities such as San Lucas Tolimán, or indeed in places further afield, may be names of Atitecos. Many names may deliberately not have been reported.

The Maximón, as Lord of the Dead and pacific mediator both, continues to have his work cut out for him in Santiago Atitlán.

The Cast:
Principal Characters

We were not always able to collect full names—names were already a delicate matter in 1979. In some cases, only nicknames were available. In a few cases, we have protected vulnerable identities with altered names. Here, we have deliberately abstained from accenting Tzutujil surnames of Atitecos. The symbol (+) indicates someone known to be dead at the time of writing.

AJCOT, Esteban: legendary "prophet" of a rain-priest lineage. See Sojuel, Francisco (+).

AJCOT, Juan: a senior story-teller nicknamed "Red Banana."

ARBENZ GUZMAN, Jacobo: President of Guatemala (1951–54) after Juan José Arévalo who had overthrown Ubico in 1945. "Deposed" by an American coup.

AJUCHAN, Nicolás: *Alcalde* of the *cofradía* San Gregorio (1978–79).

CARLSEN, Robert: American anthropologist working in Atitlán after Tarn and Prechtel. Continues work there at present.

CASTENEDA José: Director of the *Instituto Indigenista Nacional* in 1979.

CHIVILIU TACAXOY, Nicolás: One of Atitlán's most famous *aj'kuna*, mentor of Tarn in the 1950s, of Prechtel later (+).

CEREZO, Vinicio Arévalo: President of Guatemala 1986–90.

CHAVEZ, Nicolás: Head of the Reconstruction Committee in the late 1970s and rival of Prechtel's for the *primer mayor* position.

CHAYAL, Diego: *Alcalde* of *Cofradía* Animas (1978–79)

CUA POSPOY, José: a senior *principal*, member of Prechtel's mask group, nicknamed "Hatchet." A great orator.

CULAN YATAZ, Gaspar: Controversial first native Atiteco Catholic priest in 1979, "disappeared" during the Terror (+).

"DAVID": Member of a group of three friends, known here as the Brotherhood of Three, active in Adequate Technology projects in Atitlán during 1979 and in the story of the mask's return to Atitlán.

DE LEON CARPIO, Ramiro: Guatemalan Ombudsman for Human Rights. Investigates the Atitlán massacre of 1990. Later President of Guatemala.

"DOMINGO": *Catequista* friend of Juan Sisay in the 1950s, working in the *Voz de Atitlán* Radio in 1979.

ESQUINA YATAZ, Cristóbal: *Cabecera* of Atitlán in 1979. Prominent *aj'kun* friendly to Prechtel's mask group.

"EYES": see Sisay Ajtujal, Diego (+)

GARCÍA, JUAN: *Alcalde* of *cofradía* Santiago (1978–79).

"HATCHET": see Cua Pospoy, José.

"HENRY": Anthropologist, staff member of a prominent European Museum. Helps Tarn & Prechtel return the Maximón mask to Atitlán in 1979.

"JOAQUIN": Member of the Brotherhood of Three. See "David."

LARA, Celso: Prominent Guatemalan theoretician of Folklore.

"LOINCLOTH": See "Malvex."

"MALVEX": "Loincloth." Nickname of a story-teller in 1979. Prominent *aj'kun* and *Telinel* in 1979 after the firing of "Matchajpin."

"MAKUXTIN": see Petzey Tiney, Agustín.

"MARIE": Anthropologist, member of the same Museum as "Henry."

"MARIANDA": see Rianda Ajtujal, Diego.

"MAXIKAY": see Xikay Ivoy or Yol, José.

"MATCHAJPIN": *Telinel* in *cofradía* Santa Cruz in 1979, in conflict with his *cofradía*. Replaced by "*Malvex.*"

MENDOZA, Pascual: elder story-teller, known as "Weep Wizard."

MENDELSON, E. MICHAEL: French American anthropologist and colleague of Tarn's, active in Atitlán in the early 1950s.

PAKAY, Estevan: *Alcalde* of *cofradía* Santiago (1979–80)

PANSINI, Jude: American Catholic priest active in the Micatokla Mission in the late 1970s; later left the Church and worked in Social Service.

PEDRO, Nicolás: *Alcalde* of *cofradía* San Antonio (1978–79).

PETZEY TINEY, Agustín: *Alcalde* of *cofradía* Santa Cruz (1978–79). Known as "Makuxtin."

POP, Agustín: field worker for the *Instituto Indigenista Nacional*. Reported on the "Maximón Scandals" in the early 1950s.

POSPOY, Salvador: *Sacristán* and *Escribano* of *cofradía* Santa Cruz in the early 1950s. A great comedian (+).

RAMIREZ MENDOZA, Pedro: Head of a small Protestant group. Helped the *costumbristas* during the Maximón Scandals. Owner of a textile shop in the marketplace in the 1970s. Thrown from a helicopter during the Terror (+).

RAMIREZ RAMIREZ, Salvador: Town-Mayor Elect at the time of the 1990 massacre.

RECINOS, Godofredo: Salvadorean Catholic priest and leader of the *Catequistas* who launched the Maximón Scandals in the early 1950s.

RIANDA, Manuel: relative of Nicolás Chiviliu, *aj'kun* and unsuccessful candidate for *telinel* in the early 1950s.

RIANDA AJTUJAL, Diego: *Alcalde* of *cofradía* Santa Cruz (1979–80) known as "Marianda."

RODAS TOBIAS, Delfino: Town-Mayor of Atitlán during the 1990 massacre.

RODNEY, Janet: poet and printer, married to Tarn. Shared in the 1979 field work.

ROTHER, Stanley Francis: Oklahoman Catholic Priest, head of the Miclatokla Mission in the late 1970s. Murdered in his bedroom during the Terror. His heart is buried in the Atitlán church (+).

RUJUCH, Marcos: Legendary "prophet" in the Sojuel lineage. See Sojuel (+).

SISAY AJTUJAL, Diego: Nicknamed "Eyes." Prominent *principal* in Prechtel's mask group (+).

SISAY PETZEY, SALVADOR: *Catequista* cousin and friend of Juan Sisay Sisay in the 1950s. Ran his own Drug Store in the 1970s. Murdered in his store during the Terror (+).

SISAY SISAY, Juan: *Catequista* leader during the 1950s. Launched the Atiteco school of painters and acquired considerable fame and fortune with international ramifications. Murdered during the Terror (+).

SOSOF, Pedro: *Catequista* and Town-Mayor in the early 1950s. By the 1970s, he was a leading Protestant.

SOJUEL, Francisco: legendary *nabeysil* and "prophet," member of a re-appearing or re-incarnating lineage of prominent rain-priests. Lived at the turn of the century and appears to have been in nativistic political conflict with prominent landowners. Credited by some with the present form of the cult of Maximón. His family still own a *cofradía particular* containing "visionary" sculptures by S. His life needs investigating if sources can still be found (+).

XICAY IVOY OR YOL, José: *Cabecera* of Atitlán, 1978, known as "Maxikay."

TESTE: French Catholic priest from Clermond Ferrand. Order of

Lazarists. The Maximón mask which had not been burned was recuperated from him in 1952–3.

TUIZ, Felipe: young Atiteco intellectual, educated at an American inspired School of Linguistics in Huehuetenango, rival of Prechtel on many fronts, thought to have been killed as a guerilla during the Terror (+).

TZINA, Andrés: First *Regidor* in 1952, eccentric and ambivalent about *costumbre* but anti-*Catequista*.

UBICO CASTENEDA, Jorge: Guatemalan Dictator from 1932. Overthrown by Juan José Arévalo in 1944 (+).

VESEY, John: American Catholic Priest. Succeeded Father Rother. Removed after controversy surrounding his alleged lack of diplomacy and over-strictness.

"VICENTE": member of the Brotherhood of Three. See "David."

"WEEP WIZARD": see Mendoza, Pascual.

YEL, José: *Alcalde* of *cofradía* San Felipe (1978–79)

ZAPALU COCHE, Nicolás: Known as "Damian *la Oreja*," the Ear, an *aj'kun* thought to be a spy for the Police as far back as the 1950s. Believed killed during the Terror (+).

Principal Tzutujil Maya and Spanish Terms Used in This Book

For the convenience of the general reader, we have simplified transcription as much as possible. Also, we have not indicated origins from other Quiché Maya Family languages but have ranked all these as (T) for Tzutujil. Nor have we given many details of grammatical forms or pronunciation. We have, however, indicated words Mexican in origin (mostly Nahua) by an (M).

A

abaj (T): stone.

abogado (S): lawyer, attorney.

acha (T) (pl. *achi*): man, husband.

Achijab (T): Warriors, Men of Rain, Rain Angels.

aj (T): young ear of corn; man, male person; he who, he of (office, native, lineage member etc. e.g. *aj'pop*: he of the mat, i.e. prince, chief).

Ajaw (T): Lord.

aj'biaj (T/S): traveller [*viaje* (S): travel].

Aj'butalaya (T/S): Warrior, Battle-man [*batalla* (S): battle].

Aj'ch'ojacha (T): Warrior, Battle-man.

ajelbal (T): animal-soul, animal familiar.

aj'itz (T): man of evil, sorcerer.

aj'kun (T) (pl. *aj'kuna*): man of medecine, shaman.

aj'xul (T): man of the flute, flute-player.

ala (T) (pl. *ali*): boy.

Alcalde (S): 1} Town Mayor, usually: *Alcalde Municipal* (S); 2} Head officer of a *cofradía*.

Alcalde Taq Sant, or *Alcalti'* (S/T): *Alcaldes de cofradía* (S).

Alguacil (S): Lowest rank in the Indian Politico-Religious organization. At municipal service and *Cabecera*'s service.

Angel (S): Angel; Rain-Angel.

Atiteco (M/S/T): inhabitant of the *municipio* of Santiago Atitlán. Hailing from Atitlán.

Atitlán (M/T): On or near the water; place of the Water people. Lake Atitlán. Largest settlement on the lake: Santiago Atitlán.

awaciil (S/T) (pl. *alcila*): *alguacil* (S).

B

bajlam (T): jaguar, *tigre* (S).

batz' (T): thread.

Batz'bal (T): lit. spindle; the Mam's older wife.

Batzin: (T): Mr. Thread, Early Power-Man.

Batzinab (T): Little Brothers (Young Mam forms, *Mamlaab*).

be (T): road, path.

brujo (S): sorcerer.

C

Cabecera (S): Head officer of the Indian Politico-Religious organization. Head of the Town.

cacao (S): cocoa and chocolate bean, *Theobroma Cacao*, of great ritual value in precolumbian times. A shade plant for coffee.

Caja Real (S): Royal Coffer; trunk containing original colonial and other documents regarding the town, kept by *Cabeceras*.

Cakchiquel (T): a people bordering the Quiché on the south and east and the Tzutujil mainly on the east, speaking a Quiché family language. The *Annals of the Cakchiquels* is an important source book with the *Popol Vuh*.

cantina (S): bar.

Catequista (S): Member of *Acción Católica* (S) founded in Guatemala around 1945 to defend orthodox Catholicism against folk interpretations.

C.E.R.J. (S/T): *Consejo Etnico Rujuel Junam*: National Council of Ethnic Communities.

Cerro de Oro (S): lit. Hill of Gold, small volcanic area dependent on Atitlán Municipality (see map).

Cerro de Burro (S): lit. Hill of the Donkey, small hill among hills at

S.W. rim of Lake Atitlán said to be the center of the Atiteco cosmos. It is the home of dead "prophet" shamans who eventually become Rain Angels in hierarchical order and the headquarters of all Rain Angels.

cofradía (S): group of men and women committed to looking after and celebrating the *fiestas* of a group of *santos* normally for one year in the house of an *Alcalde de cofradía* and at the corresponding altar in Church. Sometimes, "the *cofradía*" is used in the same sense as "the *Costumbristas.*"

cofrade (S): officer of a *cofradía*. Normally these are an *Alcalde,* a *Juez* and *cofrades* First to Sixth.

compadre (S): also *comadre*: ritual relationship linking individuals as a result of the establishment of various kinship ties and/or religious ties.

conjunto (S): musical group or band.

costumbre (S): lit. custom. In the Guatemalan Highlands: the performance of a religious ritual.

Costumbrista (S): person who performs traditional Indian rituals, name given to *cofradía* officials and members of the Indian politico-religious organization; the traditionalist party.

cuenta (S): reckoning, counting.

cuerda (S): measure of land, usually of 32 *varas* square, approx. 1/5th-1/6th of an acre.

CH

chaj (T), (Matek Chaj): pine, Early Power-Man.

ch'ajalbe (T): road-guardian.

ch'ajalniel (T): guardian.

ch'eep (T): little finger; youngest, smallest, last.

Chejuyu (T): Cerro de Oro.

Chicacao (T): important trading town for Atitecos on the Coast, Dept. of Suchitepequez.

Chichuk (T): Volcano Elbow, Volcano San Pedro.

ch'oj (T): war, battle, conflict.

ch'ojlal: (T): lust, pleasure, crazed passion. Carlsen also has *ch'ojrik* and *rxin ch'oj* as the left-handed way of the *aj'kun* path or *aj'kuniel.*

Chokox Aq'oum (T): Place of the medecine mushroom; Mam's birthplace South-East up in the hills behind the church.

Chukumuk (T): area to North-East of town.

Chutinamit (M/T): *tinamit* (M): city-wall; name of ruins at base of San Pedro volcano, the ancient Atiteco capital.

D

dueño (S): lord, owner.

E

Escribano, Escrivano (S): Secretary or Recorder in a major *cofradía*.

F

fiesta (S): celebration, usually of a Saint's name day.

Fiscal (S): Second rank of the Indigenous Politico-Organization, just below *Cabecera*. First & Second.

Francisca Batz'bal (S/T): the spindle; more usually, thus, the whole loom; the Grandmother; the Mam's older wife.

G

güisquil (T): vegetable pear (*Sechium Edule*). The original ancestress when put to death in a sweat bath became a *güisquil* which gave rise to the original lineage tendril of humankind.

guaro (S): *aguardiente*, heavy liquor most used in *cofradías*.

goma (S): hangover.

H

hornillo (S): a tree.

huipil (T): woman's upper garment.

hwit (T): magic baton or staff.

I

ikaj, Ma ikaj (T): ax, Mr. Ax, Early Power-Man.

il, mak (T): *il*: evil, violence, crime—*mak*: guilt; pleasure-pain principle.

isote (S/T): plant *izote* (S), *Yucca Elephantipes*, remedy against witchcraft.

itzbal (T): form, toy, doll, decoy-weapon.

Itzel Vinaq (T): lit. Evil Person, Devil.

ixoq (T): woman.

Ixtulul (T): Hyeronimo *I.* Early Power-Man.

iyom (T) (pl. *iyoma'*): midwife.

Iyom Pak'lom (T): Original Deity, lit. Maturing Person, Maturing Womb, Seed-Exploder, Seed-Opener.

J

jap (T): rain.

jaspeado (S): tie-dye thread.

jay (T): house.

juicio (S): last judgement or judgement at the end of an era.

juez (S): lit. judge; second officer of a *cofradía.*

jun (T): one.

juyu (T): mountain, volcano, hill.

juzgado (S): municipality; municipal building.

K

kaaj (T): sky.

k'aam (T): rope, string, vine, one *cuerda* measure of land.

kablajuj (T): twelve.

kakaxte (M/T): ritual carrying wooden frame box, used with tumpline, containing fruit for Holy Week.

k'amalbe (T): opener of the road, guide; marriage-broker.

k'as (T): debt.

k'aslemal (T): life.

K'as ruwa (T): lit. His head is alive. Said of a live person thought to be a "prophet" and future *nawal.*

Kasueel juyu (T): lit. Pot hill, crater, topmost point of *Monumento.*

Katbal tz'ij (T): lit. Arbitrators of the word; the Municipality, the Courthouse.

Kdta' (T): Our Father.

k'exel (T): object of reciprocity; replacement; grandchild, name-bearer.

kiem (T): weaving.

kii (T): poison.

Kinom (T): woof; woven cloth while in the loom; *jocote*, a type of fruit; usually María K. Early Power-Woman.

kir (T): to untie, to open womb. *María* or *Josefa Kir*: Early Power-Woman.

k'sis (T): cedar tree, branches used in Holy Week ornamentation.

k'ix (T): thorn, *güisquil* vegetable, vagina.

kixlaan k'um (T): fruit used in Holy Week ritual.

kmo' (T): part of loom; *María Kmo'* Early Power-Woman.

kolo' (T): rope; intestine, entrails, umbilical.

kolo'be (T): rope-road; crossroads.

ko'ol (T): small.

kumatz (T): snake, often mythical.

k'un k'un (T): double-tongued drum found in *cofradías* which contain precolumbian deities.

k'ux, a'kux, r'kux (T): heart, navel, center.

kuxin (T): coffee shade tree and fruit, *Inga*; usually *Matek Kuxin*, Early Power-Man.

K'walk'oj (T): Mythical Double-Headed eagle, possibly of Hapsburg, possibly of Maya origin or mixed.

L

ladino/a (S): person defining him/herself as not Indian and eschewing Indian clothing and behavior.

licenciado (S): person having a professional diploma or university degree.

M

Ma (T): Mr. as in Makuxtin, etc.

maatz (T): ritual drink made of maize; *atole* (M).

Magdalena Castellana (S): the Mam's younger wife.

Mam (T): grandfather; the precolumbian Old God; in some parts of Highland Guatemala has calendric associations; in Atitlán: identified with the Maximón icon in *cofradía* Santa Cruz.

mangax (T): black ceremonial wool coat worn by senior members of the Indian politico-religious organization.

Martinab (S/T): the warriors, the Martín Powers, the Rain-Angels.

masat: (T): deer.

Matek (T): Diego.

Matek Staka (T/S): Early Power-Man; *estaca* (S): stake, post, planting-stick, cudgel.

matraca (S): wooden rattle, whirred especially during Holy Week.

Mayor (S) (pl. *mayores* (S); *mayori* (S/T): rank in Indian politico-religious organization, employed both at Municipality and in religious ritual.

maxan, muxan (T): large leaves, like a banana's, used for packing.

melocoton (S): lit. peach. In Atitlán, large cucurbit, *Sicana Odorifera* figuring among fruit of Holy Week ritual.

merkani (T): women once married but not currently husbanded.

Monumento (S): Holy Week structure erected over main altar in Church to have the coastal fruit hung upon it. Represents a primal hill world wherein lie the origins of Sun, man, corn. Also monumental arches at various sites outside.

mos (T): *ladino*, foreigner, outsider.

mozo/a (S): servant, accolyte.

multa (S): fine, tax, payment, sacrifice.

munil (T): not-*waya'*; dessert, fruit, slavery, vassalage, tribute.

Mundo (S): lit. world; Holy World, Maya cosmos.

muxux (T): navel, center.

muuch' (T): *chipílin* (S), *Crotalaria Longirostrata*, vegetable; usually María M.: an Early Power-Woman.

N

nabe (T): first.

Nabe Taq Siak (T): the Three First Weavings, i.e. the Martín shirts or capes.

nabeyal (T): first child; leader of a party.

nabeysil (T/S): official in *cofradía* San Juan (and San Antonio) in charge of Martín Bundle, lit. First Throne: *silla* (S) seat.

naoj (T): wisdom, knowledge.

nawal, nuwal (M/T): *nagual* (M); religious, mythical essential power; sometimes: spirit familiar.

Nawal Antiwal (M/T/S): Early (First?) Power-Man; *antiguo* (S) ancient.

Nawal Taq Achi (M/T): The First Ancestors, Power-Men.

Nawal Taq Alaniem (M/T): The First Birth-Givers.
Nawal Taq Exki (M/T): The First Ancestresses; Power-Women.
Nawal Taq Iyoma' (M/T): The First Midwives.
nikanik (T): holy fool; prophet.
nutie' (T): "my mother" (address to female official).

O

ocote (T): pitch pine splints, kindling; also the tree.
okuy (T): a tree; as in Jacobo Okuy, an early Power-Man.
O.R.P.A. (S): *Organización Revolutionaria del Pueblo en Armas*, guerilla revolutionary group.

P

pacaya (S): a palm, *Chamaedorea*, branches used as ceremonial staffs.
Pachichaj (T): Northern canton of town.
Pak'lom (T): name of hill, possibly *cofradía* San Juan as a hill. In Quiché Momostenango, it is in town and the center of the world.
palbal, palibal (T): instrument to raise oneself; throne, Angel-seat; Angel-ladder—often in a tree.
Panaj (T): South-Western canton of town.
Panajachel (T): Town on east side of the lake, a tourist destination. Highrise has disastrously begun there.
Panq'an (T): Antigua Guatemala, the Old Colonial Capital.
Panul (T): North-Eastern canton of town.
parkii (T): the *izote* (S) plant.
pataxte (T): a plant *Theobroma Bicolor* with cacao-like fruit, paired with cacao in ritual.
patin (T): savory paste usually made of fish and wrapped in banana leaf.
patojo, patoja (S): Guatemalan word for boy, girl or young person.
peq' (T): *pataxte*, sometimes cacao.
pexlak (T): succulent plant used in *cofradía* roof decoration.
petate (S): rush mat, comes in many different sizes.
pixnaq (T): kind of edible pigweed, as María P. an Early Power-Woman.

P'ko'k (T): in, at the Corral: the Lake home region.

poklaj (T): dust; as in Matek Poklaj an Early Power-Man.

pom (T): incense from resin of copal tree, *Icica Copal*.

pop (T): mat, Maya symbol of power.

Popol Vuh (T): lit. mat-book; Quiché Maya Book of the Council, the great classic of Highland Maya literature. Contains divination, myth and history materials on the Quiché populations, including the Tzutujil. See Reading List.

poy (T): puppet, doll, scarecrow, decoy, false representation to mislead an enemy.

Pral (T): Volcano Tolimán; lit. "At Her Children."

Principal (S): member of the council of senior politico-religious officers who help the *Cabecera* on important issues. People who have been through all the ranks and finished their service. *p. pasado*: one entirely retired from public affairs.

P'talpin (T): place name just South of Chutinamit. Very heavy bells in the water, only their shadow can be seen. Look with a mirror.

pueblo: a people; a town or settlement.

puub chay (T): "lightning blood"; *puub*: witchcraft weapon, blowgun. *Chay* (T) is obsidian, usually as a knife.

Q

q'amuq (T): stair-step (religious term).

q'apoj (T) (pl. *q'apoja'*): girl.

q'aq'al (T): shooting star; one's pre-birth star; majesty, glory, heat, one's fire-soul, often in a dream world. The Quiché *Pizom Q'aq'al* in the *Popol Vuh* is the Bundle of Majesty.

Q'elbal (T): Reclining place, the Throne; Cerro de Burro, the World Center.

quetzal (M/T): superb *trogon* bird; national bird of Guatemala; unit of currency roughly equal to the dollar.

Quezaltenango (M/T): *Xelaju*, *Xela* (T): Guatemala's second town.

Qij, q'ij (T): Sun, day.

q'isoum (T) (pl. *q'isoma'*): witch transforming into animal.

R

[N.B.: *R-* *(ruu-, uu-)* Pronominal prefix of the third person singular which, in nouns, indicates the possessor and in transitive verbs indicates the subject.]

r'chbal, rwachabal (T): copy, representation, fake, imitation.

Regidor (S): senior position in Indian politico-religious organization. Serves in Municipality rather than in ritual where the *mayores* are more important.

rejtal (T): sign, omen.

rey (S): king, chief.

riat kumatz (T): mythical silky-haired snake.

rilaj (T): old, venerable.

r'qan (T): foot, leg.

R'qan Sak R'Kan Q'ij: Footpath of Dawn, Footpath of Sun: the Sun's annual path across the sky.

r'k'ux (T): root, stomach, heart, seed, core, center.

r'k'ux ak'ala (T): root of child, children.

r'k'ux kaaj (T): root of sky.

r'k'ux ulew (T): root of earth.

r'kux waya (T): root of food: small hard corn cakes in Martín Bundle. The bundle in San Antonio has small representations of domestic animals.

r'k'ux xeya (T): root of waters.

r'muxux (T): navel.

R'muxux kaaj R'muxux ulew (T): Navel of Sky and Earth: Atitlán.

ronda (S): watch march, usually at night.

rox (T): third—usually in rank, as in Third *Cofrade.*

rubenom acha (T): a manufactured man (i.e. not born).

rubenom kumatz (T): manufactured, witchcraft or magic snake.

ruchulew, ruchiliev (T): earth.

r'wa, ruwa (T): head

r'wach, R'wach Ruchiliev (T): face, Face of the Earth, Original Earth Face or Skull.

r'way (R): food made from corn, sustenance; in weaving: food of the loom.

S

sacristán (S): sexton.

San Lucas Tolimán (S/T/M): town on Tzutujil-Cakchiquel border east of Atitlán & Cerro de Oro.

San Pedro la Laguna (S): Tzutujil town closest to Atitlán. Protestant sects have made heavy inroads there.

Santa Cruz (S): the Holy Cross; *cofradía* of.

santo (S): wooden statue of a Catholic saint.

Santiago (S): St. James of Compostela, patron saint of Santiago Atitlán.

Santo Entierro (S): image of buried Christ in a wood and glass coffin.

saq (T): white; light, birth, dawn.

saqsuut (T): lit. white *suut*: in Atitlán ritual *suut* white with purple stripes.

sejutay (T): flower-tendril, sprout, grandchildren, lineage.

Semana Santa (S): Holy Week, Easter.

silkum (T): whirlwind, usually sent by witchcraft.

silla (S): seat, throne.

sitio (S): house-site, house compound.

Sololá (T): Head town of the Department of Sololá, capital of Lake Atitlán area. The population is mostly Cakchiquel, another member of the Quiché Maya linguistic group.

Staka (T): usually Matek Staka, Dance King, Power-Man.

stoy (T): cloth wrap, scarf, shoulder cloth.

suerte (S): lit. luck. One's fate in life.

suut (T): head cloth. Typical is the *cofrade's* or *principal's*: red with stripes of brown, violet and an orange central stripe representing the Sun's path. These days drowned out by *jaspeado* tie-dye.

sutz' muyew (T): cape of clouds or fog.

SH (=X)

Xechivoy (T): South-Eastern canton of town.

Xesiwan (T): place at very South end of Lake, site of a house of Francisco Sojuel's.

Xetuk (T): place name to West of Xesiwan.

xjan (T): taboo, shame.

xkajkoj (T/M): brown *ixcaco* (*Gossypium Mexicanum*) cotton; *cofrade's* or *principal's suut*.

Xoa' (T): wife of the *Alcalde de cofradía*.

Xokexom (T): place name on Volcano Atitlán edge leading to Coast route.

xq'aap (T): woman's head band.

x'qunq'a kumatz (T): mythical rainbow snake, big hairy snake.

T

Ta (T): father.

telinel (T): He who carries images on his shoulder, official caretaker, dresser, carrier of the Mam/Maximón in *cofradía* Santa Cruz.

Tetixel (T): First Sun, "God the Father."

Tetiej Tetixel (T): Original undifferentiated Mother-Father Deity.

Tdta', Teeta (T): mode of address to fellow male ranked *cofradía*.

tiney (T): dahlia.

tijonel (T): *cofradía* advisor, counsellor.

Tioxa, Yuxa (S/T): (*Dios* (S): God) gods; twins, original twins.

tixel (T) (pl. *tixeli*) female *cofradía* official, usually in serving role, usually four.

tkar (T): mountain tree.

tk'r (T): loom stick or rib; as María Tk'r an Early Power-Woman.

tocada (S): set of tunes played by a *marimba* in a *cofradía*.

Todos Santos (S): All Saints; name of a well-known Maya town in Huehuetenango.

tornillo (S): wooden screw peg, knot.

tul (T): rushes used in mat-making.

tuj (T): sweat bath.

tulul (T): sapodilla fruit (S): *zapote injerto*.

TZ

tz'aaj (T): (S): *Taciscobo*; Red *Taxicoba* tree; as Matek Tz'aaj an Early Power-Man.

tz'ajtel, tz'ejtel (T): Coral Tree, *Palo* or *Flor de Pito* (S), *Erythrina Corallodendron*; seeds used for divination; Mam made from its wood as was an experimental ancestor in *Popol Vuh* while the female was made from reeds.

tz'alam abaj (T): square rock like a sacrificial altar.

Tzanchich'am (T): place name just North of town on way to San Lucas Tolimán. Many *chalets* are built here.

tz'aniem (T): to play, game of pretence.

Tzanjuyu (T): North-Western canton of town.

tz'ij (T): word, speech, statement, truth.

tzikin, tz'kin (T): bird, penis.

Tz'kinjay (T): Leading lineage of precolumbian Tzutujil; House of Birds, Capital of precolumbian Tzutujil in ruins at the foot of Volcano San Pedro.

tzoq (T): (S): *tule*; rush; as María Tzoq, Early Power-Woman.

Tzruy (T): Ancestor name as in Diego Tzruy.

tz'ubtz'ub (T): (*tz'ub* (T): suckle, breast, nipple); red-flowered plant; as María T. Early Power-Woman.

U

Uayeb: Old Yucatec Maya term for the five days between years.

Ultimo (S): the youngest, last of a line, the *Ch'eep*.

urna (S): glass case in which an icon or image is kept.

V

vara (S): staff of authority; measure of length, approx 32-33 inches.

vinaq (T): lit. twenty (fingers); a person.

vex (T): loincloth, often on a corpse, e.g. Jesucristo's statue.

Volkan (S): Volcano-Volcano: Volcano Atitlán.

W

wach (T): in front; face as essence of a person. *q'an w.*: face of yellow corn; *saq w.*: face of white corn; *rax w.*: face of black corn.

warabal, warambal (T): sleeping place, especially, here, of the Mam.

Way ya', Waya' (T): corn food-water; Our Food-Our Sustenance.

Y

ya' (T): water, liquid, liquor.

Ya' (T): Ms., Mrs.

Ya'mri: María

Ya'q'an (T): Yellow Corn-Girl.

Ya'saq (T): White Corn-girl.
Ya'xwan (T): Juana.
Ya'xper (T): Santa Isabela, the Great Midwife.

Z

zahorín, zanhorín (S): *aj'kun*, shaman, diviner.

NOTE: A long awaited Tzutujil Dictionary reached us at proof stage and could not influence this book. Consider, however, the following: "The variant of Tzutujil treated in this dictionary is that of San Juan la Laguna which, from a historical perspective, is one of the most conservative. For its part, the Santiago Atitlán variant is probably the most distinctive, having suffered a considerable amount of phonological innovation." We hear that this work has provoked controversy among Atitecos.

Selected Further Readings on
Santiago Atitlán

The reading matter on Highland Guatemala is extremely extensive and many works contain highly useful references to Atitlán. We try to hold ourselves in check here firmly.

Aguirre, Gerardo G. *La Cruz de Nimajuyu: Historia de la parroquia de San Pedro la Laguna*. Guatemala: Privately printed, Litoguat, 1972.

Asturias, Miguel Angel. "Maximón: Divinidad de Agua Dulce." *Revista de Guatemala*, Year 1, IV, 4 (1946): 18-26.

Butler, James N. & Butler, Judy G. *Tzutujil Verbs*. Guatemala: Instituto Linguistico de Verano, 1977.

———— & Fleming, I. *Tzutujil Texts*. Native American Texts Series, I, 1. Chicago: International Journal of American Linguistics, 1976.

Brinton, D.G. *Nagualism*. Philadelphia, 1894.

Campbell, Lyle R. *Quichéan Linguistic Prehistory*. University of California Publications in Linguistics, 87. Berkeley: the University of California Press, 1977.

Canby, Peter. *The Heart of the Sky: Travels among the Maya*. New York: Harper Collins, 1992.

Carlsen, Robert S. "Tradition & Mission in the Political Dynamics of a Guatemalan Town." Paper given at the 86th Annual Meeting of the American Anthropological Association, Chicago, November 1987.

————, *The War for the Heart and Soul of a Highland Maya Town*. Austin: the University of Texas Press, 1997.

Carlsen & Prechtel, Martín. "The Flowering of the Dead: Mayan Notions of Sacred Change." London: the Royal Anthropological Institute. *Man*, XXVI, 1 (1991): 23-42.

————, "Walking on Two Legs: Shamanism in Santiago Atitlán." In *The Ancient Traditions: Shamanism in Central Asia and the Americas*. Gary Seaman & Jane S.Day, eds. Niwot, Colorado: the University Press of Colorado (1994): 77-111.

Carmack, Robert M. *Quichéan Civilization: the Ethnohistoric, Ethno-

graphic & Archaeological Sources. Berkeley: the University of California Press, 1973.

———— & Morales Santos, Francisco. *Nuevas Perspectivas sobre el Popol Vuh.* Guatemala: Piedra Santa, 1983.

Carrasco, Pedro. "El Señorio Tz'utuhil de Atitlán en el Siglo XVI." *Revista Mexicana de Estudios Antropológicos,* 21, (1967) 317-331.

Chea, José Luis. *La Cruz Fragmentada.* San José, Costa Rica: Editorial Dei, 1988.

Chinchilla, Ernesto. "La Danza del Tum Teleche o Loj-Tum." *Antropología e Historia de Guatemala,* III, 2, (1951): 17-20.

Correa, Gustavo. *El Espíritu del Mal en Guatemala.* New Orleans: Publication 19, Middle American Research Institute, Tulane University, 1955.

Cua Pospoy, José: "Thirty Years Later: The Estados Unidos Goes to the Moon" translated by N. Tarn & M. Prechtel. *Sulfur,* 1, (1981): 21-27.

Dayley, Jon P. *Tzutujil Grammar.* Berkeley: *Publications in Linguistics* 107, The University of California Press, 1985

————, Perez Mendoza, Francisco & Hernandez Mendoza, Miguel. *Diccionario Tz'utujil.* Antigua Guatemala: Proyecto Linguístico Francisco Marroquín, 1996.

Douglas, William, G. "Santiago Atitlán." In *Los Pueblos del Lago de Atitlán:* 229-276.

————. *Illness & Curing in Santiago Atitlán, a Tzutujil Maya Community in the Southwestern Highlands of Guatemala.* Ann Arbor: University Microfilms, 1978.

Early, John D. "Education via Radio among Guatemalan Highland Maya." *Human Organization,* 32, 3 (1973): 331-228

Edmonson, Munro S. *Quiché-English Dictionary.* New Orleans: Publication 30, the Middle American Research Institute, Tulane University, 1965.

————. *The Book of Counsel: The Popol Vuh of the Quiché Maya of Guatemala.* New Orleans: Publication 35, the Middle American Research Institute, Tulane University, 1971.

Gross, Joseph J. *Domestic Group Structure in a Mayan Community of Guatemala (Santiago Atitlán).* Ann Arbor: University Microfilms, 1978.

————. & Kendall, Carl. "The Analysis of Domestic Organization in Mesoamerica: The Case of Postmarital Residence in Santiago Atitlán, Guatemala." In *The Heritage of Conquest Thirty Years After.*

Albuquerque: the University of New Mexico Press, 1983: 201-225.

Lothrop, Eleanor. *Throw Me a Bone: What Happens When You Marry an Archaeologist*. New York: Whittlesey House, McGraw Hill, 1948.

Lothrop, Samuel K. *Santiago Atitlán, Guatemala*. New York: *Indian Notes*, 5, 4: 370-395. Museum of the American Indian, the Heye Foundation, 1928.

———. *Further Notes on Indian Ceremonies in Guatemala*. New York: *Indian Notes*, 6, 1: 1-25. Museum of the American Indian, the Heye Foundation. 1929.

———. *Atitlán: An Archaeological Study of Ancient Remains on the Borders of Lake Atitlán, Guatemala*. Washington D.C.: Publication 444, the Carnegie Institution of Washington, 1933.

Loucky, James & Carlsen, Robert S.: "Massacre in Santiago Atitlán: A Turning Point in the Maya Struggle?" *Cultural Survival*, 15, (1991): 65-70.

Madigan, Douglas G. *Santiago Atitlán, Guatemala: A Socioeconomic & Demographic History*. Ann Arbor: University Microfilms, 1978.

McBryde, Felix W. *Cultural & Historical Geography of Southwest Guatemala*. Washington D.C.: Publication 4, the Institute of Social Anthropology, Smithsonian Institution, 1947.

McDougall, Elsie. *Easter Ceremonies at Santiago Atitlán in 1930*. Washington D.C.: *Notes on Middle American Archaeology and Ethnology* 123, the Carnegie Institution of Washington, 1955.

Mendelson, E. Michael. "Les Mayas des Hautes terres." Paris: les Editions de Minuit. *Critique*, 115, (1956): 1067-87.

———. *Religion & World-View in Santiago Atitlán*: "The Long Text." Chicago: Microfilm Collection of Manuscripts on Middle American Cultural Anthropology, no.52, University of Chicago Library, 1962.

———. "The King, the Traitor and the Cross." the University of Chicago Press for U.N.E.S.C.O. *Diogenes*, 21, (1958): 1-10.

———. "A Guatemalan Sacred Bundle." London: the Royal Anthropological Institute, *Man* LVIII, 170, (1958): 121-26.

———. "Maximón: an Iconographical Introduction." London: the Royal Anthropological Institute, *Man* LIX, 87, (1959): 57-60.

———. *Los Escándalos de Maximón*. Guatemala: Publication 19, Seminario de Integración Social Guatemalteca, 1965.

———. "Ritual & Mythology." In *Handbook of Middle American Indians*, 7, 392-415. Austin: the University of Texas Press, 1967.

Mondloch, James C. *Basic Quiché Grammar*. Albany, N.Y.: Publication

2, the Institute for Mesoamerican Studies. State University of New York at Albany, 1978.

———. "K'E?S: Quiché Naming." *Journal of Mayan Linguistics*, 2, (1980): 9-25.

Nouwen, Henri J.M. *Love in a Fearful Land: a Guatemalan Story.* Notre Dame: Ave Maria Press, 1985.

O'Brien, Linda. *Songs of the Face of the Earth: Ancestor Songs of the Tzutujil Maya of Santiago Atitlán.* Ann Arbor: University Microfilms International, 1978.

Pop, Agustín. *Diarios de Trabajo en San Pedro la Laguna.* Unpublished mss. Guatemala: Instituto Indigenista Nacional. n.d.

Ocana, Diego de. "Descripción de la Laguna de Atitlán." *Anales de la Sociedad de Geografía e Historia de Guatemala*, 9, (1932-33): 297-302.

Orellana, Sandra. "La Introducción del Sistema de Cofradía en la Región del Lago de Atitlán en los Altos de Guatemala." *América Indígena*, 35, 4, (1975), Mexico City: 845-856.

———. *The Tzutujil Mayas: Continuity & Change, 1250-1630.* Norman: the University of Oklahoma Press, 1984.

Paul, Benjamin D. "Mental Disorder & Self-Regulating Processes in Culture." In *Interrelations Between the Social Environment and Psychiatric Disorders*, 51-67. New York: the Milbank Memorial Fund, 1953.

——— & Demarest, William J. "The Operation of a Death Squad in San Pedro la Laguna." In *Harvest of Violence: the Guatemalan Indians & the Guatemalan Crisis*, R.N.Carmack ed., 119-153. Norman: the University of Oklahoma Press, 1988.

Perera, Victor. *Unfinished Conquest: The Guatemalan Tragedy.* Berkeley: the University of California Press, 1993.

Pontious, David Herne. *Diccionario Quiché-Español.* Guatemala: Instituto Linguístico de Verano, 1980

Prechtel, Martín. *Grandmother Sweat Bath: a Story of the Tzutujil Maya told in English by M.P.* Illustrated by M.P. Santa Fe, NM: The Weaselsleeves Press, 1990.

——— & Carlsen, Robert S. "Weaving & Cosmos among the Tzutujil Maya of Guatemala." *Res*, 15, Spring 1988: 122-132.

Recinos, Adrian. *Popol Vuh: the Sacred Book of the Ancient Quiché Maya.* English Version by Delia Goetz & Sylvanus Morley. Norman: the University of Oklahoma Press, 1950.

——— & Chonay, Dionisio J. & Goetz, Delia. *The Annals of the*

Cakchiquels (a.k.a. *Memorial de Sololá).* Norman: the University of Oklahoma Press, 1953.

"Relación de los Caciques y Principales del Pueblo de Atitlán, el 2.1.1571." *Anales de la Sociedad de Geografía e Historia de Guatemala,* XXVI, (1952): 435-438. N.B.: a good list of the various Colonial Documents known as *Relaciones* can be found in Sandra Orellana's *The Tzutujil Mayas.* See also Acuna, René and Carrasco, Pedro in Other Readings.

República de Guatemala. *Sexto Censo de Población, Abril 18, 1950.* Guatemala: Dirección General de Estadistica, Oficina Permanente del Censo, 1950. All subsequent data from material at the D.G.E.

Rojas Lima, Flavio, (ed.). *Los Pueblos del Lago de Atitlán.* Guatemala: Seminario de Integración Social Guatemalteca, 23, 1968.

Rother, Stanley. *The Shepherd Cannot Run: Letters of S.R., Missionary and Martyr.* Oklahoma City: the Archdiocese, 1984.

Saenz de Santa María, Carmela. *Diccionario Cakchiquel-Español.* Guatemala: Tipografía Nacional, 1940.

Sexton, James Dean. *Modernization among Tzutujil & Cakchiquel Maya: A Comparative Study of Two Guatemalan Towns, San Juan la Laguna & Panajachel.* Ann Arbor: University Microfilms, 1978.

Stresser-Péan, Guy. "Montagnes Calcaires et Sources Vauclusiennes dans la Religion des Indiens Huastèques de la Région de Tampico." Paris: *Revue de l'Histoire des Religions,* CXLI, 1 (1952): 84-90.

———. "Ixtab, Maximón et Judas." In *Actas del XXXIII Congreso Internacional de Americanistas.* San José de Costa Rica: Editorial Lehmann, 1958.

Tarn, Nathaniel, (Transl.) "Fragments from the Prayers Made on Behalf of N.T. by the Tzutujil Maya Priest N.C. of Tziquinaha, the House of Birds, Guatemala, 1953 & 1969." In *Atitlán/Alashka.* Nathaniel Tarn & Janet Rodney. Boulder, CO. Brillig Works Press, (1979): 99-104.

———. "Robert Redfield." In *Totems and Teachers: Perspectives on the History of Anthropology,* Sydel Silverman (ed.), New York: the Columbia University Press, (1981): 255-284.

Tarn, Nathaniel & Prechtel, Martín. "Metaphors of Relative Elevation, Position & Ranking in *Popol Vuh.*" Mexico: U.N.A.M. *Estudios de Cultura Maya,* XIII (1981): 105-113.

———. "Constant Inconstancy: The Feminine Principle in Atiteco Mythology." In *Symbol & Meaning Beyond the Closed Community:*

Essays in Mesoamerican Ideas, Gary Gossen (ed.). Albany: *Studies on Culture and Society* 1, Institute for Mesoamerican Studies, the State University of New York at Albany (1986): 173-184.

————. "'Comiéndose la fruta': Metáforas Sexuales y Iniciaciones en Santiago Atitlán" *Mesoamérica*, 19 (1990): 73-82.

Tax, Sol. "The Municipios of Highland Guatemala." *American Anthropologist*, 49, 3 (1937): 423-444.

————. "World View & Social Relations in Guatemala." *American Anthropologist*, 43 (1941): 27-42.

————. (ed.) *The Heritage of Conquest*. Glencoe, Illinois: the Free Press, 1952.

Tedlock, Dennis. *Popol Vuh*. New York: Simon & Schuster, 1985.

————. "The Sowing & Dawning of all the Sky-Earth: Astronomy in the Popol Vuh." In *Ethnoastronomy: Indigenous Astronomical and Cosmological Traditions of the New World*, John B. Carlson & Von Del Chamberlain, eds. Washington: Smithsonian Institution Press, 1986.

Thompson, J.Eric S. *Ethnology of the Mayas of Southern & Central British Honduras*. Chicago: Anthropological Series, 17, 1. The Field Museum of Natural History, 1930.

Tozzer, A.M. *Landa's Relación de las Cosas de Yucatán, A Translation*. Cambridge, MA.: Publications, 18. The Peabody Museum, Harvard University, 1941.

Wallace, Dwight T. & Carmack, Robert M. *Archaeology & Ethnology of the Central Quiché*. Albany: Publication 1, Institute for Mesoamerican Studies, The State University of New York at Albany, 1977.

OTHER SELECTED
RECOMMENDED READINGS

Acuna, René (ed.). *Relaciones Geográficas del Siglo XVI: Guatemala*. Mexico: *Serie Antropológica*, 45, *Instituto de Investigaciones Antropológicas*, *U.N.A.M.* 1982.

Adams, Richard N. *Crucifixion by Power: Essays on Guatemalan National Social Structure 1944-1966*. Austin: the University of Texas Press, 1970.

Annals of the Cakchiqueles. Translated by Adrian Recinos & Delia Goetz, with *Title of the Lords of Totonicapan*. Norman: the University of Oklahoma Press, 1967. N.B.: a good list of *Titulos* is to be found in Orellana's *The Tzutujil Mayas*.

Annis, Sheldon. *God & Production in a Guatemalan Town*. Austin: the University of Texas Press, 1987.

Arriola, Jorge Luis. *El Libro de las Geonimias de Guatemala: Diccionario Etimológico*. Guatemala: Seminario de Integración Social, 31, 1973.

Borhegyi, Stephan F. "Archaeological Synthesis of the Guatemalan Highlands." In *Archaeology of Southern Mesoamerica*, Gordon Willey, ed., *Handbook of Middle American Indians*, II. Austin: the University of Texas Press, 1965: 3-58.

Bricker, Victoria Reifler. *The Indian Christ, the Indian King: The Historical Substrate of Maya Myth & Ritual*. Austin: the University of Texas Press, 1981.

Bunzel, Ruth. *Chichicastenango: A Guatemalan Village*. Locust Valley, N.Y.: Monograph XXII, American Ethnological Society, J. Augustin, 1952.

Carmack, Robert M. *Toltec Influence on the Postclassic Culture History of Highland Guatemala*. New Orleans: Publication 26, Middle American Research Institute, Tulane University, 1968: 49-92.

———. *The Quiché Mayas of Utatlán: The Evolution of a Highland Guatemala Kingdom*. Norman: the University of Oklahoma Press, 1981.

———(ed.) *Harvest of Violence: The Maya Indians & the Guatemalan Crisis*. Norman: the University of Oklahoma Press, 1988.

Carrasco, Pedro. *Sobre los Indios de Guatemala*. Guatemala: *Seminario de Integración Social Guatemalteca* 42, 1982.

Coe, Michael. *The Maya Scribe & His World*. New York: the Groslier Club, 1973.

Colby, Benjamin N. & van den Berghe, Pierre L. *Ixil Country: A Plural Society in the Highlands of Guatemala*. Berkeley: the University of California Press, 1969.

Earl, Duncan & Snow, D. "The Origin of the 260 day Calendar." in Merle Greene Robertson & Virginia Fields, eds. Fifth Palenque Round Table, 1983, vol. 7. San Francisco: Precolumbian Art Research Center.

Estrada, Juan de. "Relación Geografíca Zapotitlán y Suchitepéquez (1579)." *Anales de la Sociedad de Geografía e Historia de Guatemala*, 28, (1955): 68-83.

————. "Mapa de la Costa Suchitepéquez y Zapotitlán (1579)." *Anales de la Sociedad de Geografía e Historia de Guatemala*, 39, (1966): 96-99.

Falla, Ricardo. *Quiché Rebelde*. Guatemala: Editorial Universitaria, 1978.

Farris, Nancy. *Maya Society under Colonial Rule: The Collective Enterprise of Survival*. Princeton, N.J.: the Princeton University Press, 1984.

Fox, John. *Quiché Conquest: Centralism & Regionalism in Highland Guatemalan State Development*. Albuquerque: the University of New Mexico Press, 1978.

Fuentez y Gúzman, Francisco Antonio de. *Historia de Guatemala o Recordación Florida*. Two Volumes. Madrid: Luis Navarro, 1882.

Gibson, Charles. *Spain in America*. New York: Harper Torchbooks, 1966.

Girard, Rafael. *El Popol Vuh, Fuente Historica*.Tomo 1. Guatemala: Editorial del Ministerio de Educación Publica, 1952.

Goubaud Carrera, Antonio; Rosales, Juan de Dios & Tax, Sol. *Reconnaissance of Northern Guatemala, 1944*. Chicago: Microfilm Collection of Manuscripts on Middle American Cultural Anthropology, no. 17, University of Chicago Library, 1947.

Guiteras-Holmes, Calixta. *Perils of the Soul: the World view of a Tzotzil Indian*. New York: Free Press of Glencoe, 1961.

Gage, Thomas. *The English American*. London: Broadway Travellers, 1928.

Gossen, Gary H. *Chamulas in the World of the Sun: Time & Space in a Maya Oral Tradition*. Cambridge, MA: the Harvard University Press, 1974.

Hammond, Norman. *Ancient Maya Civilization*. New Brunswick, NJ: Rutgers University Press, 1982.

Hunt, Eva. *The Transformation of the Humming Bird, Cultural Roots of a Zinacantecan Mythical Poem*. Ithaca: the Cornell University Press, 1977.

Hinshaw, Robert. *Panajachel: A Guatemalan town in Thirty-Year Perspective*. Pittsburgh: the University of Pittsburgh Press, 1975.

Immerman, Richard H. *The C.I.A. in Guatemala: The Foreign Policy of Intervention*. Austin: the University of Texas Press, 1982.

Jones, G.D. (ed.) *Anthropology & History in Yucatan*. Austin: the University of Texas Press, 1977.

Kendall, Carl; Hawkins, John & Bossen, Laurel. (eds.) *Heritage of Conquest Thirty Years Later*. Albuquerque, the University of New Mexico Press, 1983.

Kidder, Alfred V., Jennings, Jesse D. & Shook, Edwin H. *Excavations at*

Kaminal Juyu, Guatemala. Washington D.C.: Publication 561, the Carnegie Institution of Washington, 1946.

Klein, Cecilia. "Rethinking Cihuacoatl: Political Imagery of the Conquered Woman." Paper at LXIII Congress of Americanists, Vancouver, 1979.

La Farge, O. & Byers, D. *The Year Bearer's People*. New Orleans: Publication 3, the Middle American Research Institute, Tulane University, 1931.

La Farge, O. *Santa Eulalia: The Religion of a Cuchumatan Town*. Chicago: the University of Chicago Press, 1947.

Manz, Beatriz. *Refugees of a Hidden War: The Aftermath of Counterinsurgency in Guatemala*. Albany, N.Y.: the State University of New York Press, 1988.

Madsen, William. "Christo-Paganism: A Study of Mexican Religious Systems." In *Nativism & Syncretism*. New Orleans: Publication 19, Middle American Research Institute, Tulane University, 1960.

Miles, S.W. *The Sixteenth Century Pokom-Maya: A Documentary Analysis of Social Structure and Archaeological Setting*. Transactions 47. Philadelphia: the American Philosophical Society, 1957: 731-781.

———. "Summary of Preconquest Ethnology of the Guatemalan Highlands & Pacific Slopes." In *Archaeology of Southern Mesoamerica*, Gordon Wiley, ed. Austin: *Handbook of Middle American Indians*, II, the University of Texas Press, 1965: 276-287.

Millon, Rene, F. *When Money Grew on Trees: A Study of Cacao in Ancient Mesoamerica*. Ann Arbor: University Microfilms, 1981.

Montejo, Victor. *Testimony: Death of a Guatemalan Village*. Willimantic, CT: Curbstone Press, 1987.

Nash, June. *In the Eyes of the Ancestors: Belief & Behavior in a Mayan Community*. Newhaven: the Yale University Press, 1970.

Nash, Manning. *Machine Age Maya*. Memoir 87, American Anthropological Association, 1958.

Navarrete, Carlos: *San Pascualito y el Culto de la Muerte en Chiapas*. Mexico: Serie Antropológica 46, Instituto de Investigaciones Antropológicas, U.N.A.M., 1982.

Neuenswander, Helen L. & Arnold, Dean E. *Cognitive Studies of Southern Mesoamerica*. Dallas: Publication 3, Museum of Anthropology, Summer Institute of Linguistics, 1977.

Oakes, Maud. *The Two Crosses of Todos Santos*. New York: Bollingen Publication XXVII, Pantheon Books, 1951.

O'Neale, Linda. *Textiles of Highland Guatemala*. Washington D.C.: Publication 567, the Carnegie Institution of Washington, 1945.

Ordonez Chipin, Martín. "La Figura de Judas Iscariote en el Medio Guatemalteco." *Guatemala Indígena*, 8, 1 (1973): 143-172.

Paul, Benjamin D. *Life in a Guatemalan Indian Village*. Reprint from *Patterns of Modern Living*, Division 3: 468 — 515, Chicago: the Delphian Society, 1950.

———. "San Pedro la Laguna." In *Los Pueblos del Lago de Atitlán*, Tax, S. & Rojas Lima, F., eds. Guatemala: 1968.

———. "The Maya Bonesetter as a Sacred Specialist. "*Ethnology*, 15, 1 (1976): 77-81.

Paul, Lois & Paul, Benjamin D. "Changing Marriage Patterns in a Guatemalan Highland Community." *Southwestern Journal of Anthropology*, 19 (1963): 131-148.

———. The Maya Midwife as a Sacred Professional." *American Ethnologist*, 2,4 (1975): 707-726.

Recinos, Adrian. *Pedro de Alvarado, Conquistador de Mexico y Guatemala*. Mexico: Fondo de Cultura Economica, 1952.

———. *Monografía del Departamento de Huehuetenango*. 2nd. Revised Edition. Guatemala: Editorial del Ministerio de Educación Publica, 1954.

Redfield, Robert. "Coati & Ceiba." *Maya Research*, III, New Orleans, 1936.

Redfield, Robert. *Ethnographic Materials on Agua Escondida*. Microfilm Collection of Manuscripts on Middle American Cultural Anthropology 3. Chicago: the University of Chicago Library, 1945.

Reina, Ruben. *The Law of the Saints: a Pokomam Pueblo and its Community Culture*. Indianapolis: Bobbs Merrill, 1966.

Roys, R. *The Book of Chilam Balam de Chumayel*. Publication Washington D.C.: the Carnegie Institution of Washington, 1933.

Roys, Ralph, L. *The Indian Background of Colonial Yucatan*. Norman: the University of Oklahoma Press, 1972.

Sahagún, Fray Bernadino de. *Historia General de las Cosas de Nueva España*, Angel María Garibay, ed., Mexico: Porrua, 1956.

———. *Florentine Codex (General History of the Things of New Spain [Aztec version])*.In thirteen parts. Anderson, Arthur. J.O. & Dibble, Charles E. eds., Santa Fe, NM.: the School of American Research & the University of Utah, 1950-1955, and revised editions.

Saler, Benson. *Nagual, Witch & Sorcerer in a Quiché Village. Ethnology*, III, 3, (1964): 305-328.

Schele, Linda & Miller, Mary Ellen: *The Blood of Kings*. New York: George Braziller, 1986.

Scherzer, Karl. *Los Indios de Santa Catarina Iztlavacan*. Vienna 1854. Translated by E.Schaeffer in *Antropología e Historia de Guatemala*, VI, 2, (1954): 13-21.

Schlesinger, Stephen & Kinzer, Stephen. *Bitter Fruit: The Untold Story of the American Coup in Guatemala*. New York: Doubleday, 1982.

Scholes, France V. & Roys, Ralph L. *The Maya Chontal of Acalan-Tixchel: A Contribution to the History and Ethnography of the Yucatan Peninsula*. Washington D.C.: Publication 560, the Carnegie Institution of Washington, 1948.

Schultze-Jena, Leonhard. "Leben, Glaube und Sprache der Quiché von Guatemala." *Indiana*, I. Jena: Gustav Fischer Verlag, 1933.

———. "Mythen in Muttersprache der Pipil von Izalco in El Salvador." *Indiana*, II. Jena: Gustav Fischer Verlag, 1934.

———. "La Vida y las Creencias de los Indigenas Quichés de Guatemala" tr. by A Goubaud Carrera y Herbert Sapper. Reprinted from *Anales de la Sociedad de Geografía E Historia de Guatemala*, XX, 1-4, 1945. Guatemala: S.G.H.G., 1946.

Shaw, Mary (ed.) *According to Our Ancestors: Folk Texts from Guatemala & Honduras*. Norman, Oklahoma: the Summer Institute of Linguistics Publications in Linguistics & Related Fields 32, 1971.

Shook, Edwin M. "Archaeological Survey of the Pacific Coast of Guatemala." In *Archaeology of Southern Mesoamerica*, Gordon Willey, ed. *Handbook of Middle American Indians*, II. Austin: the University of Texas Press, 1965: 180-194.

Simon, Jean Marie. *Guatemala: Eternal Spring. Eternal Tyranny*. New York: Norton, 1987.

Smith, Carol, A (ed.) with Moors, Marylin. *Guatemalan Indians and the State: 1540-1988*. Austin: the University of Texas Press, 1990.

Smith, Ledyard & Kidder, Alfred V. *Excavations at Nebaj, Guatemala*. Washington D.C.: Publication 594, the Carnegie Institution of Washington, 1951.

Smith, Waldemar R. *The Fiesta System & Economic Change*. New York: the Columbia University Press, 1977.

Stoll, Otto. *Etnografía de Guatemala* (Zurich, 1884). Tr. by Antonio Goubaud Carrera. Guatemala: Publication 8, Seminario de Integración Social, 1958.

Turitz, Shari, (ed.). *Confronting the Heart of Darkness: An International*

Symposium on Torture in Guatemala. Washington D.C., Guatemala Human Rights Commission/U.S.A., 1993.

Tax, Sol. "The Municipios of Highland Guatemala." *American Anthropologist*, 49, 3 (1937): 423-444.

———. "World View & Social Relations in Guatemala." *American Anthropologist*, 43 (1941): 27-42.

———. *The Towns of Lake Atitlán*. Microfilm Collection of Manuscripts on Middle American Cultural Anthropology 13. Chicago: the University of Chicago Library, 1946.

———. "Folk Tales of Chichicastenango." *Journal of American Folklore*, LXII, (1949).

———. *Penny Capitalism: A Guatemalan Indian Economy*. Washington D.C.: Publication 16, Institute of Social Anthropology, the Smithsonian Institution, 1953.

Termer, Franz. *Etnología y Etnografía de Guatemala (1925-1929)*. Tr. by E. Schaeffer & A. Mendoza H. Guatemala: Publication 5, Seminario de Integración Social, 1957.

Tedlock, Barbara. *Time & the Highland Maya*. Foreword by Nathaniel Tarn. Albuquerque: the University of New Mexico Press, 1982.

Tedlock, Dennis. *Breath on the Mirror, Mythic Voices & Visions of the Living Maya*. San Francisco, Harper, 1993.

Thompson, Dennis. "Maya Paganism and Christianity." In *Nativism and Syncretism*. New Orleans: Publication 19, Middle American Research Institute, Tulane University, 1954.

Thompson, J. Eric S. *Maya Hieroglyphic Writing*. Washington D.C.: Publication 589, the Carnegie Institute of Washington, 1950.

———. *The Rise & Fall of Maya Civilization*, Norman: the University of Oklahoma Press, 1954.

———. *Maya History & Religion*. Norman: the University of Oklahoma Press, 1970.

Vasquez, Francisco. *Crónica de la Provincia del Santissimo Nombre de Jésus de Guatemala de la Orden de Nuestro Seráfico Padre San Francisco (1714-1717)*. *Biblioteca Goathemala*, XIV-XVII. Guatemala: Sociedad de Geografía e Historia, 1937-1944.

Wagley, Charles. *The Social & Religious Life of a Guatemalan Village*. Memoir 71, the American Anthropological Association, 1949.

Warren, Kay, B. *The Symbolism of Subordination: Indian Identity in a Guatemalan Town*. Austin, the University of Texas Press, 1978.

Wasserstrom, Robert. "Revolution in Guatemala: Peasants & Politics under the Arbenz Government." *Comparative Studies in Society & History*, 17, (1975): 443-78.

Watanabe, John, M. *Maya Saints & Souls in a Changing World*. Austin: the University of Texas Press, 1992.

Wisdom, C. *The Chorti Indians of Guatemala*. Chicago: the University of Chicago Press, 1940.

Wolf, Eric. *Sons of the Shaking Earth*. Chicago: the University of Chicago Press, 1959.

Ximenez, Francisco. *Las Historias del Origen de los Indios de Esta Provincia de Guatemala*. Carl Scherzer, ed. Vienna: Karl Gerold, 1857.

———. *Historia de la Provincia de San Vicente de Chiapa y Guatemala*. *Biblioteca Goathemala* I-III, Guatemala: Sociedad de Geografía e Historia de Guatemala, 1929-1930; *B.G.* XXIV, 1973; XXV, 1971; XXVI, 1971; XXVIII, 1975;.